MYTHICA

*A New History of Homer's World,
Through the Women Written Out of It*

EMILY HAUSER

doubleday

TRANSWORLD PUBLISHERS
Penguin Random House, One Embassy Gardens,
8 Viaduct Gardens, London SW11 7BW
www.penguin.co.uk

Transworld is part of the Penguin Random House group of companies
whose addresses can be found at global.penguinrandomhouse.com

Penguin
Random House
UK

First published in Great Britain in 2025 by Doubleday
an imprint of Transworld Publishers

Copyright © Emily Hauser 2025

Emily Hauser has asserted her right under the Copyright,
Designs and Patents Act 1988 to be identified as the author of this work.

Maps drawn by Liane Payne

A CIP catalogue record for this book
is available from the British Library.

ISBNs
9781529932485 hb
9781529932492 tpb

Typeset in 11/14.5 pt Minion Pro by Jouve (UK), Milton Keynes
Printed and bound in Great Britain by Clays Ltd, Elcograf S.p.A.

The authorized representative in the EEA is Penguin Random House Ireland,
Morrison Chambers, 32 Nassau Street, Dublin D02 YH68.

MYTHICA

www.penguin.co.uk

Also by Emily Hauser

FICTION
For the Most Beautiful
For the Winner
For the Immortal

NON-FICTION
How Women Became Poets
Ancient Love Stories

In loving memory of my grandmother, Mama,
who always knew what to say.

For Eliza and Theo, who are finding their voices.
And for Oliver, always.

CONTENTS

'Muse: tell me about a woman.'

HOMER, *ODYSSEY*, 1.1, A VARIATION

TIMELINE

IRON AGE **1050**	Amazons	1000

IRON AGE
1050

Amazons

1000

1100

Fall of Troy

1200

Linear B
Tablets

Bronze Age
Collapse

Puduhepa

1300

Petsas
House

Uluburun

AhT 20

1400

Peristeria
Penelope

Griffin
Warrior

1500

Snake
Goddess

Chania
Baby

Thera

1600

LATE BRONZE AGE
1700

Pefka

1700

Mycenae Grave
Circle B

MYCENAEANS

Hammurabi
Law Code

1800

1900

Knossos

2000

MIDDLE BRONZE AGE
2100

2100

Jewels of Helen

2500

Troy

EARLY BRONZE AGE
3100

MINOANS   3000

Note on chronology: all dates are BCE and are approximate, and follow the 'high' chronology for the Aegean Bronze Age and Sturt Manning et al's radiocarbon-based dates for the eruption of Thera (Santorini).

HISTORICA

Historical Map of the Bronze Age Aegean

THRACE

Mount Olympus

Troy/Wilusa

TROAD/TARUISA

Lesbos/
Lazpa

AEGEAN SEA

Chios

Aidonia

Mycenae

ITHACA

Tiryns

Peristeria

Sparta

Pylos

Thera

(Petsophas)

MYCENAEAN

Amnisos

GREECE

Knossos

(Pefka)

Chania/
Cydonia

Myrtos

CRETE

MEDITERRANEAN SEA

ETHIOPIA

ITHACA

DOULICHION?

ITHACA?

LIBYA

SAME?

N

W   E

S

ZACYNTHOS

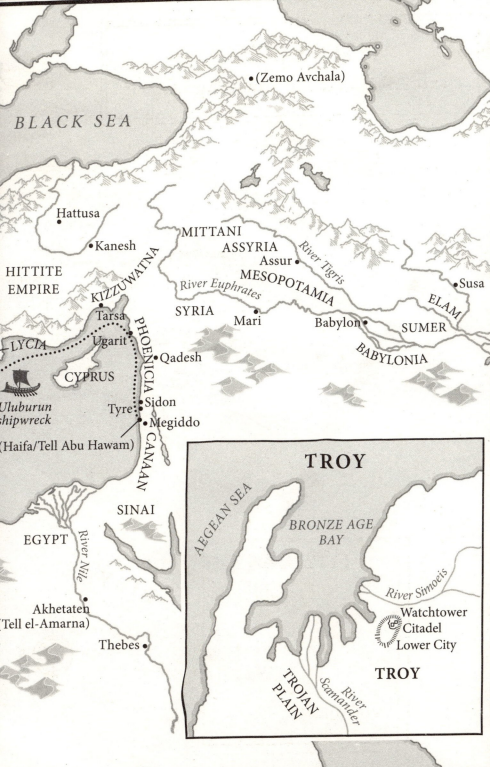

MYTHICA

Mythical Map of the World
of the *Iliad* and *Odyssey*

THRACE

UNDERWORLD

Cicones

Troy/Ilios

Mount Olympus

ISLAND OF PHAEACIANS

TROAD

Thebe

AEAEA

Lyrnessus

AEGEAN SEA

Mycenae

Scylla and Charybdis

ITHACA

Sirens

ACHAEA

Tiryns

Aegea route

Aeolia

Island of Sun

Sparta

Pylos

Laestrygonians

Cyclopes

Odyssey route

Amniso

Knossos

OGYGIA

CRETE

Lotus Eaters

MEDITERRANEAN SEA

ETHIOPIA

ITHACA

Phorcys Bay

DOULICHION

ITHACA

Palace

SAME

ZACYNTHOS

LIBYA

N

W   E

S

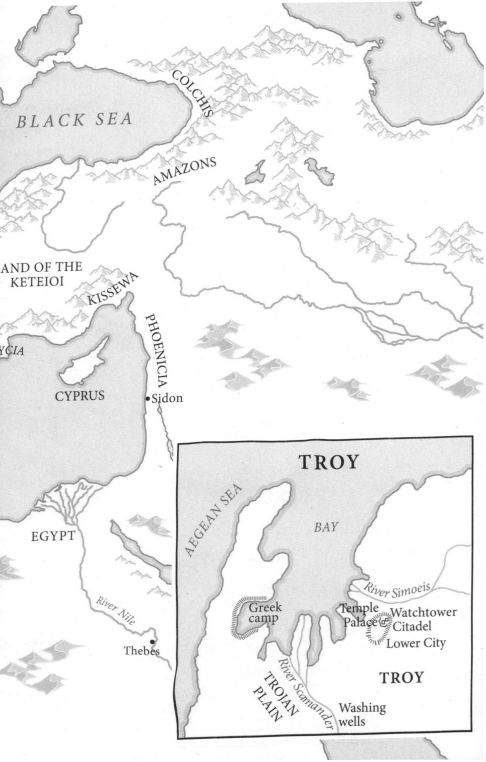

AUTHOR'S NOTE

I remember the moment I realized Homer was going to be a big part of my life. I was around fifteen, and grinding through hours of revision for my GCSEs: not a time in which many people expect to find inspiration. Over the summer I spent the sun-bleached days at my grandparents' house, living for the tea breaks that my grandmother rattled on brass trays down the corridor. I was taking ancient Greek (and acutely aware of how lucky I was: I'd travel three hours a day to get to the nearest boys' grammar where they could teach me). We'd been set a passage from the *Odyssey*: the climactic scene, near the end of the poem, where Odysseus steps up to the contest of the bow masterminded by Penelope, and announces himself at last as her husband and king of Ithaca. That morning, notes all over the ink-blotter, dictionaries propped open like white-winged seagulls in mid-flight, I'd been wading through a mire of grammar – participles, conditionals, subjunctives – in an effort to coax the enigmatic symbols into some sort of sense.

And then, like a sailor coming home, the words coming together, and the sudden thought like a swallow flying free: *I can read this.* Reading the lines out loud, wrapping my breath around the archaic Greek. Sitting on the edge of my grandmother's armchair with poems thousands of years old.

That was the beginning of a journey that, *Odyssey*-like, has taken over the last twenty years of my life. It took me, first, to Cambridge to read the *Iliad* in the shadow of King's College Chapel – where I first found, hidden in the pages of my sage-green edition of Homer, the women waiting voiceless and ignored behind the walls of Troy and in the Greek camp. It led me across the ocean to Harvard and Yale, where – in 2011 – I had the idea of opening up the world of the women of the *Iliad*, and telling *their* story, in their voices and their words, in fiction. In my novel *For the Most Beautiful* (2016), I got to step into their world. I found Briseis and Chryseis, the two Trojan women enslaved and raped by Achilles and Agamemnon, the so-called 'heroes' of the epic – the women who stood behind the entire story of the *Iliad*: and I told their tale. In the process, I discovered just how many more silenced women there were, weaving through both the *Iliad* and the *Odyssey* like an invisible thread, whose voices needed to be heard – without whom there wouldn't be any story at all. And so I decided to write this book, to uncover the real women behind the myth – women from history, the mothers and slaves and warriors and queens, who made the stories what they are.

The ancient Greeks knew, just as much as we do, that any history is subject to its own concerns in the story it's trying to tell – as well as the inevitable simplifications and reductions that come with parcelling up the messy events of the past into a coherent package that fits within the covers of a book. In traversing a huge chronological and geographical span, moving between archaeology, literature, history and myth, this book covers people and places known by different names at different periods, names that often either restrict the diversity of the many cultures in which those people or places featured, or are fraught with centuries of cultural baggage. For instance, I refer to 'ancient south-west Asia' rather than 'the ancient Near East' (a Western colonial construct). I also use 'Greeks' (a later term derived from the Latin *Graeci*) rather than Homer's Argives/Danaans/Achaeans, and 'Mycenaeans' (a modern label), but in neither case do I use these terms to suggest a national identity. Rather, I try to acknowledge complexity wherever possible, while keeping naming recognizable and consistent for ease of reading. So, for example, the ancient city we now know as 'Troy' seems in actual fact to have been called by two names – *Wilusa* and *Taruisa* – by the Hittites, the city's closest contemporary neighbours; later Greeks called it *Ilios*, *Ilion* and *Troia*; the Romans named it *Ilium* or *Troia*. 'Troy' stuck in English, and I use it throughout the book – at the same time as I explore the ancient history in which 'Troy' had many different names, in many different languages. Similarly, I call the (imaginary) home of the Phaeacians 'the island of the Phaeacians', to avoid confusion, even though it is known in Homer as Scheriē. In general, transliterations are Latinized for ease of recognition (so 'Hecuba' and 'Achilles', not 'Hekabē' and 'Akhilleus').

Quotations from the Homeric epics are for the most part from Emily

Wilson's translations; some are my own, and are indicated as such in the Notes. (Note that the epigraphs on pp. ix, 25 and 213 are my translations.) Emily Wilson's acclaimed and inspirational *Odyssey* (2018) was, unbelievably, the first time Homer's epic was translated into English by a woman. This points to a much bigger question – that this is a recovery not just *of* Homer's women, but *by* women as well; a story about the women who have studied and continue to trailblaze the study of Homer, the women classicists, historians, scientists, translators, archaeologists who have contributed so much to our knowledge about the past. I wanted to make sure that I tell their stories, too. So you will find, in these pages, not just Penelope and Helen of Troy, but also the pioneering women intellectuals – their names often lost to the record, or not recognized as they should be – who have dedicated their lives to uncovering the lost worlds of Bronze Age Greece, and of Homer.

Muse: A New Invocation

August 2017, and it's a hot summer's day in Boston, Massachusetts, but the stacks of Harvard's Widener Library are as cold as catacombs. I'm sitting in the Smyth Classics Library up in the gods of Widener, thumbing through a Greek text of Homer's *Odyssey*. Walnut desks and mismatched chairs are overseen by white plaster busts of bearded poets. There's the overwhelming, musty scent of old books, the air thick with the hush of minds at work, broken only by the tapping of laptop keys and the wind through the yellowwood trees out in the Yard. I'm searching for a particular passage in the *Odyssey*'s first book – following the invocation where the poet calls on the Muse to strike up and tell the story of 'a man' – where, I hope, I can find evidence that women in Homer's world might have been more important than we've been led to believe. Greek letters crowd the page, black ink pressing on the paper margins, and I feel myself thrill with excitement to be deciphering this ancient language – the same excitement I felt when I first started learning Greek and got gripped by the sensation of being able to unravel these Morse-code messages from the past.

As we dive into Homer's story, we're dropped into a world from over three thousand years back, an ancient land burnished to a sheen by legend and filled with a character cast of capricious gods, power-hungry kings and swaggering heroes. Greek citadels perch like crowns on rocky outcrops, each ruled by an overweening lord who spends his time doling out favours in his throne room or sallying abroad to loot gold and capture women, while wives and daughters crowd faceless in the palace shadows. What Homer is describing seems to look back (at least in part) to a real civilization of historical ancient Greeks who lived in the Late Bronze Age, called the Mycenaeans – named (by the archaeologists who discovered them) after the kingdom of Mycenae, one of the most overweening and gold-filled of them all. The ancient Greeks believed that Troy, the Trojan War, as well as the swarming Greek forces who invaded from Mycenae, Pylos and Sparta, were all certifiably, tangibly real: one ancient chronicler even gave the sack of Troy a specific date – 1184 BCE. This is (or at least, so the ancients imagined) the stamping ground of Odysseus, king of Ithaca, sacker of cities, master of disguise. And it's also the world of Penelope.

Odysseus, so the tale goes, has been gone from Ithaca for nearly twenty years, swashbuckling away in the Trojan War of legend. He'd sworn to Menelaus – king of Sparta, according to Homer, and brother of Agamemnon, king of Mycenae – to protect Helen, Menelaus' wife, the most beautiful woman in the world and so (naturally, to the loot-minded men) a prize ripe for the taking. When Helen had run off with Paris, prince of Troy, Odysseus and the other Greek kings duly banded together to get her back. The legend tells us it took ten years and a siege against Troy, a protracted war of sufficient horror and greatness for one epic poem, centuries later, to be born: Homer's *Iliad*. And then there were the exploits of the heroes' years-long voyage back to Greece – enough to fill another epic, the *Odyssey*, charting Odysseus' stunts and scrapes on his way home.

In all this, Odysseus' wife Penelope lingers in the background, waiting (so the Homeric epics tell us) on rocky Ithaca and fending off her many suitors while Odysseus has all the adventures. At the very beginning of the *Odyssey*, we meet her coming downstairs from her bedroom to find a bard singing in the palace's hall about the trials and tribulations of the Greeks on their return from Troy. Not surprisingly, Penelope, who has been spending ten years trying to forget the setbacks Odysseus must be facing, finds this a rather tactless choice of subject. In front of the suitors thronging the palace, all waiting until she finally gives up on Odysseus, she interrupts the bard, who has already struck up his tune, and tells him to sing something else. But it's not going to be that easy. Penelope's teenage son, Telemachus, who feels like flexing his authority in front of the other males, stands up and puts his mother in her place: 'Go in and do your work. Stick to the loom and distaff. Tell your slaves to do their chores as well. It is for men to talk, especially me. I am the master.'[1] And off Penelope goes.

To all intents and purposes, then, one of the most famous of all the ancient texts, telling one of the most famous ancient legends, begins with something of a mission statement: that women aren't meant to talk. Nor are they allowed to tell their own stories, their *own* myths, in their own words. The Greek term Telemachus uses for 'talking' is *mythos* – 'word' (it's where the English 'myth' comes from). He essentially says not just 'words are for men', but '*myths* are for men'. Both the myths that get told, and the words employed to tell them, are – in this manifesto – a men's-only zone.

It's a statement that has, until recently, always been taken at face value – and it's easy to see why. You can't read many of the ancient Greek myths, let alone epics like Homer's, without being told in one way or another that women are meant to be silent – seen and not heard (even better if they're not seen). In Homer's war epic, the *Iliad*, one particularly important woman – a trafficked and raped sex slave called Briseis, who is the reason the whole story exists (but we'll get to that later) – speaks only once, and gets to say about as much as Achilles' magical (male) talking horse. When women do try to have their say, then men will quickly close them down: Telemachus' refusal to hear Penelope out, and to get the poet to tell the story that *she's* asked for, is what Mary Beard calls 'the first recorded example of a man telling a woman to "shut up"' in Western literature.[2] And it's not just the mortals, either. In the first book of the *Iliad*, Hera – queen of the gods – gets slapped back (almost literally) by Zeus: when she tries to challenge him, he snaps at her to 'sit down, be quiet, and do as I say' (along with the threat of a beating if she doesn't obey him).[3] If the role of women is to shut up, it's made abundantly clear, meanwhile, that great stories are only meant to be told about the adventures of men like Odysseus. The *Odyssey*'s opening line makes the instruction to the female Muse (goddess of song and poetry) quite clear: she's only meant to inspire stories about *men*. 'Muse: tell me about a man', the story begins – where 'man' (*andra*) is the epic's first word in Greek.[4] In these legends of the Greek past, women are put firmly, and ever-so-silently, in the background, and the mythical world is made resolutely male.

But as I sit in my twenty-first-century library with the text of the *Odyssey* resting against the blinking screen of my open laptop, I wonder if there aren't different questions to be asked. Is it possible that we might be able to read past Penelope's shutting up? Can we, as modern historians, instead make space for her to speak for herself? Can we dig deeper into the past to begin to invoke the voices of Homer's women – beyond, or behind, the tale that we've always been told?

Only a few months earlier, I'd completed my PhD dissertation at Yale, based on a hunch that there was more to be discovered about the silenced women of Homer's world. The year before, in 2016, I'd published my debut novel, *For the Most Beautiful*, a rewriting of the *Iliad* that tells the untold story of Briseis and Chryseis, two Trojan women enslaved by Achilles and Agamemnon in the Greek camp. These women, like Penelope, like Helen of Troy, Cassandra, Circe and Calypso, have had to stand at the sidelines for thousands of years – both in the stories that handed them down to us, and in the scholarship that curated and interpreted them – as mere accessories to the greater theatre of epics that are, supposedly, all about men. But then, at the same time, there was the central paradox to Homer's epics that no one, to my mind, had yet satisfactorily addressed: the fundamental incompatibility between the claim the epics make that women don't matter, and the fact that in every case they are essential to the story and the myth. There wouldn't be an epic without a Muse. There wouldn't be a Trojan War without a Helen. The *Iliad* wouldn't begin without a Briseis. The *Odyssey* wouldn't end without a Penelope. I knew, deep down, that there had to be more to Homer's women than the traditional viewpoint suggested.

And then, on that August day in 2017, a magazine lands on my desk. It's a copy of *Nature*, one of the leading science journals. The glossy cover is black with a brightly coloured illustration of some recent scientific discovery, all twisting yellow helix and pink spirals. And a word I'm not expecting catches my eye: *Mycenaeans*.

I rifle through to the appropriate page, fingers sliding on the sleek magazine (I'm used to dog-eared classical texts): 'Genetic Origins of the Minoans and Mycenaeans'. It's a study published by a lab just over the river at the Harvard Medical School. The text is dense as I scan through it, full of jitter plots and complex DNA sampling methods, but what catches my eye at once are the individuals being sampled: 'Four Mycenaeans were included from mainland Greece (approximately 1700–1200 BC; from the western coast of the Peloponnese, from Argolis, and the island of Salamis).' Working through the appendix, I discover what I'm looking for: a successful DNA sample taken from the teeth of a Mycenaean Greek woman found buried in a royal cemetery adjacent to the ancient citadel of Peristeria in the western Peloponnese (north-east of modern-day Kyparissia), and dating to between 1416 and 1280 BCE.[5]

There are several reasons why this is so exciting. Our ability to extract and study ancient DNA (known as aDNA) from thousands-of-years-old biological tissue is thanks to recent scientific advances, which have had to face (and overcome) serious challenges and complications. Ancient DNA fragments are typically extremely short and subject to high levels of chemical damage in the years after death (and that's especially true when we're looking back several millennia into history). Another major issue is the problem of modern-day contamination: how can we separate the ancient DNA from the DNA of the archaeologists and researchers who have handled the sample? And not all samples provide enough endogenous DNA for analysis: from the site of Peristeria alone, twenty-six different samples were taken, but only one actually provided enough workable aDNA for the researchers to gather data. Nor does DNA tell us anything about the cultural layering of gender (as we'll see, archaeologists can look elsewhere for those kinds of clues). But when aDNA *can* be recovered, when it can be isolated from contamination and analysed in the lab, there is a wealth of secrets to uncover – like a message sealed in a bottle from the past. Biological sex can be determined with only a few thousand random sequences (compared to the three billion in a complete human genome). Family relationships between individuals can be traced through analysis of mitochondrial DNA (or mtDNA), which passes down through the maternal line and gives us a family tree wrapped up in a parcel of chromosomes. Phenotypes – observable traits like eye, skin or hair colour – can be predicted from carefully selected DNA markers. Being able to unravel aDNA from a Mycenaean grave from the Late Bronze Age world of the fourteenth and early thirteenth

centuries BCE – in the decades before the ancients said that the siege and
fall of Troy took place, when Odysseus was imagined to have sailed from
Ithaca with his ships and Penelope waited for him to come home – is like
opening up a time capsule from the world of the Trojan War.

As I look over the data on this woman – known to the researchers,
somewhat unromantically, as I9033 – the numbers from the DNA analysis, crossed with the archaeology of the context in which she was found,
begin to project a vivid picture. The archaeological evidence shows that
she was clearly a member of the ruling house: she was buried in what
is known as a tholos tomb, a beehive-like structure cut into the hillside
outside the main ancient settlement of Peristeria and reinforced with
giant masonry slabs, commonly used by the Mycenaeans for burying
their royal dead. The tomb chamber was filled with artefacts that were
intended to proclaim the occupant's high status on her journey into the
afterlife: gold leaf, beads of gold and semi-precious stones – the paraphernalia of a queen. Meanwhile, the Harvard researchers' DNA analysis
revealed that her mtDNA haplotype – her ancestral signature – was
consistent with types you would expect to see in other Mycenaean burials, showing that she, and her ancestors, were locals from the Greek
mainland. Radiocarbon dating (analysis of the decay of the organic
radiocarbon in her teeth) placed her death at around the fourteenth
century BCE. They were even able to ascertain from her genetic data
that, when she was alive, she would have had brown hair and brown
eyes – just like many of the women we see pictured in Mycenaean paintings from the same period.

All this is incredibly tantalizing, and – it would seem – a world away
from the black-and-white, two-dimensional Greek text of Homer,
replete with its careful editorial apparatus and neatly numbered lines,
that's propped in front of me. But I can't help but think that it's not – and
that there might be another lesson here, too. The archaeological site of
Peristeria – first excavated by the Greek archaeologist Spyridon Marinatos in the 1960s – is about twenty-five miles north of Pylos, a real ancient
Mycenaean site with a deep Homeric pedigree, said by Homer to be the
seat of Nestor, another Greek king and an adviser to Agamemnon. And
Pylos can claim a link to the passage I'm reading in the *Odyssey*: because,
in the epic, Penelope's adolescent son Telemachus has just decided to

go on a trip across the Ionian Sea from Ithaca to Pylos, in search of his missing father, a few short lines before Penelope bursts in on the scene and orders the bard to change his tune.

Which means that this royal woman of Mycenaean Greece lived around the same time that Homer's epic imagined Penelope, not long before the time the Trojan War could have feasibly happened, and not far away. And she's been brought back to life, from thousands of years in the past, by the debates we're having, the tools we're developing and the work we're doing now.

So the question I'm left thinking, as I look from the gleaming DNA data in *Nature* to the curling ancient script of the Greek text, is this. What if we could use modern methods – the latest advances in critiquing classical texts, the most recent archaeological discoveries and cutting-edge DNA analysis – to resurrect the real women behind Homer and return them to their rightful place, centre stage? What if we didn't just listen to the myths that men made – but paid attention to the stories encoded in the bones of the real women of history?

What if now is the time to unsilence Penelope at last?

Best Kept Silent

Over three thousand years ago, in an ancient Greece where men spoke and wrote and women went unheard, some of the world's first epics were born.[6] These epics were part of a prehistoric boxset of sung poems that were handed down over generations, passed on from one male bard to the next and rolled out at banquets for the rich and famous, where each singer would perform and re-perform his own version of a tale about the great and the good of Greece's past. And the poems were mostly focused on that most legendary of battles: the Trojan War. They were vast in length: thousands of lines of poetry (over fifteen thousand for the *Iliad* as we have it, and over twelve thousand for the *Odyssey*), recalled in performance by master singers, who would sing their tales around the fires night after night. (Comparative work in Serbo-Croatia by Milman Parry and Albert Lord demonstrated how one particularly virtuosic singer could perform, from memory, songs that reached fifteen or sixteen thousand lines – the same length as the Homeric epics.) Such epics, telling the stories of the legend of Troy, were defined in the most basic sense by their metrical form: hexameter, a metre made up of six 'feet' or rhythmic units. These units of rhythm were particularly helpful to oral poets, who, over the centuries, developed an armoury of descriptions for all the characters likely to crop up in an epic tale – stock epithets and readymade phrases like 'white-armed' or 'ox-eyed' (for women), 'swift-footed' and 'master of the war cry' (for men), to be slotted into lines at will, that would have been an essential prop to a prehistoric bard expected to recite hundreds of lines of verse from memory. Stock scenes had a similar function: narrative sequences that were common to the worlds of epic (like getting ready for battle and having an all-out war rampage, if you're a man; being told to shut up and sent back upstairs to weave, if you're a woman) were regularly repeated, and embellished upon, to keep the plot moving.

But beyond their form and poetic technique, epics were marked out, above all, by their thirst for celebrating and commemorating the exploits of heroes. In them, powerful men could see themselves reflected, and bask in the chronicles of the bold warriors and kings of Greece's glory days – what historians now call the Mycenaean (or Late Bronze Age) period, characterized above all by the flourishing of palatial hubs like Mycenae all over mainland Greece between about 1700 and 1050 BCE. But when, around 1200 BCE, a devastating wave of destruction started to sweep across the Aegean, the great Mycenaean palaces – along with their writing systems – tottered and fell. Greece slid into what used to be referred to as a Dark Age (c.1050–800 BCE) – which we're now discovering was anything but, and simply means that we don't have written accounts to tell us what was going on.[7] As far as records went, the songs about the glory days were all there was left.

When writing re-entered the scene somewhere between the mid ninth and early eighth centuries BCE (with the 'alphabet', or *aleph beth*, an import from cosmopolitan Phoenicia in the eastern Mediterranean), among the first to be consolidated and written down in the new Greek alphabet was one particular version of two of these stories: the *Iliad* and the *Odyssey*. Their alleged poet, Homer – whoever 'he' was, whenever he 'wrote' (more on this later) – became an instant celebrity in the ancient world: and, for better or worse, what he told his audiences about being a man (and a woman) stuck. These epic tales of men's valour and men's virtue would rise to become some of the most popular literature ever written – but more than that: for millennia, they played a central part in shaping who Westerners thought they were. For the classical Greeks, Homer's epics were – quite literally – their 'bible' (*biblos* means 'book' in ancient Greek). Generals would take military advice from their pages (Alexander the Great notoriously slept with a copy of the *Iliad* beneath his pillow). Philosophers like Plato and Socrates turned to Homer to understand everything from the history of war to the meaning of courage. And male writers across the centuries, from the stately Roman poet Virgil to soldiers like the English poet Rupert Brooke mired in the trenches of the First World War, recast great figures like the hero Achilles to reflect on who they were and what they did; while British public schoolboys were made to copy suitably masculine passages out of their Homer textbooks in the hope that they might turn into proper gentlemen. Western ideas and modern myths about what it meant to be a man, what it meant to rule and fight and judge, rested on the way that Homer was being read.

Meanwhile, women were shaded away into silence in the male-centric culture of classical Athens – and that mattered, because the way the Athenians thought about women, and about Homer, would have a lasting impact on the West. The Athenian historian Thucydides, writing in the late fifth century BCE and deeply engaged in the Athenian project of commingled democracy and empire, put it perhaps most clearly. Placing words in the mouth of Athens' most prominent statesman, Pericles, he proclaims that 'a woman will have the greatest glory if she's least talked about among the men – whether for good or bad'. The tragic poet Euripides, in a play written not long before Thucydides' history, has one of his characters pontificate that 'for a woman, being silent and modest is best, and staying quietly inside the house'. Another tragedian, Sophocles (author of *Oedipus Rex*), a decade or so earlier, phrased it even more simply: 'silence is a woman's best ornament'.[8] And if a woman doesn't opt in to the policy of silence, one particularly abusive poet of the seventh or sixth century BCE – who's comparing all the 'bad' types of women to different animals, including pigs rolling in filth, sex-crazed weasels and yapping dogs – complains that 'a man can't stop her barking; not with threats, not (when he's had enough) by knocking out her teeth with a stone'.[9] Any woman who wanted to tell her own tale, who wanted to write her own story, simply didn't get listened to, and women's songs, women's myths, were lost. (The numbers give the best idea of the stark reality: we know the names of at least 3,200 male authors writing in Greek – and those of fewer than a hundred women.) And the 'best kept silent' dictum tallied so conveniently with the paradigmatic scene of Penelope's silencing at the beginning of the *Odyssey*, that this way of reading Homer's (and other) women – as best kept silent – trickled into other Western cultures, which chose to adopt classical Athens as a symbolic forbear to tie in with their imperial and patriarchal values.

And so women and women's voices slid out of the record, having run through the unforgiving sieve of history (as Dame Hilary Mantel memorably put it).[10] Manuscripts of the Homeric texts copied out by medieval monks – including the most famous manuscript of all, a tenth-century codex known as the Venetus A and one of the earliest complete versions of the *Iliad* to survive – contained symbolic doodles of Helen of Troy, trapped voiceless and bemused in the margins, that speak volumes about where women and women's voices were thought to belong. The nineteenth-century philosopher Friedrich Nietzsche (whose theories were later, famously, repackaged into Nazi German nationalist ideologies) could assert that the ancient Greeks, 'from Homer to the age of Pericles', understood how 'necessary' and 'logical' it was to be 'more strict with women'. Meanwhile, the first-ever article devoted to women in Homer (written by a man, and published in 1956) spent all its time detailing how Homer's women get in the way of the hero, whose job is 'as a man [to] triumph over the trial and . . . come out of it free'.[11]

And right now, a dangerous undercurrent in online communities sees Alt-Right men's groups using ancient epic to justify misogyny and a return to anti-feminist masculinity. One thread on a forum called r/TheRedPill (part of what's known as the online 'manosphere' that embraces the so-called 'Red Pill' anti-feminist, anti-liberal ethic), for instance, uses a Greek epic poet contemporary with Homer to argue that women are always going to be more trouble than they're worth: 'the

Helen of Troy looks ambivalent about her representation in the earliest complete manuscript of Homer's Iliad, *nearly a thousand years ago.*

Greeks and Romans,' the post claims, 'were Red Pill in the extreme'.[12] This sense of Homer's place in justifying a conservative agenda has surfaced in higher education, too: at New College, Florida – where right-wing Republican Governor Ron DeSantis has been focusing his attempts to battle the liberal-ness of the liberal arts college – a new core undergraduate course on the *Odyssey* was introduced in autumn 2023 as a flagship of the redesigned curriculum, just days after trustees decided to shut down the college's programme in gender studies. A conservative activist made the connection clear, just in case anyone had missed it: 'Homer's *Odyssey* is in. Gender Studies is out'.[13] The rewriting of history to suit the needs of the present is both urgently contemporary and a centuries-old tale, and Homer's epics – so often touted as the origin story of the West, seen as a high-stakes repository of cultural values, and the ultimate and authoritatively male works that pushed out almost every woman from the canon – have been, perhaps, more susceptible to it than any other ancient texts. And so Penelope, and Homer's women, have continued to lie silent for thousands of years.

Penelope's Bones

Over the last few decades, however, the way we study the ancient world – the discipline of Classics – has undergone something of an overhaul. The recognition that the stories of the invisible actors of history – women, enslaved people, black and indigenous peoples, queer and trans individuals, those with disabilities, and all other marginal communities – deserve and need to be recovered (and often intersect with one another) has shaken up the field. Archaeologists and geneticists are sifting through material evidence and reconstructing DNA from ancient remains to get back to the bones (and beyond) of long-gone cultures. Historians are putting together clues from documents deep in the archives, previously deemed not important enough to make it into the history books, to find out more about the lost lives of the millions who were sifted out of the official historical record. Classicists like me are rereading canonical texts – such as Homer's epics – that were always seen as 'all about men', and, by virtue of the different perspective they bring, are coming up with very different conclusions that allow us to peer into a new and unfamiliar world. This is a world where we can acknowledge that, without enslaved women like Briseis who sparks the story of the *Iliad*, there would have been no story at all. A world where we find formidable gender-fluid goddesses like Athena slipping in and out of a woman's body without conforming to the female–male binary. A world where we acknowledge that the multiple powerful women in the *Odyssey* – Calypso, Arete, Circe, Penelope and many others – are the protagonists of their own stories, not just someone else's. When we look for them – when we read the Homeric texts in a way that tries to tell their story – women and women's experiences are, in fact, ever-present: from the Muses who open the epics to Helen who starts the Trojan War, from Briseis who begins the *Iliad* to Athena who helps to engineer the sack of Troy, from Calypso and Circe and Arete who rule the teeming fantastical lands of the *Odyssey*'s voyage home, all the way to Penelope who marks the journey's end.

All these silenced women populate the tales of Greek myth and the pages of ancient Greece's most famous epics, lingering in the background with walk-on roles and barely there dialogue. But, when we read them again, we are able to 'break open the stories' (as Saidiya Hartman puts it) and let their silences speak.[14] Combined with breakthrough scientific advances that give us an unparalleled insight into the experiences of women in the ancient world – like the DNA analysis that brought us the Peristeria Penelope – and the latest archaeological technologies and approaches such as bioarchaeology and radiocarbon dating, it's now possible to put texts and objects alongside each other in new ways, and piece together at last the puzzle of the silenced women of Greek legend.

Which means that what this book is attempting to do is different in several important respects from how Homer has typically been approached. In looking at the women of the past, I am setting out to dig deeper, to keep challenging and refining the way we think, acknowledging that, in exploring the variety and complexity of women's experiences, there will always be more to learn. In arguing that Homer's women matter, I'm not saying that the epics are somehow 'better', that 'we' are all derived from the Greeks, that Greece has shaped 'our' world, or any of these kinds of damaging, reductive narratives that have been used to justify the use (and abuse) of Classics – and that have frequently underpinned misogyny and patriarchal structures. In fact, much of what this book is doing is trying to push beyond the narrow confines that have tended to define Homer – moving out from textual analysis, to incorporate the latest discoveries from science and archaeology; drawing on a vein of evidence pulsing through ancient cultures from Mesopotamia and Egypt to the empire of the Hittites, in the search for ancient women. It's about recognizing that the past – any past, all pasts – are part of the ideas that make up the collective and rich collage of cultures; but equally, that it's up to us now to challenge these ideas and not be limited by them – to be critical of where we've come from, and where we're going.[15]

Above all, as we go on the journey to discover the real women behind Homer's myths, we're looking with open eyes for women in all their diversity – not some boxed-up, neatly packaged form of gender (neither hypermasculine heroes like Alexander the Great's ideal of Achilles, nor Nietzsche's silent stay-at-home wives). It's a fine line to tread, and history – as so often – provides a cautionary tale. The Victorian archae-ologist Sir Arthur Evans started excavating the palace of Knossos on Crete in 1900, and – with it – discovered the so-called Minoan civiliza-tion, predecessor of the Mycenaeans. Uncovering a number of paintings of high-status women with gorgeous hairdos and sumptuous robes on the walls of the Knossos palace, and flush with the thrill of his new-found discovery, he used them to conjure up an image of an early peaceful and nature-loving society, overseen by benevolent mother goddesses and presided over by prominent females. It's clear now that (like some of his other, highly controversial, speculations on the Minoans) this was, to a large extent, a colourful fantasy of Sir Arthur's, born of a desire for a better world than the one that had produced the horrors of the First World War. But it's a salutary reminder that our ideas around recover-ing gender from the Homeric past can convey as much about what we *want* to see and find, the positive – whether it's heroized men or mother-goddess women – as well as the negative.

While Homer's epics were interpreted in the past as 'all about men', then, and Sir Arthur Evans tried to argue the opposite for Minoan Crete, I'm not here to push us to one side of the fence or the other. I am bring-ing women to the foreground, but neither am I idealizing or generalizing them, pretending that they were always powerful or always extraordin-ary or always the same. Instead, I'm arguing, above all, that women's experiences deserve to be examined in all their diversity, that every voice deserves to be heard. But I'm also suggesting that we can find interest-ing moments at the boundaries, where at some points ancient women were more powerful or more complex than we thought, and others where they came up against constraints – all the while exploring how the conversation around gender, the ebb and flow of power and the accounts that make it into the history books have echoed down the ages. In other words, what I'm arguing is that Homer's women are the jumping-off point to investigate a bigger picture, that they're 'good to think with' – that they can push us to reflect on gender, on ourselves, on how we've interpreted the past, in new ways.

Neither am I engaged in making blanket statements about what it means to *be* a woman. Identities – impossible to recover in the hard facts of genetic sex that DNA serves up to us in a PCR tube – inevitably change and shift with ideas about who individuals believe they are: and that's where texts, and art, and artefacts, and the entire cultural production that helps shape ideas around gender can help historians of women. At the same time, a revolution in new understandings about gender has pointed out that the lived experiences and identities of women and men aren't pinned to female or male bodies (or 'sex'). Gender is, rather, the product of millennia of cultural shaping, a repeated story that has imposed the narrative of the gender binary along the lines of male/female sex. The ancient Greeks, their myths, and Homer's epics, played a central part in writing this script: and it explains why so many novelists, artists and playwrights are now turning back to the ancient world to rework these old tales into different kinds of gender stories. In this book, I use 'women' to refer to people who identify as (or who are identified as, in the historical/mythic record) women, searching for the experience of being, becoming, defining oneself as female – across multiple ancient cultures and languages, across history, literature and myth. In this sense, the gender binary will often be operationally at play. But I'm also challenging the kinds of questions we ask of the ancient sources, bringing new methods and debates to the table to critique what we thought we knew – about gender, about women and about the past.

In so doing, I freely acknowledge the anachronism of this approach, the fact that I'm presenting the voices we're interested in now as a new lens through which to understand the past. In fact, in a sense, I'm arguing that anachronism is a central part of the story. It has to be. Not only have the Homeric epics always been anachronistic in and of themselves, as part of a tradition that has continually reinvented mythic stories of the Trojan War for a new audience and a new time. The search for women's voices is only happening now because of shifts in the way we're thinking and the kinds of stories we're telling about ourselves. Novelists and poets have begun in recent years to reclaim the voices and stories of Homer's women, from where they have languished for the past three millennia in the footnotes and the margins, to fill in the gaps in the all-male tale, prising apart through the tool of fiction the story we've always been told: from Margaret Atwood's *The Penelopiad* (2005) to Guisela López's 'Anti Penélope' (2006) to the Penelope-esque Celestial in Tayari Jones's *An American Marriage* (2018); from the Sirens and Circe in M. NourbeSe Philip's *Zong!* (2008) to Madeline Miller's *Circe* (2018); from Rhina Espaillat's Helen 'On the Walls' (2001) to Pat Barker's *The Silence of the Girls* (2018) and *The Women of Troy* (2021), Nikita Gill's 'Briseis Remembers' (2019), Natalie Haynes's *A Thousand Ships* (2019) and my own *For the Most Beautiful* (2016).[16] Female classicists like Emily Wilson and Caroline Alexander have recently turned to translate Homer – Wilson's 2018 *Odyssey* was, incredibly, the first translation of the work into English by a woman – to show that women, too, have a stake in these epic texts. Meanwhile, as contemporary movements like #MeToo, Black Lives Matter and the transgender rights movement make the headlines today, it's become ever more imperative that the ways in which we narrate the past should be critically re-examined – because, as we've seen from Thucydides to Nietzsche to the Red Pill, history has *always* been made with an agenda. Bringing the stories we've been told to the table, examining historical narratives through the lens of the ideas and values we believe in, enables us to unsilence the past, to speak up for the kind of world we want to live in now – and so to write a story for the future, where all voices can be heard.

The World of Penelope

Taking a back-to-front view of history might seem unconventional: but this way of looking back at the past has actually always been the case when it comes to Homer. The Greek historian Herodotus placed Homer, the poet, at the end of the so-called Dark (or Iron) Age, around 820 BCE; while Herodotus dated the Trojan War (which he, like most of the ancients, believed was a historical conflict) at around 1220 BCE, right at the end of the Bronze Age. Later chroniclers agreed: a marble fragment recording important events in Greek history gives between 1218 and 1209 BCE as the date of the Trojan War, and the polymath Eratosthenes located the sack of Troy even more precisely at 1184 BCE. The Greek tradition suggested that – around the moment of the advent of the alphabet – Homer became the author of the *Iliad* and *Odyssey*; and that these epics, in turn, preserved a memory that looked back into the past of some four hundred years earlier. Nowadays, after centuries of heated scholarly debate and comparative work like Parry's and Lord's, looking at singers of tales in other modern cultures, this model has gradually been refined. The general consensus (founded on decades of research by my mentor at Harvard, Gregory Nagy) points, not to a single moment of transcription by a single man called Homer, but to a long evolution over hundreds of years, in which oral songs were gradually transformed, standardized and finally transcribed (from the mid sixth century BCE). They were then scripted into the Homeric texts and divided by ancient scholars into chapters (known as 'books') that give us the form in which they sit on bookshelves today – two written poems of twenty-four books each.[17] (The most unmistakable indication that these poems were originally oral comes from those stock epithets we saw above – like 'white-armed Helen' or 'swift-footed Achilles' – that are repeated to aid memorization and composition in performance.) In this view, 'Homer' – and this is the way the name will be used in this book – represents a historical tradition, a long process of evolution from the oral songs of the Late Bronze Age all the way to the written scripts that formed the basis of our modern texts. It's also a historical tradition that's resolutely male, which is why I call Homer 'he'. In this sense, the Homeric epics don't just represent a slice of history in and of themselves. The poems have, at the core of their narrative, the founding tenet that they *look back into the past*, that they preserve a memory of a time that has been and gone. The *Iliad* and the *Odyssey* were, from the very beginning, 'a poetry of the past' – a historical fiction, telling sweeping tales of mythic gods and bronze-clad heroes, gorgeous demi-goddesses and long-gone queens, imagined back on to the stage of a long-lost Bronze Age.[18] In other words, the Homeric epics began – themselves – as an anachronism.

This raises a number of questions that have vexed historians for centuries. If the Homeric epics consolidated in the Iron Age, but were set in the period of the Late Bronze Age, then what kind of world picture do they show – a Bronze Age one, an Iron Age one, or a mixture of the two? If the Homeric epics are poems, set in the realm of fiction, then did the Trojan War actually happen at all – and if so, how much of what Homer represents can be taken as definitive, historical fact? The eminent twentieth-century Cambridge historian Moses Finley put it

perhaps most forcibly, when he stated that there was -- in fact – nothing
at all to be learned about the historical, Bronze Age Trojan War from the
poetry of Homer. His view was that the Trojan War should be summarily
removed from the realm of history and returned to the sphere of myth
and poetry, until we have more evidence.[19] In Finley's eyes – summed up
in his influential book *The World of Odysseus* – all Homer's epic poems
could do for us was give evidence for the Iron Age of the tenth or ninth
centuries BCE.

It's certainly the case that we can show plenty of evidence in the
poems of the Iron Age – most obviously the presence of iron, which
didn't start to be used until after the Bronze Age (the clue's in the
name). But then there are also elements that unquestionably look
back to the Bronze Age – like the detailed description of a Cretan
boar's-tusk helmet gifted to Odysseus in the *Iliad*, which we find
buried with actual Bronze Age warriors in Crete (as well as mainland Greece) and depicted in Mycenaean wall paintings. Even the
use of an archaic language-scape points back to the Bronze Age
past: such as the personal names 'Achilles' and 'Hector' that we find
listed on Bronze Age tablets, or the word *wanax* for 'ruler' that's
attested in Mycenaean records – frequently used in Homer for
kings like Agamemnon, even though the term had fallen out of use
hundreds of years before the epics could have been written down.
It's been shown that some of the lilting phrases that sound so typically Homeric to us, like 'man-circling shield' (*aspidos amphibrotēs*),
actually have an ancient Mycenaean pedigree, preserving a version
of language spoken even earlier than the fourteenth century BCE.
It's a time capsule, passed down like an oral message-in-a-bottle,
from a much older stage of Greek – and pointing back to the long-
lost body shields that we know, from archaeology, were all the rage
in the Bronze Age.[20]

It's been argued that these kinds of details may have been added
to give a flavour of archaism, as a way to underline the pastness of
this long-gone heroic age; and that may be partly what they're doing.
But we can't forget that they're also a crucial testament to what epic
poems, originally orally sung, did and were *meant* to do – to preserve
a memory of tradition, of the past, to hand down remembrances of

genealogies and customs and long-lost places. The singers, or bards, who composed these tales of ancient heroes and passed on their craft to the next generation (and then the next – ultimately, to Homer, or someone like him), were not just storytellers or entertainers: they were custodians of the past, memory keepers who kept alive the heroic tales of a real and tangible history. We see this function of epic poetry layered into Homer's poems again and again: whether it's a description of the ancestry of a hero given as an aside during a battle, in campfire stories about the glorious men of old related among a band of warriors, or the reeled-off history of the generations of princely owners of a sceptre wielded by a king. Nor can we fail to remember that most, if not all, ancient Greeks (let alone Romans) believed that these were real events that really happened; a real Trojan War, during a real Age of Heroes, with real, redoubtable queens, superlative warriors and preternaturally gifted descendants of gods, who (so they thought) had founded the dynasties that made up their families, and built the cities they lived in. The audiences of epic would have known it as historical truth, learned at their mother's knee, that they were living in an Age of Iron – dull and blunted by comparison – following on from that last gleaming heroic age. The Trojan War was, to them, the watershed moment that sliced between the two: a world-shattering conflict that exploded into the decline and fall of an age. Epics like Homer's were a record, to the Greeks, of their own historical fabric, their sense of who they were, of the lost generations who preceded them in the shining – and tangibly real – era before their own.

So the Homeric epics are a mish-mash product of their history: both the long story of their formation over the centuries from songs into texts, and their historical stance in trying to preserve a distant, half-imagined yet remembered, past for an audience who held them as fact. There's no doubt that using the texts to look for facts about the Bronze Age is frustratingly difficult. There are certainly echoes of truth, however faint, and a historical memory that finds its foundation in the very fabric of sung oral poetry. Yet, at the same time, we have to remember that epic is, primarily, a fictional re-creation of the past for the concerns of the present – an 'ideological image of a historical society', as one critic neatly put it. Or, as another expert on the Greek Bronze Age has written, 'no epic is a realistic presentation of a society or age; rather, it is a fantasy, but a fantasy in which . . . reality keeps breaking through'.[21] It's a way of telling a story, a myth, *through* history – not a historical record itself.

But there's a different way forward. Since Finley purported to close the debate on Homer as evidence for the world of Bronze Age Greece over half a century ago, we have seen advances in science and archaeology that have uncovered new kinds of evidence about the Late Bronze Age that he couldn't have imagined. Not only that: since the 1960s we've seen a major shift in the stories we want to look for, the experiences we care about, and whose voices are allowed to speak – including the women who are the focus of this book. Finley (whose book, after all, was titled *The World of Odysseus*) pronounced, maddeningly and dogmatically, that ' "hero" has no feminine gender in the age of heroes' – as if half the population could be summarily dismissed because they didn't fit into one code of values invented by and for men.[22] If we start from *these* voices – the voices of women – and draw on new archaeological discoveries and scientific evidence for the Late Bronze Age to try to understand them and give the context for their stories, then we change the direction of the narrative. There might not have been – in fact there most likely wasn't – a Helen of Troy as Homer imagined her; but we can work to reconstruct how the idea of her might have come about, the history behind the myth – because there's real ancient documentary evidence for dynastic marriages in the Late Bronze Age between Mycenaean and Anatolian royals, just as in Homer's fictional story of Helen and Paris.[23] There might not have been a Briseis; but Late Bronze Age tablets from the Mycenaean palaces, written in an early form of Greek, show that enslaved women from Troy and its environs really were shipped to Greece. There might not have been a Hecuba; but there are historical records of Anatolian queens wielding significant power – as well as intriguing archaeological clues that the real, historical city of Troy was attacked by invaders and razed to the ground, right around the time that the ancients assigned the date for the legendary Trojan War. In other words, this is not a search for the real Penelope or the real Helen. They're male fictions, made up by a tradition of male poets telling stories about men; the two female characters are no more actual Greeks than Wonder Woman is a real-life Amazon. Instead, it's something much more interesting: a tantalizing search through the latest scientific articles, scribbled excavation reports, museum back rooms, DNA tests and centuries-old manuscripts for the real daughters, mothers, sisters, the queens, warriors, weavers, brides and midwives, the real-life women who made up the history of the Late Bronze Age world – and whose stories came to be threaded into the myths and legends of women like Helen of Troy and Penelope that would be told for thousands of years.

In focusing on the period of the Late Bronze Age, as one layer in the accretions that make up the Homeric texts, I'm taking the lead from the ideological thrust of Homer's fiction of history – that sense of pastness that permeates the epics – as well as what ancient audiences believed Homer was doing: that is, re-creating the lost world of the Age of Heroes. But I'm also switching the focus, the origin point of the inquiry, to what we can uncover about the historical women of the Late Bronze Age through recent scientific advances, critical interpretations, fictional rewritings and the latest archaeological excavations – and using those, in turn, to point a lens back on the texts and the women of Homer.

New discoveries are changing the way we think about the Homeric epics all the time. To give just one example: in the *Iliad*, there's a fleeting mention at one point of 'a folded tablet . . . inscribed with many dangerous and deadly symbols' that's used to send a message from Greece to Lycia (modern-day south-western Turkey).[24] For decades, scholars on the lookout for historical clues took this as ultimate proof of the poems' anachronism: up until very recently, the earliest-known folding writing tablets dated to the late eighth century BCE – so (the argument went) this must have been an invention added later, and couldn't possibly tell us anything about the Bronze Age. But in the last few years, a sensationally well-preserved folding wooden writing tablet has been lifted from the seabed, just off the coast of ancient Lycia in south-west Turkey, during the excavation of a Mediterranean shipwreck from the fourteenth century BCE.[25] The same artefact Homer describes; the same place; Late Bronze Age in date. So it's quite possible that – in this case – the Homeric epics were preserving a memory of one fragment of the Bronze Age all along. We just hadn't known it before.

In this way, I'm not using the epics as a fact sheet for the past, trying (for instance) to apply them to prove that the Trojan War took place, or to work out which kinds of weapons were current when (another bone of contention). I always ask, throughout the book, what new discoveries about the real women of history can do to help us understand Homer – *not* what Homer can tell us about the Late Bronze Age. Nor am I arguing that Homer presents a unified historical picture. Instead, I'm focusing in and starting from the latest discoveries we've been making about the women of the Late Bronze Age world – such as the DNA of the Peristeria Penelope – and using these to tell one story about the women of Homer and of myth, in a new way. And so, this book, too, like all books about Homer, is telling a story of Homer for our times – just like the Homeric epics did for theirs.

The Voyage Ahead to Mythica

In this book, it's the women who are going to take us on a journey through the *Iliad* and the *Odyssey*, and across the splendid, tumultuous world of the Late Bronze Age. We're going to follow them as they chart a course for us through the Homeric epics: from the war-torn plain of the *Iliad* below Troy, skimming west around the fantastical emerald isles of the *Odyssey* and then homeward bound to Ithaca. Along the way, we will come across women who lead troops into battle beside (and against) men; women who rule kingdoms with wisdom and foresight and wield the same power as a man; women who take control of their voices to tell their own stories; as well as women who have been victimized, silenced and oppressed, fallen into the margins of history. Together with new archaeological discoveries and scientific evidence, as well as the rich tapestry of cultural reworkings that have reimagined these women's stories, the voices that we uncover can be woven together into a vibrant narrative that shows us a new way into the past Homer looked back to in his epics – the gleaming world of the Late Bronze Age. Along the journey, a sequence of finds – some only recently discovered and less well known, some of them era-defining moments of archaeology – act as a way into each woman, each part of the story, along the path of recovering mythic women. And the retellings of the Homeric epics that open every chapter stand up for a new way of telling the *Iliad* and the *Odyssey* – not as a man's tale, but through the stories of women.

By putting Homer's women first, we are able to read these ancient epics in new ways. We can open our eyes to the fact that Achilles enslaves and rapes his female prisoners of war as a fundamental tenet of what it is to be a hero, or that Odysseus ties the knot on his tale with the summary execution of twelve enslaved women for being raped by his enemies – and so can see these so-called 'heroes' anew. We can look into the lives of real women across thousands of years of history who have dealt with experiences that speak to those of many women today: mothers coping with the demands of childbirth, generals rallying their troops in war, victims subjected to the trauma of sexual assault, military wives left at home to bear the burden of battle unseen, female leaders shaping society. We can make a point of putting women's experiences to the fore, and show how important it is that we do so – questioning what the one-dimensional male myth looks like from the point of view of the enslaved women, the widows, the grieving mothers, the rape victims, the traumatized siege survivors who were made to bear the cost of war, and showing that there is always a different side to the tale. We can trace how their stories – reworked because of their association with the grand Homeric epics by men from Ovid to Shakespeare to Tolstoy to James Joyce – have directed fictions about women across millennia, from supposed paragons of virtue like Penelope (what women 'should' be) to tricksy witches like Circe and power-grabbing killers like Clytemnestra (the deepest fears of male heroes). And we can ask what that means for how we think about ourselves and each other today.

But this is only the beginning. There are always more conversations to be had, more voices to uncover as the work of bringing to the fore all the individuals whom the myths, the texts and the historical records have forgotten continues to gain ground. This is just one part of that wider conversation. If we keep telling a story in which Penelope is always silent, then that's how she'll stay – silenced. It's time for her and all the others waiting in the wings to tell their stories.

So, Muse: tell me about a woman.

Iliad

WOMEN IN WAR

'This is our destiny: to be
characters in the tales told by men for years to come'

HELEN – HOMER, *ILIAD*, 6.357–8

1

HELEN

The Face

MDME. SCHLIEMANN, IN THE PARURE OF HELEN OF TROY

SPARTA, GREECE

She has always been treated as an object of beauty, and so she, too, collects beautiful things. Her chamber is her kingdom, and in the half-light when they think she is sleeping she gets up and walks barefoot, lines up her jewels and appraises them as the men appraise her.

Dawn is about to break. The distant line of the Taygetus mountains beyond Sparta is a thread of gold. Her tapestry stands on its loom, half finished, a purple shadow. She looks at her treasure, laid out on her clothes chest. Three gold cups with slender handles. A crystal dish. A silver basket, a golden spindle – gifts for entertaining one of her husband's many visitors. Earrings heavy with globes of looted amber. Hairpins of ivory ripped from the bloodied tusk of a boar. Bracelets of clasped metal that chafe her skin. All the chains of beauty.

She smooths her thumb across a crown of bronze, slides a golden necklace through her hands, drops of metal hard as seawater.

Will she take them with her when she leaves?

Troy Discovered

Early morning, 31 May 1873. Poppies thrusting themselves like open mouths through the earth as the workmen dig and toss damp soil on to the rubble pile. It's been a long season – a long couple of years since the middle-aged entrepreneur and avid Homerist Heinrich Schliemann first struck his trowel into the hill at Hisarlik, an odd-shaped mound rising out of the flatlands in Ottoman Turkey near the Dardanelles. Beneath this lump of earth these past few years, following a tip-off from British expat (and fellow Homer-lover) Frank Calvert, Schliemann has made a truly extraordinary discovery: nothing more nor less than the Bronze Age site – the real, tangible remains – of Homer's legendary Troy.

Now, they're two weeks away from shutting up the site for good as the heat of summer beckons. Some of the ruins are already crumbling away in the sun. Schliemann and his foreman, Yannakis, are eight or nine metres deep in a trench at the edge of Troy's ancient circuit wall. The other workmen, seventy or eighty of them, are scattered in various pits and cuts, and Schliemann's twenty-one-year-old Greek wife, Sophia, walks among them, a shawl draped over her shoulders.

And then, just when the hill at Hisarlik seems to have no more secrets to reveal, Schliemann strikes gold – literally.

He scrabbles at it, prising mud away. As a thin line of precious metal emerges from the trench floor, he calls Sophia down, pulls out his knife, starts to work first one object and then another free. More and more appear: thirty-four copper spears; five silver vases; two golden cups. And then, inside the largest silver vase, the trench's final secret: a treasure trove of jewellery – two splendid gold diadems, fifty-six golden earrings and thousands of tiny gold beads.

Together they wrap up the hoard, piece by piece, in Sophia's shawl, and smuggle them out of the trench. Later that evening, as dusk falls, Schliemann – still covered in dust from that day's dig – scrawls a letter to the nearby British consul: 'I am sorry to inform you that I am closely watched . . . I therefore take the liberty to deposit with you 6 baskets and a bag begging you will kindly *lock* them up and *not* allow by any means the Turks to touch them.'[1] As night falls, Yannakis sets out from the site, his shadow slipping away into the dark.

Some time later, Sophia sits in a photographer's studio in Athens. A black curtain forms a simple backdrop behind her. Around her dark hair, she has fastened the golden diadem from Troy; strands of gold hang from either side, resting on her shoulders, woven together like thread. Golden earrings gleam in her ears as she shifts on her chair for the camera, and the necklaces about her neck glint and move. The shutter opens to let the light in. The blank negative begins to take on the imprint of Sophia's face.

And as the picture spreads itself across the newspapers of the world, the word is that these are the jewels of Helen of Troy.

*

This, at least, is the story as Schliemann's letters and diary entries tell it. It's a sensational tale, full of theatricality: era-defining archaeological discoveries, a covert husband-and-wife partnership and a spot of make-believe dressing up (something the Victorians were very fond of). As Schliemann published his finds and Sophia's image went the nineteenth-century version of viral (passed around on Schliemann's calling cards), the spectacle burst the bounds of Troy and became truly global.

Recent archival research, however, combining Schliemann's personal diaries and correspondence alongside his publications of the finds, newspaper reports and court records, has uncovered the full story. It turns out Schliemann went on to smuggle the hoard on a ship out of Turkey and into Greece – he had, by now, dubbed it 'Priam's Treasure', after the legendary king of Troy from Homer's *Iliad* – for the staging of that famous photograph of Sophia in Athens. Having spent a vast sum of money on the Trojan excavations, he wanted the collection for himself, and claimed (as European antiquarians often have – most famously in the case of the Elgin Marbles) that it was safer in his hands than in its native land. The Ottoman government, to whom half the collection legally belonged, understandably disagreed. When it came to confiscating the jewels, however, they found that they were gone. Schliemann had hidden them: and the Ottoman state had to make do instead with an unsatisfactory pay-off. The treasure was sent for public display in the South Court of what would later become the Victoria and Albert Museum in London, from 1877 to 1880; it then moved to Berlin, as a gift to the German nation (and a record of Schliemann's achievement) 'for all time'.[2] The Ottoman Empire, Britain, Germany – everyone wanted a slice of the prize. All these great nations wanted to claim that they had a link to the greatest nation-building propaganda exercise of them all: Homer's Trojan War, the time-honoured victory tale that Schliemann's trowel had proven to be true – and the ideal origin story for these burgeoning nineteenth-century empires.

But two burning questions still remained: were these really Helen's jewels? And more specifically – were they really the jewels of Homer's Helen?

In Search of Homer's Helen

Helen is by far and away the most famous of Homer's women, and her story is as seductive as her legendary beauty. The legend begins when Aphrodite, goddess of love and sex, promised Helen to the Trojan prince Paris as his prize if he judged her the most beautiful of the goddesses. When Paris picked Aphrodite, events were set in motion that would trigger an ancient world war: because Helen was already wed to the Greek king Menelaus, who – through her – had gained the kingdom of Sparta. Menelaus was more than a little put out when his beautiful wife, and with her his claim to the throne, abandoned him for Troy. And so he gathered up the Greek allies, and sailed to ravage Troy and get her back.

It will come as no surprise that it's Helen, and not her husband or the Greeks, who is routinely blamed (both in Homer and by later Greek and Roman writers) for starting the Trojan War. (There is a stock phrase that peppers the Homeric epics: it all happened 'because of her'.) It's probably fair to say that most ancient Greek men (whose wives were their legal property and who handed out severe punishments for a woman's infidelity) thought – when they listened to Homer – that, by leaving her husband and forfeiting her homeland, Helen was guilty either way. For them, it hardly mattered whether the legend said she was doled out as a prize by the gods, trafficked (or raped) by Paris, or if she went of her own accord. By the time of the Elizabethan playwright Christopher Marlowe (a contemporary of Shakespeare), Helen could be reduced to a famous (and damning) line of poetry in his *Doctor Faustus* that turns Helen into nothing but a body that's to blame for war: 'the face that launch'd a thousand ships'.

Homer, however, starts in the middle of the story – and he's much more interested in examining a more complicated, more nuanced version of Helen, one that shows her working through the monumental repercussions of what has happened to her, than in condemning her outright. Instead of the supernatural beauty contest, the night-time assignations in Sparta or the flight across the Aegean in Paris' ship, we first meet Helen in a remarkably quiet and contemplative scene in the third book of the *Iliad*, sitting inside the walls of Troy, weaving a tapestry in which

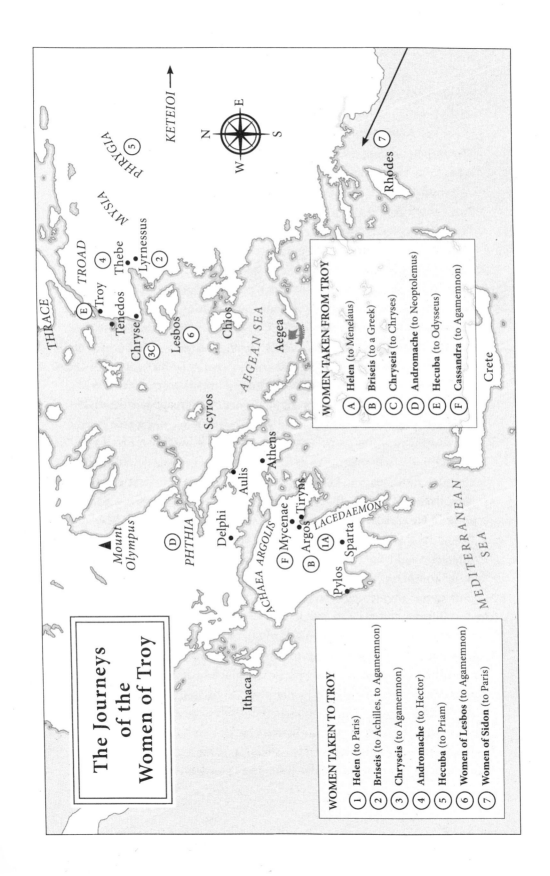

The Journeys of the Women of Troy

WOMEN TAKEN TO TROY

1. **Helen** (to Paris)
2. **Briseis** (to Achilles, to Agamemnon)
3. **Chryseis** (to Agamemnon)
4. **Andromache** (to Hector)
5. **Hecuba** (to Priam)
6. **Women of Lesbos** (to Agamemnon)
7. **Women of Sidon** (to Paris)

WOMEN TAKEN FROM TROY

A. **Helen** (to Menelaus)
B. **Briseis** (to a Greek)
C. **Chryseis** (to Chryses)
D. **Andromache** (to Neoptolemus)
E. **Hecuba** (to Odysseus)
F. **Cassandra** (to Agamemnon)

THRACE

TROAD

MYSIA

PHRYGIA

KETEIOI →

Troy
Tenedos
Chryse
Thebe
Lyrnessus
Lesbos
Chios

AEGEAN SEA

Aegea

Scyros

Mount Olympus

PHTHIA

Delphi
Aulis
Athens

ACHAEA
ARGOLIS

Mycenae
Tiryns
Argos
LACEDAEMON
Sparta
Pylos

Ithaca

Crete

MEDITERRANEAN SEA

Rhodes

N E S W

she's worked scenes of the war that she has caused. It couldn't be clearer that, in spite of her divine ancestry (her father was rumoured to be Zeus, king of the gods), Homer is setting up for us a tableau of a very human Helen, who is taking the time to reflect on the costs of the battle being fought for her beyond the city walls.

The quiet doesn't last, though: inevitably, the real battles of men intrude into this contemplative, female space. Summoned by Priam, king of Troy, to give an insider view on the Greeks he can see from the battlements of the city, she reluctantly goes up to the towers of Troy to gaze from the walls over the plain at the Greek forces, and identify the leaders to the Trojan king. In a scene that could have been extremely uncomfortable, not to mention incriminating (at one point, Priam points out Menelaus, the husband she left behind, among the Greek troops), Homer deftly conjures sympathy for Helen: she searches in vain for her brothers, Castor and Pollux, among the Greeks, 'not knowing,' Homer tells us, 'that they were already buried in the life-giving soil back in Sparta, her home.'[3]

This nuanced, thoughtful and sympathetic Helen reappears throughout the rest of the epic. Summoned by Aphrodite to have sex with Paris, she refuses with a sharp and witty comeback. 'Go to him yourself and sit beside him,' she snaps. 'Give up the path of gods and let your feet never turn back again to Mount Olympus! Spend all your time taking care of Paris, crying for him, until he makes you either his slave girl or his wife!'[4] No mortal can, however, prevail against the gods, and Helen is forced into Paris' chamber. Yet even here, she has something to say for herself – and she doesn't pull her punches, either. 'I wish that you had died out there,' she says bluntly, turning away from him and averting her gaze, 'defeated by that strong man who used to be my husband.'[5] Just as Telemachus tells Penelope to shut up in the *Odyssey*, however, Paris orders Helen to stop telling him off: he doesn't want to hear her complaints. He has 'never been more attracted to her', he says (with a cringing inability to read the room): he just wants to go to bed.[6] So Helen tries to talk to someone else. When Hector, the eldest prince of Troy and leader of their armies, returns to the city a little later to bring Paris back into the war, she asks him to sit with her in her chambers and tries to work through her guilt. Relentlessly shaming herself to him as a 'bitch', she makes it clear that she feels that she is to blame for the Trojan War.[7]

Because of her and Paris' 'folly and delusion', she says, she has made everyone suffer – Hector most of all.[8] With extraordinary prescience and not a little metapoetic foreshadowing (that serves to hint at her very special status within the poem), she predicts their fate: to become 'characters in the tales told by men for years to come'.[9] When Hector meets his end towards the epic's close, Helen is one of the women who leads the lament at his funeral – claiming that Hector protected her from the spite of the other Trojans and their wives, the only one in Troy who saw her as she really was.

Helen's own comments, as well as what others say about her, make it quite clear that she is being presented as the cause of the war, the reason why Troy is being besieged. She is, in other words, the explanation for why the epic poem we know as the *Iliad* exists. But recent research, building on the new way of looking at the past that has started exploring the roles of women, is also showing that she provides us with a unique insight into the many expressions of her voice – unparalleled among women, who, as we've seen with Penelope in the *Odyssey*, are often told to stay silent. Through her upbraiding of Aphrodite and Paris, her self-reproach to Hector, her lament among the people of Troy, she speaks out of the text, allowing us to break down the ostensible story that women stay silent and 'words are men's concern'. This is a Helen who is in full control of her voice and who is able to reclaim her story. This is a Helen who speaks out in the full awareness that her tale will be told by men, that she will become fodder for the songs and the epics of men, and that she wants to have a say in how her side of the story is passed on. This is a Helen who is able to step back from the war and weave a narrative of the battles that are being fought around Troy, from her point of view, in her own way – just, in fact, like the poet Homer does. When we go out in search of the women of Homer and read their tales with an ear to what they have to say, we can see beyond the battles that make up much of the epic, the ebb and flow of Achilles' anger and the final showdown with Hector. And we can see that it is actually a remarkable woman, Helen, who precipitates the entire action of the war, whose strong and independent voice punctuates the epic, and whose determination to tell things her way means she gets, at least in part, to hand down her own story 'for people in the future' – like us.

But it's not just in the *Iliad* that Helen takes on an important role. She has a part to play in the *Odyssey*, too. At this point, the war has now been won by the Greeks – following Odysseus' famous trick with the Trojan horse – and Helen has been reunited with Menelaus (who was set on killing her during the capture of Troy, but – so the story goes – was unable to resist her charms when she, ever resourceful, gave him a flash of what he was missing). Here, in the *Odyssey*, among the olive groves in her father's ornate palace at Sparta, she is back with the husband she regretted leaving and surrounded by the props of a queen; although her jewels aren't mentioned, there are plenty of allusions to golden cups and silver bowls. And she is a world away from the Helen of the *Iliad*. She and Menelaus entertain their recently arrived guest in style – Telemachus, Odysseus' son, who has sailed to Sparta in search of news of his father – and regale him with tales of Troy. If either Menelaus or Helen find their reminiscences of the war she started, and he finished, a little awkward, they don't show it; if anything, Menelaus is keen to demonstrate that he endorses Helen's stories of what happened at Troy: 'well spoken, wife', he says.[10] And in any case Helen has the ideal solution to ease the tension: a 'drug of forgetfulness' – probably opium – which she hands out to her guests. It's easy to imagine that, after all that has happened, Helen is quite happy to help her husband – as well as herself – along the path to trying to forget the past.

Forgetfulness and erasure, as we see it in the *Odyssey*, becomes a key theme around Helen that other, later – though still ancient – authors pick up on. Poets, rhetoricians and playwrights like Stesichorus, Gorgias and Euripides take Helen's story, as it was narrated in Homer, and tell it in new, and strikingly different, ways. In these texts – coming to a peak during the years of Athenian democracy now known as the classical period, in the fifth century BCE, when debates about right and wrong and the role of the law were raging – Helen becomes a focus for discussing who was really to blame for the Trojan War. An extraordinary story arises, best exemplified in the drama *Helen*, by the renowned tragedian Euripides, which premiered in Athens in 412 BCE. The tale goes that the gods sent a ghost Helen, an *eidōlon*, to Troy instead; the real Helen actually spent the war vacationing in Egypt. In this, entirely different and rather startling, strand of Helen's tale, she is excused of all responsibility for the battle – because, in fact, she never went to Troy at all.

Will the Real Helen Please Step Forward

Which means that our search for the 'real' Helen is not just a modern concern, and not just an issue of Schliemann's, either – it's an ancient one, too. When Schliemann was excavating at Troy and searching for Helen's jewels, he was digging into a much deeper issue. This wasn't just about whether he'd found Helen's jewels. It was about whether Helen ever went to Troy at all, whether she even existed, or whether she was simply a ghost, an *eidōlon*, of Homer's – and our own – vivid imaginations.

To some extent, in Schliemann's case at least, she was just that – a Homeric fantasy. Schliemann thought he had found Homer's Troy, and, in a way, he was right: we now know that he was in the right *place* – the site Calvert found, and Schliemann began to excavate, is the site of what the ancients called Troy. But the way that archaeology works – the way that *history* works – is that the past is rarely preserved without the accretions of later generations. There are, of course, notable exceptions: one of the most famous is Vesuvius' eruption in 79 CE that led to the total burial of the towns of Pompeii and Herculaneum, conserving them to be discovered again hundreds of years later. But, for the most part, we tend to live with our past. When a building outlives its purpose, we add new parts or build on old foundations. We reuse objects handed down to us and surround ourselves with heirlooms that have meaning. At Hisarlik, the circuit wall that Schliemann thought belonged to Homer's Troy was just one layer in a site that was rebuilt and repurposed over thousands of years. And these remains were far too deep to date to Homer's Troy: over a thousand years too deep. 'Priam's Treasure' dates to a layer of the city known to archaeologists as Troy II, to around 2400 BCE – more than a millennium *before* the Trojan War should have taken place.

Modern excavations at the site of Troy, however, have told us a lot more about the evidence for a Trojan War at Troy than Schliemann could ever have imagined. Careful peeling away of the layers of the site, and

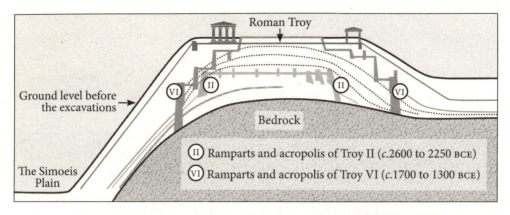

*Section – looking from the west – through the site of Troy (after Dörpfeld).
Schliemann failed to realize that the Late Bronze Age remains of Troy
lay close to the surface, due to multiple levellings of the hilltop over the
centuries. Instead, he used dynamite to blast through most of Late Bronze
Age Troy – so destroying what could have been 'Homer's' city.*

dating of the stratigraphy by precise comparisons of the pottery finds alongside radiocarbon dating, allows us to reconstruct a timeline for the various occupations of the mound of Hisarlik, from the Early Bronze Age Troy I all the way to the late Roman Troy IX. And it's at the layer of the site now dated to around 1230–1180 BCE, known as Troy VIIa – and right around the date that the ancients set for the Trojan War, traditionally placed at 1184 BCE – that archaeologists have found evidence that, suggestively, seems to point to an enemy attack and the destruction of Troy. Skeletons of unburied bodies lie in the streets of both the citadel and the recently discovered lower city. Bronze arrowheads are scattered everywhere. Houses, their carcasses blackened by fire and filled with ash, have been burnt to the ground. As recently as 1995, heaps of sling bullets have been found throughout the lower city, ready to be used by Troy's defenders. Meanwhile, the fabulously grand, and slightly earlier, parts of the city – Troy VI, with its towering gates, high walls, broad streets and splendid palace, still very much in use at the time of Troy VIIa – seems to be a fitting candidate for the poetic inspiration for Homer's depiction of a wealthy, broad-pathed Troy with its shining halls, opulent houses and massive gates.

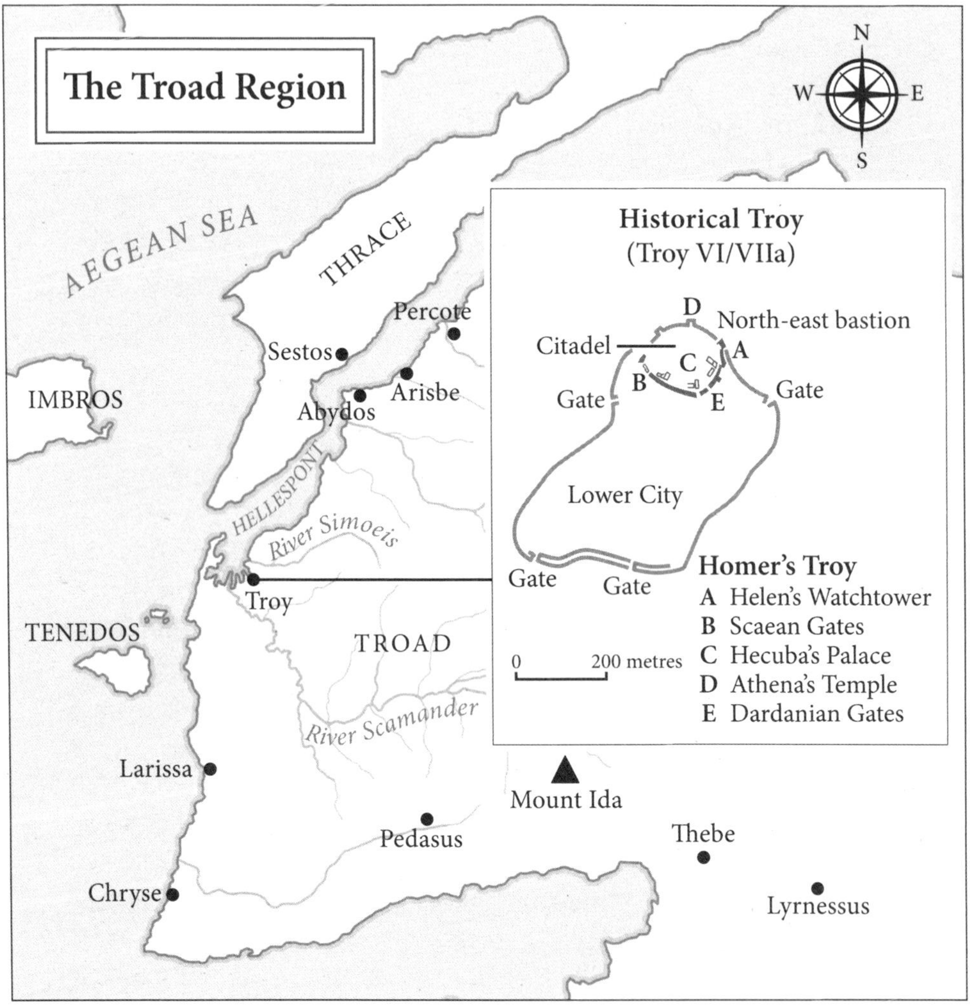
The Troad Region
N
W
E
S
AEGEAN SEA
THRACE
Percote
Sestos
Arisbe
IMBROS
Abydos
HELLESPONT
River Simoeis
Troy
TENEDOS
TROAD
River Scamander
Larissa
Mount Ida
Pedasus
Thebe
Chryse
Lyrnessus
Historical Troy
(Troy VI/VIIa)
D
North-east bastion
Citadel
A
C
B
Gate
E
Gate
Lower City
Gate
Gate
Homer's Troy
A Helen's Watchtower
B Scaean Gates
C Hecuba's Palace
D Athena's Temple
E Dardanian Gates
0
200 metres

But – as tempting as it may be (and Schliemann certainly allowed himself to get tempted) – we have to approach all these conjectures with caution. While Troy VIIa does seem to have been attacked and destroyed by fire, it's essential to note that there is no concrete archaeological or textual evidence at the site of Hisarlik (or, indeed, anywhere else) for who these attackers were, let alone that they were the Greeks described by Homer – nor that this was a ten-year siege of the magnitude that

Homer depicts in the Trojan War. There's still an ongoing debate as to when this war (if it did happen) might have taken place, with scholars putting it in anywhere from Troy VI to Troy VIIa, from the thirteenth century BCE (Carl Blegen, who excavated Troy in the 1930s, favoured a date of 1250 BCE) into the early twelfth. The reason this later date would be a problem for Homer's Trojan War is that, if the city of Troy really did fall around 1190/80 BCE – as the general consensus now suggests – then it would have been destroyed at the same time as, or even after, many of the Mycenaean palaces on the Greek mainland had already gone up in flames – meaning the attackers couldn't have been Mycenaeans, unless their palaces were being burnt precisely *because* they were away. Nor is there any written record, until Homer's epic poem several centuries later, that a woman named Helen ever went to Troy. If Homer was remembering some kernel of truth in the *Iliad*, it seems likely to me that it's a telescoped version of the Late Bronze Age Troy VI and VIIa, set in the context of the mass destruction that swept across the Aegean world, that is the Troy of Homer's epics: a once-proud city crouching in the ruins of its former grandeur, attacked by enemies and scarred by fire, magicked with the wave of a mythopoetic wand into the Trojan War of legend.

No matter how much Schliemann wanted it to be, then, the treasure he had found in Troy II could never have been Helen's jewels.

When I visited Troy myself, however, in the search for the real women behind Homer – on a sun-streaked day in May very like that morning when Schliemann found his spectacular treasure – I couldn't help but see how Schliemann might have got carried away in his speculations about Helen. It's a hugely complicated site, difficult to pick apart, even for an ancient historian. Walls scramble over other walls, cutting through and over them; piles of stones from one layer of the city's past sit next to those from hundreds of years earlier. As I wander across the hillocks and between the tumbling buttresses from different centuries, swallows chattering above me in the sky and the horizon dominated by the flatlands down below that stretch towards the coast, I try to imagine what it must have been like for Schliemann – and the later excavators of the site, Wilhelm Dörpfeld, Carl Blegen and Marion Rawson, Manfred Korfmann – to piece together this fractured jigsaw puzzle from the past. Above all, as someone who works on a day-to-day basis with

The sloping walls and battlements of the real Troy – just as Homer described them. To the north lies the great watchtower where Homer imagined Helen of Troy looking out over the Greek troops.

Homer, I'm blown away, just like Schliemann was, by the many, almost uncanny, resonances between the Homeric texts and the Trojan site. While Schliemann, in his haste to reach his goal, ironically destroyed much of the layer of Troy that experts would now date to the time of the Trojan War, some parts of Troy VI/VIIa still remain, picked apart by later excavators: most notably the monumental eastern run of the stone-built defensive walls, as well as impressive gates and a 25-foot-high watchtower. Homer describes these walls in the *Iliad* with the precision of an engineer: 'three times Patroclus tried to climb the angle of the high wall', he says (describing the Greek warrior's ill-fated attempt to enter Troy).[11] And that's exactly what we find at the archaeological site of Troy: curiously angled ramparts built of stone that would have been expressly designed to fend off attacking enemies. In the legend of a Trojan War that was handed down the centuries in oral memory and embellished into epic, it seems that some memory of Troy's great fortifications was – dimly – preserved. Standing here along the walls on the colossal watchtower of Troy, the salt wind blowing into my face from the sea, it's all too easy to imagine that a woman like Helen might once really have stood here too, gazing out over the battle plain as she is described by Homer in the *Iliad*.

And, as mistaken as Schliemann might have been in dating the treasure to the time of Homer's Troy, the inextricable link he forged between the jewels and the figure of Helen – the anachronistic draping of 'Helen's' diadem and necklaces on his wife Sophia – did do one very important thing. It changed, for the first time in hundreds of years, the way people thought about Helen. For centuries, with the site of Troy lost to history, Helen had been a figure fashioned purely of myth, a poetic construction of Homer's imagination – an *eidōlon*, just like the ancient Greeks had argued. Now, for the first time since the Roman era, with the discovery of the undeniably real stones and fabric of the city of Troy, it suddenly became possible that there could, once, have been a woman in the pattern of Helen – not, perhaps, historically real in the sense Schliemann would have wanted her to be, with a set of her personal jewels locked up in a Trojan treasure chest, but a distant memory (warped through time and poetry) of a prehistoric queen. More than that, it was only now – exactly a hundred and fifty years ago – that it became possible, for the first time since antiquity, to actually forge a link between the texts of Homer and the archaeology of Troy and the Bronze Age: to suggest, not just that the texts had some relationship to history, but that Homer's Helen, too, might find some basis – however tenuous – in the past.

This was a massive blow to the establishment opinion on Homer in the nineteenth century when Schliemann was digging at Troy. To the venerable classicists, enthroned in their Oxford and Cambridge colleges like Olympian gods and authoritatively pronouncing on the right way of reading the Homeric texts, Schliemann's 'poetical fancy playing around unwritten legend' (as one eminent professor of Greek put it) was nothing more than an iconoclastic attempt to turn Homer into a cheap historical phenomenon and, in turn, to undermine the grand, timeless ideals of the epics.[12] For the ancient Greeks, however, this would hardly have come as a surprise. To them, Homer wasn't the distant, illustrious and upright paragon of the Victorians: his epics were a cross between a local history guide, a national treasure and an instruction manual, providing up-to-date information on everything from battle advice to how to worship the gods. Above all, they believed – almost universally – that what the epics recounted was true, incontrovertible fact: that the Trojan War had really happened, and that it belonged to the Age of Heroes that had preceded their own. Victors in the ancient Olympic Games proudly derived their family lineages from warriors of this heroic age: one of the most sought-after prizes at the Games was to have a bespoke hymn composed that showcased the victor's family tree, all the way back to what they regarded as their very real epic ancestors. In fact, many ancient Greeks believed they would literally have become extinct as a nation if the Greek (or 'Achaean', as Homer calls them) heroes who went to Troy hadn't made it back home again.[13]

And Helen, more than any other of the Trojan War legends from that lustrous Age of Heroes, was a familiar, tangible presence to the later Greek inhabitants of Sparta. A historic queen and an icon to her people, she was worshipped in cult centres (known as hero cults; we find many of these dedicated to the heroes of the Trojan War) around Sparta. The greatest of these, perched on a hilltop overlooking the ridge of Mount Taygetus at Therapne – around one and a half miles south-east of the Spartan Acropolis – welcomed worshippers of Helen as an embodied queen, and wife of Menelaus, that people could relate to: a real person, not a god. Here, at the spot where Helen and Menelaus were believed to be buried, devotees of Helen could bring offerings to ask for a good harvest or a successful breeding season at the farm: like the mid-seventh-century BCE bronze flask discovered at the site, inscribed with words to the effect: 'from Deinis to Helen'.[14] Meanwhile, young Spartan girls – surrounded by flickering torches and garlanded with hyacinths – would sing bridal songs about Helen's marriage to Menelaus on the eve of their wedding.[15] At Helen's shrine, men and women alike would flock to identify with the very real young girl from the Age of Heroes who had become a wife; the trophy who had had to navigate a life of possession; the famed beauty who had filled the world's spotlight; the Spartan who had left the banks of the Eurotas river, only to come home again.

Many Helens

The ancient Greeks would also have known that we always – for better or worse – bring a part of ourselves to the search for 'the real' Helen. The archaic citizens of Sparta, who brought her their dedications and worshipped in her temple, looked to their hero to ensure the survival and cohesion of their community. Meanwhile, Schliemann's near-obsessive desire to find Homer's Helen – and Troy – had its beginnings in a contemporary cultural movement in German philhellenism that looked to the Greek past as the origin of Western civilization. But Schliemann's cultivation of the past wasn't just political – it was deeply personal, too. In decorating his wife with Helen's jewels, he was playing out a troubling personal fantasy: the idea that he could actually have an ancient Greek woman, or even Helen herself, for his own. When Schliemann decided to marry a second time (his first marriage ended in divorce), he asked his Greek tutor to find a 'black-haired Greek woman in the Homeric spirit', who knew her ancient Greek, to be his wife.[16] Presented with three photos, he chose Sophia. Their offspring would be Homeric children (their names were Andromache and Agamemnon). Their partnership at Troy would allow them to follow in the footsteps of Homer's heroes. Dressing Sophia in (what he thought were) Helen's jewels was, in many ways, the crowning moment in which he declared to the world that he had managed to create a Homeric wife – to possess his own Helen.

This combination of sexual and symbolic appropriation of Homer's Helen into men's wishful fantasies – her 'grafting', as one critic has called it – has patterned her story across history.[17] In many ways, Helen's trafficking is the beginning of history in the West. Herodotus, the so-called 'father of history' whose *Histories* (published in the mid 420s BCE) are generally identified as the earliest example of the modern historical genre, opens his inquiry by tracing the cause of the enmity between Persians and Greeks. (His subject is the fifth-century BCE Persian Wars.) The answer: the seizure of Helen by the Trojan prince Paris, which Herodotus identifies among the first of several tit-for-tat traffickings of women across the Aegean.[18] In other words, once men begin to write – whether epic, like Homer, or history, like Herodotus – they make Helen their subject. Just as Helen had predicted in the *Iliad*.

Echoes of Helen – both idolizing and demonizing this much-trafficked figure – resound across the centuries from then on. The Roman poet Ovid imagines steamy love letters written between Helen and Paris, and mockingly places an ageing Helen in front of a mirror, wishing she had her youthful beauty back.[19] In fashionable Pompeii, an astonishing new discovery made in 2024's recent excavations shows a painting of a rather reticent Helen lingering behind Paris on the wall of a well-to-do's dining room – serving up a ready topic of conversation for classically versed dinner guests. Meanwhile, Christopher Marlowe's late sixteenth-century *Doctor Faustus* – in which the famous line about the thousand ships appears – presents Helen as the Devil's ultimate temptation to Faust (Faust, naturally, is unable to resist). Little wonder that Renaissance pamphlets counselled good Christians against naming their daughters Helen – given all the associations with adultery, women's sexuality and (last but not least) the fall of civilization.[20] English Pre-Raphaelite painters, influenced by the heady atmosphere of Romanticism and nineteenth-century classicism, were rather more sympathetic, conjuring up a Helen – like Dante Gabriel Rossetti's 1863 portrait – dressed up like a classical statue of Aphrodite, with thick golden locks, plump curves and sumptuous robes. In the twentieth century, meanwhile, riffing off Marlowe, science fiction writer Isaac Asimov claimed to have invented a new unit of female beauty: the 'millihelen', or the amount of beauty required to launch a single ship (if Helen's face could launch a thousand, then a millihelen would be sufficient for one). And in Derek Walcott's epic poem *Omeros*, from 1990, Helen travels to the Caribbean, metamorphosing into the love interest of two fishermen in St Lucia, Achille and Hector, at the heart of an exploration of the ways in which European colonialism has erased black identities, past and present. These Helens – seductresses and tormentors, Helens of Troy and Helens of Antilles – chart the afterlife of, and continuing obsession with, Helen's ever-shifting ghost.

But this isn't just a story told by men. Women have also had something to say in re-creating Helen's tale: and it's not just modern women, either. Sappho, the first and most famous female poet of the ancient Greek world, composed a poem around 600 BCE in which she twisted the narrative around on its axis. Instead of blaming Helen for the Trojan War, she turns the tables: she's not going to talk about Homer's wars, his 'armies of ships'; love is going to be the subject of her poetry instead.[21] In doing this, Sappho can say that, as a woman and a lover, she understands Helen in a new way: just as Helen took matters into her own hands and pursued the love she wanted when she went after Paris, so Sappho, too, can't stop thinking about the woman she loves. For Sappho, putting Helen first means foregrounding her own voice, and her own kind of poetry as a woman in a world of men.

Just as Sappho engaged with Homer by moving the focus, so contemporary women writers face up to the male tradition of turning Helen into a beautiful object and silencing her voice. Instead of placing Helen on a pedestal or vilifying her as the Devil's temptation, these modern reworkings by women – from Sandeep Parmar's *Eidolon* (2015) to Anne Carson's *Norma Jeane Baker of Troy* (2019) (a fusion of Helen with Marilyn Monroe) and Claire Heywood's *Daughters of Sparta* (2021) – are trying to critique the world that produced Helen, and showing what it looks like when expressed in her own voice, when we tell her side of the tale. And, as the poet Rhina Espaillat points out, it's often about much more than just Helen: 'The future finds its Troys in every Sparta.'[22] This Helen, like all the Helens that have gone before, is very much a product of our times: refusing to be silenced, telling her own story – as problematic and complex, even difficult, as that often is. She's not the subject of men's song any more.

The Face That Launched a Thousand Ships

These metamorphoses of Helen are as much a part of her story as Homer's is. But an essential part of the work is also in peeling back these layers, in excavating away the many guises that Helen has been forced to wear, the many mythical accretions she has accumulated, like barnacles clustered on a bronze statue on the seabed. This is the work of reconstructing the Bronze Age Helen: a real, flesh-and-blood woman, remembered in Homer's epics and turned into a legend; not necessarily even 'Helen', or beautiful, but a memory or a testimony to the many living, breathing women who made up the Late Bronze Age world.

If recent novels have worked on giving Helen back her voice, it's Helen's face that has been a source of fascination for millennia. In a way, by dressing up Sophia in what he thought were Helen's jewels, Schliemann was trying to do what men have done for thousands of years:

to put a face to Helen's name. Helen's face has always posed problems, stretching right back to antiquity. The Greek painter Zeuxis (active in the classical period of the fifth century BCE) was trying – so the story goes – to paint Helen, and struggling to find a woman beautiful enough to pose for him. And so he did the next best thing: he assembled five of the most attractive women he could find, and created a composite image with the best features of each one – attempting, collage-like, to reconstruct a kind of perfect beauty.[23]

So what might a woman like Helen really have looked like? The evidence from Mycenaean wall paintings from Greece, including one from the Mycenaean palace at Tiryns from around 1300 BCE, show white-skinned women draped in jewels with breasts like helium balloons crammed into their bodices, rouged cheeks and lustrous dark hair. Helen's whiteness is a major feature of her representation (as with all ancient Greek women, depicted with lily-white skin on everything from walls to water jars), and probably one of the reasons that she was so appealing to later European writers invested in constructing a lineage back to a white classical past.[24] Homer calls her 'white-armed' on her first appearance in the *Iliad*, and in later depictions of Helen on Greek vases she is painted in a pale slip that makes her whiteness shine out from the dark surface of the pot.[25] Similarly to the Mycenaean wall paintings, a sculpted plaster head of a woman (or perhaps a woman-headed sphinx) from Mycenae, an incredibly rare find dating to the thirteenth century BCE, also has moon-bright skin. White lead oxide, which women would have applied to their faces and bodies to make them appear whiter, was available in the Late Bronze Age, and archaeological finds from women's graves in later periods have shown the dried-up remains of lead carbonate still contained within the make-up jars that were often buried alongside their female owners.[26] (One of these jars, known as a *pyxis*, is represented in the wall painting in the hands of the Tiryns woman.) Along with their white skin, these Late Bronze Age women would have boasted dark-lined eyes – probably using kohl, which we know from organic remains and written recipes was current in Egypt at the time – and rouged cheeks, with red rosettes sometimes painted in saffron or henna on cheeks, foreheads and chins, hands and arms (as we see on the Mycenae plaster head). And while almost all Mycenaean wall paintings show dark-haired women, Helen was famous for her luxurious golden curls (the Homeric word, *xanthos*, covers everything from golden hair to bay-coloured horses and sandy river-water).[27] One gorgeous Late Bronze Age painting from the island of Thera, a lush scene of women gathering saffron surrounded by riotously coloured vegetation, depicts a young woman with striking golden-red hair and blue eyes. An early Helen, perhaps?[28]

But a face is much more than the make-up that creates the mask that people see. A face – the real face – is part of the bones and tissues of our body, the flesh-and-blood fabric. Because the soft tissues that make up the surface of the face gradually decompose over time (unless preserved by artificial processes like mummification), the question of what the skeletons dug up from Bronze Age tombs would have actually looked like has always been something of an enigma to archaeologists.

Until recently, that is. In the last couple of decades, with the development of techniques from forensic anthropology and DNA analysis to technologies like radiocarbon dating and 3D digital printing, our ability to reconstruct the faces of the people of the past has made leaps and bounds. Taking into account everything from eye, skin and hair colour (all of which can be derived from DNA traces) to dental and bone ageing (which can be used to determine the age the person died) and using radiocarbon dating to provide an accurate historical context, the scientists, archaeologists and forensic artists who undertake facial reconstruction – whether in order to identify murder victims for forensic investigation, or to allow us to see what ancient people might have looked like – start from the premise that it is possible to reconstruct the layers of muscle and skin over the skull structure to rediscover the full picture of a face one can no longer see. These layers are either physically sculpted with clay over a cast or 3D-printed replica of the skull, or generated on a computer to create a 3D digital image. With these kinds of techniques, we can – for the first time – peer back into the eyes of the past. And we can see if Helen's face looks back at us.

In 1986, a team at the University of Manchester – who pioneered one of the current major methods in facial reconstruction, now known as the Manchester method – decided to apply what they'd learned to seven skulls found in a grave circle at the Bronze Age site of Mycenae, legendary seat of Homer's King Agamemnon (and another glittering

archaeological gem of Schliemann's, excavated by him in 1876).[29] One
of these – excitingly, for the search for the real women behind Homer –
was a woman. Known as Γ (or gamma) 58, she belonged to a group of
skeletons uncovered in what is known as Grave Circle B at Mycenae.
This is a royal cemetery from the seventeenth to sixteenth centuries BCE
containing twenty-six graves along with finds of extraordinary wealth
and splendour, discovered by accident in the 1950s by a group of workmen excavating a nearby tholos tomb (like the one where the Peristeria
Penelope was found). Such burials are testament to the enormous
wealth and power of royalty and their extensive trade connections in
Greece at the beginning of the Late Bronze Age. Royal individuals are
buried here with all the pomp and luxury Mycenae had to offer: from
imported pottery from the Cyclades and Crete, boasting international
trade links, to the most expensive clothing trimmed with gold and all
the latest finery. Women, in particular, were dressed up for the afterlife
in the utmost magnificence, with golden diadems, necklaces of golden
flying birds, set with amber, cornelian and amethyst, and silver earrings,
their clothing adorned with bronze pins with rock-crystal heads. And
they were surrounded by all the paraphernalia that goes with beautifica-
tion: one was buried alongside her cosmetic bowl, cut out of pale pink
crystal in the shape of a duck. These were wealthy and important females
who wanted to demonstrate their affluence, as well as their beauty, to
the world: just like the Helen we see in the *Odyssey* surrounded by her
golden cups and silver spinning-basket.

Γ58 has a lot to tell researchers, many secrets locked into her bones.
She was tall for the time – 1.61 metres – and strongly built, characteristic of the physical health (based on a good diet and health outcomes)
that we'd normally expect to find in burials of a ruling elite.[30] Evidence
from her teeth showed that she died in her mid-thirties; signs of arthritis
in her vertebrae and hands are perhaps evidence of repeated weaving,
a common (and physically wearing) activity among women (and one
which we have seen Helen undertaking in the *Iliad*). But bones are – as a
famous sixteenth-century anatomist put it – just like tent poles to a tent:
the job isn't finished until the tent fabric is up.[31] And so the laborious
work of bringing Γ58 back to life began. Painstakingly, the Manchester researchers started to assemble and reconstruct the various parts of

The face that launched a thousand ships?
A reconstruction of a real Late Bronze Age woman from Mycenae –
home, in legend, to Helen of Troy's sister, Clytemnestra.

her face – casting the skull, layering it with clay, sculpting the mouth, nose and eyes.[32] The face that emerged is heart-shaped, with relatively small and widely spaced eyes; the mouth is full, the jawline strong and forehead pronounced. (The hairstyle – the hair gathered back with long tresses falling over the shoulder, and a band and loose curls over the forehead – is conjectural, based on contemporary wall paintings.)

In the last few decades, however, technology has moved on in unimaginable ways. Facial reconstructions can now be re-created digitally – and even, with the latest available tools, using AI. As part of the research for this book, I teamed up with a specialist in digital facial reconstruction (who goes by Juanjo Ortega G., or @imperiumromanum_27ac) to develop the Manchester researchers' clay model – and to generate an astonishingly lifelike face for this millennia-old prototype for Helen of Troy. Using a digital AI program, Juanjo gathered together historical and literary evidence to input criteria for the re-creation, and layered these over the Manchester mock-up to bring Γ58 to breathtaking, vivid life. It is incredibly exciting to think that, for the first time since she was laid beneath the ground over three and a half thousand years ago, we are able to gaze into the actual face of a Bronze Age royal woman – just like Helen.

And it truly is a face to launch a thousand ships.

In the literal sense, of course, quite obviously, Γ58 isn't actually Helen. Γ58 died around the beginning of the Late Bronze Age, several hundred years before the supposed date of the Trojan War, and was buried in Mycenae, a kingdom across the Peloponnese from Sparta. More than anything else, we have to remember that Helen (daughter of a thunder god who metamorphosed into a swan to rape her human mother, hatched from an egg, and objectively and flawlessly gorgeous) is a resolutely fictional character, woven into the tapestry of epic. Yet Γ58 still has things to teach us about being a woman in Helen's world. By combining the rich grave goods – the paraphernalia expected to go with female beauty – buried beside Γ58 with the reconstruction of her face in three dimensions, we can begin to build up a portrait of a woman something like Helen, in all her different and complicated facets. Here we find a world where a woman could be powerful and beautiful at the same time, using the ornaments of wealth and beauty – jewels, cosmetics, clothes – to be remembered, as Homer's Helen puts it, 'by men for years to come'. Here we find a woman whose face we can look at, not through the many masks and preconceptions layered upon ancient women in literature and art (and Helen most of all), but as she would actually have looked – a window back in time that allows us to see her with fresh eyes. And though her lips of clay can no longer move, perhaps she, too, was able to speak in a voice of authority when she lived, just as Helen speaks out in Homer. Γ58, and the secrets she is unlocking about the elite women of the Late Bronze Age, gives us a rare and fleeting glimpse into Helen's world – a mirror reflecting Helen's shadow.

The War Goes On

Schliemann thought he had found the jewels of Homer's Helen, but he was wrong. Meanwhile, modern researchers are piecing together the clues in the Homeric texts and the evidence provided by wealthy

Mycenaean women buried with jewels of their own, to bring these women back to the forefront – to put a face to the nameless women who stood behind Helen.

But there is one final postscript to the story of Helen's jewels. We left them in Berlin, dedicated in Schliemann's will to remain there under his name 'for all time'. (One can't help but think he was channelling Helen's voice when he made that stipulation.) Once again, however, Schliemann made the wrong bet. In the spring of 1945, in the closing act of the Second World War, the Soviet Red Army stormed Berlin and – as the city fell beneath the Soviet flag – took possession of the Anti-Aircraft Tower, where Germany's most valuable antiquities were being safeguarded: including an apparently non-descript box, labelled MVF 1, containing Priam's Treasure. Held in secret for decades, along with around two million other items captured as 'restitution in kind' for Russia's losses during the war, the location of the jewels was only revealed to the international community in the 1990s in a series of exposé articles by two Russian journalists.[33] They now sit in the Pushkin State Museum in Moscow, presiding over another war – Russia's invasion of Ukraine, which has forced nearly 6.5 million Ukrainian refugees to flee their homes and which a historic vote of 143 member countries in the United Nations General Assembly has publicly condemned.[34] And so the war goes on. And the terrible cost of war, which is so much a part of Homer's Iliadic story – and the so-called jewels of Helen – continues to be exacted.

If refugees are one of the dire human costs of war, then so – in the ancient world – were enslaved people. In the fictions of Homer – in the lived history of the Bronze Age – defeat in war meant the horrifying prospect of slavery to the victors. These enslaved victims were the beaten-down survivors of ancient campaigns of terror: women and children. In the *Iliad*, during his visit to Troy – in which Helen predicts to him the endlessness of their own war as a subject of future song – Hector, prince of Troy, makes it only too clear that he knows exactly what it will cost the women of Troy if he loses. It is not the pain of seeing his brothers fall in the dust beneath the spears of his enemies that he fears, he says: it is the horrors that his wife, Andromache, will have to endure, when 'one day some bronze-armed Greek will capture you, and you will weep, deprived of all your freedom'.[35]

Evidence of these real enslaved women, who were captured in their multitudes across the Bronze Age Aegean as cities fell in swathes to enemy armies, is notoriously hard to find. If women are invisible and silenced in the records of history, then enslaved people are even more so. But, eighty years or so after Schliemann dragged his jewels out of the mud of Troy, another discovery was going to revolutionize the world of the Bronze Age – because the records of history themselves were about to be uncovered. It was in the wake of the Second World War, on the other side of the world in 1940s New York, that another piece in the puzzle of the real women behind the myth was about to be found.

2

BRISEIS

Slave

She knows herself to be among the nameless. It's dark, and fire dances on the buildings, and she no longer has a name.

The smell of burning and sweat and blood in her nostrils is gut-churning. Next to her, chained to her arm, a daughter of someone has to urinate on the ground, panting as she does, and some of it spatters disgustingly on to her leg. They've all been stripped to their tunics, and she wonders, in this tangle of bodies, if they will ever unravel themselves. A nameless bunch of arms and legs, herded up in the wreckage of their hometown and penned like pigs waiting for slaughter. She is one of many, not even a number, and they tell her she is lucky for the lot she's drawn. Achilles' slave. I'd kill for that, they say.

Yes: and he did, too.

Enigma

A cigarette burns in Alice Kober's hand as she leans over one of her index cards. The other cards are bundled into empty Lucky Strike cartons lined up on the dining table. The packs she's smoked, the library slips and church circulars she's cut up to get paper to write on (she hasn't owned a notebook since the war), the nights worked after a full day's teaching high-school-level Virgil at Brooklyn College – all to get here.[1] Hundreds of thousands of squares of paper and blotted ink. A life's work, littered among the dinner plates.

She's squinting at a grid scribbled on the back of the cover of an exam book. It is 1949, and outside her window in the New York suburb of Brooklyn a taxicab horn blares. The grid is crossed by tiny symbols that she has inked into place, single shapes made up of lines and arcs, organized neatly into columns and rows. This is a code from thirty-two centuries ago that no one, yet, has managed to crack, thrown into relief in the dim light cast by her desk lamp. Over the last two decades, she has travelled by ship from New York to Oxford to see the nearly two thousand inscriptions of this unidentified Bronze Age script – known as Linear B – unearthed in excavations in Greece, and kept there unpublished. She has worked in the freezing temperatures of the Oxford colleges (post-war strictures mean heating is a luxury the scholars can't afford), laboriously copying out thousands of tiny symbols in a cramped hand. She has amassed piles of index cards, covered with the signs of Linear B – measuring, precisely, where each one appears in words, which symbols it comes next to, how it changes across the inscriptions. Solving this riddle – this enigma – where she doesn't know what kinds of sounds the symbols represent, or even what language she's looking for, is like trying to solve a crossword puzzle without any clues.[2]

The sign that's caught her attention is an image of a woman – crude, but unmistakable: breasts marked by two dots either side of a scrawled loop that curves around a woman's body. It appears again and again on what Kober knows, just from looking at it, from years of living and breathing the inscriptions, is a list. Alongside it, the other symbols change and shift in myriad different patterns, but to Kober's eyes – behind her bottle-bottom glasses – a pattern is emerging. The symbols change when the image of the woman appears. Which means she's altering the words around her. Something is happening to the words of the text when they cross into a woman's world.[3]

Kober's hands are not as steady as usual as she makes a tiny check mark on the card. Tired as she is, worn down from days filled with a crippling teaching load and nights spent toiling away at her dining table, she knows what this means. The language is starting to unlock its secrets. The first secret: *it has gender* – words that are grammatically masculine, and words that are feminine.

She leans back, draws on her cigarette, listens to the late-night revellers on the street outside.

She knows that she is close to the end, now. Close to solving the mystery.

Code Woman

Tragically, Kober would not live to finish the job. She died the following year, paving the way for Michael Ventris – a gifted young architect and amateur enthusiast who would eventually (though too late) acknowledge the debt he owed to Kober's work – to crack the code of Linear B, only two years after her death, in 1952.[4] As so often in the history of women, Kober and her hours of hard and unglamorous work remained invisible for years, obscured by the oh-so-appealing figure of Ventris, with his romantic schoolboy passion for Linear B, his amateur decipherment of the ancient world's hardest puzzle, and the apparently unending fascination with the myth of the tortured genius.[5] But it was the joint labour of this unsung hero of Linear B – a woman, a tireless expert, a respected professor of Classics – alongside Ventris's triumphant sprint over the finish line, that led to one of the biggest discoveries in the history of ancient Greece.

The decipherment of Linear B was an astonishing achievement, and it took the world by storm. On 1 July 1952, a few months after Queen Elizabeth II ascended the throne, Ventris announced his breakthrough on BBC radio. It marked the unlocking of a code that had been bolted shut for millennia, that opened up unhoped-for secrets about the Mycenaean Bronze Age – written in the hands of actual Bronze Age scribes. It all started with the discovery – first in 1900 on the island of Crete, then later in 1939 on the Greek mainland at Pylos – of thousands of unremarkable-looking clay tablets, covered with minute symbols in a language no one recognized. These still-malleable clay tablets were kept in archive rooms in Bronze Age palaces across Greece before being destroyed at each year's end, like short-term receipts in an office filing cabinet waiting to go through the shredder. But then the unexpected happened. The mysterious wave of devastation that triggered the collapse of the Mycenaean palaces all over Greece around 1200 BCE – whatever that was: earthquake, or invasion, or war – brought with it fire, and fire, it turns out, was exactly what history needed. Inadvertently fired to kiln-like temperatures in the massive conflagration, the soluble clay of the tablets was transformed into hard, durable ceramic, and thus they were preserved, by chance, for thousands of years. These, in other words, are the palaces' final account books: a record, fixed in time, of the moment before the fire that lit up the last twilight of the Greek Bronze Age.

But the question remained about what language they were written in – and, of course, what they were saying. It was, in fact, Kober's breakthrough discovery that the symbols showed signs of being what linguists call an 'inflected language' – that is to say, a language whose word endings vary according to their role in the sentence, as well as their gender – that built the bridge for Ventris to cross over towards decipherment.[6] Because it was finally accepting what Kober had been proposing all along that enabled Ventris to suggest – and, only a couple of weeks later, prove – that Linear B was, in fact, contrary to everyone's expectations (given its strange syllabary and its appearance far away in Crete), an early form of Greek.

What this meant was nothing short of revolutionary. It provided proof, conclusively, of another missing piece in the search for the world that Homer had recalled in his epics, which Schliemann had started when he uncovered Troy. It showed that the Mycenaean inhabitants of Greece, the kings at Pylos and Mycenae, did, in fact, speak a kind of Greek – just as Homer had said they did.

It wasn't all exciting news, though – at least, not at first. When Ventris and others, including the Cambridge professor John Chadwick, set about translating the thousands of tablets with the newly unlocked code, it turned out that these weren't the literary masterpieces, the songs of Homer, the sweeping tales of gods and men, that classical scholars might have hoped for. They weren't even personal letters scribbled on clay that might have given researchers a glimpse into the thoughts of the people of the Late Bronze Age. Instead, they were lists – stacks and stacks of bureaucratic lists, carefully compiled by the palace administration and evidence of the vast network of industries they supported, from textile production to the manufacture of luxury perfumes, from livestock management to food processing. Production goals and records; notations of expenditure; names of suppliers and receivers of goods; inventories of property holdings and commodities exchanged – all were noted down on the tablets by the palace scribes with meticulous accuracy.

Not quite the poetry of Homer, then. But for me, in the search for the real women behind Homer, these tablets are invaluable evidence. In fact, it is here that the trail begins in earnest, precisely because of the specific (and apparently idiosyncratic) nature of what the tablets record: because they shed light on a side of society that we hardly ever see represented in the archaeology, and only hinted at in the Homeric texts. I'm interested in one tablet in particular. It was discovered at Pylos in Greece in 1939 by the archaeologist Carl Blegen, from the University of Cincinnati, who had just finished a stint excavating at Troy and who, at Pylos, had uncovered a stunning Mycenaean-era palace, complete with an archive room filled with hundreds of clay tablets dating to around the thirteenth century BCE. (He subsequently dubbed it the 'Palace of Nestor', after the Homeric king of Pylos who appears in the epics as the aged adviser of the Greek king Agamemnon.) Known to researchers as PY Ab 194, the tablet is – at first sight – lacklustre, to say the least:[7]

.a GRA 3 TA DA
.b pu-ro] ki-si-wi[-ja] o-nu-ke-ja MUL 7 ko-wa 3 ko-wo 6 NI 3

At Pylos, 7 Chian women who make o-nu-ka, 3 girls, 6 boys, 288 litres wheat, 288 litres figs, 1 DA 1 TA

It doesn't make for very thrilling reading. But unpack it a bit, dig a little deeper beneath the surface, and there's a wealth of information to be uncovered. These are women who are being listed because of the food rations the palace is providing for them, a record of the palace's outgoings for this particular workgroup.[8] We know they're women, not only from the feminine plural that gives us their name (ki-si-wi-ja means 'Chian women'), but also from the specially added ideogram: the very same symbol of a woman that led Kober to uncover the gendering of Linear B nouns (now transcribed as MUL, from Latin mulier for 'woman'). More than this, they're highly specialized textile workers operating in the heart of the palace at Pylos, experts at decorating a finely ornamented cloth border known as o-nu-ka.[9] They've been allocated two female supervisors to oversee their work, one 'TA' (a supervisor for the group) and one 'DA' (a higher-ranked supervisor), both likely women.[10] And they're accompanied by their children: three girls (ko-wa: it was Kober, again,

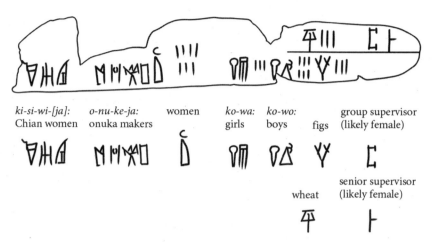

| ki-si-wi-[ja]: | o-nu-ke-ja: | women | ko-wa: | ko-wo: | figs | group supervisor |
| Chian women | onuka makers | | girls | boys | | (likely female) |

senior supervisor
wheat   (likely female)

*The silenced majority: a Linear B tablet from Pylos lists women weavers,
their children and rations. The sign for 'women' is represented
with a head and skirt.*

who first guessed that this was a feminine-gendered word) and six boys
(*ko-wo*), who also get a share of the food. From the outset, this is a fascinating glimpse into the origins and occupations of actual, historical
women: not the mythological women of legend, nor the literary women
of Homer; nor are they imagined or idealized women, like the silent
wives of later classical Greek texts. In fact, the Linear B tablets provide
us with one of the largest sets of evidence for women in any period of
ancient Greek history. (One imagines that Alice Kober would have been
glad to know that the code she worked so hard to decipher would reveal
so much about women's history.) In place of the evidence we usually get
from burials – which tend to privilege high-status elites, and capture
individuals in death – this is tangible, and highly specific, evidence of
the day-to-day lives of ordinary women who are on record as operating
in a real Mycenaean palace.

But more than this, what's particularly interesting, for our purposes,
is that they're identified as being from Chios. Chios is a mountainous
island in the eastern Aegean, down the coast from Troy. Although later
colonized by Ionian Greeks (it was, in fact, said in ancient times to have
been the birthplace of Homer), Chios in the Bronze Age was at the heart
of a flourishing criss-crossing network of east Aegean trade routes that

put it in contact with Troy to the north and the Cycladic islands to the west, as well as the Mycenaeans of Greece. The question is – how did these Chian women get all the way across the Aegean and over the Greek mainland to Pylos? And what were they doing there?

Enter Briseis

It's Homer that gives us the way in. To understand who these Chian women were, we need to turn to Briseis – an enslaved woman who first appears at the opening of the *Iliad*, captive in the Greek camp in the hut of Achilles, who has claimed her as his war prize. Homer has a specific word in Greek for this kind of war booty: *geras*, a term meaning 'something captured in war' that, disturbingly, covers everything from tripods (a sort of ancient casserole-dish stand with three legs) to actual women. The whole problem that begins the *Iliad* – literally, the start of the epic, the moment where the curtain rises and the drama begins – is that Agamemnon, king of the Greeks, has been forced by the gods to give up his own war prize: another enslaved woman, captured in the war around Troy, by the name of Chryseis. Demanding retribution – for otherwise, Homer tells us, he will lose face in front of the Greeks if he has to part from his *geras* and all the other leaders keep theirs – and stung by Achilles' slights on his honour, the king resolves publicly (ignoring all advice to the contrary) to seize Briseis by way of recompense. Achilles flares up in a demonic rage at the loss of his prize – the *Iliad* opens programmatically with the word for his 'wrath' (*mēnis*). And so the stage is set for a conflict that will propel the whole poem, that will lead us on the tortuous path through Achilles' enraged withdrawal from the war, to, ultimately, his tragic return.

In the grand sweep of the Homeric *Iliad*, as the narrative careers along the course set by these blustering heroes and kings with their easily offended pride and buffed-up honour, it's been easy in the past to lose sight of Briseis – the enslaved woman and victim who actually started it all. Here is a woman traded back and forth between the Greeks, her body the property of men, who crops up throughout the poem mostly in painfully offhand cameos of rape: 'Achilles slept inside the well-built hut, and with him lay the beautiful Briseis.'[11] In spite of the fact that she's the reason the entire plot of the epic exists, she's given only a few lines of dialogue, towards the end of the poem: about the same amount of speaking time as Achilles' magical male talking horse (yes, he has a talking horse), who erupts into speech just after Briseis' only lines in the epic.[12] A blistering example of upstaging.

But, looking for Homer's women – and when I was writing *For the Most Beautiful* – I've been fascinated by the possibility of mining the Homeric text for all the details it can tell us about Briseis in particular. My idea was to see if there was a way we could bring this character who lay hidden at the heart of the *Iliad* – captured into slavery, raped by the man who killed her family, traded back and forth between men – back into the foreground. Searching through an obscure passage in the second book of the *Iliad*, in which Homer details all the Greek ships – the 'thousand ships' launched by Helen – that came to Troy, I unearthed an often neglected passage that tells us more about this long-overlooked character. She was, Homer tells us, taken captive by Achilles when the Greeks razed the town of Lyrnessus, on a campaign of terror around the Troad (the area around Troy) that also saw the devastation of another city, Thebe.[13] Achilles later boasts of the destruction of Lyrnessus himself. 'I ravaged it,' he says, 'and took away the women as captive slaves [*lēiades*], robbing them of their day of freedom.'[14] These parallel war raids by the Greeks – smaller attacks on neighbouring cities to accompany the larger siege on Troy – crop up throughout Homer, both in the *Iliad* and the *Odyssey*: they're clearly seen as a singularly calculating necessity to feed, equip and, above all, reward a marauding army in the Homeric economy (particularly in the long nine years that precede the tenth year of the war, in which the *Iliad* opens). And among the most highly prized of the possessions taken in these raids – clearly, as Agamemnon and Achilles' reactions show when they're faced with losing them – are the women. With their men slaughtered, local women in the epic like Briseis are driven to a horrific existence, enslaved by their Greek captors and the killers of their fathers, husbands and brothers – utterly powerless victims of war, subject to the soldiers' every whim, including rape. And yet the *Iliad*, with its focus on men and men's power, tells us very little about how it feels to be a woman in war, enslaved, raped, trafficked: Homer gives us just one brief glimpse of the horror of Briseis' loss of freedom as she's shuttled from one rapist slaveowner to another – 'unwillingly', the poet says. How much oppression, of how many women, lies behind that one word.[15]

The reference to the town of Thebe in Briseis' story isn't incidental. It connects her to another woman, Andromache, wife of the Trojan prince Hector. Andromache, we're told, came from Thebe, the same town that Achilles and the Greeks destroyed when they laid waste to Briseis' Lyrnessus. When Hector visits Andromache in Troy in the sixth book of the *Iliad*, she begs him to think of the consequences of war on women, reminding him that she's lost everything in the raid that – in the early years of the war around Troy – devastated her home. Similarly to Briseis, Achilles slaughtered her father and her seven brothers, she says; he enslaved her mother before freeing her for ransom.[16] But Hector isn't entirely blind to the outcomes of war. He knows only too well, he says, that there will come a time when Troy will fall. And when that happens, he predicts Andromache's future: dragged away by a bronze-clad Greek warrior, she will be shipped to Greece as a slave, set to carry water or to weave at the loom at some other woman's bidding. What he fails to mention is the fact that she will also certainly be raped.[17]

Another vision of what happens to women after the Trojan War appears in the epic that follows its fall, the *Odyssey*. Odysseus, voyaging on his way home from Troy and leaving the smoking ruins of the city in his wake, hears a bard singing the tale of Troy's fall. The legend has clearly already made its way to far-away lands. He hears the poet tell the tale of the Trojan Horse that Odysseus invented, how the Greek warriors poured from inside the horse and 'sacked the city; how they scattered out, destroying every neighbourhood'. Odysseus, upon hearing the tale, melts into tears, and 'his cheeks were wet with weeping, as a woman weeps':

> as she falls to wrap her arms around
> her husband, fallen fighting for his home
> and children. She is watching as he gasps
> and dies. She shrieks, a clear high wail, collapsing
> upon his corpse. The men are right behind.

> They hit her shoulders with their spears and lead her
> to slavery, hard labour, and a life
> of pain. Her face is marked with her despair.[18]

It is an extraordinary, shattering simile. At the moment where the poet (very much on the pattern of Homer) memorializes the Greeks' victory at Troy, at the moment where Odysseus might be presented as the triumphant conqueror and respond with pride to his role as the daring strategist, the narrative is sliced open by the disruptive power of women's grief; testifying to their terrible experiences, behind and beyond men's acts, of the devastation of war.

Clearly, there is a pattern being established here. The Homeric battle campaign at Troy sets up an inevitable paradigm: women, not only from the city of Troy but from all its surrounding towns, are being rounded up and hauled back to Greece as war prizes. The economy of the *Iliad* – and the epic makes this clear from the very start, with the opening quarrel over Briseis and Chryseis – rests on the conversion of *raped and enslaved women* into *men's glory*, through the accumulation of enslaved women as war trophies that attest to a man's prowess. This is the reason, plain and simple, why Agamemnon and Achilles get so angry at the start of the *Iliad*. Achilles' wrath – his programmatic *mēnis* that drives the poem forward – is the pique of a man whose trafficked woman has been taken from him and so has reduced the aggregate of his honour. The gleaming epic of heroes like Achilles is, when you flip the coin to its grittier side, powered by the oppression of women. But, at the same time, this is a bigger story than the acts of violence perpetrated against women in one war. The capture and rape of the women of Troy is explicitly justified, by Homer's Greeks, as repayment for Paris' original seizure of Helen. Nestor, one of the Greek leaders, tells the Greeks with brutal calculation that nobody should sail back home 'before he shares a Trojan woman's bed to pay for Helen's sufferings and struggles'.[19] In other words, this is a war that started because one man sexually assaulted and captured one Greek woman, Helen; but this has become a war that is entirely about possessing, and raping, *as many non-Greek women as possible*. The framework of the legend of Troy rests on, and is brought to completion by, the rape of women. Whether or not Helen might actually have gone of her own accord with Paris is a moot point, in the eyes of the Greek men. It's all about the rhetoric of payback, commodification, and rape in revenge. Achilles says as much, hurling back his insults to Agamemnon: 'Why should the Greeks make war against the Trojans? Was it not to retrieve a woman, Helen?'[20] All of which explains why, in this war that is waged by men to capture women, the epic begins with Briseis: one victim among many, rounded up in the Greek camp, when the Greeks came to Troy. One raped and trafficked woman, enslaved to boost men's egos, converted into currency to bolster their glory, and scapegoated as reparation for Helen's loss. And Andromache, when Troy falls, when boatloads of enslaved women are shipped back to Greece, will be one of the many to come.[21]

Which brings us back to the (historical) Pylos tablet, and the Chian women. Although they're never specifically called slaves, there are clues within the tablets that these women are – like Briseis, like Andromache – exactly those kinds of enslaved foreign victims, deported back to Greece, that Homer mentions. First and foremost is their eastern Aegean provenance, linking them with Troy, not far away from Chios on the east Aegean seaboard, and the growing (historically attested) expansionism of the Mycenaean Greeks into the east. And the Chian women aren't alone: other tablets found in the archive room in the palace at Pylos list groups of women workers from other areas nearby in the eastern Aegean – Miletus, Knidos, Halicarnassus, Lydia (all in modern-day western Turkey) and Lemnos (an Aegean island). We even find one enslaved woman listed on the Pylos tablets who – incredibly – seems to come from Troy itself: *to-ro-ja*, or *Trōia* – a real-life Trojan woman.[22] All these groups of women are united by several distinct characteristics, aside from their eastern-Aegean ethnicity. They are assigned to low-status, labour-intensive and back-breakingly repetitive tasks: flour-grinding, wool-carding, linen-working, and so on.[23] They are treated as an undifferentiated mass, without any individual identity: none of these women are given a name, apart from their ethnicity (other, higher-status women do get names in the tablets: Kessandra, Karpathia and Philopatra are just a few examples).[24] They are totally dependent on the palace for their survival, through the food rations apportioned to them. They are separated from the men (these tasks are for women only); their children are co-opted into labour too, with the boys taken away from their mothers to labour in the fields as soon as they reach maturity.[25] Finally, at one point in the tablets, they're listed alongside a cluster of Linear B symbols that, when sounded out, gives us a single word: *ra-wi-ja-ja* (or *lawiaiai*). Astonishingly, this word seems very likely to be the Linear B, older Greek version of exactly that same term which Homer's Achilles uses to boast about his capture of Briseis and the women of Lyrnessus: *lēiades* – captive women slaves.[26]

In other words, it's highly likely that these real, historical women from the eastern Aegean (and their children), recorded in the tablets at Pylos and set to work at the loom, were taken captive in war, deported to Greece and coerced into labour there as enslaved women. Just like Briseis and Andromache in Homer. It's a shudderingly, almost disturbingly real testament to the actual experience of women like Briseis: captured on the east Aegean coast by the Greeks, forced to work for their economy as enslaved women, trafficked to Greece to live on rations and break their bones with weaving – never seeing their homes again.

Twenty-First-Century Briseis

Evidence like the Linear B tablets can open up for us an unparalleled window on to a world that, within the society of Mycenaean Greece, was one of the most marginal, the least talked about, the least visible. They allow us a glimpse into the lives of the hundreds of women who were very likely enslaved, trafficked across the Aegean as part of the trade in human capital, and who were probably the victims of a growing Greek expansionism – an expansionism that the legend of the Trojan War, tellingly, celebrates. By crossing these real-life texts from 3,200 years ago with Homer's epic portrait of enslaved women like Briseis, we can start to read the Pylos tablets in new ways. We can begin to understand these massed groups of anonymous women, whose names and identities have been lost to the historical record, as individuals. We can start to reconstruct a narrative about what their lives might have been like.

But we can also begin to tell a new story about the *Iliad*, too.

On-the-ground evidence for the reality of being a woman in war in the Late Bronze Age compels us to direct our attention to the lived reality of the Iliadic battles: to prise our gaze away from the glory of male heroes to confront the terrible cost of war. Recent work on women in Homer has shown that the *Iliad* invites this reading, too.[27] There are moments when the worlds of women and men collide in ways that show the poet conjuring up the women's lost world of peace, the what-could-have-been that women represent, and the reality of their future suffering that marks the horrors of war – from Andromache and Hector's final shared moment (though they do not know it), as they stand at the gates of Troy holding their infant son and overlooking the battle; to the washing wells that Hector races past during his final duel with Achilles, 'where Trojan wives and pretty Trojan daughters laundered the shining clothes in former times, in peace, before the sons of Greece arrived'.[28] It is Homer's ability to flesh out the full cost of war, in the shadows that lurk behind the heroes' blazing glory, that makes the sacrifices endured by both the men and the women of Troy even more compelling, and underlines their pathos.

But it is Briseis, more than any other woman from Homer's epics, who is recently being brought to the fore in a new way. A cluster of modern novels written by women has recently endeavoured to reclaim her story: not just rereading her role in Homer, but giving her a voice once again. Women writers are putting Briseis back at the forefront of her own tale to show, in her own words, the full implications of this character who is both central to the story of the *Iliad* – who sparks the quarrel of Achilles and Agamemnon that sets the narrative in motion – and, at the same time, utterly marginal. These novels – my own *For the Most Beautiful* (2016), Pat Barker's *The Silence of the Girls* (2018) and *The Women of Troy* (2021), and Natalie Haynes's *A Thousand Ships* (2019) – give Briseis a voice to flesh out the brutal reality of war, seen through a woman's eyes.

In so doing, they are, at the same time, drawing on another strand of the ancient Greek reimagining of the Trojan War: a tragedy by the classical Athenian dramatist Euripides – the same tragedian who penned *Helen* – known as *The Trojan Women*. This play, foregrounding the bleak aftermath of war and the grim reality of the situation faced by the Trojan women – Hecuba, Cassandra, Helen and Andromache – as they await enslavement to the Greeks, was first performed in Athens in 415 BCE.

It is no coincidence that, a year earlier, the Athenian empire – which had slowly been garnering power and wealth over the course of the fifth century BCE, and which was currently embroiled in a long-drawn-out conflict with its rival, Sparta – committed its most abhorrent act of unprovoked aggression: the destruction of an island unwilling to bow to its might, by the total slaughter of the men and enslavement of all the women and children.[29] Euripides' portrait of the horror and futility of war, in the suffering of the Trojan women, could not be a clearer commentary on Athens' increasingly troubling imperialism.

But the recent flush of novels telling Briseis' story, while they look back to Homer's flashes of insight into the women's world, and Euripides' revolutionary foregrounding of the women after Troy, also do something new. By zeroing in on Briseis, with her central role in the narrative of the *Iliad*, they do more than use the Trojan War as an arena to explore the costs of war: they focus a lens, uncompromisingly, on Homer's *Iliad* itself. For me, when I was retelling Briseis' story, this was about more than just a woman's rewriting of war: this was a woman's rewriting of Homer, from the perspective of the silenced and the enslaved – redressing centuries of violence done against women across history, *and* in the texts that have recorded history. As women writers have taken centre stage in Homeric reworkings in recent years, they have shown how the canon of Western literature – where male writers for centuries wrote about men, with the *Iliad* seen as the originary text and the most masculine of them all – can be rewritten in the female voice. No longer is it about Achilles' anger, Achilles' pride, and the stories of men: now it is Briseis' loss, her trauma, her own words as evoked by women writers, that articulate Homer's epic in a new way. Through Briseis, the *Iliad* becomes a work that we can engage with on a different plane, that highlights the deep injustices, acts of oppression and sexual violence against enslaved women, while acknowledging (and interrogating) the central place that the Homeric epics have held. We can critique hundreds of years of obsession with the *Iliad* as a glorious tale of men's valour, how it has been used and abused to validate everything from empire to patriarchy, to bring out another side – to shed a light on the world of Andromache, as well as Hector. We can re-evaluate centuries of valorization of so-called heroes like Achilles by drawing attention to women like Briseis, standing in the blood-spattered backdrop to his choice to fight for glory. By rewriting Briseis' story, we can give Homer's women the agency, at last, to step forward out of the shadows and tell their side of the tale. And so – just like the twentieth-century cracking of the code from Pylos that gave us the millennia-old enslaved women from Chios – we can begin to learn more about the women of the past, and the kinds of stories we want to write for our future.

Briseis, Chryseis, Cressida

Briseis has found a new place in women's writing in recent years, but it's not the first time she has cropped up in literary retellings. Even in the ancient world, a flurry of fan fiction retold the Trojan War story – from a fake diary purporting to be written by a Trojan soldier called Dares the Phrygian (a late Latin translation of a Greek forgery), to a pretend 'official history' of the Trojan War by a Greek commentator.[30] Dares, in his account, calls Briseis 'Briseida' – a name that reappears in later medieval romances on the Trojan War that used Dares as their sourcebook, such as the French poet Benoît de Sainte-Maure's hugely successful twelfth-century *Romance of Troy*.

But it is here that something interesting happens. Because, as the texts and accounts filter down through the literary tradition, Briseis – or Briseida – starts to fuse with another Homeric woman: Chryseis, enslaved by Agamemnon, and Briseis' counterpart in the Greek leaders' quarrel. (It's the loss of Chryseis – when her father, a Trojan priest, delivers an impassioned speech to Agamemnon and prays to Apollo to bring a plague on the Greeks to get his daughter back – that makes the Greek king turn to Briseis, Achilles' prize, instead.) For Benoît de Sainte-Maure, Briseida is now a priest's daughter, like Homer's Chryseis, embroiled in a courtly love triangle between a young Trojan prince, Troilus, and a Greek warrior, Diomedes. By the time this much-adapted story reaches medieval England (via the Italian poet Boccaccio) in the late fourteenth century, Briseida has become Criseida and then (in an epic of Chaucer's) Criseyde – cementing the fusion between the two Homeric women. And it's only a matter of time before Shakespeare picks it up and delivers it on to the stage at the Globe Theatre in London, with his *Troilus and Cressida*, probably performed in around 1603.

Briseis and Chryseis – Homer's two enslaved women whose trafficking sets the stage for the drama of the *Iliad* to begin – are inseparable in Homer. Their story goes together: two women who are both totally powerless and, at the same time, lie at the crux of the narrative – and the intertwining of their stories stays that way for much of their literary afterlife. But, in many ways, Chryseis – in spite of the apparent privileging of her name and her identity as a priest's daughter that makes its way into the later stories about her – is the more silent, the more difficult to bring back to life, of the two. Once her father succeeds in recovering her, she is shipped back home halfway through the first book of the *Iliad*, never to be heard of again; in contrast to Briseis, whom Homer allows to speak once (in her lament for the death of Achilles' partner Patroclus), Chryseis doesn't say a single word. Her role, it seems, is to be drowned out by her father's voice in the drama of his determination to set her free, and his brazen run-in with a king; to be cast in his shadow as a sheltered young girl, and silent daughter. So how do we go about finding Chryseis – the girl who never speaks?

3

CHRYSEIS

Daughter

She says nothing, not because she has nothing to say, but because none of them will listen. All the men are talking, talking – her father most of all – deciding what will happen to her, and no one thinks to ask her what she wants. A war trophy in the Greek camp, polished and primped and stacked on Agamemnon's shelf; or a dressed-up bride back home, delivered by her father to the highest bidder, like a cow dragged by the neck for sacrifice. Does it really matter which she is?

The sea lies flat and burnished in the low sun like a sword blade. Wind blows spray in her face and blasts what they are saying back at her. Her father's threats. Agamemnon's bluster. Achilles' rage. It's all so many words.

Why speak, when your words don't matter?

Pompeii of the Aegean

It's the end of May in 1967, a dry day, and Greek archaeologist Spyridon Marinatos has opened a trench in a scrub-covered field, towards the coast just south from the village of Akrotiri on the island of Santorini. This excavation has been years in the making, but war – two world wars, then the civil conflict that cannonballed across Greece – has made it hard, lately, to look to the past. Now all is quiet: a breeze rustles the leaves of a couple of olive trees at the field's edge, and cicadas thrum gently. Marinatos's workmen lay out their trowels and buckets on the grass and set to work with their pickaxes, not saying much. In the distance, the sea glitters steel-like around the giant curve of Santorini's rock, the arching ridge of cliff that looms like the rim of a cauldron out of the sea.

For decades – ever since the Santorini bluff started being mined in the mid nineteenth century (a cheap source of cement, given the unusual qualities of the volcanic rock) for the construction of the Suez Canal – bits of pottery and plaster, even ancient walls, have been emerging from the quarries. The miners toss them out, unthinking. But geologists have started to suggest that Santorini (or Thera, as the ancients called it) was hit by a volcanic eruption of extraordinary magnitude, thousands of years ago – an eruption that had blown out the volcano's centre, leaving behind the unique caldera surrounded by the crescent-shaped island, and burying the earth in a thick blanket of pumice and ash. These experts are now beginning to argue that the primitive finds that littered Santorini's mines might have belonged to the victims of that first prehistoric eruption: that, buried under hundreds of feet of hardened rock, a lost ancient city lies hidden, Atlantis-like, waiting to be discovered.[1]

This is what Marinatos – himself a seasoned excavator through the recent slew of Bronze Age discoveries across the Aegean – and other experts along with him, including renowned archaeologist and Harvard professor Emily Townsend Vermeule and Penn Museum scientist Dr Elizabeth Ralph, have come to find. They are not the first to look. They know as well as anyone how much luck is involved in choosing a place to start, deciding where to dig a trench. They know they may have to dig elsewhere, try again, before they find their lost Atlantis – if they ever do. But within a couple of hours they get their first, extraordinary glimpse of what's to come. First to emerge out of the pumice are fragments of prehistoric pottery painted in swirls of black, white and red – instantly recognizable as Bronze Age tableware, thrillingly similar to models discovered elsewhere across the Greek islands.[2] Next come walls, then stairs leading down into the rock-hard earth: clues that what they have hit are upper levels to houses that are two, or even three, storeys high. News of the finds reaches the villagers at nearby Akrotiri, and some of them leave the tomato harvest to walk down over the dusty fields to help.[3]

As trenches are opened one after another over the next few weeks, more and more houses are uncovered, their doors supported by millennia-old wooden beams, their walls cloaked in fresh-seeming plaster in jewel-bright pinks, whites and greens – and the extent of what the team has found begins to emerge. This is a Bronze Age town that has been perfectly preserved for over three and a half thousand years beneath Santorini's hardened ash. It is a portal in time back to a community that

*The Pompeii of the Aegean: the buried Bronze Age city of Akrotiri, Thera,
as it looks now.*

existed on this fractured clifftop island that, until now, was lost. A town
that was the victim of a cataclysmic eruption from the Theran volcano
around 1600 BCE, which triggered frosts across the globe as far away as
modern California, which wrote itself into the glacial ice of Greenland
and sent towering tsunamis crashing across the Mediterranean.[4] For the
first time in thousands of years, it is possible to wander down a Bronze
Age street. It is possible to linger in a prehistoric village square, to look
up at the edifices of several-storey-high buildings, painted in shades that
evoke dream-like images of its multicoloured world. It is possible to peer
into homes preserved almost exactly as their owners had left them –
cups still standing on pantry shelves, pots of paint abandoned beside
half-plastered walls.[5] As more and more of the site reveals its secrets, it
becomes clear that this was, in its heyday, a bustling Cycladic harbour
town, connected to the major trade centres on Crete, with grand public
buildings and private residences, linked to a brand new wastewater
disposal system and decked out with vivid frescoes of ships and seaside
villas, of red and blue crags burgeoning with lush ochre-stemmed lilies

and swallows spiralling across painted skies. This is a city forgotten in time, and captured in rock.

This is the Pompeii of the Aegean.

On the Threshold

Homer's Chryseis is a young woman teetering on the edge of a conflict of literally epic proportions. The narrative of the *Iliad* opens with a famous line that has echoed down the centuries: 'Goddess, sing of the cataclysmic wrath of great Achilles, son of Peleus.'[6] The background to the hostilities unfolds in the following lines. Chryses, Trojan priest and father of Chryseis – taken as a captive, as a *geras*, by Agamemnon in war – has approached the Greek king to demand his daughter's release. When Agamemnon refuses to part with his prize, Chryses draws on his divine connections and prays to the god Apollo, who brings down a plague on the Greeks with his deadly arrows. Homer describes the corpses heaped in stinking piles, picked over by dogs and carrion birds, their flesh pockmarked with the rings of Apollo's arrow-strikes. Surrounded by dead and dying soldiers, Agamemnon has no choice but to give in; yet he will only do so, he says, on condition that his greatest warrior, Achilles – who has challenged Agamemnon's honour – gives up his own prize, Briseis. Under serious duress (and the intervention of the goddess Athena), Achilles at last complies; his pride fatally wounded, he withdraws from the war. And so the stage is set for the drama of the *Iliad* to begin.

In the set piece of her father's unsuccessful appeal to the king and the epic's opening quarrel, Homer's Chryseis lingers in the background, cast in the role of silent daughter (her very name – which means 'daughter of Chryses' in Greek – emphasizes her dependence on her father) and enslaved woman. The task Homer wants her to perform is not to speak, but to spark the conflict between men through the value they place on her – either as her father's possession, or as her captor's. Agamemnon makes her attributes as his prize quite clear: 'figure, height, intelligence, [and] skill', he says, enumerating (like a shopping list) the qualities he values.[7] Chryseis is a young woman in a world dominated by men, moving from being her father's property into the world of war and then back into her father's domain: a liminal figure, on the boundary between a woman, a concubine and a wife, caught between peace and war, her father's world and her captor's.

If Chryseis occupies a silent world in Homer's epic, then we will have to look to a different medium to let her speak – and fortunately the ruins on Thera provide exactly the kind of access point we're looking for. Some of the most spectacular of all the discoveries at Akrotiri (as it is known: we don't have its ancient name), when it was uncovered fifty years ago, were the paintings splashed across the walls of its prehistoric homes. There are images of young women plucking crocuses in verdant landscapes, men hunting leaping deer, fishermen out in the bay with their nets: scenes that seem to speak to a rich and vibrant Bronze Age world. Of course, we need, from the beginning, to treat these frescoes with caution: they're not, by any means, snapshots of 'real life'. Although they're striking for the sheer (and unexpected) number of women they represent, almost all the women are elite, depicting a very specific slice of society, and are staged in poses and scenes that seem to be highly ritualized in nature.[8] Rather, like the photographs we surround ourselves with in our own homes that construct a narrative of how we want to remember ourselves, what we care about, and who we want to be seen to be, these three-and-a-half-thousand-year-old paintings are carefully curated sets of ideological portraits – a way of conjuring up an airbrushed Theran society that tells us more about the stories they were telling themselves and each other than they do about the 'real' world of women. They're also around three to four hundred years older than any feasible historical setting for the Trojan War – meaning that using them to talk about the women of Troy is a bit like using Shakespeare's Juliet to talk about twenty-first-century British women: we need to be careful about context, paying attention to the very particular world of Thera and its religious, historical and social landscape. And yet, in spite of all this, what these paintings *can* do is stand as a vivid and real Late Bronze Age testament to how the Therans broadcast the experience of daughters from elite families – and, in so doing, give us a new insight into the ways in which liminal young female figures, usually lost to the historical record, were understood. We can start, in other words, to find the hidden daughters of history – just like Chryseis at the opening of the *Iliad*.

I'm drawn to one particular image that might be able to give us a new way into understanding Chryseis. It's a painting of a young girl quite literally on the threshold: squeezed on to a narrow strip of plaster beside a door, in what was probably the attractive living room of an impressive two- or three-storey house in Akrotiri that dominates an open town square and is now known as the West House.[9] She wears a long robe and has a gold hoop earring at her ear; her full lips are slicked in red (a common sign of female sexuality and fertility), her head close-shaved (shown by blue paint) with a lock of dark hair on her forehead and a ponytail at the back, and in her hands she carries an incense burner. When first discovered, she was subjected forthwith to all the typical preconceptions about the roles of women and summarily dubbed a priestess, the West House transformed (with the fickle wave of the

A three-millennia-old townhouse: the West House at Akrotiri. Note the large window looking out on to the town square.

prehistorian's imaginary wand) into a sacred shrine.[10] But comparisons with other paintings across Akrotiri have shown that all young figures, male and female alike, are portrayed with blue shaven heads, and that the shaved head and lock of hair probably indicate children at various stages of the rites of passage into adulthood.[11] It's much more likely, then, that this was a local grandee's family home, and that this girl – along with the two boys who are depicted in the same room, their heads also shaved, proudly displaying their catches of fish – was one of the young members of the household.[12] Recent research suggests that it's even possible to guess at her father's occupation: probably an affluent and cultivated textile manufacturer, to judge by the large quantity of weaving equipment (mostly loom weights, used to keep the tension on the threads hanging down from the loom) that was found in another room of the house.[13] Perhaps, like Chryseis who was praised for her work by Agamemnon, this young woman just on the cusp of adulthood also took part in the work of weaving cloth in her father's home – along with her duties in giving ritual offerings, shown in the painting by her sprinkling of saffron on to the incense burner.

Her story doesn't stand alone, though. Just as her portrait interacts with those of the young fisher boys on the other walls to tell a narrative about her family, so it does with the paintings that run along the upper wall of the room she's been placed in, like a technicoloured comic strip. A fleet of ships, with leaping blue-and-yellow dolphins at their prows, sails towards a prosperous city, teeming with high buildings in reds, yellows and blues that cling to the hillside of the blue-red crags behind. On the opposite wall, men dressed in long white robes assemble in a war council; out at sea, more ships make for land – some caught in a sea battle, where warriors fall overboard and spill black gore as they drown, others disgorging their soldiers on to land to march into war, clad in red-brown oxhide body shields and boar's-tusk helmets, with swords and spears at the ready.[14] (As we saw in the Introduction, real archaeological examples of these kinds of boar's-tusk helmets have been found in Late Bronze Age burials.) Above them, oblivious to the battle going on below, is a world of peace – a stone-built well, next to a couple of feathery trees and a brushwood sheep enclosure, where two long-haired women collect water in their pitchers. Just like the washing wells of the *Iliad*, 'where Trojan wives and pretty Trojan daughters laundered the shining clothes in former times, in peace, before the sons of Greece arrived',[15] this watery women's world sharpens the gory battle scenes that envelop it – and makes a dismal prediction of the future of women captured in war: to carry water as an enslaved woman, just like Hector predicts in the *Iliad* (with knowing specificity) to Andromache.[16] Meanwhile, the fleet conjures up Homer's catalogue of the thousand ships launched for Helen – the voyage across the sea to a great city echoing the Greeks' campaign across the Aegean to Troy and their return, the marching warriors the 'bronze-clad Achaeans' with their boar's-tusk helmets and towering body shields (both explicitly mentioned as part of the Greeks' armour by Homer in the *Iliad*).[17] And the assembly of men gathered on the hilltop in council evokes the opening drama of the *Iliad* – particularly against the backdrop of the war below.

We shouldn't imagine this as some kind of literal transcription of Homer: the Homeric epics, as we know them today, wouldn't be written down for hundreds of years. It is, in a much more fluid way, a tale that inhabits the narrative thought-world in which Homer's epics had their roots – that gives us a striking picture in another, differently tinted medium of the swirling forces of war and peace, the dramas of women and men, that formed the stories acted out upon the Late Bronze Age stage, and that would, later, come to shape epic tales like the *Iliad* and *Odyssey*. It's been suggested that these vibrant epic scenes, painted on the walls of a Theran townhouse, are actually visual evidence of a far longer tradition of heroic oral poetry that stretched right back into the Late Bronze Age, as far as the fourteenth century BCE and possibly earlier.[18] Martin West, the virtuosic scholar of Homeric Greek, has even shown that it is possible to excavate fragments of Mycenaean verse, characters and names, embedded in Homer's text like a prehistoric fly trapped in amber: remnants of a much, much older oral epic poetry that's now lost to us, and which we might just be able to glimpse in the Theran ship scenes.[19] These images, in other words, hidden for thousands of years by an accident of nature, may provide crucial visual evidence of what oral poets were singing about in the Bronze Age and the kinds of legends that would eventually trickle down into epics like Homer's.

Meanwhile, new research into the geology of Late Bronze Age

Thera – before the mega-eruption that would blow out the caldera and cover Akrotiri in a mantle of pumice and ash – has shown that the gorgeous city being approached by the fleet of ships displays all the physical landmarks of the volcanic landscape that surrounds Akrotiri: the high ring of hills protecting the harbour; the characteristic dark lumps of weathered volcanic rock and fractured dykes; even the bands of colour undulating across the mountains, the horizontal layering of geological deposits that are so characteristic in the cliffs at Santorini.[20] In other words, what we seem to see here, brushed in glowing colours across the walls of a textile manufacturer's living room, is a sweeping pre-Homeric epic tale that has been deliberately transposed into the specific pre-eruption landscape of Bronze Age Thera. Just as we can read through the priestly figure of a young woman on the threshold into Chryseis, here, in the grand narratives about peace and war that form the backdrop to Bronze Age life on Thera, we can find the wider context of the Late Bronze Age spelled out. We can see how the painted narratives that ancient Therans wanted to tell might interweave with Homeric-style tales about war, peace and a woman's world; how they saw women – as both emblems of peace and playthings of war – stepping into their place in the never-ending spectacle that played out across Aegean history.

Here on the walls of this millennia-old villa, painted out like a script, we see the full story her family wanted to tell about the world in which this young woman lived. Here, at the threshold, is an idealized image of a young girl in the process of initiation into the roles she will play in adulthood. Here is a daughter, engaged in the roles that her gender dictates, on the threshold of maturity and sexuality, and yet still cradled within the domestic space of her father's home. And here is a young woman who will have a part to play – like Homer's Chryseis – in the constant wars that are the growing pains of the hustling cities of the Late Bronze Age Aegean.

Sisterhood

What we also find here is a young woman who – alongside her brothers – is envisaged as having her own part to play in the family unit. This is a message that was, until a few years ago, hard to take seriously. In the Homeric epics, it is very clearly through marriage, not birth, that women are seen to gain status in peacetime. Daughters like Chryseis are visualized as the movable elements of a household, transitioning flexibly from their father's home to that of their husband, to whom they are meant to deliver children of their own. Andromache marries out of her father's family in Thebe and moves away from her seven brothers, to become Hector's wife in Troy and give him a son. Penelope is given by her father Icarius in marriage to Odysseus, leaving her home in Sparta for Ithaca (she also bears him a son, Telemachus).[21] Assimilated into their husbands' families, these women are patently defined, in Homer, by men. Male heroes and kings in the epics, on the other hand, often give their names and lineages (one of the many functions of the oral poetry that underpins the Homeric poems was to preserve a memory of family histories), and for these male warriors, it is, quite naturally, their father's family tree that they trace – the line goes up through father, grandfather and into the men of their ancestry, with the women seen as add-ons to the patriarchal dynasty. Achilles (in the very first line of the *Iliad*) is the 'son of Peleus'; Agamemnon (six lines later) is the 'son of Atreus', and so on. Linear B tablets back up this custom, using patronymics to identify elite men (never women) – like Alektryon, the son of Eteokles, who is specified on a tablet from Pylos.[22]

In the archaeological record, before it was possible to analyse the DNA of the skeletons found in Mycenaean tombs – and thus to understand vital data such as (accurate estimations of) their sex, where they came from, how old they were, how they were related, and so on – burials were traditionally assessed to accord with this pattern. High-status 'females' – labelled as such by archaeologists of the late nineteenth or early twentieth century, on the assumption (based on prevailing ideas about gender) that jewellery, mirrors or spindle whorls were always associated with women – who were buried alongside 'males' (those with weapons) were usually interpreted as wives who had married into the dynasty. Men, in this version of history, were the age-old roots, trunk and branches of all ancient family trees; women who remained in the record had to have been grafted on from elsewhere.

But in the last few years, this story has started to be challenged. Here, it's a case, not of reading further into the slivers of women's experience that Homer serves up for us, or using the Homeric epics to illuminate Bronze Age iconography, but of challenging the historical accuracy and one-sidedness of the androcentrism that the poet holds up. This is what advances in the study of the ancient DNA of human skeletons found in Bronze Age dynastic tombs have started to do, bringing up a series of surprising findings, and overturning what used to be known about the roles that daughters, and sisters, played in the world of prehistoric Greece. The first unexpected discovery was in 2008, back at Grave Circle B, in Mycenae on the Greek mainland, when the Manchester researchers who had taken on the facial reconstruction of the Bronze Age skeletons decided to go further and take DNA samples to work out the relationships between the individuals to whom they'd given a face. With the number of people buried in the Grave Circle – thirty-five burials covering three or four generations – the conjecture had naturally already arisen that this might have been a family plot, the after-death residence of one particular dynasty.[23] Γ58 – the woman whom we met in Chapter 1 as a way of imagining a face for Helen – was buried in the same grave as a man. Aged around thirty-three, he is known as Γ55. The grave goods associated with him show that he was clearly a high-status leader: he was the only individual in the entire grave circle to be buried with an ornate death mask with a stylized representation of a face, made out of a flat sheet of precious electrum.[24]

Until then, relationships between Γ58 and Γ55 and others buried in the graves had been suggested, but no one had, as yet, proposed that Γ58 and Γ55 might themselves have been related. In fact, given their similar ages and the traditional narrative that women lived in the shadow of men, exerting power and influence through their husbands, they had been assumed to be connected by marriage – with Γ58 buried alongside Γ55 by virtue of being his wife. But the facial reconstruction had thrown up an interesting possibility, because their reconstructed portraits were strikingly similar: widely spaced eyes and broad cheekbones, prominent forehead, heart-shaped face. The idea was that these two individuals could, in fact, have been related to each other by blood.

And that's exactly what the follow-up DNA analysis, almost twenty years after the initial reconstructions, has recently confirmed. Γ58 and

Γ55 don't just have the same facial characteristics in common – they share, deep down in their tissues in the DNA the researchers managed to extract, the same mitochondrial DNA (mtDNA) haplogroup, genetic material that is passed down solely through the maternal line. The way they were buried makes it clear that they were interred within a few months of each other: we can tell that Γ55's joints were still intact, linking his bones together, when his body was moved aside for Γ58 to join him.[25] Their close age, and their shared maternal DNA, means that they were, in all probability, brother and sister – not husband and wife. (It's worth adding that, while a sibling marriage is theoretically possible, it's highly unlikely: the DNA data shows that first- and second-cousin marriages were much more the norm.)[26] This matters, not just for what it tells us about kinship and burial practices among the elite in the Mycenaean world, but because it shows that Γ58 was accorded this distinguished burial, not through a marital connection, but by right of her own authority through her high birth. This was a woman who had value in Bronze Age society, not because she married a man, but by her birthright: as a high-status daughter, like Chryseis, and like the young girl from Thera.

Another, more recent, study gives us an even more comprehensive picture of the important role elite daughters might have played in the way relationships were structured within their families in the Late Bronze Age.[27] Early in 2023, an international group of researchers led by the Max Planck Institute in Leipzig, Germany, published one of the largest studies so far of ancient DNA from across the Bronze Age Aegean. Samples of aDNA were extracted from ninety-five Bronze Age skeletons buried throughout mainland Greece and the Greek islands. The researchers' main aim was to learn more about mobility and migration patterns of populations across the Aegean in the Bronze Age, but in unlocking the information encoded in the prehistoric remains, they uncovered several other remarkable findings that they hadn't expected. At one site on mainland Greece, in particular – a Late Bronze Age cemetery known as Aidonia, not far from Mycenae – the patterns of relatedness between the individuals (revealed by their DNA) showed an intriguing tendency. The traditional, Homeric interpretation of Greek dynasties based on the paternal line would tell us to expect that relatedness should always run through men (a phenomenon known as patriliny): grandfathers, uncles, fathers, sons should be related to each other, while wives come into the family unit from outside, and daughters in turn marry externally into other dynasties.

The DNA, however, tells a surprisingly different tale. At Aidonia, archaeologists found three women buried in the same chamber tomb from around the sixteenth century BCE who, as this new study shows, were related to each other: two of them first-degree relatives (so, sister/sister or mother/daughter), and the other either a grandmother, a half-sister or an aunt. In a patrilocal system, in which a wife moves to live with her husband's family, we'd expect to see patterns of relatedness between males – but here, it's possible that we could have up to three generations of women from the same family buried in the same tomb.[28] In fact, intriguingly, it has recently been suggested that it is precisely female burials associated with objects that run counter to traditional gender norms – women laid out with warrior kits, for example, or other grave goods typically associated with men – that were deliberately meant to signal that these elite women were successors in the line of descent (or matriliny), crossing over what might normally have been expected of their gender.[29] Ironically, this means that – before DNA analysis could confirm the sex of the human remains – traditional methods of sexing remains, according to modern gender norms around the grave goods buried alongside them, always ended up confirming the old story about patrilineal descent, even when women were hidden in plain sight in the mortuary record.

This is noticeably at odds with the Homeric model of daughters as mobile tradable goods, marrying, and moving, far away from their homes to bolster their husbands' patriarchal line. Here daughters are commemorated alongside their birth families, just like Γ58 with her brother at Mycenae. They are memorialized together as they were in Aidonia, commemorated by their descendants as a sisterhood of women who brought the family together and celebrated the line of succession, even after they died. In counterpoint to Homer's silenced daughters, the story written into DNA gives us intriguing hints of the roles that sisters and daughters played in the structuring of the family unit: a role that was sufficiently important in life to be commemorated in death.

Of course, this was by no means always the case. Many (if not most) Mycenaean burials do appear to privilege men and the male line, just as we'd expect in the patriarchal society of Mycenaean Greece. The story that is emerging is simply that they didn't *always* follow the traditional pattern: that in some cases (often, it has to be said, the elite ones: it's usually elites who are selected for visible burials), women might have been able to play a different part. And in fact, when we look a little deeper, the exceptional examples of high-status daughters that we find at Aidonia and Mycenae are, in fact, backed up in occasional instances in the Homeric texts, too. The best-known example of them all is one we have already come across in the search for Homer's women: Helen. For Helen – in spite of having two brothers, Castor and Pollux (just as with Γ58 and her likely brother) – is, in fact, famously, the female heir to the kingdom of Sparta. (It's there that we meet her in the *Odyssey*, when Telemachus pays a visit in search of his father.) When she marries Menelaus, a prince of Argos, it is he – not she – who moves, and joins her, and who rules alongside her in the palace at Sparta; when the kingdom passes on, it goes not to Menelaus' sons, but to Helen's daughter, Hermione.[30] In other words, in the case of Helen – possibly Homer's most extraordinary woman of all – the Spartan line follows matrilineal, not patrilineal, descent. Just as with the re-evaluation of the burial of Γ58 and the chamber tombs at Aidonia, a more nuanced rereading of the Homeric epics uncovers a different world from the uniformly homogenous, male-orientated society that both the Mycenaeans and Homer projected, and archaeologists and Homerists have posited: one that, on occasion, went against traditional patriarchal norms, and allowed for a different configuration in the case of a few outstanding, high-status women.

What this shows, among other things, is that the histories that have been told about both mythical and real women in the ancient world derive as much from modern interpretations as they do from Homer's, in the tendency to make sweeping generalizations about the past (for example: if Mycenaean Greece was patriarchal, then it always was; if Homer was more interested in the world of men, then he always was). Post-antique ideas about what should and shouldn't be associated with a 'female' burial, forcing women into gender-stereotyped boxes, has tended to diminish and flatten the story around gender in the Late Bronze Age – which could be a lot more unconventional, a lot more boundary-crossing, than used to be thought. And nowhere is this more

Hers, not his: an electrum face mask buried with the woman in Grave Circle B, Mycenae (17th–16th centuries BCE).

evident than back in the grave of Γ58 at Mycenae. Because scholars are now saying that it is almost inevitable that the death mask in precious electrum, with its depiction of a delicate, hairless face – the only such relic to be discovered in the entire Grave Circle, and immediately assigned by archaeologists to a man – didn't belong to the supposedly high-status brother at all. It was discovered too far away to have covered his face. It was, in fact, much closer to where Γ58 originally lay.

And so this highest of status-markers, this costly representation of a face for all eternity, might actually, in all likelihood, have been hers.[31]

Beyond Greece

New discoveries in the field of aDNA, then, are leading to new ways of unravelling the past, new inroads into explaining the evidence from archaeology that go against the grain of previous interpretations. They can shed light on how a young woman like Chryseis – the wordless daughter of the *Iliad*, bartered back and forth between men – might, in fact, have experienced a different reality from the narrative that Homer's women have inhabited for millennia: one where she could have owned her position in the family as a daughter, not be traded in and out of it. In a sense, this confirms the picture we're uncovering in other places, like the wall paintings at Thera: where not only is a daughter pictured as a valued member of the household, as at the West House in Akrotiri, but elsewhere women depicted in the wall paintings represent female communities that seem to hold value and power, like the high-status group of prepubescent female saffron gatherers shown in the mountain meadows at Akrotiri who seem to gesture to a sensuous, revered world of women's groups and women's rites. In fact, a recent interpretation of these crocus-picking women has connected them to a strange sunken basin nearby topped with a painting of a woman dripping blood – suggesting that the young saffron-gathering women are celebrating their first period (saffron, after all, has important medicinal properties and would have been used to regulate menses), and that these kinds of basins were used for women's menstruation, as young girls like Chryseis celebrated the defining rite of passage towards womanhood.[32]

Just as aDNA research and new readings of the frescoes at Thera are reclaiming the stories of women like Chryseis, fiction, too, is giving us a new way of bringing her experience to the fore. In the last few years, Chryseis has transcended the role of the courtly love interest of Troilus that defined her post-antique reincarnation as Shakespeare's Cressida, and has come forward, like Briseis, to tell her own story. In my *For the Most Beautiful* and Natalie Haynes's *A Thousand Ships*, the women of the Trojan War step forward to tell the collective tale of female suffering, in their own voices – staging, through the joint drama of Chryseis' and Briseis' silencing at the *Iliad*'s opening, that this is just as much a woman's story as it is a man's. Chryseis speaks out at last, in a new realm that – like the recent discoveries at the chamber tombs at Aidonia – resists the typical Homeric narrative, bringing together a community of Trojan women and tapping into the collective power of their voices to retell this ancient tale of gods and men from a woman's point of view.

Unlike her ancient counterpart, a contemporary Chryseis can use words of her own.

But the comparison with the women's community at Aidonia also brings up a problem with the evidence we've been using to look for Chryseis. And it's a problem that, just like our view of a patriarchal Bronze Age Greece that may, in fact, have been far more complicated and many-layered, goes straight back to Homer. So far, in my search for the real women behind Homer, I've been drawing on the world of Bronze Age Greece: the burials at Mycenae, the Linear B tablets at Pylos, the chamber tombs at Aidonia, the wall paintings at Akrotiri. The songs that told legendary tales of spear-wielding heroes and epic wars – like the marching warriors and water-carrying women on the wall at Thera – circulated around Greece from the middle of the second millennium BCE (and possibly even earlier). They would have been sung by itinerant bards who spoke an early kind of Greek, fashioning a Greek (or 'Achaean', the word that's used in Homer) identity that presented their heroes as formidable conquerors and founders of the Greek city states. The Homeric texts were no different; in fact, if anything, they're even *more* Greek – and that's not just because they were written down, sometime in the archaic period, in what's now known as the Greek script. They also underwent a significant process of what could be called 'Athenianization' around the sixth century BCE, when the tyrants of Athens (just before the century that would bring democracy) began to consolidate the fluid, oral Homeric texts into a fixed version that fitted into their idea of what it meant to be Athenian, and (consequently, in their eyes) what it meant to 'be' Greek.[33] Homer became what one critic has called 'a spokesman for the Athenian empire'.[34] The Homeric *Iliad* and *Odyssey* were performed at Athens' national festival, the Great Panathenaia. Images of the sack of Troy were sculpted on to Athens' most famous building (and the crowning monument of empire), the Parthenon, as an advertisement of Greek victory over the barbarians. The 'Achaeans' (*Achaioi*) of Homer, originally used to denote the scattered members of various Mycenaean city states, were homogenized and imagined as proto-Greeks through the skewing power of Athens' Panhellenic imperial ambitions; one ancient Greek scholar even claimed that Homer had been Athenian himself.[35]

This essential Greekness of Homer has important ramifications for the portrayal of the Trojan women. Chryseis – whom Homer tells us was a Trojan captive of the Greeks – confusingly has a quintessentially Greek name, that both means 'Goldie' in Greek and 'daughter of Chryses' (her father's – also Greek – name; although Trojan, he speaks perfect Greek in the opening of the *Iliad* when he addresses Agamemnon). The Trojan wife of Hector, Andromache, has a name that means 'man-fighter' in Greek (we have Linear B equivalents from the tablets for these kinds of early Greek war-names for women, such as *Wi-ja-da-ra*, 'she who has men due to her strength'); and Andromache, too, conducts her conversation at the gates of Troy with Hector in flawless Homeric Greek. When the queen of Troy, Hecuba, prays to the gods to bring help to the Trojans at Hector's request, she goes (with aching irony) to the temple of the Greek god Athena. Almost all Homer's so-called 'Trojan women', in fact, have Greek names: they speak Greek; they worship the Greek pantheon. This is a kaleidoscopic vision of a world that has been shaken up and re-focused through a highly coloured Greek lens.

Which means that we're engaged in something of a catch-22 when we look at the women in the *Iliad*. Most of them (with the exception of Helen) are Trojan – but they're written about in a Greek text that was used to broadcast Greek ideas and identities to an ancient Greek audience. Using comparative evidence from Bronze Age Greek sites to think about the women, in this sense, sort of works: if we want to recover the kinds of women the Homeric texts might have been attempting to capture, in their delivery of a Greek version of the past, then it makes sense to look to Greek evidence. But what if we want to break down, and push past, the veneer of Greekness that Homer presents? What if we want to go beyond the illusion of an all-Greek world that Homer conjures up? What if we want to find the real women of Troy – beyond Homer?

4

HECUBA

Queen

TROY

She knows, already, what her son has come here to say. Like the other women who watch from the walls, she has grown experienced in war, these past ten years: watching her sons die, one by one, like bits of carrion picked off the bone by birds. She has seen the plague that festered in the Greek camp, the stinking piles of soldiers. She has watched the truce they tried to make – the Greeks and Trojans – break like a shattered spear, when the men realized it wasn't Helen they were fighting for. She has seen Achilles leave to nurse his wounded pride, watched Diomedes step forward to splatter her sons' blood on his ancestral shield. She heard them shouting to each other, Hector and her other sons, as they let the Trojan line fall back towards the gates. A mother does not easily forget the sound of her children's fear.

She goes down to the treasury, where the royal seals lie side by side. Walks to the chests where the costliest fine-threaded robes are kept, puts key in lock and opens the lid. There they lie: women's treasures, years of skilled work and the richest dyes, worth their weight in gold. Woven by women her son captured in a raid south in Sidon, and took as slaves. They worked their fingers to shreds on these: she watched them at their clacking looms. And on the plain below, the Trojan men fight to make sure their wives won't suffer the same fate.

This is what women do in war. This is what a woman's world looks like. These are battle trophies, woven in blood-red: a scream for help that no one hears.

She slides out a gleaming robe, folded edge sharp as a blade, and runs it through her fingers.

Now it is time to ready her own weapons.

Queen of the Land of Hatti

Excavation season at Gözlükule in southern Turkey has begun. Hetty Goldman is in her second year of directing the dig here at the ancient port town of Tarsus, and she's thankful it's not raining. The first time they came here, in April 1934, scouting out where to start the first trench, their car was almost swept into a local river (the Ceyhan) as their ferry floated away on the rain-swollen current.[1] But today, in the spring of 1936, it's warm and bright, good for digging. A school playground nearby fills the air with the busy noise of children. The cemetery on the other side is silent.[2]

The site at Gözlükule – a dusty, scrub-covered mound that juts out of the flat Cilician plain at the edge of modern Tarsus – is a warren of jagged gashes in the hillside and deep pits, dug over the last few years by Goldman's team. Fragments of Roman wall stick out at angles, part of a gateway that once led to the sea where ships would have set sail for Cyprus – now crumbling and coated in dust. Several metres down, other walls have started to appear: low corridors of mud brick and stone criss-crossing each other and then disappearing into the solid face of the undug earth. Goldman knows, already, that what she has found is a Late Bronze Age building: with an expertise honed by excavations all over the Aegean, she has swiftly categorized the scraps of pottery discovered here into Late Bronze Age types. She knows, from the quantities of Hittite ware, that this prehistoric city must have been a significant outpost of the Hittite Empire – a vast central Anatolian power that was, by the middle of the second millennium BCE, one of the major imperial players in the ancient Mediterranean and south-west Asia, controlling swathes of land from the Aegean coast near Troy to the west all the way east across Turkey and into Syria, and ruled by the formidable Great King and Great Queen from their central capital in Hattusa (modern-day Boğazkale in Turkey).

But Gözlükule is a challenging site, even for an experienced excavator. When, over a thousand years after the mysterious collapse of the Hittite Empire in 1200 BCE, the Romans (unleashing their own imperial ambitions and expanding their provinces into the east) sank foundations into the hill at Tarsus, they destroyed many of the early layers Goldman is looking for. The same happened during the Islamic period; then again when drain systems were plumbed into medieval and modern buildings.[3] The stratigraphy – the precise layering of deposits one on top of the other that allows archaeologists to construct timelines and place objects in their historical context – has become a frustrating mess.

So when Goldman finds an undisturbed, sealed pit dating to the Late Bronze Age, crammed to the brim with the prehistoric equivalent of landfill, it's only natural to wonder what she might find. At first, it's nothing very exciting. A couple of insignificant pieces of metal. A bead bracelet. Then a fragmentary tablet, pressed with the tiny imprints that mark the cuneiform script of the Hittite language.

And then it appears. A tiny, round clay seal impression, insignificant-looking at first: the kind of stamp found across the Hittite world in official seals. This one has cuneiform running around the broken edge, the word *Hebat* just visible, alongside the Hittite word for 'daughter'. But what catches Goldman's eye at once are the miniature hieroglyphs patterned down the centre – a local Anatolian alternative to cuneiform (that had been imported from Mesopotamia to the east).[4] Minuscule box-like hieroglyphs spell out the sounds *pu-tu-ha-pa*; either side of the vertical glyphs, a mirror image of a head appears in profile, wearing a trailing veil encircled by a disc-shaped coronct and gazing towards the central inscription. These symbols represent titles: the coronet is 'Great'; the veiled face 'Queen'.

And, through the haze of the day's heat and the dust coating her fingers, it becomes clear what Goldman has found: the personal seal of Puduhepa, one of the last Great Queens of the Hittite Empire.

Queen of Troy

Homer's Hecuba is not a historical Hittite queen, but the legendary queen of Troy – a city that, as Schliemann discovered, was situated on the outer fringes of the ancient Hittite Empire, which real queens like Puduhepa once ruled. Homer provides a bit of backstory to flesh out his epic character, giving her an origin in Phrygia – a kingdom that, historically, was situated in west-central Anatolia (modern Turkey), bordering the western edge of the Hittite heartland and largely incorporated into the Hittite Empire (probably with the help of loyal puppet rulers, a common Hittite policy) during its flourishing in the Late Bronze Age. She is, according to Homer, the daughter of a king called Dymas, who is said to have held sway 'on the banks of the river Sangarius' (the modern Sakarya river).[5] Not coincidentally, perhaps, this is the site of the actual Phrygian capital of Gordion (some of its massive later fortifications still survive), a major city located on the ancient trading route westwards from Mesopotamia, and it may have been near here – on the main route from the great inland empires towards the far-away ports of the Aegean Sea – that Homer imagined Hecuba's father once ruling. When she married Priam, king of Troy, however, Homer's Hecuba would have had to leave for Troy on the shores of the Aegean on the north-western Anatolian coast. Here, like Andromache, she would have made a new home in her husband's kingdom: the wealthy, and strategically important, city of Troy – located at the mouth of the narrow channel that links the Aegean to the Black Sea, controlling access to one of the major connecting points between the western world of Greece and the great eastern Anatolian plateau.

Arriving in Troy, Hecuba, so the story goes, entered a palace that was already replete with royal sons and daughters from Priam's other wives and from his concubines. In the sixth book of the *Iliad*, at the moment we first meet the Trojan queen, Homer sketches out the splendid architecture of the Trojan palace on the city's windy citadel where, since leaving Phrygia, she spends her days: in particular, a courtyard with a portico made of polished stone, around which the bedchambers of Priam's sons and daughters are arranged – fifty for the sons, and twelve for the daughters.[6] Nineteen of these sons, we are told, are Hecuba's; the other thirty-odd have been fathered by other women in the court. While Hecuba is clearly the chief and favoured wife – her sons (like Hector) are legitimate, the others are referred to as bastards – she is not the only royal consort, not the only mother of the children of the king.[7]

The picture Homer paints in Book 6 of the *Iliad*, however, makes it very clear that – in her role as a queen, as a ruler of Troy alongside

Priam – Hecuba stands supreme. At this point in the epic, the Trojan army is in crisis. Even though the Greeks have had to do without their best fighter – since Achilles withdrew from the war, his pride wounded because of Agamemnon's seizure of Briseis – the Trojans have not had an easy time of it. A duel between Paris and Menelaus, which was meant to settle the issue of Helen once and for all, ends at a stalemate when the Trojans (lured by the pro-Greek goddess Athena) break the truce. Fighting breaks out again, and the Greeks immediately seize the upper hand. One of the warriors and a favourite of Athena, Diomedes, above all, is determined to prove himself the best of the Greeks and engages in a swashbuckling, blood-spattered parade of slaughter. Trojan warriors are falling left and right beneath the pitiless Greek advance, as the battle surges over the plain. And so, as book six opens, Helenus – another of Hecuba's sons – calls his brother Hector to make an urgent retreat back to Troy, to take the only option left to them: to beg their mother, the queen, to gather the women of Troy and formally supplicate the goddess Athena to take pity on the Trojans – to stop Diomedes in his tracks.

As Hector ducks through the Scaean Gates – the famous main gates of Troy's citadel in Homer – and climbs up to the royal palace, we move from the theatre of war beyond the walls of Troy, and dive into a women's world. This is a different place, as we will see, filled with a character cast of mothers, sisters and wives; a quiet space of weaving, apart from the gore-splattered battle; a realm of captive women and waiting wives; a place that threads together, like Helen's tapestry, the longing for a return to peace and the dread of what might happen if the war is lost. And it is here, at the heart of Troy's palace, that – before any of the other Trojan women – Hector meets his mother, Hecuba, the queen.

She guesses, immediately, why her son has come: it can only be, she remarks, that the Greeks are pressing hard on the city, and that he needs her to pray to the gods. At once, with the ease of a lifetime spent in command, she gathers together her female attendants and the older women of the city; selects, from her royal treasury, her grandest and most richly woven robe (Homer's word is *peplos*). Not just any robe, though: this is a garment that was woven by enslaved women from Sidon (modern-day Lebanon), who – the poet takes care to inform us – were brought back by Paris on his return to Troy with Helen.[8] The Greeks aren't the only ones to capture women in battle raids, then. Hecuba might, perhaps, have taken a moment to reflect on the provenance of her offering, and the suffering of women it encapsulates in her son's double capture of Helen and the women of Sidon, before serving it up to the war goddess. In any case, blithely ignoring the portent of female oppression she holds in her hands, she lifts up the handiwork of enslaved women and goes in an all-female procession up to Athena's temple in the citadel. There, in the company of Troy's women elders and on the orders of the queen, the priestess Theano can spread the *peplos* on the goddess's knees and promise plentiful sacrifices (twelve young cows, to be precise) if Athena shatters Diomedes' spear.[9]

It's a powerful scene of desperately voiced supplication from Troy's victims that stops the bloody Iliadic narrative of war in its tracks. For a moment, we are drawn into the intimate world of women, and get a sense of the vital roles and numinous religious influence to which these prominent females – queen, elders, priestess – could lay claim. In the past, however, when critics have looked at the passage, it's not (unsurprisingly) the women that have been the focus, but rather the curiously Athenian flavour of the scene. In fact, it's even been suggested that this passage was a later interpolation by the pre-democratic tyrants of Athens, given what we know about the standardization of the performance of the Homeric epics that went on during the sixth century BCE.[10] This is because the Homeric description of the offering of a *peplos* to Athena is highly reminiscent of one of Athens' most prized national festivals: the Great Panathenaia – that same festival at which the Homeric epics were, later, performed. This great civic celebration, in honour of Athens' patron goddess, Athena, is most famously memorialized in the frieze of the Parthenon (currently held at the British Museum as the Elgin Marbles), which depicts the Panathenaic procession as it winds around the Parthenon temple, culminating, at its centre, in the image of a young girl handing over the *peplos* that would have been used to clothe the statue of Athena. Just as the women of Troy come together in the *Iliad* to dedicate a *peplos* to Athena, so, the theory went, later Athenians privileged a mirror-like reflection of their own festival – centring around young girls, female priestesses and the dedication of the *peplos* to Athena's statue – within Homer's epic.

But, as obvious as it might have seemed to seek out the typically Greek elements of Homer, we're much more interested now in directing our gaze past the marble-clad mirage of Athens and towards the diverse and global world that forms the backdrop to Homer's epics. In particular, a recent groundbreaking study by Mary Bachvarova has argued that south-west Asian epics and stories of real figures from Asiatic history could have been transferred orally by bards travelling between Anatolia and the Greek Aegean.[11] The Hellenocentrism of previous scholars has led them to ignore the overwhelming evidence that the world of the ancient Aegean, from the Bronze Age all the way into the archaic period and beyond, was well networked and deeply interconnected. We know that major hubs of contact for trade between Greece and Anatolia popped up across Cyprus and the western Aegean coast of modern Turkey – the gateway into south-west Asia – and flourished for centuries before Homer's time, and again into the Iron Age.[12] We also know that there are unmissable correspondences between Homeric and ancient epics of south-west Asia – most famously, the Mesopotamian *Epic of Gilgamesh* (though there are plenty of others).[13] And then there are the historical figures, like the great Akkadian conqueror Sargon the Great and his grandson Naram-Sin, whose stories migrated into myths retold across the centuries from Mesopotamia to Syria to Anatolia, and whose tales find echoes in characters in Homeric epic.[14] These correspondences have to be more than just coincidental: there are simply too many of them, and they're too close, to be purely down to chance.[15] Histories, legends, even word patterns were clearly being shared between these ancient cultures, a treasure trove of stories exchanged between them along with the trade in physical goods. It's likely that festivals on the Aegean coast, at the fertile boundary between the worlds of the Greeks and south-west Asia – with a headline programme of performances on the religious festival circuit, by bards from a melting pot of cultures – played a crucial part in this trade in myths and histories that would, eventually, trickle down into the epics of Homer.[16]

And this kind of new research into the global, and particularly south-west Asian, backdrop to the Homeric epics – the epic stories flooding in through Anatolia, the historical personalities from millennia of rich south-west Asian history – gives us a hint that there may be another, older layer to the scene of the Iliadic women's supplication. If we dig a little deeper, we can in fact find an Anatolian model for Hecuba that demonstrates that – beneath the Greek accretions – we might just be able to uncover in Homer the memory of real-life, powerful Bronze Age Anatolian queens.

Then the Ships Came

Puduhepa, Great Queen of the Hittites, whose royal seal was found by Hetty Goldman at Tarsus in 1936, ruled the Hittite Empire from its capital, Hattusa, alongside her husband Hattusili III from around 1267 to 1237 BCE.[17] She was one of the most powerful of all the queens to rule the Hittite Empire (or the Land of Hatti, as they called it – the term 'Hittites' comes from the Bible): she is shown in both the Hittite texts and iconography as Hattusili's valued chief consort and very much his equal partner. Hattusili met her at her home in south-east Anatolia – an area known as Kizzuwatna, in which the city of Tarsus (where Goldman ran her excavation) was located. He was on his way back from Syria, where he had fought the largest battle of the era against the Egyptian pharaoh Ramesses II: the Battle of Qadesh, in 1274 BCE. When Puduhepa arrived at Hattusa as Hattusili's bride, there were – just as in Hecuba's case – multiple princes and princesses at the palace, the offspring from previous marriages, along with concubines and second-rank wives. But Puduhepa was clearly held in high esteem, as both Great Queen and Chief Priestess of the Hittite realm (a function traditionally held by the chief consort of the king), throughout her life. She corresponded personally with some of the most powerful rulers of the day on matters of state, including Ramesses II himself. She arranged dynastic marriages – a key element of international diplomacy, since royal marriages often lay at the heart of peace alliances – and was instrumental in arranging the highly prominent marriage of at least one of the Hittite princesses to Ramesses II (part of the ongoing peace negotiations after Qadesh). Her personal seal (just like that found by Goldman) was often set alongside her husband's in matters of international diplomacy, attesting to the unusual power she was able to wield and her equal status to the king.

Indeed, when Hattusili drew up the Qadesh peace treaty with Ramesses fifteen years after the battle, Puduhepa's seal was stamped on to the treaty alongside her husband's.[18] Even after Hattusili's death, she continued to wield considerable political influence throughout the reign of their son, Tudhaliya IV, and she died, aged about ninety, around 1200 BCE – at the very moment in time that archaeological evidence has suggested that the historical city of Troy VIIa was attacked and fell to enemy forces.

So what might this queen who married into her husband's kingdom, ruled an Anatolian empire that bordered Troy, and lived and died around the time of its attested historical fall, have to tell us about the legendary Hecuba's world?

The first instance in which Puduhepa and Hecuba, the Hittites, the Greeks and Troy come together is in a text that seems to have been authored by the Great Queen herself. It's a votive prayer, written on a clay tablet discovered among the thousands of texts (personal letters,

The Great Queen Puduhepa, pictured on a Hittite rock relief, making an offering to the Sun Goddess Arinna Hebat: the queen (right) wears her priestess's robes, while the goddess is enthroned to the left.

diplomatic agreements, collections of laws and prayers) found in archives uncovered at Hattusa, and dating to the thirteenth century BCE.[19] In it, Puduhepa – as Chief Priestess – is supplicating the gods, including one goddess in particular: Hebat (a goddess from her home region in Kizzuwatna whom Puduhepa was responsible for introducing into the Hittite pantheon). Her request is simple. She promises gifts – sacrifices of an ox and eight sheep, and gold – if the gods save her husband's kingdom and bring destruction to her enemy, a Hittite renegade by the name of Piyamaradu.

We know about Piyamaradu from other diplomatic correspondence in the Hittite archives, and it seems he caused the Hittite king and queen no end of trouble. A rebel against Hittite authority over an extraordinary career of disruption that must have lasted more than thirty years, he attacked Hittite vassal cities over the course of the thirteenth century BCE in an attempt to foment anti-Hittite rebellion. One of his targets included a city in north-west Anatolia called Wilusa (which appears elsewhere in conjunction with another place name, Taruisa – to which we'll return later). At Wilusa, a major foreign power called Ahhiyawa became involved (and later continued to provide protection to Piyamaradu); there was some sort of 'hostility' around the city between the Ahhiyawans and the Hittites that came to an end in the mid thirteenth century BCE under Puduhepa's husband King Hattusili III.[20] What brought the Ahhiyawans to Wilusa, we don't know – though it's clear that the Hittites had a particularly vested interest there, having recently signed a treaty with the Wilusan king, Alaksandu, promising to come to his aid as allies and kill his enemies in war in return for imposing Hittite control over the region. But all that's in the past now, Puduhepa's husband writes with a flourish of magnanimity, in a personal letter to the king of the Ahhiyawans: 'about the matter of the land of Wilusa concerning which he and I were hostile to one another, we have made peace. Now hostility is not appropriate between us.'[21]

This might sound like so much prehistoric squabbling, until we uncover the real political players, the history-changing international dynamics at play behind the scenes. Because most scholars now agree that the *Ahhiyawa* of the texts at Hattusa is a Hittite version of ancient Greek *Achaia*, the land of the *Achaioi*, or 'Achaeans'. This is not only one

of the words that Homer uses in his epics to describe his heroic Greeks
and legendary invaders of Troy; it's also the term that the real, historical
Mycenaeans most likely used to describe themselves.[22] So if Ahhiyawans
are Achaeans – historical Bronze Age Greeks remembered by Homer as
the Achaean heroes of old – then what about the city of Wilusa? Can we
do any further digging to discover more about the hidden identity of this
north-west Anatolian city, fought over by Bronze Age Achaean troops?
Well, the first clue lies in Homer: because, in the epics, the city of Troy
has two names that are used interchangeably, probably originally desig-
nating the city of Troy and the region that surrounded it.[23] These are Troy
(*Troiē*) and *Ilios*, the root of the epic's Greek name, *Iliad* – a word that,
in Homeric Greek, would actually have been pronounced *Wilios* (the
'w' was later dropped). Wilios and Wilusa: the echo is uncanny. But it's
not just that. The historical city of Wilusa that appears in Hittite records
crops up, at one point, next to another name – Taruisa – that seems to
have been used for the region nearby.[24] The match between the north-
west Anatolian Wilusa/Ilios (the city) and Taruisa/Troy (the region) is so
close that most scholars now agree that Wilusa was, in fact, the city that
Homer remembers as Ilios – or Troy.

Once these matches are made – Ahhiyawans as Achaeans (what we'd
call Mycenaean Greeks), Wilusa as Troy – the other correspondences
start to pile up. We know from the Hittite archives that Wilusa, ruled
by Alaksandu, was allied with the Hittites. Homer gives the names of
some of the allies who were said to have supported the Trojans, among
them the *Kēteioi* – a word that appears to be an echo of the term the
Hittites used to refer to themselves, the Hatti.[25] On the other side, the
letter sent from Hattusili III to the Ahhiyawan 'Great King' talks about
the king *and his brother*, acting in concert in the hostilities; could this
king-and-brother pair be remembered in Homer as the Achaean King
Agamemnon and his brother Menelaus, perhaps?[26] Meanwhile, the
name of the Wilusan king, given in the Hittite records as Alaksandu,
bears an unmissable similarity to a name that crops up frequently in
Homer: Alexandros, more commonly called by the other name Homer
gives him, Paris – the Trojan prince whose theft of Helen started the
Trojan War. (The debate about this rather odd double naming of Paris
is ongoing, but it seems likely that Paris is probably a local Anatolian

name added to the epics to give a bit of exotic colour, while Alaksandu was an alternative that could easily be assimilated into the Greek *Alexandros* for the poems' audience.)[27] Could the Hittite treaty with Alaksandu of Wilusa and their campaign against the Ahhiyawans in the thirteenth century BCE be remembered and adapted, in the Homeric epics, in the figure of Alexandros of Ilios (Paris of Troy) and the war he triggered? Could a diplomatic letter written by Puduhepa's husband to an Ahhiyawan king, reminding him of the war that once went on around Wilusa, be hiding the secret of an epic tale? Could the *Iliad* be preserving the lingering memory of a real Late Bronze Age Anatolian king who fought with his allies around Ilios/Troy (Wilusa/Taruisa), against the marauding invaders of Achaean (Ahhiyawan) Greece, led by their king and his brother?

The correspondence with Homer is by no means perfect – and we shouldn't expect it to be. If anything, trying to push for an exact match undermines and devalues the flexibility of legend, the power of stories and myths to reframe the past. (For instance, Paris/Alexandros doesn't lead the Trojan troops in Homer, and the conflict recorded in the Hittite texts is between the Ahhiyawans and the Hittites – not the Trojans – over Troy. We don't even know the scale of the dispute, which could – by different readings of the Hittite texts – have ranged from anything from outright war to a diplomatic spat.) Products of hundreds of years of oral transmission, the Homeric epics were consolidated in a context quite different from that of the Late Bronze Age. More than anything, we have to remember that the *Iliad* and the *Odyssey* are, first and foremost, poetic narratives; and it is the nature of narrative to stir up history in the cauldron of myth, and thus to reinvent the past in ways that speak to the present.

But what we do have in the Hittite archives, and Puduhepa's prayer, is written evidence for something like a Trojan War, which could later be magnified and mythicized by Homer – some kind of conflict stirred up, around the thirteenth century BCE, by the Ahhiyawans/Achaeans around the city of Wilusa/Taruisa/Troy. It was, perhaps, this shimmering memory – most likely woven together with the (at least) three other historical battles that we know, from Hittite records, were fought during the Late Bronze Age at Wilusa – that was polished to a sheen by the

Greeks, transmitted at the feasting table in the retelling of heroic legends over the centuries and, finally, transformed into the epic ten-year Trojan siege of Homer's *Iliad*.

Anatolian Queens

And this is where we return to Puduhepa's prayer to the goddess Hebat for help against the warrior Piyamaradu. Because what Puduhepa is doing in her three-thousand-year-old prayer – a queen promising sacrifices to a female deity if she intervenes to protect the kingdom from a marauding intruder, who is fighting with the Greeks around the city of Troy – is remarkably similar to the poetic scene of Hecuba's supplication to Athena in the *Iliad*.[28] While this isn't about direct imitation or historical commentary, but rather a shared tradition of oral memory handed down across the Aegean and evolved from history into legend, the details nevertheless align to hint at a story pattern that shows continuity with an Anatolian model where a queen like Puduhepa gained near-equal status with her husband the king, and acted as Chief Priestess of the realm. Here, just as with Hecuba, we have a queen with high status within her kingdom, and a key role in safeguarding the realm through her proximity to the gods. Here, too, we have an intercession – by virtue of the queen's priestly connections – with a goddess. And here, above all, we have a prayer to destroy a specific enemy warrior, one who is historically associated with the Greeks (Piyamaradu receives protection from the Ahhiyawans, Diomedes is a Greek warrior), and a promise of sacrifice in return for victory.

The argument for a historical Hittite prototype for Homer's powerful queen figure with favourable, and deeply political, access to the divine is all the stronger, because there was no equivalent for the role of queen (in this sense) in the world of prehistoric Greece. While the highest position for a man in Mycenaean society documented in the Linear B tablets is that of *wa-na-ka* (Homer's (*w*)*anax*, 'king' or 'lord', a title given in the *Iliad* to King Agamemnon), there is no analogous word in early Greek for 'queen'. Neither Helen nor Clytemnestra are called 'queens' in Homer, and although Penelope in the *Odyssey* is given a term – *basileia* – which would come (in later Greek) to mean a queen, in Homer it seems to be a specific term for Odysseus' wife that tries to convey her unusual role as regent in protecting her husband's realm during his prolonged absence in the Trojan War.[29] If we look to the historical records of the Linear B tablets deciphered by Kober and Ventris, none of the ruling elite documented there are women, and no woman ever holds a secular office in the Mycenaean palace administration.[30] A realm in which women *could* hold power in Late Bronze Age Greece, on the other hand, was in the sphere of ritual, as high priestesses – a role which was specifically set apart from political power, in a separation of sacred and secular that the Hittite queens would never have understood. These priestesses could attain high status within the area of cult, operate as key-bearers of the sanctuary, and were even, on occasion, granted leases of land as a special mark of honour (as in the example of a priestess called Eritha at Pylos, who, as the Linear B records show, leased both private and public land).[31] What Mycenaean Greek women couldn't do, it seems, was wield signifi-cant political power – and certainly not alongside a priestly role. They couldn't be a queen in the way their Hittite counterparts were.

So when the Homeric epics present the image of a legendary Trojan queen initiating offerings to the gods for the safeguarding of her city, it seems that – in the context of centuries of historically attested conflict and diplomatic relations between the Ahhiyawans and the peoples of Anatolia – the poems are trying to make sense of an Anatolian-type Hecuba for a Greek audience. They are evolving out of an almost ethno-graphic picture of an Anatolian Troy, specifically through the Trojan women, that sets it in the context of the Hittite borderlands, and situ-ates it within a remembered historical environment and customs. But the idea of a queen who was also a priestess was probably just one step too far for a Greek audience, who weren't used to women in positions of political power, and whose priestesses operated solely in the context of their religious sanctuaries. By introducing the figure of the priestess Theano (the one who, on Hecuba's orders, actually makes the prayer to Athena in the *Iliad*), Homer neatly separates the royal and priestly functions of an Anatolian queen like Puduhepa, to create a shared sup-plication between a queen (Hecuba) and a priestess (Theano).[32]

There is a hidden clue that the *Iliad* is, perhaps, handing down an echo of Puduhepa, the Anatolian queen and Chief Priestess, in Hecuba and Theano's joint scene. In her brief appearance here, the priestess is given another name, *Kissēis*. This is an epithet that has always been taken to mean 'daughter of Kisseus' but – lately, now that we're starting to challenge the Hellenic-only version of Homer and search for non-Greek traces – has been reread as 'Kissewan, from Kizzuwatna', the birthplace of none other than Queen Puduhepa herself.[33] Similarly, recent work to reconstruct the missing parts of the inscription around Puduhepa's seal, found by Goldman at Tarsus, suggests that it reads 'Queen of the Land of Hatti, Daughter of the Land of Kizzuwatna, Beloved of Hebat' – a neat conjunction of the themes of queenship, birthplace and divine favour by a goddess that are also to be found in the poetic Homeric scene.[34] And there are other Anatolian echoes in Hecuba's supplication in Homer, too: above all, the group of old women Hecuba summons to join her – a specifically Anatolian feature, where 'Old Women' female ritual practitioners are listed again and again in the Hittite texts with specializations in healing and oracles.[35] It's possible, then, that Theano and Hecuba together, the priestess from Kizzuwatna and the queen of an Anatolian city surrounded by Hittite ritual elders, unite in supplication to a goddess as a way to infuse the epic of the *Iliad* and create a tangible historical backdrop – the shadowy remembrance of a real, and redoubtable, Hittite queen.

Reading the fictional character of Hecuba through the historical figure of Puduhepa, we can see that there's a lot more in Homer about her that isn't Greek. Even her name – unlike many of the other Greek-influenced names that Homer gives the Trojans, such as Andromache or Cassandra – may have an Anatolian root that connects her to a Kizzuwatnan goddess, Kubaba. This draws a parallel once again with Puduhepa – whose name (Pudu-*heba*) includes that of another Kizzuwatnan goddess, Hebat – while, at the same time, underlining Hecuba's non-Greek identity.[36] We can thus see the Homeric epics preserving a memory – lingering, perhaps, and hidden behind the resonances between ancient Anatolian rituals and secret codes like *Kissēis*/Kizzuwatna – of these real, powerful queens, engaging with the international conflicts that were playing across the Aegean and manipulating the power structures available to them to engineer the outcome of war, right across the Bronze Age Anatolian world.

Nations United

The tragedy of Hecuba, of course, is that she's praying to the wrong goddess. Instead of Puduhepa's Hebat, she appeals to Athena – a Greek goddess, patron of the Greek army and situated squarely within Homer's Greek epic. As much as the *Iliad* might sketch out a representation of the Anatolian aspects of the Trojan women, it is, at the end of the day, an epic that has its roots in Greek – written in the Greek language (the women's supplication is in Greek, not the Hittite-related Luwian language the Trojans would probably have spoken), and peopled with Greek gods. And Homer's pro-Greek goddess – quite naturally – denies Hecuba's request.[37]

In this sense, both as a woman and as a non-Greek, Hecuba is on the wrong side of history. But there's always another side to any tale. And, in 1984, the speculative (but intriguing) suggestion was put forward that two scattered lines preserved in the Hittite archives might, in fact, give a hint of those other voices, of a Trojan or Hittite version of the Trojan War. '[And they sing:] when they came from steep Wilusa', goes one of the fragments; 'when the man came from steep [Wilusa]', goes the other.[38] Extremely, almost achingly, brief, the lines nevertheless provide tantalizing evidence of a possible alternative epic tradition of Troy, told from the other point of view. The most convincing clue of all: 'steep Wilusa', an unmissable Hittite analogue for Homer's 'steep Ilios' (a stock formula in the *Iliad* for Troy).[39] In fact, it's recently been argued that the Anatolian version of the legendary fall of Troy came first, and that it was later appropriated and colonized by the Greeks, through their interactions with Anatolian poets, assimilated into what would become the *Iliad* (and, ironically, one of the founding texts of Western culture).[40] The gesture to something bigger is hugely tempting – a *Wilusiad*, perhaps? – and it's possible that, as more and more fragments of Hittite texts continue to be found, more of the Anatolian epic of the Trojan War might be uncovered.[41] What might this *Wilusiad* have looked like?

How might Hecuba have been described in the words of the Hittites who knew Puduhepa, rather than through Greek eyes? In a *Wilusiad*, might she and Theano have prayed to the correct goddess? And might she, then, have been granted her wish?

We don't know whether the historical Puduhepa was as successful in her prayer to Hebat to rid her kingdom of Piyamaradu, as the legendary Hecuba was unsuccessful in her appeal to Athena. It's likely she wasn't, as there's evidence that Piyamaradu continued to cause trouble for the Hittite Empire into the reign of Puduhepa's son, Tudhaliya IV.[42] But we do know that Puduhepa was eminently successful in another area of international diplomacy: the peace treaty with the Egyptian pharaoh Ramesses II, following the Battle of Qadesh, on which she signed her name and impressed her seal alongside her husband's. Recorded both in Egyptian hieroglyphs carved into the walls of Ramesses' temples, and in Hittite clay tablets discovered at Hattusa, this text is not only a monumental achievement in securing peace between two great ancient powers; it is also, remarkably, the oldest known peace treaty in the world. In honour of its pledges of eternal peace, lasting friendship and mutual alliance, a modern replica of the treaty is displayed in the head-quarters of the United Nations in New York: a reminder of the ideals that have underpinned international diplomacy for millennia.[43] And so, hanging on the walls of the UN, passed every day by members of the General Assembly, lies the earliest peace treaty in history – as ratified by the signature of an ancient Anatolian queen.

If Puduhepa was an outstanding leader for her times, and took strides – both in the Qadesh treaty and in the marriage alliances she forged between at least one, and maybe two, of the Hittite princesses and Ramesses II – to secure peace for her husband's empire, she was, however, first and foremost a royal wife. It was her marriage to Hattusili III, just like Hecuba's to Priam, that established her as a Great Queen. On the Qadesh peace treaty, the imprint of Puduhepa's seal lies next to her husband's. In Homer, meanwhile, Hecuba holds sway over the women of Troy, and earns the right to approach the gods on her city's behalf, as Priam's wife. And so, to find out what it meant to be a wife in the Late Bronze Age, we turn next – not to Homer – but to the sterile white clean-room of a modern-day laboratory in Germany.

5

ANDROMACHE

Wife

TROY

She thinks back to their wedding day, in the evenings when she lies alone in her bed, in the nights when their son wakes and screams at the shadows that drip down the walls. She remembers the sounds of castanets clattering in the streets as her chariot rattled through the gates into the city. She remembers the men dancing and the women swaying and singing outside their bedchamber and placing crowns of violets on her hair. She remembers waiting, and Hector stooping under the roof beam as he came in.

Her mother always told her to keep her teeth clean. Strong teeth would do her well in her marriage, she said. Teeth hold back words that shouldn't be spoken.

Now her mother is dead, her father is dead, and her marriage is scarred by the war that has ripped it apart like a festering wound slashed open again and again. Ten years of horror. Ten years of fear shuttering her mind like an electric shock, a bolt of power driving her mad. Ten years of waiting here alone and wondering if the screams on the battlefield are his, if the next bloody corpse to be hauled through the gates, mouth fouled with dirt, will be his – and still he keeps going, he won't stop. Won't understand why she asks him to come back. They can barely speak to each other now.

Strong teeth, she said? If only she had teeth strong enough to rip out her enemy's heart and drag her husband from the battlefield, like a dog trailing its kill. Then that might be enough.

White Teeth

The lab technician at the Max Planck has a lot of teeth. Hundreds of them.

Each white tooth is in its own bag, neatly labelled in black ink. *KUK005. XAN023. I5427.* Eirini Skourtanioti – doctoral student in the archaeogenetics lab – has laid them out meticulously in sequence in the sampling room, along with the other bones collected under the blue-bright lights of the Max Planck Institute for the Science of Human History.[1] A network of researchers across Greece, Germany and North America have been hard at work for the past few years, together with excavators, gathering teeth and bones from archaeo- logical sites throughout the Aegean: a rocky cliff tumbling over the sparkling waters of Paros; a dank cave filled with skeletons on a Cretan mountainside. Skourtanioti has just completed the data set with a visit to Chania in Crete, with its brightly painted harbour front, collecting the first material from the ancient city ever to be analysed for DNA. All the precious ivory-like fragments, the messages-in-a-bottle from the past, have now made their way back to the Max Planck labs near Leipzig – where they wait to be drilled open and scraped like pearls from an oyster.

In the clean-room, the technician peels open a bag, picks out a tooth with her forceps, places it carefully on aluminium foil. Leans forward, then, with a high-pitched whirring, the diamond saw blade slices through the pulp chamber of the tooth, shredding it into powder. Collects the powder on some folded paper, picks it up and tips it into a plastic test tube, labels another bag. Cleans her workspace, adjusts her latex gloves.

Then starts again.

It's a laborious process, but for the Max Planck team – led by Philipp Stockhammer and Johannes Krause, Skourtanioti's doctoral supervisor – the results are well worth the grind. While the assembled teeth scattered over the workbenches might look like extractions by an overzealous dentist, they actually come from ninety-five millennia-old skeletons from across the Bronze Age Aegean – making up what the scientists know will be, in 2023, one of the largest data sets to be collected to date.[2] And once the tooth powder can be sampled and DNA extracted, they will have a wealth of information to reveal.

Our teeth are the keys to a past that we carry locked within our jaws. We all have teeth, after all; across different ethnicities, different national- ities, different genders and time periods across history, we are connected by our teeth. They link us to our roots (quite literally), recording unique data about our age, our diet, even where we were born. This is because the enamel that forms on our teeth when we're children, unlike all the other parts of our body that change and are replaced over our lifetimes, remains unaltered – and, as we'll see later, it contains distinct chemical traces of the environment we grew up in. And, after we die, teeth are often the best-preserved part of a skeleton (protected by the enamel, a super-hard mineral compound), which means they provide one of the best chances for archaeologists and scientists to recover ancient DNA, even from thousands-of-years-old specimens.

What Skourtanioti and the team are interested in here, in particular, are the traces of aDNA that can be extracted from the inner chambers of these ancient teeth. Their aim is to generate a map of the prehistoric Aegean that traces genetic shifts, tracking the movements of different populations across the Bronze Age. But, while they're peering into the secrets wrapped up in the intertwined ribbons of DNA, they also want to look for something else: what's known as ROH, or 'runs of homozygosity'. Homozygosity is a word derived from ancient Greek: *homo-* meaning 'same', and *zygo-* from the Greek for 'yoke, join two things together' (used in the Homeric epics for yoking horses to a chariot, for instance, and, later, for getting married; used in biological terminology for the zygote, a cell created from the genetic material of two parents that get 'yoked' together). So 'homozygosity' is the measure of the genetic similarity between one person's maternally and paternally inherited chromosomes, generated by comparing how many stretches of DNA with

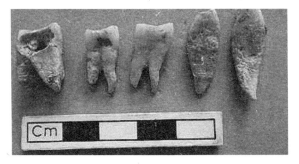

Deep roots into the past: teeth from XAN023, an adult female who lived in the 13th century BCE, *Cydonia (modern Chania), Crete.*

the same variants they have: the more closely related their parents are, the more 'runs of homozygosity' they will have in their genetic make-up. Finding out information about precise relationships is something that very recent advances in aDNA extraction and analysis have made possible: if archaeologists in the future dug up my children's bones, for instance, without examining their DNA they wouldn't be able to tell how related (or not) my husband and I are to each other. But by checking the runs of homozygosity written into their genetic code, scientists would be able to confirm that we don't, in fact, share a close genealogical relationship.

These Bronze Age teeth, on the other hand, are about to reveal something of a surprise.

Keeping It in the Family

Contrary to all Skourtanioti's expectations, what came out of the results were levels of parental relatedness unprecedented in earlier studies of prehistoric Aegean DNA. Across the Aegean, from Crete to the Greek mainland to the eastern Aegean islands, and across the Bronze Age, the genetic data was suggesting that first- and second-cousin marriages (what biologists would call endogamy or consanguinity) were not only routinely practised, but in fact, in some contexts, the findings paralleled present-day communities that practise endogamous first-cousin marriages.[3] Kinship marriage was a social practice that wasn't recorded in the Linear B tablets (concerned, as they were, with the inventory records of the Mycenaean palaces), and that couldn't, until now, be traced with any precision in the archaeological remains. What the DNA has allowed scientists to do is to access each ancient individual's genetic birth certificate, as it were – to measure the degree of relationship between their parents, and so, by mapping all individuals together, to trace patterns of marriage between women and men across Bronze Age Greece. Take two of the women (possibly sisters) we saw in Chapter 3 at Aidonia, for instance, buried in the three-woman matrilineal tomb: their mother and father were closely related (either first or second cousins). And they weren't alone. The findings uncovered by Skourtanioti and her team suggest that prehistoric people throughout Greece and the Aegean islands were opting for pairings with their first or second cousins, arguing for a Bronze Age system of kinship marriage that transcends time (over hundreds of years) and place (across the Aegean world). In fact, a recent analysis of hundreds of ancient genomes crossing from Europe into West Asia has unearthed similar evidence of first-cousin unions at Pylos in Greece (the home of many of the Linear B tablets).[4] And a pilot aDNA study by a group of archaeologists and scientists at the Early Bronze Age settlement of Titris Höyük – hundreds of miles away on the trade road across the Euphrates river, near Bronze Age Kizzuwatna, the region in south-east Anatolia that would be Puduhepa's homeland – hints at additional early evidence (though without ROH) for kin-based family units, closely related extended families who practised intermarriage.[5]

The early data suggests that this is a phenomenon that was unexpectedly common across the Bronze Age Aegean world, and raises many questions about exactly *why* these kinds of marriages were taking place. Perhaps prehistoric populations wanted to keep their farmland and their olive groves (a key source of subsistence that would have required generations of cultivation) in the family, and marrying close relations was one way of doing it. Perhaps it was simply another means of enforcing a patrilineal and patrilocal family structure, where men married into their father's kin group (such as, for instance, their father's brother's daughter) and were thus able to keep women from moving away to marry into families elsewhere. Whatever the case, the DNA has opened a window on to the little-seen realities of a woman's world in the Bronze Age Aegean, showing us that, for a girl coming of age and looking to start a family, marriage to one of her close cousins would likely have been on the cards.

Endogamy might seem unfamiliar to us – and it's something that seems to be unfamiliar in the Homeric epics too, which found their final form hundreds of years after the end of the Bronze Age in the twelfth century BCE. Instead of showing routinely practised kinship marriages among the societies of Troy or Ithaca, Homer's epics instead relegate the practice of consanguineous wedlock to the edges of their world – in the superlative realms of the divine, and in the mythical fantasy lands encountered by Odysseus on his journey home. The children of the god of the winds, Aeolus – six sons and six daughters – are married to each other. The brothers spend their days feasting on the gorgeous cliff-ringed island Odysseus visits, and they spend their nights sleeping in a sumptuous palace beside their sisters, 'the wives they love'.[6] Hera and Zeus, queen and king of the gods and parents to many of the Olympian deities, are, famously, brother and sister as well as husband and wife. Meanwhile, the powerful queen of another luscious semi-mythical island frequented by Odysseus, Arete, is the niece (brother's daughter) of the king, her husband.[7] Perhaps, in the otherworld of Olympus and the strange half-realities of the fantasy lands of the Aegean that Odysseus comes across, the Homeric epics retain (and circumscribe) some memory of the Bronze Age past, of a society that used to keep marriage – and women – closely within the family. The families of Aeolus and Arete in particular are unusually close-knit, living together in a concord that seems to be confined to the wondrous, far-distant islands of Odysseus' travels: an almost unreachable, past ideal of peace and family unity, expressed through intermarriage – a family so harmonious it can generate a family of its own.

Father, Mother, Brother, Husband

It's an ideal that the *Iliad* makes particularly clear can't be achieved. If peace, in the remembered past of Odysseus' travels, allows families to come together and marriages to be made, it's war that tears them apart. In times of war – and particularly among elite rulers, whose job it was to protect their kingdoms – marriages would have had to be forged to build alliances, designed to bring other kings (and their armies) into a partnership. We find archaeological evidence for these kinds of extra-familial unions – between local rulers and outsider women who have been brought into the family to marry – at Mycenae (legendary kingdom of Agamemnon) in Greece, in a group of burials known as Grave Circle A (not far from Grave Circle B, where Γ58 was found). Here, teeth again are the key, but in a different way from Skourtanioti's study. In a research project published in 2009, the teeth of eleven Late Bronze Age individuals from Grave Circle A were sampled for traces of strontium – a naturally occurring element that crops up in different forms, and which makes its way into our food (via the water that trickles off rocks into the soil) and so into our teeth.[8] Isotopes of strontium occur in specific ratios depending on the geology that makes up the bedrock of where you live, and they find their way into our food (plants drawing chemical nutrients from the soil, animals eating plants) – so that the chemical make-up of olive oil pressed in Greece, for instance, will be noticeably different from that produced from an olive tree in Troy. And, because we are what we eat, the traces of the rocks we live on make their way into our bodies through the building blocks of our food. What's unique about the enamel on our teeth is that – unlike the rest of our body, our blood, our bones, our skin, all of which is continually reconstructing itself based on the nutrients we put into our bodies – enamel consolidates from what we eat in childhood; and it stays that way for the rest of our life (and for thousands of years after we die). So the strontium isotope ratios written into our teeth contain information that was locked in when we grew up as children, while our bones reflect the traces of the last seven to ten years of where we've lived. And archaeologists, digging up skeletons that have lain in the ground for millennia, can unlock those traces, and so deduce where the people of the past were born, where they lived, and where they died.

The skeletons at Mycenae had some pretty interesting information to reveal. Of the eleven sampled only two could be definitely established as Mycenaean locals (that is, born and bred in Mycenae) – and both of them were males. Meanwhile, of the three individuals who had a strontium isotope ratio showing that they were non-locals at birth (in other words, that they'd moved into Mycenae; most likely as part of a marriage union) two were the only securely identified females of the group. One of these non-locals, in particular, known as MYC2/III, was clearly an elite female: buried with a treasure trove of gold objects, including a sizeable gold diadem on her head, and a gold-and-silver clothes pin, she was laid to rest alongside two wealthy men decked out in gold (one of whom was probably her husband).[9] It's likely that women such as MYC2/III who were brought in from outside Mycenae in marriage would have been highly dependent on their husbands as the source of their wealth and financial security. That much is clear from the Linear B tablets at Pylos, where a list of seven wives of high-ranking Mycenaean officials makes it quite plain that these women have little to no property to call their own (in fact, the most one of them owns is a pair of sandals).[10] In other words, these wives have high status through their marriage, but no economic or financial security, except through their husbands. But MYC2/III wasn't just a wife: she was also, fleetingly, a mother. She was laid to rest with a baby laid tenderly on her chest, all that remains of the infant now a cloud of delicate gold foil that once covered its tiny body. While the sample size of the study is small, it produces a suggestive early picture of a marital pattern, and a nascent family, at Mycenae, where high-ranking men took in non-local elite wives in order to consolidate political alliances with outside families – and to start a dynasty of their own. Tragically, in the case of this wife and her child, it wasn't to be.

This kind of dynastic alliance – a marriage beyond the walls, a husband who is a prince and an elite wife from outside, a young baby who begins (and ends) a dynasty – appears in Homeric epic in the figures of Andromache and Hector. Andromache, as we have already seen, is the daughter of a local king from a city called Thebe, who married the heir to the Trojan throne; Homer explicitly tells us how she left Thebe, in the shadow of a wooded mountain, to come to Troy.[11] While DNA, strontium isotope analysis and the Linear B tablets may give us information about patterns of marriage in the Bronze Age world, what the Homeric epics can do – from the other side – is to provide a picture, in narrative, of the emotional, lived experience of marriage as it is imagined in war: and, in the *Iliad*, that means the destruction of family, the devastation of husbands and wives. The *Iliad* is set against the backdrop of a marriage that has been torn apart: Paris' seizure of Helen from Menelaus is the initial wrecked marriage that, in turn, tears apart both Trojans and Greeks, causing husbands on both sides to be slaughtered and Trojan wives to be captured and trafficked into slavery. And it is the moment at which Hector and Andromache meet – poised halfway between the worlds of war and peace, men and women, colliding with each other between battlefield and city at the Scaean Gates of Troy – that the fragile rawness of their marriage, and its fracture in war, is encapsulated in one of the most moving vignettes in the entire *Iliad*.

Waving the soldiers off to Troy? A vase from Mycenae (c.1200 BCE) shows
a woman waving farewell on the left, as warriors march off to battle –
likely how Homer imagined the Greeks in the Trojan War.

Andromache and Hector come together as the very last of Hector's
three encounters with the women of Troy in Book 6 of the *Iliad*: first
his mother, Hecuba, whom he charges with the supplication to Athena;
then his sister-in-law, Helen, who invites him to rest and sit beside her in
Paris' perfumed bedchamber; and finally, his wife, Andromache. In this
world of women behind the walls of Troy, Hector is already drastically
out of place.[12] He can't drink the wine his mother offers him, because – he
says – it will weaken his courage in war. He can't help her with the ritual,
because he is covered in blood and muck from the battle. He brings his
huge gore-spattered spear with him into Paris and Helen's bedroom – a
spectacular misfit for their intimate chamber.[13] But Andromache – the
woman whose name means, with plunging irony, 'man-fighter' – is just
as much out of place as her husband is. When Hector searches for her
in the spots he'd expect to find a woman – cloistered with her enslaved
women at home; demurely visiting her sisters-in-law; engaging in the

women's ritual supplication at the temple with the queen – he fails.[14]
Instead, he's told, she has run up on to the walls of Troy with their infant
son Astyanax to see the world of men, desperate to find out what has
happened to the Trojan army on the plain below. War is turning this
marriage upside down: Hector, the general, is knocking at his own door
behind the city walls, while his wife surveys the troops from the battlements. Husband and wife are trying, desperately, to engage with each
other's divided worlds.

But war has torn them apart. As Andromache sees Hector about to
leave back to the battlefield through the great Scaean Gates, she hurries
down to meet him. She tries – knowing, perhaps, that this is her only
chance – to summon for him a picture of her world, her values. And
all she wants is to keep him safe, for him not to die, for her to have a
husband and for their child to have a father. She doesn't care about his
so-called glory, his commitments to his troops: what about, she seems
to say, his commitments to her – to their – son? She begs him to follow
a more defensive strategy, predicting that if he goes back to fight on the
front line he will die, telling him that she has already lost almost everything. Her father and seven brothers were killed in the war by Achilles,
her mother enslaved before her untimely death. Hector is all she has left:
he has become everything to her. And so she makes a gut-wrenchingly
powerful appeal: 'Hector, you are my father and my mother. You are my
brother, and the vigorous man whose bed I share.'[15] This is not a metaphor: it is the truth of her situation. She cannot afford to lose him too.

Of course, it's already made clear – from what Homer says – that,
in the biological sense, Hector isn't Andromache's father, her mother
or her brother. This isn't a case of extreme endogamy, as we see in the
Odyssey in the children of Aeolus; it's not even a cousin union, which, as
the DNA has shown, was commonly practised in the Bronze Age. But
Andromache talks about her closeness to Hector in a way that articulates the closeness of marriage along the lines of the structures of kin.
This woman, who had to move away from her family to marry into the
Trojan dynasty, who has lost her parents and brothers to war, is attempting to express the ineffable bonds that connect a family together, the
deep ties of blood and belonging – and to show that she feels that, too,
in their marriage. In a sense, her losses and traumas in war have forcibly

transferred those kinship ties on to her husband. This isn't marriage within the family – it's marriage that, through the fractures of war, has *become* her only family.

The trouble is, Hector – as a Homeric man, as the heir to Troy, as the leader of his troops – has his own allotted role that he has been born and trained to fulfil, his own obligations to another group of men. He can't understand her vision of marriage-as-family; he cannot *afford* to understand it – because their city is under siege, because his community plays out on the wider stage of Troy, because all the men and women of the Trojans depend on him to survive. His response slides past hers. He cannot merely play the part of a defender (even though 'defender, holder' is what his name, Hector, means in Greek), he says, because to fail to do his duty as the Trojans see it would be to reject everything, his family, his birthright, the deaths of his brothers and soldiers, his obligations as prince and husband: to protect Troy and to win glory for himself and his father by fighting on the front line, to fulfil the expectations of a hero within the remit of a man's world. And yet, in spite of all this, tragically, he declares that he knows in his heart that Troy will fall. He

On a silver vessel from Late Bronze Age Mycenae, warriors attempt to ward off attackers with slings and bows, while the women watch from the walls above – just like Andromache and Hector.

knows Andromache will one day be captured and taken into slavery – and he would rather die before he hears her screams as she is dragged into captivity. But, for him, there is no other way. He has no other choice but to fight. And so the failure of words, the inability to make meaning match up in this torn world where women and men can't talk to each other, rattles on.

This, then, is a marriage between a woman and a man, a wife and a warrior, that is fundamentally divided along the fault lines that shudder through the *Iliad* across the contours of gender: the woman who longs for peace, and the man who has had war thrust upon him; the mother who wants to protect her family, and the prince whose life plays out before his people; the wife who has lost everything, and the hero who has everything to lose if he fails. This is an attempt – and a failure – to reach into each other's worlds. This is about trying to reach an agreement, a way of thinking the same (*homophrosunē*, or 'like-mindedness' in Homer's Greek), a marriage of true minds (to quote another, later, great poet). 'For nothing could be better,' Odysseus comments in the *Odyssey* (engaged in his own attempt to return to his wife and reunite his marriage), 'than when two live in one house, their minds in harmony, husband and wife.'[16] Andromache and Hector can't think, or talk, in the same way: war has ripped apart their marriage, and what they believe marriage is about – the ties she feels to her family, for her; the status he holds in his community, for him.

All they can do is share a moment with their son, as the baby boy – unused to the world of battle – recoils at the bristling plume of Hector's helmet. Wife and husband smile, and Andromache laughs through her tears as Hector removes his helmet and she passes the infant into his arms for a last embrace. For one heartbeat, the war is suspended as a family are allowed to come together, sharing a moment of closeness – even if they do not know that it is for the final time.[17] Then Hector sends his wife back home, back to their divided lives, back to being trapped in their irreconcilably opposed gender roles – using almost exactly the same words that Telemachus uses to shut up Penelope: 'Go home and do the things you have to do. Work on your loom and spindle and instruct the slaves to do their household work as well. War is a task for men – for every man born here in Troy, but most especially, me.'[18] The soldier says goodbye, and the military wife has to watch him go.[19] In the polarities that the conflict around Troy has thrown up like battle ramparts, a woman's world and a man's simply cannot coexist. Homer's audience knows, as Hector and Andromache know, that Andromache will end up enslaved, and Hector will end up dead. They know that baby Astyanax will be tossed like rubble from the walls of Troy by the Greeks when the city falls.[20] He will not be buried on his mother's chest, as MYC2/III's child was with her. And Andromache will have to bury her husband herself. Her bones, and her teeth, will not lie beside his.

Looking to the Future

In one sense, then, Andromache and Hector's predictions are right. He will die, she will be enslaved. But they're not as successful at predicting further into the future about another, less immediate aspect of their afterlife – the way their stories will be told. Helen, in fact, warns Hector of this during his meeting with her just before his encounter with Andromache: they will, she says, inviting him to linger, tempting him to reflect that he will one day be remembered in epic, be 'characters in the tales told by men for years to come'.[21] Andromache and Hector, however – understandably, perhaps, given the fate that's awaiting them and their son – are too preoccupied with the here and now to wonder, as Helen does, about the ways that people to come will tell their story.

But tell their story they did. The first to jump into the fray was Sappho – the same poet who rewrites Helen's story as a love match. Sappho moves the focus from the traumas of the divided world of war to the joyful moment of Andromache and Hector's wedding day – the herald running to announce that Andromache's ship over the salt sea from Thebe has arrived, the crowds of women thronging in the chariots yoked to oxen by men, the pipe and lyre and the songs of virgin girls, the smoke of incense and the cries of praise by men and women for the marriage of Hector and Andromache.[22] As with her reconfiguration of Helen as a lover rather than a face that launched a fleet of ships, Sappho resists Homer's depiction of Andromache and Hector's parting at the Scaean Gates and produces her own version that attempts to heal the trauma of

Homer's uncompromising gender divide – that moves back in time to a world of peace, at the budding moment of the bride and groom's first meeting when Andromache's marriage was full of hope, when women's voices could resound in celebration in accord with men's, even as we know what is to come.[23]

Other poets take up Andromache and retell her story, though in different ways from Sappho. The Athenian playwright Euripides, for instance, turns the focus to the devastation that follows the fall of Troy, and traces Andromache's brutal treatment as an enslaved woman to Achilles' son in Greece.[24] (These plays would later set the tone for the seventeenth-century French playwright Racine, who scripted a drama about Andromache of such sweeping tragedy that it established him as one of the leading dramatists at the court of King Louis XIV.)[25] But her afterlife isn't just confined to poetry – she also finds a place in works of art. The moment when Hector hands back her baby, and the eyes of wife and husband meet, was a commonplace in Roman wall paintings: historians tell us that it was sufficiently poignant to move one stern Republican matron (the wife of Julius Caesar's assassin, Brutus, no less) to tears.[26] In 1769, Swiss-born Angelica Kauffman (a hugely successful Romantic painter, and one of only two women artists to be elected among the founding members of the Royal Academy of Art in London) produced a shadowed, moody painting of Andromache and Hector's final parting for the Royal Academy's first-ever exhibition. When I go to see it in its current home in the Georgian mansion of Saltram in Devon, I'm struck by how the spotlight is on Andromache, her bright-white skin drawing attention in the darkness to the clasp of her hand with Hector's, while he seems to hesitate, his body yearning towards her and his helmet tilting uneasily on his head, longing to linger by her side. Like Sappho's poem, Kauffman's painting is an act of healing: a work that puts Andromache back in the centre, that insists on the equality of gender, and imagines a world where Hector pauses in Troy, beside his wife, one moment longer – where women and men stand side by side.

But how could Andromache have ever known that this is where things would end? How could a woman predict the future – without the gift of prophecy?

6

CASSANDRA

Prophet

TROY

In her dreams, she sees things. Burning. Fire. Often she smells singeing hair, and flares dance in front of her eyes, orange-red and gold, bursts of colour like torch brands. Sometimes she sees them when she wakes.

She sees her brother Hector back at war, the screaming dark cloud of death around him wherever he walks. She sees them digging their dead into the ground, Trojans and Greeks, bodies black with flies and a meal for vultures, and she sees – blurred, smoke-like – the ones who will die next, as if they are already ghosts. A battlefield of phantoms. She sees an army of Trojan wraiths crawling up the walls of the Greek camp, yelling ghoulishly in their battle frenzy, and she sees the Greeks cowering in their graves.

But there is one vision that returns to her more often than the others. Three Greeks trailing across the shore in a swarm of sand. Achilles, alone with Patroclus, clashing chords on a lyre. A question in the darkness, and a choice like fire – the only choice there is.

She knows what his choice will be: she can smell the burning already. She knows what will happen to her. The jagged gash of blood between her legs when she is raped at the foot of a god. The mad raving she sings across the waters. The axe blow that splinters his skull.

This was one of her earliest revelations, when the visions first started. For prophecy is not, after all, a hard business, when you know this one rule: men make the fate they want. The future belongs to them. She – and all her sisters – are contingent, like flames in the wind, on what men choose.

Oracle

It's spring 1907 in the Crimea, the sky through the window free of clouds and washed by the last rain so that it gleams like hammered gold, and Lesia Ukrainka is, as always, scribbling in her notebook. The front page, corner turned down in her hand and mottled in the half-light from the garden, has been headed in careful looping ink with two words. One is Кассандра – *Cassandra* – the title of the drama she is writing, the latest in a body of work that has already made her famous in her lifetime and will see her become the foremother of modern Ukrainian literature; the other, Українка – *Ukrainka* ('Ukrainian woman') – a pen name. This, here, is her disguise, like a binding around a book, like a spell: a carefully chosen word that serves both to hide her and to assert her cause. A name that was assumed at the age of thirteen, when she became certain that she was, above all things, a Ukrainian, and a woman. When she knew that language was the only way she could express herself – when even the act of writing in the tongue her mother taught her was forbidden by the Russian Empire.[1]

Ukrainka – celebrated poet, political activist, polymath in command of eight modern languages as well as Latin and ancient Greek – emerged into adulthood during the turbulent last decades of the nineteenth century, at a time when Ukraine's fervid hopes for political independence from the Russian tsars (who had controlled them since the empire-building era of Catherine the Great) were beginning to stir. As a young girl, Ukrainka had to watch as her much-loved aunt was arrested and exiled to Siberia, in a wave of persecution against political activists in St Petersburg. The shock of her aunt's fate, the punishment that awaited women who opposed the Russian regime, was the friction to the flint of her imagination – sparking her first poem, 'Nadiya' ('Hope'), written at the age of nine. Now, at thirty-six and closeted in her house here in the Crimea, close to dying (she has suffered nearly all her life from crippling tuberculosis of the bone), she is finishing one of her last.

She has always had a sense of the future: numinous, glowing. She remembers, as a child at home in her family's village in Volhynia, listening to the piano, a circle gathered round – a tune for dancing – and standing there with a tear on her cheek and a white chill in her bones, as if she knew that the illness was coming.[2] As the Ukrainian words for *Cassandra* pour from her pen, she knows herself, again, to be a prophet. 'Who has seen the naked truth?' Cassandra's brother asks. 'I have – I have seen it, and much too often!' Ukrainka's Cassandra retorts.[3] She knows that there must be – that she must call forth – a realm in which women can speak back to patriarchy, to claim a name for the women history has forgotten. The ink from Ukrainka's pen flows across the page like a river: 'Brother,' she writes in Cassandra's sonorous voice, 'you do not know the cost of women's sacrifice . . . Oh, they are legion: the nameless women who had made much harder and unsung-of sacrifices!'⁴ She knows that the revolution that has swept the Russian world, only two years before, the bloody mutinies that came so close to toppling Tsar Nicholas II, are only the beginning. There is more still to come.

And yet – as spring blazes into summer, and unrest continues to flare like wildfires across the tottering Russian Empire – she also knows that there is danger in calling forth from ancient myth the Trojan seer, whose predictions of ruin were never believed. And Troy went up in flames all the same.

She can only hope that, this time, they are listening.

Half a year before, and on the opposite side of the Black Sea, excavations at Boğazkale are starting. Hugo Winckler, a bespectacled archaeologist and Assyriologist supported by the German Oriental Society, along with Theodore Makridi Bey of the Istanbul Museum, are about to attempt to dig into a rocky massif that looms up behind the Turkish village, around a hundred miles east of modern-day Ankara. For decades, British, German and French travellers have been picking up bits of clay tablets stamped in cuneiform script that lie scattered on these craggy outcrops; some of the larger slabs have been known to make their way on to the antiquities market, handled by local dealers who specialize in such things. An expert in reading and interpreting the cuneiform texts from Mesopotamia, Winckler is searching for a juicier prize, however. His curiosity has been piqued by the similarity between the unknown language on these tablets and some as-yet-undeciphered ancient letters written in cuneiform discovered far away at Tell el-Amarna in Egypt. He wants to follow the clues that these finds are hinting at, to prove that this was once a flourishing and important city, with links to some of the weightiest empires of the ancient world.

What he does not know is that he is, in fact, about to uncover the lost capital of the Great Kings of the Hittite Empire itself.

The weather is warm and muggy, and the local Turkish workmen have

rolled up their sleeves, sweat beading their necks as they haul wheelbar-
rows and pickaxes up the grass-covered slopes from the village towards
the rocky gorge. Winckler's plan (simple as it is) is to begin at the base
of the cliff outcrop known as Büyükkale, or 'Big Castle' in Turkish, and
work his way up.[5] His luck is quite extraordinarily in – perhaps unsurprisingly, given the number of finds already made by chance visitors to
the site; and yet the magnitude of the discovery is beyond anyone's hopes
or expectations. That very first summer, preserved in the ruins of storage chambers within an ancient palace buried beneath the ground and
blackened by fire, he uncovers thousands of hardened clay tablets – just
like the Linear B archive, except that these are written in cuneiform.
Shaded from the beating sun and with new specimens brought to him
daily as the workmen continue to dig deeper into the trenches, Winckler
sets about – with the feverish enthusiasm of a philologist – the monumental task of copying out and deciphering the thousands of fragments
of clay. Even though he does not know the language that covers most of
the tablets, from the few that are in Akkadian (the lingua franca of its
day, and a specialism of Winckler's), he can tell at once that it is a quite
exceptional archive. Some of them are letters. Some of them are prayers.
Some of them are diplomatic texts – including a royal copy of the post-
Qadesh treaty with Ramesses II that confirms beyond doubt that what

Hattusa: the once-great capital of the Bronze Age Hittite Empire.

he has found is, in fact, nothing less than the capital city of the Hittites: Hattusa, the great beating heart of the Hittite Empire itself. All were baked to hundreds of degrees and so preserved in the red-hot fires that raged across the city around 1200 BCE, when the kingdom of Hatti fell.

And one of them – speaking across thousands of years – is an oracle of the future.

But it does not predict its own civilization's fall.

How to Become a Prophet

Cassandra is not a prophet in Homer. In the *Odyssey*, she crops up only once at the moment of her murder. The ghost of Agamemnon in the Underworld conjures the scene: Cassandra, already a captive slave, shrieked and clung to his body, the Greek king says, as Clytemnestra's weapon fell and the halls swam with blood. In the *Iliad*, meanwhile, she appears in two scant scenes: first, as a demure and attractive bride who is said to be 'loveliest of all' of Priam's daughters; then as a dutiful sister, the first to spot her father bringing home the body of her dead brother Hector.[6] She does not speak more than a few lines to call the Trojan men and women to witness Hector's corpse; elsewhere she is either wailing piteously (as in the *Odyssey*) or entirely silent (in the *Iliad*'s first scene), a passive object to be traded between her father and her husband-to-be. She certainly does not deliver a prediction. The infamous story of her prophetic voice, her unheeded warnings of the fires that would destroy Troy, finds its roots instead in another – now lost – epic from the cycle of poems about the Trojan War: the *Cypria*, attributed by some in antiquity to Stasinus of Cyprus, an early, semi-legendary Greek poet. All that's left of this lost epic masterpiece is a much later summary of its plot in prose; but it's possible to unpick, from later tragedies by the classical dramatists Aeschylus and Euripides that looked back to the ancient tradition, how her story must have gone.[7] The god Apollo – archer god and deity of the lyre, poetry and prophecy – gifted Cassandra with the power of prediction in return for sex.[8] When she broke her word and refused him, the god cursed her with never being believed – so twisting his original gift into a burden, and, without silencing her, effectively removing all power from her utterances. Her story continues as, a virgin priestess of Apollo with prophetic powers and no audience for her prophecies, her body is instead subjected to horrific violations: first during the sack of Troy, as she clings for safety to the statue of Athena and is raped by Ajax of Locris; then as the enslaved woman of Agamemnon carted off to Greece.

Scenes litter classical literature and art in which the prophetic, but never believed, Cassandra attempts to make her voice heard. Proclaiming that Hecuba's dream, while pregnant with Paris, of giving birth to a torch of fire predicts Troy's fall in flames.[9] Warning, as Paris returns from exile as a shepherd boy on Mount Ida to take his place as prince of Troy, that he will be the destruction of the city.[10] Shouting the truth about the Wooden Horse as it is dragged into Troy, while the Trojans chant choruses of victory and clothe the temples in festive branches.[11] Screaming as Ajax prises her off Athena's statue to brutally rape her (a particularly popular scene among Greek and Roman painters).[12] Singing a frenzied wedding song as she stands, decorated in the sacred ribbons that mark her as Apollo's priestess, in the smoking ruins of the city amid the women who will be led away into slavery, foretelling that her enslavement to the Greek king Agamemnon will be her act of vengeance and break apart his house.[13] Shrieking like a wild beast as her chariot approaches Agamemnon's palace in Mycenae and Clytemnestra steps out to welcome them, as the vision of a house awash with blood takes hold of her, and she sees the axe that will fall on Agamemnon's neck and hers, when Clytemnestra kills them both.[14] But Apollo's curse follows her wherever she goes: she can never make anyone believe her.[15]

Cassandra's powerful, and powerfully ignored, voice rings out across the centuries through classical literature, as a warning against what happens when we fail to heed what women say, and to draw attention to the price they have paid for millennia, like Cassandra, simply for telling the truth. The denial of any meaning to her words, the refusal to listen to her, stems from her attempt to take agency over her own body by refusing the advances of a man. And so her unheeded predictions of Troy's fall are not just a commentary on the vagaries of prophecy; they are also a stark reminder, inscribed into every one of Cassandra's words, of all the women of the war, like Helen, like Briseis, whose bodies were transgressed, whose voices were not heard. The twist that Apollo's curse takes on Cassandra makes salient the lot of every woman in the drama of the Trojan War: their bodies treated as objects by men, and their voices silenced – even when they attempt to speak.

Which explains, perhaps, why Cassandra's prophetic voice isn't mentioned in the *Iliad*. Like the men of legend who refused to listen to her, Homer is simply the first man in recorded history to ignore what she has to say.

An Early History of Women Prophets

But it's not just Cassandra that he ignores. Later commentators give us a fascinating testimony that suggests they thought that Homer actually stole some of his verses – in some accounts, the entire form of epic poetry (made up of hexameter, or lines of verse consisting of six metrical 'feet') – from the words of inspired women prophets.[16] There's no real way of knowing whether this is true or not: the (male) historians (Pliny, Plutarch and Pausanias) who tell us this lived centuries after the Homeric poems were composed, while women's voices and identities as poets are often untraceable. As the feminist writer Virginia Woolf would put it hundreds of years later, 'I would venture to guess that Anon., who wrote so many poems without signing them, was often a woman.'[17] There is, however, one clue that reaches past 'Anon.' to give us the name of (what the Greeks believed was) a real female prophet, whose verses Homer supposedly borrowed: Daphne, daughter of Tiresias (a seer whom Odysseus encounters in the Underworld in the *Odyssey*).[18] There's no evidence that Daphne was a historical woman: her name – 'Laurel' in Greek – connects her to the laurels of Apollo, god of prophecy at the great mantic temple of Delphi where she was said to have been a prophet, so it's more probable that she's standing in here for the generic role of women in ancient Greek prophecy. And yet it's important to acknowledge that, for the Greeks, Daphne (and the other early women prophets whose names crop up in the ancient texts) was very real. In the Greek imagination, Daphne was the first in a line of real, historical female seers at Delphi – and, for some at least, Homer plagiarized his poetry from her divinely inspired words.[19]

It's easy to see how such claims could be made. Female prophets had an unusually high status in the Greek world: the Pythia, the oracle at the temple of Apollo at Delphi, was consulted and held in great esteem by kings and armies throughout Greek history. And oracles did, in fact, deliver their predictions in Greek hexameter poetry – the same metrical verse form as Homer's epic. These female seers, crouching on their tripods above the smoking vapours seething through cracks in the rock at Delphi – thought by the Greeks to be the very centre of the world – were said to be possessed by the prophetic god Apollo who has 'a mind that knows all', and who delivered his verse oracles through them.[20] This is highly reminiscent of how the ancients imagined poetry to come about. Vouchsafed, again, by the god Apollo (god of both prophets and poets), the male poet was said to be inspired by the divine Muse who (Homer tells us) 'knows all'.[21] Poets and prophets come together in the ancient Greek imagination, connected by their divinely imparted knowledge, their unique connection to the gods (especially Apollo) and their verse offerings.

But there's also an essential gender difference between the two. The female prophet, the Pythia at Delphi, was seen as a vessel for the words of the male god Apollo, her body and her voice to be inhabited by his when her mortal frame (like Cassandra's) was forced to deliver the god's message, whereas the epic poet is never an unconscious instrument of the Muse: his poetry is a combination of a divine gift and a product of his own personal craft and skill.[22] And, while the bard conveys his own words to an audience in songs – as in the figures of the male bards (like the one Penelope asks to change his tune) in the *Odyssey*, as well as Homer himself – the oracle at Delphi wasn't actually allowed to deliver her message herself: her words were interpreted and explained by men, known as 'speakers-on-her-behalf'. The Greek word for this: *prophētēs* (*pro* meaning 'for', *-phētēs* from *phēmi*, 'I speak'), or prophet.

All of which paints a tellingly different picture from the high-status role of female oracles that we started with. Their bodies possessed by a male god, their voices channelling his words, and their own verses 'interpreted' by men who quite literally spoke for them and took over their role as prophets. These were women, like Cassandra, who had a voice, yet had no say in their own words; who had a body, but didn't own it; whose speech was snatched from them and reconstrued by men.

No wonder, then, perhaps, that Homer was said to have stolen the words of a female seer.

This theme of men ignoring women's prophecies is one that doesn't just hide behind what the ancients thought about the composition of the Homeric epics; it lies at the heart of the story of the *Iliad*, too. Prophecy, and fate, is a gendered theme that runs through the epic, drawing male heroes towards their inevitable deaths, and Troy to its fated fall. In Greek mythology more broadly, the Fates – female goddesses, called the *Moirai* – are said to spin the thread of mortal life, and to allot humans their portion (which is what *moira* in Greek means) of good and evil at their birth.[23] In Homer, however, it's largely the overweeningly masculine Zeus who dishes out good and bad to mortals, who weighs up human fates (as at the moment of Achilles and Hector's duel, for instance, when he places their deaths in the balance on his golden scales) and who deals out prophecies to the other gods of what's going to happen, both in the *Iliad* and in the wider Trojan War.[24] This near-total replacement of the ancient, mysterious, female Fates by Zeus – father of the gods, patriarch of Olympus – has been read as a deliberate subordination of these antiquated female divinities to the patriarchal Olympian system.[25] And this kind of dynamic of male suppression and silencing is replicated explicitly elsewhere in the poem, as in the first book of the *Iliad* when the female deity (and his wife) Hera attempts to challenge his plans, and he threatens – disturbingly – to shut her up by beating her.[26]

So when another goddess tries to make a prophecy elsewhere in the *Iliad*, we can almost expect that it will be swept aside by the epic's chief male protagonist. By Book 9, we have arrived at a crisis point for the Greek troops. Zeus is determined to make the Greek army suffer, after he promised Achilles' mother – the goddess Thetis – to avenge her son's loss of honour, after the seizure of Briseis, by inflicting terrible losses on Agamemnon's troops. The Trojans – led by Hector – have gained ground, protected by Zeus, and have pressed the Greeks back behind the defences of their camp. King Agamemnon calls an emergency assembly, where – on the advice of Nestor, king of Pylos – it's resolved to send ambassadors to offer Achilles gifts, including Briseis, and persuade him

back to war. But Achilles is having none of it. He still detests Agamemnon, he spits, and gains nothing from the war, when the king takes
all for himself and gives him no chance to win wealth and glory. He
has options, he says, granted to him by his goddess mother Thetis, who
prophesied that he would have the choice between two fates: 'If I stay
here and fight, besieging Troy, my chance of ever going home is lost, but
I shall have a name that lasts forever. Or if I go home to my own dear
country, I lose my glory but I gain long life.'[27]

A short life and glory, or long life and ignominy, then, are Achilles'
twin destinies. But when the course of events takes a different turn, when
his companion (and likely lover) Patroclus is brutally slain by Hector
and Achilles determines in a black cloud of grief to return to the war to
avenge him, Thetis – emerging from the sea like a silver fish – cannot
persuade him to remember her prophecy, that he has a choice. If he goes
back to war, she reminds him, his own death will inexorably follow; but
Achilles, blinkered by anger and riled by grief, can no longer see that his
destiny is his to choose. He is a man trapped in the masculine imperative of vengeance, the chain of heroic slaughter that means that, after
Hector killed Patroclus, Achilles will kill Hector, and Achilles himself
will in turn be killed. He must in the end, he says, go back to battle to
win fame and glory among men, and make the Trojan women weep with
grief.[28] The imperative of epic demands nothing less. This is the plan of
Zeus, which has determined that Troy will fall. This is the code of heroes,
which demands glory for men and makes women mourn. This is the
stipulation of Homer's epic, that Achilles returns to war so that the story
can go on. This is the male plan, not the female. And Thetis, the mother
who reared her infant son so carefully, the goddess who once predicted
that he had the chance of a long and peaceful life, is left alone on the
shoreline.

Prophet, Priestess, Princess

The empty echoes of Cassandra's voice are replicated in Homeric epic –
not explicitly, where she's silenced – but in other prophetic female
figures, like Thetis, as well as the shadowy women seers like Daphne

whom some ancients believed stood behind Homer. Yet women prophets were not only central to the prehistoric (and historic) Greek world; they had an important role to play across the Bronze Age Mediterranean. And their Anatolian counterparts might have more to tell us about Cassandra (who was, after all, in the legend, a Trojan). In the ancient heartlands of Mesopotamia in particular, divination had been honed to a refined art since the third millennium BCE – the interpretation of dreams, portents and omens, the examination of the movements of the stars and the inspection of the entrails of sacrificial animals, all in search of signs of the will of the gods. These various signs and their meanings – the hidden script of the language of the gods that was written into all creation – were gathered into vast dictionaries, glossaries of omens and their meanings, and were passed, gradually, into the Hittite Empire that had spread across Anatolia by the late fourteenth century BCE, so that the Hittite rulers, too, could learn the gods' plans for their burgeoning lands. Oracular experts would delve into the intestines of sheep, scan the skies for birds in flight, or watch snakes swimming in a bowl of water, asking a series of questions about a problem that had arisen – why was there a plague, for instance, and what could be done? The omens would be interpreted, to determine which of the thousand Hittite gods had been offended (thereby causing the issue), and what was required by way of recompense. These questions and their answers were then meticulously recorded by a scribe on clay tablets, so that the appropriate action could be taken.

One such oracle tablet – now referred to as *AhT* 20 – was uncovered during Hugo Winckler's early excavations at Boğazkale, among the thousands at the royal archive at Hattusa.[29] Originally found in fragments (later fitted together by scholars), it displays the neat wedge-like stamps of the cuneiform script and is written in the Hittite tongue – the previously unknown language that was deciphered in 1915 (nine years after Winckler first struck a spade into the ground at Boğazkale) by the brilliant Czech linguist Bedřich Hrozný. Dating to around 1310 BCE – the height of the Hittite Empire, as well as the period of the historical city of Troy's great wealth and pomp before it was attacked by enemy invaders – the tablet is a record of inquiries into the reason and cure for a dangerous illness that afflicts the Hittite king, probably Mursili II (father of Puduhepa's husband, Hattusili III).[30] In an ironic twist for our search for Cassandra, who was able to speak but was not believed, other texts suggest that Mursili had, in fact, lost the power of speech; perhaps it was this that he was seeking to remedy by consulting the oracles.

What's remarkable about the rituals documented in *AhT* 20 is that they provide historical evidence from the Late Bronze Age for the elevated roles that women could play as oracles within the predominantly patriarchal hierarchy of the Hittite world (just like the mythical Cassandra and Daphne, and the historical Pythias in Greece), as well as further clues about Anatolian–Greek interactions, and the influence they might have had on the ritual depiction of women in the *Iliad*. As Mursili's agents search for the source of the king's trouble, they peer into the guts of a sheep – checking the flap of the liver, counting the coils in the intestines, noting the presence of tapeworm blisters. But they also routinely turn to check their results with a respected female practitioner, known as a *hasawa*. These highly skilled women probably started out as midwives (*hasawa* means '[she] of birth'), but they developed over time into eminently skilled ritual professionals, with a specialism in certain types of oracles, as well as healing practices.[31] Interestingly, these ritual practitioners are also known in the Hittite texts by the term 'Old Women' – which suggests, as we've already seen, that the crowd of old women summoned by Hecuba for the supplication of Athena in Book 6 of the *Iliad* may actually be a reference to these specifically Hittite female ritualists.[32]

Other women fill out the rest of the text of *AhT* 20, demonstrating their unusually important role in divination: a priestess is mentioned, by the name of Mezzulla; an unnamed female dream interpreter's elucidation is quoted word for word; even a princess makes an appearance. Called Massannauzzi, we know that she was Mursili's daughter – her name is attested elsewhere in a letter from the Egyptian pharaoh Ramesses II.[33] And she may, perhaps, have played a key part – not only in seeking her father's cure, but in fostering diplomatic relationships between the Ahhiyawans (or Achaeans/Greeks) to the west and the Hittites. At one point in the text, the omens are inspected as to whether the king should bring 'the deity of Ahhiyawa and the deity of Lazpa' to Hattusa.[34] Bringing another god into the pantheon of the thousand Hittite divinities was common practice, and in this instance is usually interpreted as summoning into the Hittite Empire the statues and worship of a Greek (Ahhiyawan) god, as well as a god from the island of Lesbos (Lazpa in Hittite), just off the coast of Troy – a key site of interaction between Greeks and Anatolians. We know that Massannauzzi was married to a vassal ruler who had strong political ties to Lazpa/Lesbos. So it's been suggested that it could have been she – an Anatolian princess with connections to the Greeks via the eastern seaboard of the Aegean – who heard of the efficacy of these Greek deities, and recommended that her father adopt them into the Hittite pantheon, and give them due worship as a way to cure his disease.[35]

Hidden behind a king's desire to safeguard his own body and political power, then, we find an elaborate network of women in this Late Bronze Age Hittite world who are working together in the sphere of ritual: specialized female oracle practitioners, priestesses, dream interpreters, and a princess with global connections to the web of deities that criss-crossed the Aegean world. While these may not have been women who controlled their own destinies, they joined together, at least, to claim what power was possible to them, to attempt to predict (and, perhaps, influence) the future of their king and their country. And they find a reflection, a refraction, a memory, in the storyline of the *Iliad*, too. Recent research has suggested that the Homeric epics (and the early network of oral poetry, connecting Anatolia to Greece, which forms their backdrop) preserves a reminiscence of Anatolian ritual, not only in the supplication of the gods by the priestess queen Hecuba and her group of Old Women, but also in the opening of the *Iliad*.[36] During the attempts at a purification for the plague that Apollo brings on the Greeks because of the loss of Chryseis (just like the attempts to cure the sickness of Mursili), Achilles demands 'a priest or prophet or somebody who knows the ways of dreams'.[37] Achilles' Anatolian-style counter-plague measures of oracles and dream interpreters are a curious echo of the powerful positions occupied by women in curing plagues, referred to in Mursili's plague-prayer tablet. Perhaps a trace of the Hittite women of the oracles, the way they spoke to the fate of an empire through the interpretation of dreams and portents of the future, trickled through the oral tradition into Achilles' request – and later emerged in the powerful female figure of Cassandra: the prophet, priestess, princess of Troy, who once tried, too, to read the vagaries of what was to come, and to warn in vain of the horrors that would destroy them all.

End of the World

The divination of prophets like Cassandra and the Hittite 'Old Women' was essential, because of the sheer lengths to which the gods could go to act out their displeasure. Nowhere was this more salient than in one of the oldest and most powerful myths: that legend of ultimate destruction, the flood. One ancient Babylonian epic called the *Atrahasis* – fragments of which were found at the Hittite capital of Hattusa (and the narrative makes its way, too, into the Bible in the flood story of Genesis) – tells how the great god Enlil, angry at the swelling numbers of the human population, decided to send a flood to wipe them all out. In the Greek tradition – narrated once again in the almost entirely lost epic the *Cypria* that tells us of Cassandra's run-in with Apollo – Zeus uses a war, rather than a flood, to relieve the earth of its burden of mortals. But it's not just any war: it's the *Trojan* War. A rare fragment of this other ancient epic gives a glimpse into the tale:

> There was a time when countless throngs of men were trampling
> all the land, and weighing down the wide expanse of earth.
> Zeus saw it and he sighed, and in his complex mind
> he chose to take the weight of men off nature's chest,
> to spark the fire and set alight the Trojan War,
> and so by death to lift the load. The warriors at Troy
> kept being killed. And Zeus' plans came true.[38]

Which makes Cassandra's predictions about the fall of Troy pretty important. It means that the Trojan War, repeatedly foretold by Cassandra, was actually – within the larger framework of the legend – part of a much larger-scale plan for the destruction of human civilization. Like a Greta Thunberg of ancient times, she was trying to tell everyone about the end of the world, the overburdening of the earth that was going to cost the lives of them all. In the ever more uncertain world of the twenty-first century – as climate disaster looms, population numbers swell and parts of the planet become uninhabitable – it's hard not to see the endless catalogue of deaths in the *Iliad* as a salient reminder of a very ancient fear. How long will it be until the earth can no longer hold 'the countless throngs' of humans?[39] And what will happen when it can't?

In the ancient world, diviners like the Hittite Old Women (and their records on tablets) were deemed essential to making sure these kinds of calamities didn't take place, or – if the gods really were determined to bring about destruction – that ancient kings were forewarned and knew what to do about it. And it wasn't long after our oracle that just such a catastrophe struck. Shortly after 1200 BCE, around the same time as the historical fall of Troy that the legendary Cassandra predicts, the Hittite capital of Hattusa, too, was destroyed. The twentieth-century excavators found the city littered with ash, charred wood, piles of mud from melted mudbricks, collapsed walls and fortifications. The palaces had been abandoned by the royals, rooms emptied, store chambers cleared of all portable possessions, long before they were put to the torch – as if the king and his family knew the attackers were coming.[40] Did the hours of snake-watching and entrail-gazing in their shadowy temples pay off, in the end? Or did they have their own powerful-voiced Cassandra, who warned them ruin was on its way? And did they listen, this time?

Modern science suggests that there were other, more prosaic though no less terrifying, omens of impending doom – an ultimatum furnished by nature, not Cassandra. A study published in *Nature* in 2023 by Sturt Manning of Cornell University and his collaborators, searching for evidence of possible climate-induced causes for the Hittite collapse, investigated the data provided by ancient juniper trees, excavated at the site of Gordion in the Hittite lands (the city, incidentally, that lay near the kingdom said to be ruled by Hecuba's father).[41] By analysing the growth of the tree rings – narrower tree rings indicating less growth, due to less water – along with stable isotope analysis, the scientists have been able to show evidence of ancient climate change between the thirteenth and tenth centuries BCE, resulting in significantly less rainfall (and so, critically, lower grain production, crop failures and a crisis in the availability of food) across the land-locked Hittite Empire. Most crucially of all, through the chronology developed from the tree rings, they were able to pinpoint with minute accuracy the peak of this centuries-long dry period: an extreme, three-year drought, between 1198 and 1196 BCE – right at the time of the Hittite collapse.

While periodic droughts were (and are) common in the region, the sheer length of this 'megadrought' – lasting over hundreds of years – and the sharp upswing of its peak just after 1200 BCE, would have been unlike anything the Hittites had experienced or could have prepared for.[42] Famine would have struck as resources became depleted: the ancient sources confirm that there were, indeed, grain shortages – and these texts match up in their dates to the timeframe that Manning and his team have identified as the critically dry period. In fact it's Puduhepa herself, queen of the Hittite Empire, corresponding with the Egyptian pharaoh Ramesses II in the thirteenth century BCE, who first bears witness to the early danger signs of what was to come. 'I have no grain in my lands,' she tells him baldly.[43] As food stocks continued to dwindle over the decades and Hittite rulers bombarded Egypt with requests for food relief, populations would have been forced to move, leading to mass migrations, unrest and potential internal rebellions – all of which could have reasonably paved the way for invasions by foreign attackers.[44] (This would also neatly explain the planned exodus of the royal family at Hattusa, who may well have been forced to abandon the site and move elsewhere to escape from the drought and the famine, long before any invading armies got there.) Drought wasn't by any means the only cause of the fall of the Hittite Empire, however – it was one part of a wider global crisis, and the millennia-long drama that continues to play out (with more relevance than ever today) between the natural resources we rely on and our fragile, overburdened civilizations. But it was, as seems likely, the spark to the bone-dry kindling that lit the flames – and that brought Hattusa down.

Perhaps it is because her prophecies turned out to be true – because cities like Troy, and Hattusa, really did fall – that Cassandra's name has echoed with eerie resonance down the centuries. Women writers, in particular, seem to have been drawn to the figure of the female prophet who was gifted with foretelling the future, only to be ignored – and some have drawn on Cassandra to channel their anxieties around global disasters, including the increasing threat of climate change. Doris Lessing, British-Zimbabwean winner of the Nobel Prize in Literature and writing in impassioned resistance to the Soviet–Afghan War in the 1980s, called on Cassandra to encompass the catastrophes of poisoned oceans, ravaged rainforests, the Cold War, the destruction of Chernobyl: 'You could say the whole world has become Cassandra, since there can be no one left who does not see disaster ahead. They are all of them preventable, preventable.'[45] Others, like the German novelist Christa Wolf, who penned a *Cassandra* around the same time as Lessing – in East Germany, 1983 – propelled the Trojan seer to the forefront of the Homeric tale to formulate a critique on patriarchy, the maleness of the literary canon and the objectification of women, as well as to channel dark predictions of impending nuclear war.[46]

Which brings us back to Lesia Ukrainka: another Cassandra, who prophesied imminent disaster and war that would bring about the end of an empire.[47] Over a hundred years after Ukrainka first wrote *Cassandra*, in the autumn of 2022 – shortly after Russia's latest devastating invasion of Ukraine – the play crossed Europe to premiere onstage in the UK, in its first-ever performance in a new English translation by Nina Murray. As the lights go down and the eerie voices of the cast pierce the darkness in a haunting lament, I, along with the rest of the audience, can't help but feel a shiver of apprehension. Ukrainka's Cassandra – emerging strident-voiced and booted on to the stage, sharp-lined in the half-light – seems to step out from beneath the shadow of the current ongoing Russian attacks and the largest refugee crisis to engulf Europe since the Second World War, calling on us all with uncanny directness. 'I can sense it, I see disaster coming, but I cannot show it,' she rails, pointing out with unfocused eyes beyond the stage. 'I cannot say, watch here, or over there – where it will strike. I only know when it is already and can't be escaped. When no one can do anything at all. If only it were possible, I'd have stopped it by myself.'[48] Cassandra does not cease to proclaim her message of the devastation of war, to draw attention to the suffering of the victims of terror. The only question is who, now, will hear her.

Cassandra's message is all the more powerful, because she is a mortal who has been granted the vision of the gods. Unlike humans, embroiled in the conflicts and politics of the day-to-day, pushed and pulled by desire and fear and hate, Cassandra can see with a clear eye and speak with a god's voice. 'The piddly concerns of our human life are foreign to you, oh, godlike!' one character in Ukrainka's drama remarks.[49] It is Apollo's curse that lifts her up from the mortal sphere and makes her speak at cross-purposes in words that humans fail to understand. And as Cassandra's eyes lift from the Trojan plain and turn west towards the peaks of Olympus, so too do ours. We ascend to the realm of the gods.

7

APHRODITE AND HERA
Seducer and Matriarch

Her lover lies unmoving on the bed, sprawled across the sheets, flushed and swollen like a body on a battlefield, like the distended Greek corpses that litter the plain. In the morning light that slices through the shutters, carefully, slowly, she is putting on her armour:

A robe made at the loom by the war goddess with fibres of bronze-rust red, rubbed in scented oil that smells like sex.

Golden clasps pulled across her breasts, taut as a throbbing thread stretched tight, all white skin and gash of nipple.

Earrings trailing down her neck like sweat. Belt around her body like a baldric for a sword sheath, but what it holds is her hot blood and flesh and redness.

She has seen the gold-flecked sap pour from her body, so she knows she has it. She knows that she can bleed.

Why shouldn't they, too?

Touching a Goddess

The women emerge from the pit in broken body parts, sheared-off ceramic. White balloon-like breasts with pert red nipples. A single twisting arm, milk-white, wrangling a snake. Wasp waist and flaring hips ensnared in a skirt. A bodice clasped by a knot at the bust. A sheath-like belt, dotted with saffron crocuses.

It's near the end of the 1903 excavation season at Knossos in Crete. Arthur Evans – British prehistorian and Keeper of the Ashmolean Museum at Oxford – has been digging here with his team since the spring of 1900, when they first ran a fluttering Union Jack up a flagpole and broke ground on a hillock outside the capital of Heraklion.[1] Flowers – pink anemones and blue irises – have started to push through the soil like fingers, but the skeletons of Ottoman rule (the last horrendous massacre of 1898 that set Heraklion ablaze) are still visible in the burnt olive groves that loom against the distant sky.[2] Locals call the hill *ta pitharia* – 'the pots' – after the rows of ancient storage jars found there by the site's first excavator, a Cretan, Minos Kalokairinos.

Now, after four seasons of laying the earth bare, Evans has revealed far more than pots. A labyrinth of walls that snake beneath the mound forms the ground plan of a massive prehistoric palace: filled with brightly coloured frescoes of twisting acrobats and gorgeous dancing women, gold rings stamped with luscious plant life, pottery vessels wrapped with the looping tentacles of octopus and majestic stone-carved thrones set against vivid wall paintings of waving palm fronds. What Evans has uncovered is a previously unknown Bronze Age civilization, at the crossroads between Anatolia, the Cyclades islands, Egypt and Greece, that became a dominant power in the Aegean from around 2000 BCE – well before the flourishing of the Mycenaean Greeks on the mainland. He calls it Minoan: after the legendary King Minos of Crete (memorialized

The real labyrinth? The Bronze Age palace at Knossos, Crete.

several times in Homer), for whom the craftsman Daedalus built the mythical labyrinth to house the terrifying Minotaur – half man, half bull – which Theseus escaped, guided by Ariadne's thread. As excavations proceed, and Evans uncovers a twisting complex of hundreds of rooms in this sprawling palace, along with ancient sealstones showing mysterious images of bull men, he has been seduced by the hope that this might, indeed, be Minos' fabled palace – that this seat of prehistoric Aegean power, with its network of cramped and winding passages, might in fact have been the ancient labyrinth of legend itself.[3]

But Evans is not just looking for a mythical king; he is also searching, with increasing fervour, for a goddess. For the last few years, he has been hunting for evidence of Minoan gods, and has been inching towards an idea that there may have been a supreme kind of Mother Goddess worshipped on Crete – enticed, in large part, by the representations of women that explode from Minoan art, dancing across blue-skied courtyards, riding in chariots in long-plumed caps or worshipping goddesses in meadows blooming with flowers. Now, nearing the close of the 1903 season, Evans has revealed (more or less) the full extent of the palace site – and, hidden under the paving stones of a storage chamber just south of the Throne Room, has uncovered one last secret. Two stone-lined pits, filled with precious objects that might once have belonged to a shrine, many of them, apparently, carefully broken: jewellery, furniture inlays, votive plaques.[4]

Most spectacular of all are the fragments of three faience figurines, 20–30 centimetres high, dating to around 1600 BCE. These miniature, dislocated parts of women's bodies – of the two best-preserved models one has no legs, another is without a head – confront the gaze with their bare, bouncing breasts, their tiny waists circled by tight-knotted belts, their hands clutching at snakes. For Evans, fingering these dismembered figurines in the shadowed pit of this ancient palace, there can be no question that the larger of them, at least, is a goddess – fecund and fertile, with plaited snakes entwining her loins (conjuring, for this turn-of-the-century archaeologist, a potent cocktail of associations with women's dangerous allure, from the temptation and downfall of Eve to the snake-haired Medusa with her petrifying gaze), her breasts bared for all to see.[5] There can be no question, for Evans, that this, at last, is the clinching evidence for a supreme female deity among his precious Minoans: a Mother Goddess, a giver of life, a fertility divinity and Lady of the Underworld who dies and rises again like the crops of the earth, a voluptuous and fruitful guardian of nature.[6] And so, three and a half thousand years after this totem of her body was secreted away, he can claim to have touched a goddess.

Web of Seduction

In March 2023, on a rain-washed spring day, I paid a visit to the *Labyrinth* exhibition at the Ashmolean Museum in Oxford, looking this time, not for ancient women, but for some very old goddesses. It would be easy to confuse the two in this labyrinthine tangle. Everywhere I looked in the dark, twisting passages of the exhibition with its black-painted walls and glittering coins in glass cases, I was confronted by spotlit images of women – some divine, some mortal – being seduced, and often raped, winding through the Cretan story like Ariadne's thread. Europa, a Phoenician princess whom Zeus, the king of the gods, disguised as a bull, abducted to Crete and raped (Minos, legendary king of Knossos, was their son). Pasiphae, the wife of Minos, whom the sea god Poseidon punished by forcing her to fall passionately in love with a bull and copulate with it – so giving birth to the half-bull, half-human Minotaur. Ariadne, Minos and Pasiphae's daughter, who told the Athenian prince Theseus how to escape from the Minotaur in the labyrinth by retracing his steps with a ball of thread, and was then unceremoniously dumped on the island of Naxos when they fled together across the sea (she was later rescued and made the consort of the god Dionysus). This legendary ancient Cretan world – from what the myths were telling me – seemed to weave a web of seduction, an irresistible attraction that pulled women and men across the Mediterranean, a jewel of the Aegean ripe for the taking that everyone desired; an upside-down, criss-crossing world where gods could have sex with mortals, where deities could become beasts and beasts could mate with men, and where, above all, sexual violence against women shuddered through history like a beaten drum.

Stopping in front of one object on my way through – a slender gold

seal-ring, emblazoned with a woman and man stepping on to a decked-
out ship – I couldn't help but think that these tales seemed to be forerun-
ners of the story of Helen and Paris: another illicit sea crossing, another
tale of east meets west, another cataclysmic seduction. And it is for this
reason that we are going back in time and leaving the Anatolian heartlands to sail west across the Aegean towards Crete: because, to fully
understand the backdrop to Homer's world and Homer's women, we
need to meet another weighty ancient civilization, that of the so-called
Minoans. This fabulously rich and cosmopolitan society, flourishing in
the cultural melting pot of Crete, reached its peak in the second millennium, up until around 1450 BCE (when it seems to have been taken
over by Mycenaean invaders). The island sat like the central gem in the
crown of the flourishing network of Mediterranean trade – stretching
from Egypt to Cyprus to Thera to the Greek mainland – that turned it
into a fertile breeding ground for the spread of objects and ideas, and
saw the burgeoning development of its own unique and hugely influential culture. On no one, perhaps, did it have a greater impact than the
Mycenaeans of Greece, who – as their own civilization was taking off in
the mid second millennium – directed their gaze south to the cosmopolitan zenith of Minoan Crete, birthplace of legends, long-established
seat of power and vigorous wellspring of culture and art. When the
Mycenaeans started writing Linear B, it was the Minoan script that they
borrowed – known as Linear A, among the earliest-known scripts in
the ancient world, the language of which is still undeciphered. When
the Mycenaeans painted their pots, they copied the lustrous styles of the
Minoans. When elite Mycenaean women dressed up, they adopted fashionable trends straight from the Minoan catwalk: wall paintings from
the palaces on the mainland, like the Tiryns fresco we met in the search
for Helen, show Mycenaean women proudly modelling the distinctive flounced skirt, slim-waisted silhouette with wrap-around belt, and
gaping bared-breast bodice of the Minoan elite.

So when, at the Ashmolean in Oxford, I wound my way through the
passageways to the exhibition's centre, and reached a diminutive altar-
like plinth at the heart of the labyrinth where the two most complete
so-called 'Snake Goddesses' stood, I recognized not only a goddess, but
the distant cousins of the kinds of women and goddesses who would

later be memorialized in Homer's songs. These twin females, one larger, one slightly smaller, both sculpted from faience (a kind of glazed quartz ceramic), are intensely, almost painfully, corporeal. In complete control of their sexuality, they seem to invite the viewer to focus on their bodies, to take in a woman's physicality and explore, by looking and touching, the way that a body is ornamented through dress. These women have breasts, skin, fingers, a stomach; the snake that twists over the larger figure's pelvis binds itself in a knot above her genitalia. This is a distinctly female, distinctly human body – even if Evans (no doubt taking in the chthonic snakes, powerful stance and abundant connotations with fertility and nature worship) immediately accorded at least one of them goddess-like status. A key clue, in Evans's mind, was the presence of what he called the 'Sacral Knot', looped braided cords that project from the bodices between the figures' breasts.[7] These mysterious knot-like loops were discovered all over the site of Knossos, depicted across frescoes, votive figurines and sealstones, and were taken by Evans to be one of the most revered sacred symbols of the Minoans.

Yet there has been much debate over how we read the otherworldly connotations of this humanoid pair: do we call the larger one a goddess? A high priestess evoking the form of a female deity? Or are they a set – a goddess and her acolyte? Or are they, perhaps, two goddesses – like Hera and Aphrodite, set side by side?[8] Gazing at the two of them at the end of the sinuous journey that has taken me past the legendary Cretan world of Europa, Pasiphae and Ariadne, I can't help but think that the slip-page between the human and divine that we see in the ancient myths of women raped by gods is part of the point here. These are women who stand for a world where a goddess might look like a human, a human like a god – where a woman's body, as the victim of the male gaze and desires, is the point where gods and mortals collide.

And this brings us to another kind of desire, one that's driven archae-ologists and historians across the centuries: the desire to claim an interpretation about history as the truth, the temptation – initiated by the ancient objects themselves – to fabricate a fiction about women and package it up as fact. Nowhere is that more evident than in the case of the Snake Goddesses. When Evans extracted the figurines from their underground cist, he immediately hired the Danish artist Halvor Bagge

to 'restore' the missing pieces – endowing the larger so-called goddess
with a skirt, and the smaller with a head, second arm and beret-like
headpiece complete with oddly perching cat. (This kind of highly controversial 'reconstitution', as Evans called it, was a characteristic strategy of
his: witness the garishly painted concrete reconstruction of the Throne
Room and Grand Staircase of the palace at Knossos, which visitors
often find frustratingly difficult to disentangle from the actual ancient
remains.)⁹ Evans then commissioned plaster replicas of the 'completed'
goddesses to be cast and sent back to the Ashmolean Museum in Oxford
(where he was, as we've seen, the Keeper) – the very same reproductions
at the centre of the *Labyrinth* exhibit.

These twin figurines – the originals at the Heraklion Archaeological
Museum in Crete, the painted replicas in Oxford – became a starting
point for an increasingly fervent (and gender-binary) narrative that
would consume Evans's thinking about the Minoans, and that would
become one of his most famous, and most hotly debated, legacies. The
ubiquity of women in Cretan iconography, and above all the discovery
of the Snake Goddesses, led Evans over the years to construct a fervid
vision of a pre-patriarchal society overseen by a primal, maternal,
fecund Great Mother Goddess – the archetype of the feminine divine.
For Evans, the Minoans represented an 'older matriarchal stage of social
development', signalled above all by their worship of a Great Mother
Goddess.¹⁰ Yet this myth of his own creation seems to have been largely
that – a twentieth-century myth. It's possible to trace the (sometimes
paradoxical) contemporary ideas around gender that played on Evans
to lead him to the Minoan Mother Goddess: from Sir James George
Frazer's hugely popular *The Golden Bough* (1890) with its hypothesis of
a Great Mother Goddess as the ancestor of all so-called 'primitive' religions across the globe, to Johann Bachofen's theories of the matriarchal
evolution of societies (propounded by Cambridge classicist Jane Harri-
son, who was familiar to Evans), to Romantic notions of the natural
primal feminine, to the progressively feminist Victorian image of
the New Woman.¹¹ In Evans's mind – misled, it has to be said, by a series
of forged artworks, purporting to be Minoan originals, that exploded
on to the market in the wake of his Knossos discovery – the women
of Minoan Crete slipped and metamorphosed into the modern Victorian

Knossos gets a European makeover: this fresco of a Minoan priestess was nicknamed 'La Parisienne' by Sir Arthur Evans for her slick make-up and coiffure.

lady, a very of-its-time, fin-de-siècle combination of original mother, spiritual feminine ideal and à la mode New Woman.[12] One particularly urbane-looking female on a Knossos wall painting (supposedly a priestess) was even nicknamed *'La Parisienne'* by Evans's team for her slick, red-lipped, contemporary look. (It's worth noting that this overlapping of past and present in Evans's gender story was by no means accidental, but part of a desire to promote the 'Europeanness' of Crete – suggesting that the Minoan civilization marked the beginning of Greek, and European, predominance.) All of this reached its pinnacle in what was perhaps Evans's most bizarre anachronism of all, focused (just like the Mother Goddess theory) around the figures of the Snake Goddesses: the time-travelling of the Victorian practice of waist constriction back to the ancient Minoans – as laid out in the lavishly illustrated four-volume compendium of his discoveries, *The Palace of Minos at Knossos* (1921–35) – transforming the Snake Goddesses' bodices and wasp-waisted belts into the original body-contouring Victorian corsets.[13]

So, standing at the centre of the Ashmolean's *Labyrinth*, I couldn't help but feel that I was being ensnared by an alluring, and potentially dangerous, mesh of disguise. Where does the imagination of a modern male archaeologist end, and women's history begin? Was I looking at goddesses or mortals? Originals or reproductions? Proto-Europeans or prehistoric Cretans? Did the Minoans really worship a Great Mother Goddess? Did these sumptuously dressed goddess-women, whom we know influenced the fashions of Mycenaean Greece, have any kind of actual power; and how far can we trust visual representations (which are all we have for Minoan Crete: until Linear A is deciphered, we don't have any contemporary texts to rely on) to tell us the real story? And what, with their electric eroticism and tight-belted aura of seduction, might this powerful pair of so-called goddesses have to do with the women, and the female gods, of Homer's world?

So how do we untangle this labyrinthine web? Is there a way out of the maze? Or is getting caught in the net actually where the story starts?

What a Tangled Web We Weave

In the *Odyssey*, a male bard on the fantasy island of the Phaeacians (where Odysseus has stopped off on his travels back from Troy) tells a titillating tale to amuse his all-male audience. It's the story of how Aphrodite, goddess of sex and love, got caught *in flagrante delicto* by her husband, the hobbling craftsman Hephaestus – how he trapped her and her lover Ares, the god of war, naked and writhing in the middle of the act, by means of a cunningly devised net above the bed that ensnared the adulterous pair.[14] This knotted net – Homer's word is *desmos*, which means 'bond' or 'knot' – tangles the lovers together so the (male) gods can come and have a good laugh (while the female gods stay demurely at home: the sight of Aphrodite's luscious body is for male eyes only).[15]

If the tangled web is used in the *Odyssey* by a man to ensnare a woman, in the *Iliad*, by contrast, we encounter a quite different kind of woven object, one that foregrounds instead a woman's world. This is an extraordinary magical love belt, belonging to a goddess, that invites us into seeing women's clothing, not as a constraint, but as a weapon of their own sexuality. And it gives us a new viewpoint for looking back at the seductive bodies, and costumes, of Evans's Snake Goddesses.

As we arrive at Book 14 of the *Iliad*, the Greeks are faring no better than they were before. Achilles has refused Agamemnon's offer of Briseis, and remains stubbornly in the Greek camp. Without him, his fellow warriors continue to suffer losses, and the Trojans – led by a triumphant Hector – eventually even manage to storm the Greek fortifications down by the shore.

It's at this point that the Greek forces are in dire need of some divine intervention, and that we now head to Olympus to meet Homer's goddesses. These are some of the powerhouses of the narratives of both the *Iliad* and the *Odyssey*, driving events forward and fighting tooth and nail for their favourites: above all, Hera and Athena, who are both committed champions of the Greeks. But, by now, Hera's attempts to safeguard her protégés are languishing – Zeus, her husband and king of the gods, continues to threaten her to stay out of the war – and so there's only one thing to be done. She needs help from Aphrodite to get her way with her husband.

The first step is to freshen up. She retires to her rooms in her palace on Olympus (Homer mentions that Hephaestus, Hera's son, has fitted it with a lock that no one else can open: perhaps he's learned a lesson in the value of home security after Aphrodite's adulterous excursions in their marriage bed), and starts her beauty routine. She cleanses her body with fragrant ambrosial oil, combs and plaits her shining hair. She shrugs on an ambrosial robe woven by Athena, and pins it across her breasts with golden clasps, wrapping around it a tasselled belt. Then for the finishing touches: triple-drop earrings, a veil bright as the sun and a pair of killer sandals.[16]

Ready for battle, she sallies forth to Aphrodite. Her request: to borrow a fabulous aphrodisiac, a legendary 'decorated belt' that, we're told, carries with it divinely erotic properties and makes anyone who wears it irresistible. Cleverly (because Aphrodite is pro-Trojan), Hera doesn't reveal her plan to get round Zeus, but claims she needs it to sort out an argument between the old river god Oceanus and his wife, the mother goddess Tethys. Because of their quarrelling, she says, it's been a long time since these two ancient gods slept together and, Hera pleads, she wants to help. And so Aphrodite takes from around her breasts the 'decorated belt', which, the poet tells us, is woven through with 'every seductive spell': 'lovemaking, intimacy, desire, and flirty talk'.[17] Armed with her weapon of choice, the queen of the gods heads off to seduce Zeus. She's successful (of course – with her plan and Aphrodite's charm, how could she not be?) and he, after the deed is done, immediately falls asleep, leaving Hera free to rampage around the battlefield and give the Greeks a bit of moral support.

The way this scene is gendered shows the story of sex and seduction from the woman's point of view (in contrast to Hephaestus' very male-orientated capture of his errant wife in his bed). Here, as in Hecuba's palace and Helen's chambers at Troy, we enter a scented, secret, markedly 'feminine' world – not only eavesdropping on Hera's whispered intrigues with another female god, but gaining a voyeur's view into the highly intimate private realm of her bedroom, too. The gender-coding of this seductive domain is marked by the detailed description of the way Hera dons her clothes: translating into the female sphere a classic Homeric stock scene – the warrior's arming with sword, shield, helmet and spear (typically recounted before he goes into battle and displays his peak fighting moves, known as his *aristeia*, 'show of excellence'). Even the word Homer employs for the sex belt Hera takes from Aphrodite – *himas* – is most often used for the chin straps of soldiers' helmets.[18] Instead of a warrior arming for battle, here we have a woman readying herself for amorous combat: an *aristeia* in the field of erotic, rather than martial, encounters. Just like a mortal warrior, this goddess is distinctly human in shape, and ready to go to battle against her male opponent on her own terms, equipped with the weapons supplied to her by her superlative goddess comrades-in-arms.

Unlike the male warrior, however – and along the lines of the Snake Goddesses – Hera is possessed of a markedly feminine body: she has 'gorgeous skin', long hair, and breasts.[19] Even her clothes, Homer tells us, are made for her by a woman: Athena, the goddess (among many other things) of craft, and the epitomization of the well-known role of women in the ancient world as weavers and producers of textiles, made her robe. Meanwhile Aphrodite's belt is, as we saw, adorned with 'every seductive spell' – which suggests, not only that there are figurative erotic scenes woven across the fabric, but also that the belt has, itself, some kind of magic, some ability to make the images it portrays come true. (We might compare the first time we see Helen in the epic, weaving the battle scenes that are at that very moment taking place beneath the walls.) In this women's realm, it is women who are creating the gorgeous, resonant clothing (like the rich attire of the Snake Goddesses, like Hera's robe made by Athena, like Aphrodite's belt) that enables them to exercise their erotic powers to the full; women who are stitching their own stories as a magical means to make a tale come true; and women who are trading these clothes between each other to build a world where they can seduce men to get their own way.

So what might Aphrodite's bewitching sex belt have actually looked like? It's possible to imagine that the ubiquitous girdles nestling under the voluptuous breasts of both Minoan and Mycenaean women, from the tight-waisted Snake Goddesses to the well-endowed females parading across the painted walls of palaces in Crete and mainland Greece, might have inspired the idea of an erotic love belt. We might even imagine the Snake Goddesses as one potential incarnation of the sex goddess: breasts bare and full, a belt fastened around them just like Aphrodite's and brandishing a snake (a standard symbol of sexual fertility) in each hand. Evans certainly associated other goddess images with Aphrodite, whom he saw as an aspect of the Great Mother. But there's an even closer, and more specific, Cretan connection to the Homeric scene. When Hera leaves Olympus (skimming over the snowy Thracian hills, stepping across the Aegean to Mount Ida near Troy, where the king of the gods is holding court) and approaches Zeus, doused in perfume and girded with the sex belt, he is simply unable to resist her: 'such strong desire,' he says, 'has never suffused my senses or subdued my heart for any goddess or for any woman as I feel now for you. Not even when I lusted for . . . the famous Europa, child of Phoenix, and I fathered Minos on her.'[20] In other words, Zeus says he wants Hera so much, he wants her even more than he did Europa – mother of Minos, founder of the legendary line of Cretan rulers. If Hera reminds him of anyone, dressed up in her finery and encircled by a love belt, it's a Cretan princess. (And if it's more than a little discomfiting that the male god thinks he's complimenting his wife by comparing her to his adulterous rape victims, she doesn't comment on it.) Is it possible that the mention of Europa, as Hera charges in with Aphrodite's sex belt, might be a distant memory – just like the one it evokes in Zeus – of the splendidly attired, erotically charged, deeply girdled women of Crete?

But there are other associations here too, and from further afield. Homeric scholars have long struggled with the problem of why Aphrodite's belt should be worn on the breasts (and why Homer is so ambiguous about its placement to start with: when Aphrodite hands it over, she tells Hera to place it 'in her *kolpos*', which can signify anything from the breasts to the lap to a fold of the clothes), and why the belt itself isn't called by the more usual Greek word, *zōnē* (the root of modern English 'zone').[21] It's likely that the ambiguity in the Greek is, itself, the central clue. The Homeric poems are quite literally struggling for words, because they're drawing on models absorbed from ancient south-west Asia – in particular, the transcendent presence of the ancient Mesopotamian goddess of love and fertility deity, Ishtar, often equated in antiquity with Aphrodite. Gods (and ideas about gods) could be traded with sublime ease across the cosmopolitan, global Bronze Age world – as with the deity of Ahhiyawa, summoned into the Hittite capital to cure the sick king Mursili. We know the names of some of the later Bronze Age Greek gods through the evidence of the (Mycenaean) Linear B tablets, and some of them bear unmistakable resemblances to their subsequent Homeric counterparts: *Di-we* for Zeus, *E-ma-a* for Hermes, *Po-se-da-o-ne* for Poseidon, *Di-wo-nu-so* for Dionysus, *E-ra* for Hera. (We also find *Pa-ja-wo-ne* for Paion, the healer god, mentioned as the physician of the gods in Homer and later associated with Apollo: it's been suggested that Paion was the Ahhiyawan god summoned by the Hittite king Mursili.)[22] Interestingly, some of the female gods of the Olympian Greek pantheon are missing – Aphrodite and Athena, most conspicuously – while others suggest a complex and layered pre-Greek past. One in particular, *po-ti-ni-ja* (later Greek *Potnia*, 'Lady' or 'Mistress'), garners different epithets that gesture to her many guises. In the tablets at Knossos, she receives offerings of honey as the local 'Lady of the Labyrinth' (*da-pu-ri-to-jo po-ti-ni-ja*); in Homer, we find Artemis, the hunter goddess, as 'Mistress of Animals' (*potnia thērōn*); while elsewhere in the Linear B tablets at Pylos, suggestively, she is 'the Lady of Asia' (*po-ti-ni-ja a-si-wi-ja*).[23] This goddess was probably an international import from the Anatolian region of Assuwa – an ancient confederation of city states in the north-west of Anatolia, whose name apparently provides the origin of our modern term 'Asia', and (curiously enough) included the city of Wilusa (that is, very likely, Troy).[24] And the trade in gods didn't just go one way: in the Hittite treaty with Alaksandu of Wilusa (perhaps Paris of Troy), a Wilusan god is given by name – Apaliuna – who seems, remarkably, to be a Wilusan version of the Greek god Apollo. The equation is buttressed by the fact that Apollo is one of the key pro-Trojan gods in Homer, that he was said in legend to have built the walls of Troy with his own hands, and that a similar-sounding deity (probably a Hittite version of Wilusan Apaliuna) is described in Hittite texts as a plague god – just like Apollo at the start of the *Iliad*.[25]

If Troy and Greece seemed to have enjoyed a particularly fertile exchange in gods, so, too, was there a flourishing trade in deities from further afield. This interchange didn't just mean the wholesale export of gods, but could also involve the neat amalgamation of deities with similar powers and attributes (a phenomenon known as 'syncretism').[26] One particularly common syncretism in the ancient world incorporated the Greek Aphrodite into a whole family of potent south-west Asian and north-east African goddesses: in particular, the Phoenician Ashtart, the Egyptian Isis and, above all, the Mesopotamian goddess Ishtar – to whom, in fact, the Greek goddess Aphrodite (said in legend to have been born out of the waves in Cyprus, an island with deep ties to the ancient civilizations of south-west Asia) probably owed her origins.

And there is one particularly striking correspondence between the Mesopotamian Ishtar and Homer's Aphrodite. The goddess Ishtar is commonly depicted in her ancient statues naked and wearing a saltire, a kind of belt that – significantly – crosses between the breasts, then

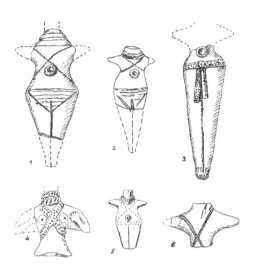

Naked goddesses from Syria to the Indus Valley (c.14th century BCE),
with the distinctive saltire slung across their breasts.

wraps around the waist like a girdle. Ishtar – or Inanna, as she was
known in her Sumerian (southern Mesopotamian) incarnation – was
particularly well placed to stir up impassioned words of poetry in her
followers, who poured forth giddy praise for her bounty and beauty.
The earliest-known named author in world history – who, remarkably,
was a *woman* – was a Sumerian priestess by the name of Enheduanna,
who wrote deeply personal hymns devoted to Inanna (over one and a
half thousand years before the Greek poet Sappho). In several of these,
Inanna pointedly appears as 'crowned with lustrous desire' and 'clothed
in awesome radiance', sketching a portrait of a love goddess arrayed in
her erotic attributes – written by a woman poet – that seems to fore-
cast Homer's Aphrodite, quite literally girdled in sex.[27] And in another
Old Babylonian hymn exalting the dizzyingly gorgeous love goddess,
dating to the sixteenth century BCE, Ishtar is 'clothed in love, adorned
with ripeness, seductive charm, and sex' – a remarkable similarity to
Aphrodite's girdle woven with 'lovemaking, intimacy, desire, and flirty
talk'.[28] So perhaps Homer's erotic breast belt, worn on the body of a sex
goddess, is a testament to Greek exchanges with a Mesopotamian way
of thinking about the seduction of the divine – borrowed for a moment,

just as Hera borrows from Aphrodite, from the fecund, fertile Mesopotamian goddess of love.

Bondage

But it's not only powerful Mesopotamian goddesses who seem to have used love belts to their advantage. A magic spell from Assyria – an ancient Mesopotamian empire north of Babylon, with its heartlands on the banks of the Tigris – provides sensational evidence of the everyday association, at the end of the second millennium, between women, woven belts and occult erotic encounters. The spell, discovered on a clay tablet at the Assyrian city of Ashur and dating to around 1000 BCE, is stamped in minute cuneiform script under the intriguing title 'Incantation to be recited when the husband of a woman is angry with her':

> You weave together into a single strand the tendons of a gazelle, [hemp,] and red wool; you tie it into fourteen knots. Each time you tie a knot, you recite the (i.e., preceding) incantation. The woman places this cord around her waist, and she will be loved.[29]

The incantation that the woman was supposed to recite while tying the knots in her triple-ply is frustratingly fragmentary, but we can just make out that it invokes Ishtar – the love goddess commonly worshipped as Aphrodite's Mesopotamian equivalent. Fascinatingly, the ritual seems to be designed for a situation exactly like the fabricated story that Hera makes up for Aphrodite when she goes to her for help: the falling-out of a husband and wife (Oceanus and Tethys, the river god and mother goddess). And Aphrodite's prescription in Homer is distinctly similar to the Ishtar spell above: a specially designed cord or belt, woven by a woman, tied around a woman's body to ensure 'she will be loved' (a word that incorporates both affection and sexual desire – just like the attributes woven into Aphrodite's belt).

The efficacy of the Assyrian ritual seems to be assured by the physical process of knotting.[30] Aphrodite's belt isn't explicitly knotted, but we can find other traces of magical and erotic knots in Homer – above all, the knotted net (*desmos*) of Hephaestus in the story told by the Odyssean bard, which entraps Aphrodite and acts as a form of marital bondage, tying wife to husband. Hephaestus' net is notably gender-reversed in comparison to the Assyrian spell: here, we have a knot made by a man instead, to bring back his errant wife. (This is a classic marker of Hephaestus' marginal, subordinate status in the Olympian pantheon, as a disabled god. He was born with a disability and was, he says in the *Iliad*, horrifyingly, tossed off Olympus by his own mother Hera when she found out that he was disabled.[31] Hephaestus' marginalization and gender reversal is one link in the chain of cultural values in Homeric epic that suppresses, and connects, femininity and physical disability.[32]) Another kind of knot we find in Homer is a form of bondage taught, this time, by a woman to a man: a particularly complicated kind of knot that we hear Odysseus learned from Circe, the powerful goddess of Aeaea (as well as wand waver and expert in magic potions: she turns Odysseus' men into pigs) with whom the Greek lingered (and had sex) for a whole year on his return journey. Just as Hephaestus tries to bind Aphrodite to him through knots, so, with her symbolic lessons in bondage, Circe attempts to tie Odysseus to her. And in a way, it works: even though he does in the end sail away, we're told he remembers her knotting lessons when he's on the last stop of his travels, and is tying up a chest of gifts he's planning on taking home: 'he shut the lid and tied a cunning knot that he had learned from Circe'.[33] It seems that, in Odysseus at least, Circe's bondage tutorials have found an attentive pupil.

There's one other knot that is worth turning back to in this tangled web of associations: and that's the Sacral Knot. This strange symbol of a narrow strip of cloth, knotted into a loop with two loose ends of patterned textile falling away, crops up everywhere in Minoan and even Mycenaean art – in stone, in ivory, in faience, in paint – and constitutes a centuries-old mystery. Often, as in the looped cords between the breasts of the Snake Goddesses, they're associated with women: a Late Minoan golden ring showing a buxom female figure bent to the ground, twisting to look at a knot that seems to float ethereally in space, provides a good example. For Sir Arthur Evans, this sign was clearly the mystic personal calling-card of the Minoan Cretan Goddess, worn as a cult badge by the Snake Goddesses and their priestesses alike. His most convincing argument for this lies in the parallels he drew between the Sacral Knot and the contemporary Egyptian *tiet* or 'Isis Knot': a knotted symbol associated with the potent Egyptian mother goddess Isis who straddled life, death and rebirth, and which was commonly worn in ancient Egypt as a protective magical amulet.[34] Similar knotted signs, like the looped hieroglyph ankh that represents the word for 'life', appear elsewhere in Egyptian symbology as protective icons that convey sympathetic magical support and guarantee prosperity and success.

But it's not just Isis that these knots are entangled with. Back in Mesopotamia, the goddess Inanna (Ishtar's Sumerian counterpart) makes an appearance on a stunning one-metre-tall alabaster vase from around 3000 BCE, uncovered by archaeologists in the goddess's temple complex in the ancient city of Uruk. The relief, carved with exquisite delicacy into the surface of the stone vessel, details a procession winding its way up the vase to Inanna's temple at the very top, where the goddess is represented waiting ready to graciously receive her offerings. Behind her stand two gigantic and unmissable symbols, comprising a loop at the top, with two narrow ribbons of unequal length trailing to the ground. In the past, these were interpreted as simple bundles of reeds representing the door jambs to Inanna's temple, but it's been convincingly shown that there are unmistakable parallels with the so-called 'Sacral Knot' of Crete, with the knot at the top twisted slightly to one side and two narrow strips falling from the tie that are – as often in the Cretan examples – of different length.[35] Moreover, it seems that this symbol was deeply and intrinsically linked to Inanna (in other words, it wasn't just an architectural feature or pictorial decoration): a knotted sign in early Sumerian script, associated with the goddess, appears to have exactly the same shape. And, of course, the knotting spell of the Assyrian tablet directly invokes Ishtar–Inanna to aid the woman in her erotic binding enchantment.

So Aphrodite's love belt, the knotting spells of Assyrian housewives and the knots and baldric of Ishtar–Inanna all seem to entwine into one interconnected mesh of associations. But if we go back to the *Iliad*, there are clues that the poem is not just signalling the equivalence between Aphrodite's love belt and Ishtar–Inanna's knotted cord or baldric – it's actually commemorating its links with Mesopotamian traditions of storytelling, too. Hera's made-up tale about trying to heal the rift between Tethys and Oceanus – a mother goddess (whose children are the river gods and ocean nymphs) and a god of the rivers, who are said to be the progenitors of all the other gods (only here, nowhere else in Greek literature) and whose argument and separation triggers a fault line down the cosmos – bears a marked resemblance to a Late Bronze Age Babylonian epic, *Enuma Elish*, that tells the myth of the creation.[36] One scene in the *Enuma Elish*, in particular, recounts the original cosmic union between the sea goddess Tiamat and the river god Apsu, the primeval parents of all gods; it charts their quarrel, and their separation. (It's even been suggested that the name of the mother goddess Tethys, as recorded in Homer, actually derives from that of the Mesopotamian female divinity Tiamat: in Akkadian, Tiamat is *Temtu*, which would in turn have been pronounced *Tethu* in ancient Greek).[37] And the fact that Homer actually signposts this as an act of storytelling – Hera is spinning a yarn for Aphrodite to get what she wants – hints that the ancient Greek poem might be advertising its adoption of a series of Mesopotamian storytelling motifs. What's happening, it seems, is the incorporation of a patchwork of mythical, magical foreign storylines into the Greek epics, in the attempt to articulate this nebulous otherworld of powerful women and goddesses: a Babylonian tale of quarrelling ur-gods; an Assyrian-style approach to the goddess of love, with the magical amulet of a cord tied around the woman's body to solve a marital rift; and a Mesopotamian Ishtar-like love belt.

The End of Ariadne's Thread

The mystic belt, then, with its magical binding properties – the cord of knotted fabric – is a symbol that entwines deeply, and inextricably, around women, in the realms of both the human and the divine. It is a sign that binds women together, across the burgeoning civilizations of the ancient world, from the parading Mesopotamian worshippers at the smoking temples of Ishtar to the Assyrian wives at home furtively tying husband-placating knots into hemp and wool, from the snake-brandishing, belt-busting Cretan priestess deities all the way to the defiant Olympian goddesses of Homer; a sign that takes its cue from their intricate connection to textiles – as weavers, as makers of objects – and harnesses a deep and intractable power to make what they want happen. It is a knot that laces women into their desires, a form of bondage that hints that they might take sexual agency in a world that often denied them the right to act, a tapestry that interweaves female power, eroticism and the sacred role of mother goddesses and goddesses of love across the fantastical, magical imaginary of the ancient world. And, although it plays out largely on the stage of the gods in the myth, epic and religion we've looked at, it's possible – through the Assyrian spell in particular, which doles out love recipes to ordinary wives trying to solve marital problems – to imagine how real women in the Late Bronze Age might have used the symbol of the knotted belt as a way to express (and effect) their erotic mastery. It's this that I find particularly liberating about the intimate exchange between Hera and Aphrodite in the *Iliad*: two powerful women (goddesses, yes, but also women), working together to get exactly what they want; an example of unfettered female sexuality that helps to offset some of the many other instances where mythical women are raped into submission, silenced, enslaved or simply written out of the record.

Returning to the so-called Snake Goddesses, then, I don't think we have to go all out with Evans's Victorian-Edwardian conception of a revered, omnipotent, originary Great Mother Goddess, the primal she-god who is the forerunner to the Olympian male – a narrative that, in any case, sets up a problematic story of 'progression' from primitive female to cultivated male. Instead, we can adopt a more global view to embrace the complex, shifting and multicultural forms that were circulating in the Late Bronze Age world around women's sacredness and their sexuality: sometimes with religious resonances, sometimes magical; sometimes with a local flavour, sometimes tapping into wide-reaching shared concerns; sometimes knotting together the sacred and the sexual into a complex tapestry, sometimes keeping them apart; and sometimes – just sometimes – granting women an extraordinary, vital power to achieve their sexual (and other) goals.

And yet a woman's body often wasn't her own. For almost all women in the ancient world there would have been one aspect of inhabiting a female body that they weren't able to choose, whether they wanted it or not – and that was the experience of becoming a mother, from the swelling of pregnancy to the racking of birth to the dripping and seeping of breastfeeding. The presence of goddesses of sex, fertility, birth and motherhood across the ancient world (from Aphrodite to Ishtar to Isis) testifies to the pervasiveness of mothering; Evans, in fact, saw the enlarged breasts of the taller of the Snake Goddesses as distinctly maternal (swollen with milk, perhaps) and it was in large part this that clinched her identification, in his eyes, as a Great Mother Goddess.[38] The myths encircling Crete tell a similar story: Zeus' rape of Europa impregnates her with the legendary King Minos; Ariadne – whom Robert Graves (of *I, Claudius* fame) imagined as the Mother Goddess herself – was abandoned by Theseus to become a mother to the sons of the wine god Dionysus; Pasiphae's desire for the Cretan bull (forced on her by the vindictive god Poseidon) saw her giving birth to a half-beast, the Minotaur.[39]

A new poem cycle by Fiona Benson, titled 'Translations from the Pasiphaë' and published in 2022, pushes to the fore the theme of motherhood, as a raw, fearful, truthful, overwhelming force in the Cretan legends, and offers a startling take on the traditional tales told in the past about marginalized communities – both women and people with disabilities.[40] Here, the Minotaur is not a monster but a disabled child, protected from a slow death by exposure on a mountainside (a cruel but common fate for unwanted children in the ancient world) by his mother, Pasiphae – who is recast in the myth, not as a lustful Jezebel, but as a victim of her times who fights through as a powerful and protective mother (against the oppression of Minos).[41] Pasiphae can forget the trauma of her violated past, consumed as she is by her love for her son. With the all-embracing concentration of a mother's gaze, she picks out every feature of his tiny body that she loves:

> He was beautiful, my son.
> In his sleep, he shone.
> I kissed the wet tufts of his fur,
> his damp snout,
> his long and delicate jaw.[42]

Jennifer Saint's recent novel *Ariadne* (2021) similarly pivots to focus on Pasiphae's motherhood, placing Ariadne in the intimate world of her mother's chambers watching the agony of her birth as the raking horns and hooves of the infant scrape her insides – then the indiscriminate and exhausted tenderness as Pasiphae sits at a window, clutching her baby to her in a bundle of blankets.[43] And it's the physical, visceral experience of giving birth that brings us all the way back to the belt of Aphrodite, of Hera, goddess of women in childbirth, and of the Snake Goddesses: because, in the ancient world, it was the act of untying a woman's girdle from around her waist, as the contractions began, that came to symbolize the onset of labour. After a successful birth (never a given before the advent of modern medicine), these women's belts or girdles would later be dedicated at the shrines of Greek birth goddesses – goddesses who earned themselves, in time, the resonant epithet of *Lusizōnos*: 'Belt-loosener'. We even appear to have evidence, from one Linear B tablet found at Pylos, of a 're-zoning' ceremony for women after birth, where new mothers would come together to symbolically re-belt their changing bodies.[44]

So if seduction through bondage was the prelude to sex, then motherhood – with its concomitant loosening and retightening of the belt – is where Ariadne's thread runs out. It's the end of the labyrinth, where the dark winding passages of myth open out into the stark reality of being a woman, in history – and the beginning of the next chapter in a woman's world.

8

THETIS

Mother

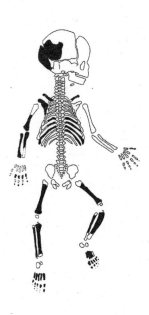

*She cannot get away from being a mother. She shifts shape: it's her gift –
from flecks of water to face-melting flame. She can pour from the mould of
a goddess into the slick dripping maw of a lion and out again.*

But she is never not a mother.

*She can slide and stretch into different skins, but she cannot escape the
stretch marks from that one, terrifying transformation. She remembers
the jagged pain when that other shape plunged into her, how her body
distended though she hadn't tried to change, how the contours of her skin
stretched and bulged: strange lumps in her abdomen, elbows, heels, driving
like stakes into her inner organs. And she remembers the lunging and tearing as the labour pains took hold, how her body shook and sweat poured,
and she wished her bones would melt and she could be free of this blood-
and-body chain.*

*And then he slipped out: tiny, warm, folded into blankets, with the
smallest pinkest nails, like shells. And the terror of her exhausted love for
him was too much. Fragile as driftwood. Warm as sand. And as they cut
the cord and blood splashed round her thighs, she wanted to lay her body
down on him like the waves wrapping the shore and never let him go.*

Baby Toes

The bones, small and delicate as a bird's, emerge from the sieve, soaked
and shining with water, trailing a smear of mud. Archaeologist Anaya
Sarpaki has been bent over in the lab painstakingly sifting the soil
lifted from the shallow pit, running it through the mesh with a hose, to
extract the minutest of organic remains. Now she feels the bits of grit
slip between her fingers, and fumbles for the mud-flecked pieces of the
human puzzle that are beginning to surface in the rush of water: flakes

of skull, then ear bones the size of drawing pins, twelve ivory teeth and ten miniature toes.

She cradles them in her hands as the water sluices through her fingers, clear and vital as amniotic fluid.

And she knows that she is holding a baby.

It's autumn 2014, and the pastel-splashed harbour of the city of Chania (ancient Cydonia) in Crete is returning to its warm, languid hum, the odd musician plucking a bouzouki and locals dipping beneath the awnings of red-and-ochre shops as the summer's tourists drain away. The team of archaeologists has been digging here since the 1970s at the Agia Aikaterini Square, up behind the harbour in a quiet tree-lined plaza. Stone walls run over each other in a dusty maze across the reddish earth, interspersed with scattered paving slabs from a prehistoric court-yard, and half-formed runs of staircases. And it's in one forgotten corner, by a wall behind the crumbling remains of a sprawling townhouse from the Late Minoan city of Cydonia, that the team have unearthed three soil-blackened stone slabs – covering the grave of a baby boy.[1]

As Sarpaki meticulously picks the bones out of the sieve, it's clear to her, as well as the rest of the team (including specialist in osteology Photini McGeorge) that there will be plenty of clues to unlock. Bones might not be able to speak, but they still have a lot to say. Measurement of the radius (part of the forearm) and comparison to expected growth reveals that this is a 39-week foetus: a full-term infant, who probably never made it beyond the first few hours of his life. The unerupted baby teeth tell a similar story: teeth begin to develop in the womb, even if they don't appear until several months after birth, and the extent of crown formation in particular (a newborn baby, for example, can be expected to possess incisors with over half of the crown already complete) gives a timeline that provides an approximate gestational age. They also reveal that this baby had a low birth weight, since defects present in the enamel (known as enamel hypoplasia) correlate to a less well-nourished, under-weight infant at birth; and lesions on the inside of the bones of the skull suggest either bacterial infection (transmitted to the foetus through the placenta), or perhaps foetal distress due to poor maternal nutrition. It's impossible to determine the cause of death for sure, but the signs point to a combination of nutritional deficiency during pregnancy, along with an infection developed either in utero or during or after birth (poor hygiene at delivery was, sadly, a common killer of both mother and child).[2]

It might seem an out-of-the-way, meagre burial – a few small bones without any gaudy grave gifts, covered with a couple of hasty slabs – but the way this infant has been laid to rest has lots to tell archaeologists and historians used to interpreting the messages conveyed by these kinds of mortuary practices. Burials like this one, inside a house or settlement – rather than in an external cemetery – are known as 'intramural' (from *intra muros* in Latin, meaning 'within the walls'). Although these kinds of burials were common on mainland Mycenaean Greece (as well as ancient south-west Asia) throughout the Bronze Age, they don't appear in Crete in the earlier periods (the Minoans preferred to bury their dead outside the city fortifications).[3] The dramatic appearance of intramural-type burials like this one across Crete around the sixteenth and fifteenth centuries BCE appears to bear witness to one of the most conspicuous cultural upheavals in Late Minoan history: the invasion, and takeover, of the old Minoan strongholds – particularly thriving harbour towns like Cydonia, a hub for booming trade and (coincidentally) the closest port to mainland Greece, so a natural means of approach for an invading force – by the warlike Mycenaeans from the north. And this matches up with other evidence, too. A vivid blemish of destruction flares around 1450 BCE through the ancient palaces and towns across Crete, from Knossos to Cydonia, as the former citadels burn and fall; gradually rebuilt over the years, they are replaced with a strict Linear B-based admin-istration and impressive gold-bedecked Achaean-style warrior tombs, which point strongly towards the imposition of a Mycenaean identity.[4] Meanwhile, new analysis of the DNA extracted from ancient skeletons provides fascinating evidence that, at Cydonia in particular, a lot of new genes (most likely from the Greek mainland) were being mixed into the Cretan pool over the last few centuries of the Bronze Age. The bones of the Cydonia baby, in particular, revealed a mixed Minoan and Mycenaean genetic origin, as shown by aDNA analysis. This little boy is demonstrating genetic traces, in other words, of an influx of Mycenaean Greeks.[5]

So the burial of the Cydonia baby is a key link in the chain of Crete's

An early Homer? This fresco of a bard, from the throne room in the Late Bronze Age palace at Pylos (c.1300 BCE), shows what the original Greek bards who sang songs of the Trojan War in this very hall might have looked like. The bird likely represents the singer's 'winged words' (a common formula in Homer).

Briseis' story: one of the early papyrus fragments of book 1 of Homer's Iliad, *written in the second century CE, preserves the tale of one of the enslaved women who initiates the conflict of the* Iliad. *Here, she is called Achilles' 'trophy' (geras).*

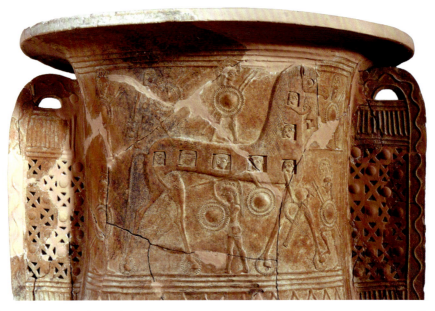

The Trojan Horse: this is the earliest known depiction of the legendary wooden horse (from an eighth-century BCE vase from Mykonos), and suggests that the Trojan War saga was being told around Greece some time before the Homeric epics were written down.

Women collect water, while men march to war wearing boar's-tusk helmets and body shields, on this fresco from the buried city at Akrotiri, Thera (c.1600 BCE). Boar's-tusk helmets and body shields were out of use by Homer's time, but both are described in the Iliad as part of the Greeks' fighting kit – memories of a long-lost age.

An artist's interpretation of the historical city of Troy, as it would have looked in the thirteenth century BCE, before it was attacked by invaders. Homer imagined Helen of Troy standing on one of these watchtowers.

Linear B, the script of the Mycenaean Greeks, was deciphered only decades ago. On this fourteenth-century BCE inventory tablet from Knossos, you can clearly see the signs used to indicate chariot wheels – just like the chariots Homer describes the Greeks using in the Trojan War.

Beauty standards: a woman with lead-white skin and impossible breasts is depicted on the walls of a Late Bronze Age Greek palace (c.1300 BCE). She carries a box of make-up (a pyxis).

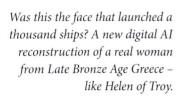

Was this the face that launched a thousand ships? A new digital AI reconstruction of a real woman from Late Bronze Age Greece – like Helen of Troy.

This fresco of a young girl stands at a threshold in the West House, a Minoan townhouse in Akrotiri (c.1600 BCE). Did a girl like her once live here?

A modern digital recreation of one of the rooms of the West House: note the fresco of the young girl to the left of the door, and the ship frieze above it.

An early epic? A Late Bronze Age fleet of warships sets sail – a precursor, perhaps, to the thousand ships setting off to Troy?

The Greek ships arrive home (an early Odyssey*?): note the distinctive features of the hills and city, which are identical to those of Akrotiri, Thera, where this painting was found – making it, potentially, the world's earliest map.*

This sixteenth–fifteenth century BCE ring may have an epic story to tell: a woman and man, his hand on her arm, prepare to board a ship, while a god hovers overhead. An early Helen and Paris, perhaps?

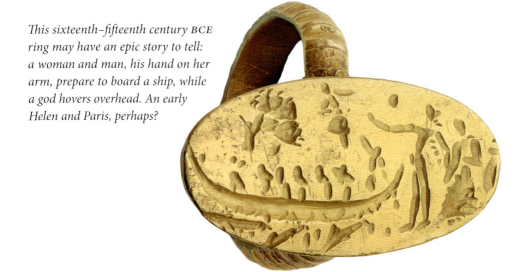

Ariadne's labyrinth: an early twentieth-century reimagining of the so-called Queen's Megaron in the Bronze Age palace at Knossos, Crete. Fantastical images like these helped to support Sir Arthur Evans' controversial 'reconstitution' of the ancient palace, and its women.

Fantasies of females: three heavily restored women from the palace at Knossos (sixteenth–fifteenth century BCE). The parts of the fresco that actually survived are visible as brownish fragments; the rest is a speculative early twentieth-century reconstruction.

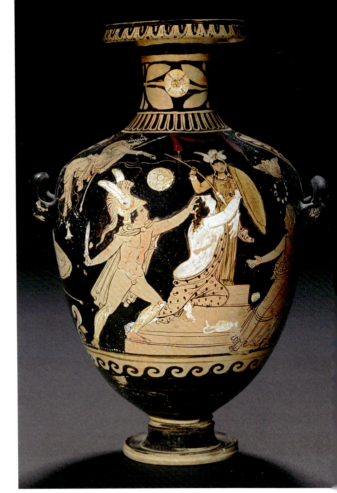

The rape of Cassandra, as she clings to the statue of Athena during the fall of Troy (from a later fourth-century BCE vase). This was the act of violence that precipitated Athena's wrath against the Greeks, and meant that many of them never reached their home.

Real-life Amazons: one of many real warrior women's skeletons from Scythia, buried here with a large dagger and two arrowheads. Long thought to be men, skeletons like this one are now being reassessed through ancient DNA.

past. But there's more to the story than the sweeping grand narrative of invasion, migration and social and cultural change – as interesting as all that is. Because the grave of this baby, in the corner of a house on a tree-shaded hill, was dug by someone. Someone dressed their newborn for the last time, wrapped the infant in a shroud and scattered him with earth; someone laid him in the ground, put flowers and wooden toys beside him perhaps, and sealed the place with stones. Burials tell us as much (if not more) about the living as they do the dead; and in the ancient world, the rites of lamentation and the preparation of the dead were the province of women above all. This was an infant who was hidden beneath the floor by someone – most likely a mother – who wanted to keep her baby with her in the house, to try to find some way to deal with her loss, to process her grief.

Birth would have been a terrifying and highly dangerous undertaking in the Bronze Age world – for mother and child alike. In one especially dismal prehistoric settlement in mainland Greece, over half of the hundred children buried there had died in the first month of their life.[6] Not far from the baby at Cydonia, another infant burial, this time of a premature foetus, thirty-seven weeks old, was discovered under the floor of a domestic area for the preparation of food.[7] Struggling through pregnancy and birth to give life to children who died was a woman's reality, until very recently – but I don't think that would have made it any less raw, any less searingly painful. To treat these burials like neat pin markers that allow us to map cultural change takes away the traumatic and heart-rending loss to a mother that each and every one represents. Scarring the red-brown earth across the Aegean world, the graves of the lost newborns and infants gouged out of the floors of family homes and stitched back up again each stand for their own pock-mark of terrible loss and longing – tucked up in baskets as if they were sleeping, wrapped in blankets as if their mothers longed to keep them warm, nestled with the toys they never used and the clay baby feeders they would never need again. What would it have been like to live with an infant who was of the world but not in it, under the paving slabs slapped by the soles of your children's feet, knowing every day that your baby boy was there? Would that have been a source of comfort – or an unrelenting, unforgettable pain?

A Grief She Can't Forget

The *Iliad*, Homer's so-called epic of war, is consumed by the gut-wrenching anguish of a mother learning to live with her grief for her son – and it is she, veiled and cloaked in black and 'the grief she can't forget' (as Homer puts it), who brings the poem to its close.[8] Just as Helen starts the Trojan War, and Briseis and Chryseis initiate the conflict of Homer's war epic, it is another powerful, and powerfully sidelined, woman – a mother – who stands behind every twist and turn in the Iliadic story, who propels and directs this supposed tale of heroes all the way from the opening book to the last; who realizes the desires of the epic's greatest warrior, and who is, in many dark and untapped ways, mightier than the king of the gods himself.

Her name is Thetis. And she is the mother of a boy: Achilles.

In the masculine, attention-grabbing melodrama that thrusts itself into the foreground of the Iliadic plot – the noisy wrangling of a king and a soldier over their wounded pride, the blood-spattered vaunting of warriors on the battlefield, the dauntless heroes who lust to burnish their glory and the seething forces of vengeance and honour that take them down – it has been all too easy to forget the shadowy, slick figure of Thetis who slips in and out of the poem from the salt depths that are her home. Thetis is a sea nymph: daughter of the old sea god Nereus, who dwells surrounded by corals and weeds at the dark bed of the ocean. In Homer, we hear her backstory, purportedly in her own words. She remembers how Zeus 'forced' her into being raped by a mortal man, Peleus, 'even though it was entirely against my will' (Thetis is careful to make the lack of consent unequivocally clear); she then gave birth to his son, Achilles.[9] As to why Zeus coerced her into being raped by a mortal, Homer doesn't say; but we know what's going on behind the myth from later versions of the story. The legend goes that Thetis was initially hotly pursued by both Zeus (king of the gods) and Poseidon (god of the sea). But when a prophecy was made that Thetis would bear a son greater than his father, both retreated, and Zeus compelled her to wed a mortal man, Peleus, instead: a neat way to neutralize the threat to the supremacy of the king of the gods.[10] Thetis fought back against the man she'd never asked for, transforming into, among other things, fire, a bird and a vicious-toothed lion in an effort to escape. But in the end Peleus (with the help of a male god) bound her tightly with a rope while she slept – and so raped her.[11] Which is how Achilles came to be born.

Thetis' subjugation and victimization makes for a troubling backdrop to the legend of Achilles, the greatest warrior the world has ever seen: because the excellence of the hero comes, quite literally in the myth, from the oppression of a woman. (We've seen this elsewhere in the *Iliad*, too, with Briseis and Chryseis, whose enslavement and conversion into trophies of honour is precisely what gives heroes their status.) Yet there's also an intriguing layer to the myth that firmly roots Thetis' power – even her power over Zeus – in her identity as a mother: her ability to give birth to a conqueror. Because of Zeus' dictate that diverts her disruptive reproductive potential away from the gods, her son is not born a deity, however, but a supremely gifted mortal. And so Thetis is in a strange and precarious position as the drama of the *Iliad* begins: because she is not only a terrible goddess whose unrivalled status as the mother of a conqueror has threatened the domain of even the strongest of gods, but also a helpless victim and a grief-stricken mother, who wants nothing more than to shield her mortal son from death, and knows that she cannot.

From its opening lines, the *Iliad* is articulated by Thetis' desperate attempts as a mother to safeguard her son and to come to terms with the awful knowledge that she has given birth to a man who will die: a paradox, born of the chasm between immortal mother and mortal son, the gaping divide between a mother's drive to protect and a hero's need to succeed, which leads to a paralysing and inconsolable grief for her son even while he's still alive. In the *Iliad*'s first book, as Achilles howls with rage on the Trojan shore after Agamemnon has seized Briseis, he cries for his mother. Thetis rises, wrapped in mist, from the grey brine, and asks, with barely concealed bitterness: 'Why did I go through such a terrible birth? Why did I mother you?'[12] Thetis' evocation of motherhood is deeply felt, personal and visceral, her words punctuating the epic with the physicality of the memory of her son's birth. Later in the poem, in Book 18, at the fatal point at which Achilles decides to go back to war – knowing that he will die – she digs deep to invent a new word that had never existed before in Greek (and would never be used again), to try to describe her experience of being, and becoming, a mother to Achilles. She is, she says, *dusaristotokeia*: 'the worst-and-best-child-birther'.[13] It's an astonishing term, one that embodies the mixed terror and joy of motherhood, and captures the paradox that it is Achilles' status as 'best' (*aristos*) of the Greeks that will realize her own 'worst' fears. She remembers how, after giving birth in the expansive chambers of Peleus' halls, she brought Achilles up, how she tended him carefully, like a tree, and he 'shot up like a sapling'.[14] Yet every cherished memory is shadowed by the knowledge that her son's life will be cut short – not only because he is subject to the mortal condition, as the offspring of a human father, but also because, at this very moment in the epic, he has chosen his destiny, by finally going back into battle after the death of his partner Patroclus, and taking part in the Trojan War. It was Thetis, after all, with his mortality forever at the front of her mind, who had made him the prophecy that he could choose between two fates: glory in battle and a short life, or a long life in anonymity at home.[15] Achilles' decision to fight – his resolve, at the poem's climax, to return to the front line of battle – seals for her the certainty that his death is coming soon.

And yet, in spite of her impotence in the face of fate and her son's inevitable death, with a forcefulness and fierceness that recalls Hecuba's determined solicitation of the gods on Hector's behalf, she does everything she can both to nurture and protect him and to further his cause. When an incensed Achilles demands reparation for the insult to his honour by Agamemnon's theft of Briseis, Thetis dashes to Zeus to ask him to bring Achilles glory, by granting victory to the Trojans and slaughtering the Greeks under Agamemnon's command until the king realizes his mistake and begs Achilles to return.[16] Zeus – reminded of how she once single-handedly saved him from an uprising of the gods (another clue, if we needed one, that this is truly a powerful goddess), and mindful too, no doubt, of the favour she did by not bearing him a son who would overthrow him – accedes to Thetis' plea.[17] And so Thetis' request is what sets the course for the entire epic.[18] The early acts of the *Iliad* are governed by Zeus' ruling, derived direct from 'the plans of Thetis', that the Trojans should win until Agamemnon has no choice but to recall Achilles.[19] It is not until Achilles determines to return to

war after the death of Patroclus (who went into battle to aid the ailing
Greeks, and was slain at the walls of Troy by Hector) that the king of
the gods rescinds his Trojan favour. Even then, when Achilles is set on
duelling with Hector, and Thetis is cut through with grief at the inevitable untimely death she knows will follow, Achilles' mother still
continues to protect her son: darting up to Olympus like a falcon, she
asks the blacksmith god Hephaestus to craft divine armour for Achilles,
a magical marvel wrought in bronze and silver and gold that launches
Achilles back into battle like an incandescent flame.[20] And when we see
her last, in the *Iliad*'s final book as Achilles' destiny unravels towards
its predicted end – Hector's lifeless corpse, unburied and sullied by the
dust, at his feet, his own death waiting in the wings – it is Thetis who
is charged with the all-important task of ordering her son to desist
from his enraged abuse of Hector's corpse. Achilles, blinded by grief,
has been engaged in the ultimate savagery in the honour-driven world
of Homeric heroes, refusing to bury his enemy and instead dragging
the body behind his chariot around Patroclus' tomb, in a twisted vigil
of near-sociopathic grief. Thetis' message – direct from Zeus – is that
Achilles must, by order of the gods, stop this act of impiety: he must
ransom Hector's body to his father, King Priam, thereby sparking the
final act of reconciliation (and burial) that will bring the poem to its
close. Thetis appears to Achilles dressed in black, as if her son is already
dead and gone. And yet, a mother still, she strokes his hand, reminds
him – even as she instructs him to return Hector's corpse – not to give
in to his own obsessive grief, to enjoy the physical pleasures of a mortal
life – food, sleep and sex. For, she says, 'death stands already close at
your side, and overwhelming fate'.[21]

It's often been said (and written) that the *Iliad* is the story of Achilles'
glory. And that's what the *Iliad* itself broadcasts: epic poetry is labelled in
Homer as 'the tales of the glory of men', while *kleos* (the word for 'glory'
in Greek) can also mean 'poetry', the oral epic that preserves a hero's
renown.[22] But flip it on its head, and it's also the tale of Thetis' unforgettable grief.[23] It begins with the story of a victim who was forced to
become a mother, pushing to bend the rules of the world to her will and
demand everything she feels her child deserves. It centres on a mother
who will do anything to protect her son, even when she knows she is

powerless to change what will happen. And it ends with a mother who has gradually, excruciatingly, come to terms with the naked concrete fact that her child's life is going to be cut short, that she will have to watch it happen, and find some way to keep on living anyway.[24]

But Thetis is not the only immortal mother in Homer to feel the acute, keening loss of a human son. In fact, it's Hera (herself a mother) who reminds Zeus – tempted to snatch one of his own sons, the Trojan ally Sarpedon, from the war as he faces up to meeting his doom – that it is not within the rights of the gods to intervene in the deaths of heroes.[25] Yet, while Zeus might be able to restrain himself, goddess mothers throughout the *Iliad* won't be stopped from protecting their mortal progeny. Thetis throws herself at Zeus' knees to bring Achilles glory, and sends her son into battle shielded by the divine armour she has brought him from Olympus; similarly, Aphrodite envelops her son Aeneas in her arms on the battlefield to protect him from slaughter (pierced by Diomedes' spear, she ends up wounded and bleeding ichor, the divine version of blood).[26] Perhaps the difference between Zeus in his detached composure and Aphrodite and Thetis, with their compulsive intervention on their sons' behalf, is precisely the physicality of motherhood inscribed into their bodies. Just as the immortal equivalent of blood spills from Aphrodite on to the Trojan plain, so even the goddesses on the dizzying heights of Olympus experience the full, raw reality of childbirth.[27] In a hymn attributed to Homer that gives a visceral account of the god Apollo's birth, his goddess mother Leto falls to her knees and clutches at the trunk of a date palm as the contractions of labour grip her body.[28] And in the *Iliad* – remarkably, stunningly, in the midst of a gory battle scene on the Trojan plain – the poet pauses to compare the Greek king Agamemnon's hot dripping wound, ripped open at spearpoint in the manly realm of mortal combat, to the deadly pain wrought on women in childbirth by the goddess who controls the contractions, Eileithyia, whose 'piercing, cruel arrow strikes a woman in the agony of labour, shot by the goddesses of labour pangs'.[29] If men's deadliest enemy is war, in other words, then the killer of women is childbirth. And the only remedy – just as when Hector was defeated in battle and retreated back to his mother's world – is for women to pray to the gods.

Birth Cave

Like Homer's other goddesses – like Hera, for instance, whom we found on the Linear B tablets – the birth goddess Eileithyia, too, had a well-documented history as a deity who was worshipped and called upon by women in the Bronze Age. And it's here – in a dank, dripping cave in the middle of Crete where Eileithyia's worshippers once gathered – that we can start to understand why Homer is able to compare a man's battle wound to a woman's contractions in labour, why Thetis' remembrance of giving birth to Achilles is so scarringly vivid, and why a woman's experience of motherhood can underpin the story of the *Iliad* so compellingly. It is here, in a Cretan cave, that myth, poetry and history come together, to point to the real measures that women took to help them with childbirth – the beginning of the long and perilous journey of pregnancy, labour and motherhood that has defined the lives (and deaths) of so many women throughout history.

In Book 19 of the *Odyssey*, Odysseus – already arrived back on Ithaca, disguised as an old beggar and in private audience with Penelope – is spinning one of his many intricate yarns for his wife. Assuming the mask of a Cretan prince (so as not to give his identity away: he is, after all, we are told, a master of disguise, though the jury is out as to whether or not Penelope may have already recognized him), he describes his fake 'homeland' of Crete with a rush of lyricism: it is a lush and fertile island, he says, crowned by Knossos, ruled by the legendary King Minos. Odysseus' ship, so he claims, was blown off course to Crete on its way back from Troy, and dropped anchor at the Knossian harbour Amnisos, 'beside the cave of Eileithyia'.[30] What's fascinating about this story (apart from showing how important Crete was in Homer's world view) is the throwaway comment, neatly tucked into Odysseus' fabricated story, about a cave dedicated to the ancient goddess of birth: because a Linear B tablet unearthed at the palace at Knossos, which we can now read thanks to Michael Ventris's decipherment, appears to back up Homer's knowledge of ancient Crete – specifically listing Eileithyia's name (*e-re-u-ti-ja*, in Linear B) alongside the place name, Amnisos.[31] (Interestingly, it was this word, 'Amnisos', or *a-mi-ni-so*, that actually provided one of the keys to Ventris's decoding of Linear B.)³² The legend went, in later times, that this mystical cave at Knossos' old harbour was Eileithyia's birthplace: certainly Crete seems to have been a central focus of her cult worship (the fact that it makes its way into the *Odyssey* testifies to that), and it may be that she originated as a prehistoric Cretan goddess who was later promoted to chief birth goddess in the Greek pantheon.³³

In the late nineteenth century, a Cretan local from Heraklion by the name of Christoforos Anerrapsis came across Eileithyia's ancient cave, not far from Knossos under an escarpment of rock crouching above a river that winds lazily down to the sea. The shadowed hollow, accessed behind a fig tree, oozes in the darkness with grey mineral water that has left behind weird stalagmites in haunting formations: above all, a pile of rock that resembles a sinuous female figure cloaked in stone, an odd hunched boulder at her feet that might recall a child.³⁴ Her outline would have shone grey-white in the gloom, smoothed and polished by the touch of the hands of the countless women worshippers who ducked through the cave mouth to lay offerings at the altar beneath her feet, and prayed, hands outstretched in the womb-like dark, for the safe delivery of their child. When I visited the cave myself to investigate this aeons-old landmark and pay my respects to the ancient birth goddess, as both a historian and a mother, it wasn't hard to imagine how such a place – murky and silent, inhabited by these otherworldly dripping silhouettes – could have been conceived of as holy.

The mounds of broken offerings left in this deserted hollow speak to the power that goddesses like Eileithyia, with the lure of a safe and speedy childbirth, could hold over the women who worshipped her: and the all-too-real fear that gripped them. On the wind-whipped peak of one particular mountain, Petsophas, on the north-east coast of Crete, women would gather in crowds as night drew in to light a bonfire – like a beacon, sparking above the steely waves below. Here, along with the bloody sacrifice of animals, they would toss fist-sized clay figurines into the ravenous flames: miniature pregnant women pinched out of reddish earth, their bellies swelling and vulvas dilated as they squat, legs spread, over birthing stools; beside them, thumb-shaped incised balls of clay, minuscule newborns swaddled in cloth. (These are the predecessors of commonly found Mycenaean figurines that show women

nursing infant children, known as *kourotrophoi* – 'child-nourishers'.)
Accompanying these literal, three-dimensional prayers for a successful
birth were other votive depictions of animals, and they seem at first to
be an odd choice: weasels, tortoises and puppies. However, it's recently
been shown – by delving into later classical medical texts as well as the
evidence for midwifery practices across the ancient world, from Egypt
to Mesopotamia – that these particular animals were the source of drugs
that would have made up a fundamental part of a midwife's toolkit.[35]
Weasels, the Roman historian Pliny the Elder tells us, were an essential
repository (in the form of a liquid secreted by their uterus) of an oxyto-
cic drug – one that induces or strengthens uterine contractions, and so,
crucially, by ensuring a stable delivery and assisting with the expulsion
of the afterbirth, dramatically reduces the risk of postpartum haemor-
rhage.[36] Tortoise meat was similarly used, from Egypt to Babylon, to
induce labour, as were the milk of bitches and their placentas. All would
have been administered by local wise women and midwives to heavily pregnant mothers-to-be, desperately gulped down in the hope that
contractions would be quick and strong. The gaping chasm of anxiety
that lies behind these collected mountain-peak votives is clear: a plea
to the gods born of the terror of obstructed labour, the birth pangs of
Eileithyia that left a woman labouring for days or that ended in unstop-
pable bleeding, one of the major causes of both maternal and foetal
death.[37]

New data from the bones of females who died in Bronze Age Crete
gives us a picture of the bleak reality faced by such women. Long-term
analysis of multiple burials across sixteen different Cretan sites, undertaken by Photini McGeorge – the anthropological expert who was
charged with examining and identifying the bones of the baby buried at
Cydonia – shows that peak mortality for women was in their most fertile
years, between the ages of twenty and twenty-five: concrete evidence, in
other words, that the fears of the women at Petsophas were correct, that
becoming a mother was likely to be the main reason a woman died in the
Bronze Age Aegean. (Men, by contrast, had an average life expectancy
of around thirty-five.)[38] In a particularly harrowing grave – also found at
Cydonia, in a collection of tombs discovered in 1987 outside the Bronze
Age settlement – the bones of a teenage mother-to-be were discovered

with a foetus still in her womb.[39] Dead pregnant women, their bones
mixed heartbreakingly with those of their infants who never survived,
litter the mortuary record of the Bronze Age Aegean world, the forgotten
victims of the most virulent killer of over half the ancient population –
from the Late Minoan burials at Cydonia on Crete to Mycenaean
cemeteries on the mainland.

Just as with the Cydonia baby, it's hard to come in like a coroner
and determine the exact cause of death over three thousand years after
the event and in the absence of any written accounts. (And archaeologists in the past rarely bothered with mothers and babies, anyway.)
But clues from the bioarchaeological record (the skeletal markers of
diet and disease that are written into our bones and teeth) give some
indication of the cycles of chronic malnutrition, juvenile conception,
and complications in gestation and childbirth that would have led to
the failed pregnancies of so many women and – ultimately and all too
often – their deaths. A recent study of the skeletons of Mycenaean
women and men buried at Pylos, on the Greek mainland, provides
striking evidence that women (in particular, lower-status women) did
not have as much access to meat in their diet as men.[40] By examining
the traces of stable isotopes (particularly carbon and nitrogen) that had
built up in these ancient Mycenaean bones from foods consumed in the
last ten years before death, the researchers were able to show that men at
Pylos ate significantly more animal protein than the women – a finding that accords with both the archaeological evidence from Linear B
tablets, which indicates that men would have been the sponsors and
beneficiaries of lavish, state-held, meat-based sacrifices and feasts at the
nearby Mycenaean palace, and the testimony of Homer, where meat-
rich barbecue feasts are a key male-bonding activity between heroes.[41]
And this wasn't just the case among the elite: the Linear B tablets reveal
a gender difference in diet at the lower end of the social scale, too.
Analysis has brought to light that enslaved men at the palace (among
the worker groups, like the Chian women we saw at Pylos in Chapter 2)
received two and a half times the food ration of females.[42] This systematic, socially structured deficiency in female diet can be shown to have
created poorer health outcomes among women across the board – in
particular, a much higher incidence of dental decay, abscesses and tooth

loss in comparison to men, indicating a significant disease burden on the female population of Pylos.[43]

The chronic poverty of women's diet compared to men's isn't just a feature at Pylos, however; it's found across the Bronze Age Aegean world.[44] It is evidenced, not just in the make-up of women's bones, but in the malformation (or hypoplasia, comparative to men) of the enamel on their teeth, indicating that disease and malnutrition were present early on in youth, when the enamel was first laid down. Perhaps most tragically of all, it can be traced in the development of the pelvis: if a female's diet is insufficient in early childhood, the birth canal flattens, leading to a much more difficult labour later in life.[45] The higher a female's pelvic ratio index (a measure of pelvic capacity), the more open her birth canal. Modern American women display an average index of 91.6; women in one particularly dire worst-case-scenario Bronze Age Greek cemetery, on the other hand, showed a remarkably lowered ratio of 73.4.[46] These numbers, as dry as they might look on paper, bear witness to the hideous downward spiral that drove many ancient women's lives (and deaths). Chronically malnourished as they grew up in comparison to their male peers, they were weakened by diseases of nutritional deficiency, such as anaemia and osteoporosis – brought on by lack of vitamins and minerals in their diet – and were more vulnerable to attacks by pathogens throughout their lives.[47] When they became pregnant as undernourished teenagers (like the mother buried at Cydonia; it's been shown, in one sample, that first pregnancies occurred on average at the age of nineteen, below the threshold of the biologically optimal childbearing age of twenty to twenty-four), their chronic malnutrition and disease history paved the way for complications during gestation.[48] And then, as they approached the final hurdle of labour, drained and exhausted, the flattening of their pelvis and narrowed birth canal (itself a product of years of malnutrition) placed both mother and child in mortal danger at the harrowing moment of birth – as the infant tried to push its way through ill-adapted bones, as the woman attempted to draw on a body maimed and depleted by a lifelong lack of sustenance.

So it's striking that the *Iliad* compares the gut-wrenching throes of labour to a deadly bleeding battle wound, that it sets the silent killer of women alongside the loudly glorified slaughter of men. It's striking that the *Odyssey* describes Eileithyia's dank birth cave as one of the defining features of the Cretan landscape. It's an evocative hint that – even within the hyper-masculine world represented in Homer's epics, with its self-avowed concerns with glory-seeking war and the military hero – the trauma of birth, the mothers and wives and daughters who were taken to the Underworld through the mortal toll of pregnancy and its end, was a dark shadow that flitted through everyone's lives, and made itself known to all.

No wonder, then, that Thetis calls her birth 'terrifying'. No wonder that she has to summon new words (*dusaristotokeia*), like ghosts, to describe it – as both the most important, and the most shudderingly traumatic, experience of a woman's life in the ancient world.

The Lost Babies

But childbirth did not mark the end of this long and dangerous road. There was also the awful possibility that, after months of problematic gestation, poor nutrition and infection, the infant wouldn't make it beyond the first few hours or days of life, while the mother survived. The impact of this loss would not only have been felt in the burden of grief on the barely recovering mother. It also meant that, without a new-born to nurse, she was left without the contraceptive protection that breastfeeding provides.[49] Unable to recoup her strength and without any kind of prophylactic defence, she was likely to fall pregnant again before she had fully healed – meaning that her next embryo would be drawing on an even more depleted body, had an even lower chance of coming to term or surviving its early weeks – and so the damaging cycle went on. This kind of appalling catch-22, of maternal exhaustion and infant mortality, seems to be recorded in one of the most gruesome groups of burials on the Greek mainland, at a Bronze Age (pre-Mycenaean) settlement called Asine, not far from ancient Argos. Here – just like the baby at Cydonia – the tiny bones of foetuses, infants and children have been found carefully placed beneath the floors of houses in the lower town, nestled together beneath the walls of the buildings. Of the 103 children recovered from the site, 60 per cent had died in the first month of their life – an exceptionally high mortality rate that points to the worst-possible scenario for a woman of multiple failed pregnancies and deliveries.[50]

Other sites give a less dramatic, but equally bleak, record: at nearby Lerna, just round the bay from Asine, the number of children dying in the first month drops to 25 per cent – yet it's still the case that nearly half of the entire population died within their first five years of life.[51] Back on Crete, among the burials at Cydonia that include the teenager and her foetus, almost half of the graves belong to children, many of them younger than five years of age.[52] And at the Late Bronze Age cemetery at Armenoi, not far from Cydonia, nearly a quarter of the children buried there had died at or not long after birth, and over half before they were five.[53] Their bones showed traces of infectious diseases – deadly pathogens that entered through the mother's bloodstream during pregnancy or were ingested or introduced by infection after birth, attacking a young child's brain, heart, bones and other vital organs.[54] It's possible – tragically – that it was forced early weaning among mothers (who, most likely, weren't able to produce sufficient milk due to their own systemic malnourishment) that deprived young children of the essential protective antibodies contained in breastmilk, making them more susceptible to disease.[55] At Asine and Lerna, for example, children seem to have been given milk alternatives as early as three months of age, and were no longer nursing at all by four to six months. This is exceptionally early (compared to current World Health Organization guidelines, where breastfeeding is now recommended for at least two years), especially since the evidence of malnourishment from the enamel formation on the teeth in these infant burials suggests they weren't getting adequate nutrition elsewhere.[56] The likelihood is that their mothers simply didn't have any other option. And we have an idea of the kind of diet these young children were being given: new techniques of residue analysis, which enable researchers to identify the biomolecular components of organic remains on ancient cookware, have revealed traces of honey, mixed with a potent cocktail of wine, barley beer and mead, on a child's clay feeder bottle from Midea, buried in the foothills above the graveyards of Lerna and Asine.[57] It's probable that this heady combination of honey and fermented products was administered as a combination of nourishment and sense-numbing drug during the final days of a child's life – a mother's last attempt to provide some small comfort to a daughter or son floundering in the grip of a fatal illness.

These kinds of infant feeders – miniature terracotta jars with little spouts, the ancient version of today's toddler trainer cups – are found carefully buried with children across the Bronze Age Aegean world, alongside animal playthings and even what appear to be little pull-along toys on wheels. One infant grave – discovered, like the Cydonia baby, tucked under the floor of a Late Bronze Age house-cum-pottery workshop just outside the citadel at Mycenae on the Greek mainland – is exceptionally richly endowed. Three vases and a stunning necklace of gold, precious lapis lazuli and blue glass beads were found, laid beside two tiny fragments of human bone – so small, they suggest that this infant was probably preterm; yet the parents chose nevertheless to honour their baby with costly gifts and keep them close by, beneath the floor of the living room. One of the vases, in particular, was a specially made, bespoke sippy cup, with a built-in lid and strainer mouthpiece, little holes perforated in the clay to allow a

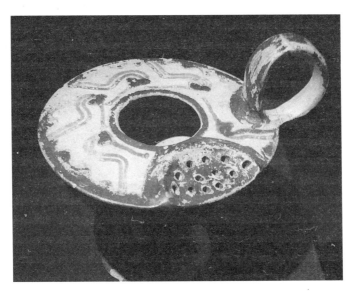

A sippy cup made by Bronze Age parents for a child who would never use it (Mycenae, 14th century BCE).

child to drink more easily, and decorated around the outside with an attractive winding pattern of ivy. This seems to have been a beautifully crafted custom piece produced specifically by the family of potters who lived and worked at the house, and who laid their lost baby to rest beneath the floor: a heartfelt gift for a member of the family whom they knew would never fulfil their destiny to become a worker of clay among them.[58]

The remains of children hidden beneath the floors of houses across the Bronze Age Aegean world, from Cydonia to Mycenae, bear witness to an unspeakable sense of loss that must have haunted their families in a way we can barely begin to imagine. It is almost always newborns, infants and young children who are buried in this way, under the floor of the family home – suggesting that there was a particular bereavement, a need to come to terms with a life cut short, a deep-seated craving for togetherness, after the death of a child (even if, or perhaps because, it happened so often). A couple of Late Bronze Age clay coffins, painted with scenes of mourning in sketchy red-and-black silhouettes and excavated in the late twentieth century at Tanagra near mainland Thebes, provide a startling, and deeply moving, window on to the emotional last moments of laying a departed Mycenaean child to rest. On one of them, outlined in abstract orange-red, two women bend over a dead girl to prepare her for burial, clothing her carefully in all her finery and laying her out on a funerary bed of criss-crossed reeds; beside the bier, two female mourners tear their hair in grief, mouths almost gruesomely distorted in their stark despair at the little girl's loss. On another of the coffins, two women – their eyes slanted in pain – lower a child, now nothing more than a mute shape wrapped in a tiny shroud, into its final resting place. Occasionally, in the archaeology of some actual burials, we are just able to trace the impression of such cloths, now long disintegrated, that were once wound round the tiny bodies laid in their graves. The evocative painted outline of the little bundle, and the way the women's hands linger around it – longing not to let it go – is moving beyond words: a testament to the very real loss that inscribed itself into these women's lives, and that, like the imprint of a shroud, left its indelible mark.

What the vignettes sketched on the Tanagran coffins make clear, above all, is that – just like the perilous journey of birth – the voyage towards death was, by and large, a woman's world.[59] Just as women were charged with bringing children into existence, so it was up to women to mourn their loss, to lament them and to prepare their bodies for burial. This woman's world of visceral public grief, an outpouring of loss at a young life cut short, is echoed in the *Iliad*: when Hector's body is at last brought back to Troy, it is his mother, Hecuba, along with his wife Andromache and sister-in-law Helen, who raise their voices in a stirring, emotion-laced lament for him. And it is *their* resonant voices – a desolate mother howling at the death of her son, a wife desperately grieving her husband and the father of her child, an outcast bemoaning the loss of her protector – not, as is so often thought, the voices of men, that see Hector to his grave and bring the epic of war to a close.[60] And yet, as compelling as Homer's portrayal is, the archaeological evidence – from the mud figures tossed into fires on mountain peaks, to the teenage mothers buried curled up with their unborn infants, to the graves of children kept under domestic

Burial and lament were a woman's world in the Late Bronze Age and Homer. Here, four women bury and tear their hair for a lost child: on a young girl's coffin from Tanagra in Greece (14th century BCE).

floors – reveals the grim irony that, in reality, mothers and their babies were far more likely to die of natural causes in pregnancy and birth than as victims of armed conflict.[61]

Unless, of course, your child went on to fight in the Trojan War. Unless your child became Achilles.

A Life Cut Short

All of which brings us back to Thetis. Because her role in the *Iliad* has always been seen – in the way that women have always been read, in history as well as literature, for millennia – as important only insofar as it tells us about, and furthers the narrative of, the man Achilles. Her supplication of Zeus is significant, we are told, only because it increases Achilles' glory. Her prophecy about her son's twin fates is pivotal only because of the choice that Achilles will make to go back to war. Her dread that his life will be cut short is an epic theme that fleshes out the vulnerability and pathos of the male mortal hero – and so on.

But the clues that we can dredge up from the ancient bones of women and children from the Late Bronze Age world, the flashes of terror we can see in the dripping shadows of an eerie birth cave on Crete and the weird distorted figures tossed into a glowing fire on a mountain peak, tell a vibrantly different story. Thetis' need to protect her son from death would have been something that many ancient mothers could identify with. This was a dark and dangerous world, as we have seen, where to be a mother, more often than not, was to struggle through the deadly hazards of pregnancy and labour only to grieve for a life cut short – a world strewn with the macabre skeletons of infants who died before their parents and were buried beneath the homes they lived in, whose lifespan could be measured in days and weeks, not years. The story of Thetis' grief, traced throughout the *Iliad*, is at its core the harrowing tale of a mother coming to terms with her child's foreshortened life. Achilles' 'fate runs faster after him than any mortal's', she wails to Zeus, when she makes the plan that starts everything off; she only 'birthed him for so short a life', and knows it is his 'destiny to live so very short a time, not long at all'.[62] The danger to Thetis of giving birth to Achilles – the sharp birth pangs that Homer says are just as deadly as the dripping wounds of war – are part and parcel of her child's short life: the very same treacherous journey, through delivering a baby to watching them die, that would have scarred so many mothers' lives.

Yet this shared reality of a woman's life is also magnified – in the way that myth often does – by being translated into the realm of the divine. Shifting the experience of losing a child on to an immortal goddess forced to bear a mortal son throws the tragedy of loss into sharp relief. No mother will find the untimely death of a child more unimaginable, more devastatingly unthinkable, than an immortal deity who almost gave birth to a deathless god. It's perhaps for this reason that a cluster of myths sprang up around Thetis that depicted her desperately trying to reverse the mortality of her son. Early, rather more gruesome versions, possibly contemporary with Homer, show Thetis tossing her children into a cauldron of boiling water to test whether they were mortal; this becomes, in later authors, a maternal trial-by-fire designed to make Achilles deathless (Peleus screams when he sees Thetis holding the baby in the raging flames; she drops the infant on to the floor and vanishes into the depths of the sea).[63]

The most famous rendition, however, is the myth of Thetis descending to the Underworld and dipping her son by his ankle into the oozing black waters of the Styx – as if reabsorbing him into her birth waters – in an attempt to protect him with a veneer of immortality.[64] Achilles' ankle, untouched by the divine panacea, thus remained his weakest spot, and this – so the story goes – was where Paris' arrow struck and at last brought his death, at his 'Achilles heel': the medical name later given (by classically versed anatomists) to the tendon at the back of the heel, and a phrase we still use today to describe a fatal vulnerability or flaw. First appearing over eight hundred years after Homer in a half-completed epic from the Roman Empire and a popular subject in Roman art, the scene went on to become particularly fashionable in Roman-influenced Renaissance and neoclassical art. The Flemish painter Peter Paul Rubens painted an oil landscape in the 1630s in which a flushed Thetis leans to douse Achilles in the swirling Styx, the Underworld with its unhappy souls waiting to cross the river of death looming moodily in the background. Meanwhile, a marble sculpture by the British sculptor Thomas

Thetis dips the infant Achilles in the River Styx in an attempt to make him immortal (c.1st century BCE).

Banks (now at the Victoria and Albert Museum in London), commissioned for a Colonel Thomas Johnes in 1789, bizarrely transplants the faces of Johnes' wife and his beloved infant daughter Mariamne on to the figures of Thetis and Achilles – creating a personalized modern version of this age-old myth for an eighteenth-century Welsh M.P.[65] Perhaps Johnes had hoped that invoking the ancient story, by commissioning this statue to sit in his family home in Wales, would act as some kind of amulet to protect his young daughter. If so, he was wrong: tragically, just like Achilles, she predeceased her father and left him heartbroken when she died at the age of twenty-seven.

If later male poets and artists were obsessed with Thetis' quest to make Achilles invulnerable, however, the *Iliad* is conspicuous for its refusal to give Thetis any recourse to protect her son from his mortal fate. In Homer, crucially, there is no cauldron-boiling, no fire-scalding, no Styx-dipping; from the beginning of the *Iliad*, from the very first pronouncement that she 'birthed him for so short a life', the immortal goddess has to learn the hardest lesson a mother can – that she cannot save her son from dying. Achilles has a mortal body, he bleeds like any other hero. As one Trojan acerbically comments, after Achilles has been wounded on the arm and black blood spurts on to the ground, 'the man has flesh that can be pierced by bronze. He only has one life and he is mortal.'[66] When Thetis asks Hephaestus in the *Iliad* to make immortal armour to shield her son, it is in the full knowledge that it will not stop his death – only delay it a little longer. One of the most recent (and most compelling) reworkings of the legend of Thetis and Achilles, Madeline Miller's *The Song of Achilles* (2011), noticeably follows Homer's lead to puncture the myth of Achilles' invulnerability. As Paris stands on the Trojan ramparts, nocking his arrow to point at an Achilles who cannot be protected by his goddess mother, he asks the god Apollo: 'Where do I aim? I heard he was invulnerable.' And Apollo drily replies: 'He is a man. Not a god. Shoot him and he will die.'[67]

In the end, Thetis, goddess as she is, is just like any other mother. She has experienced the physical journey of birth. She has nurtured and nourished her child. She has tried to protect him from the fate that would take most children, and herself from the grief that consumed most mothers – and then come to face the fact that all her fears are coming true. Her process of reconciling herself to the devastating, haunting grief of a mother who sees her child's life cut short – drawing on the real lived experiences of the women who prayed in caves and buried their dead babies across the Bronze Age Aegean, who, though not immortal, were still left behind to grieve for the children they had lost – lies at the very core of the *Iliad*'s tragic narrative; just as much as the glory of a man.

But not all women were forced to watch their sons die from the sidelines of the battlefield. There were some women in the ancient world who were able to fight in war alongside men – and some who were even among the most famous warriors of them all.

It's time to meet the Amazons.

9

PENTHESILEA

Warrior

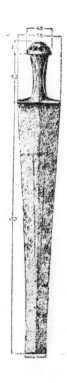

She rides into Troy past the ashes of Hector's pyre, sword at her belt rattling against her bronze greaves as the horse sways, and all she thinks as the raw, bone-dry smoke hits the back of her throat is: there is a warrior who failed. There is a warrior who ran too slow.

Her vision has always been white-sharp as the point of her battle axe. But when you have seen as many skulls shattered to splinters, as many brains pooling like spring floods on the marsh plain, then it makes itself clear. To kill or be killed. To fill the groove of your sword blade and paint with another's fluorescent blood, or to spill your guts for the dogs and birds. That is what it is to be a warrior. That is what she has come to do.

The walls of Troy rise pale around her, barely registered in her falcon gaze. What she sees are the tips of the Trojans' spears gleaming like a wolf's obsidian eyes. What she hears are her Amazons' hoofbeats drumming like arrowheads on the hollows of her eye sockets. What she smells is sweat and blood and smoke and death: some of it already done, and some of it to come. Some of it hers.

And her muscles flex like ropes, taut as a bowstring. Imprinted on each, one old and long-learned impulse, taught as she played in the grass like a lion cub around her mother's blood-smeared spear.

To kill.

Skin and Bone

December 1927, near Tbilisi, Georgia, cold enough to turn the knuckles white. Georgij Nioradze – air misting in front of him like a dying breath – is digging. He's been called here by farmers who have turned up human remains in their fields; they won't work any more with the pale bones scattered over the half-ploughed land, like a plain of the dead. Further along the slope of the hill, a grey building blots the washed-out sky: the Soviet Children's Labour Camp, a local *gulag*.[1] He can just make out the barbed wire that forms a jagged web between the watchtowers and the skeletons of trees. Behind, it is eerily quiet – no voices, no shouting, no life at all. He doesn't know what they do within those tomb-like walls. He doesn't want to know.

He carries on unearthing the grave beneath the field, losing himself in a time before history, when the atrocities of men were less thorough. And the dead start to emerge into the wintry daylight, their bones not far below the surface as he pulls them from the soil and dusts them off with his brush. A skull, split by a spear or pointed axe. An arm trapped under a bronze sword, bangles dangling around the emaciated bone. Skeletal fingers slung with loose rings. A line of blood-red carnelian beads. An iron dagger, and a spear point that lies across the jawbone and cenotaph-like teeth of a horse.[2] Everything Nioradze has been taught, all he has ever learned in his studies from Tbilisi to Moscow, Berlin to Hamburg, points to an ancient warrior burial: the gorgeous metal weapons, the traces of a battle blow to the skull, the horse interred beside the fighter-rider. And the curious mixture of bronze and iron weapons dates it to that turbulent time of transition, when the Bronze Age tumbled into the Age of Iron – around 1000 BCE.[3]

He sits back on his heels, thinking, fingering a fragment of pelvic bone, brittle as a dead leaf. This is, no doubt, an astonishing find. It will make his name back at Tbilisi: tangible evidence, held in his cold hands, of a flourishing prehistoric Georgian warrior-culture. The sword in particular is unique, a testament to local bronze-working with its engraved pattern of spirals tracing the channel of the blood groove down to the tip. The ornamentation reminds him of decorative patterns he has seen on pots recently uncovered at the site of Troy, far away along the coast of the Black Sea: the grandest of connections, to the legendary fighters of the Trojan War and Schliemann's golden haul, for this lonely discovery in a freezing Georgian field.[4]

But, as he holds the bone up to the grey sky, and feels the pockmarked surface rough under the skin of his thumb, there is just one thing that troubles him.

This warrior has the bones of a woman.

And Then the Amazon Came

This is the story of the discovery of the real Amazons. For hundreds of years, the Amazons – fierce women warriors who, so the ancient Greeks said, dwelt around the shores of the Black Sea, who fought on horse-back and were as skilled in battle as the most intrepid of heroes among men – had been assumed to be nothing but a myth: another invention of the fervid Greek imagination (just, so they said, like Troy). The Amazons certainly occupied the minds of ancient men, the stories they told, in a way unequalled by almost any other female figures in antiquity. Later commentators, from the travel writer Aristeas to the Greek historian Herodotus to the Roman geographer Strabo, placed them at the fringes of the Greek world, anywhere from Thrace to western Anatolia, to the southern or northern coasts of the Black Sea and the Sea of Azov, all the way to the Caucasus – covering a vast sweep of land that would become synonymous with the steppes of the Scythian nomads.[5] Amazons crop up in epics battling the Greek heroes whose names echo down the ages – Hercules, Theseus and Achilles. They make their way into the founding legends of ancient Athens, where (so the ancients believed) the graves of

Equals to men: breast-baring Amazons battle nude male Greeks on a temple relief from Bassae, Greece (5th century BCE).

the Amazons who rode from the east to burn down the Athenian Acropolis could still be seen. They are splashed across the headlines of ancient art, from the imposing sky-high marble sculptures of the Parthenon to the painted terracotta cookware of everyday life, coolly trampling nude male warriors with their horses and impaling them with their spears.

And they also write themselves into some of the oldest tales of Greek literature – including the poems of Homer. To Homer – who mentions the Amazons twice in the *Iliad*: they have a part to play in his legendary world, if only on the sidelines – the Amazons are described with a particularly resonant epithet, the Greek term *antianeirai*.[6] This is a fascinatingly complex word, a compound adjective in the feminine made up of two elements: the prefix *anti-* ('against', but also 'in comparison to') and *aneir-*, from *anēr*, the word for 'man' (which, incidentally, is the first word of the *Odyssey*, and defines the epic project as a tale of the 'deeds of men'). The Amazons, then, in the words of the *Iliad*, pose a unique, and challenging, gendered combination: they are 'women against men' – as warriors in combat, and as women who oppose the established (Greek) rules of male superiority. But they are also, at the same time, 'women comparable to men': women who are as outstanding as men and, extraordinarily, can be compared with them within the medium of epic, as fighters in their own right. Priam, king of Troy – who is the first to use the word in the *Iliad*, during a lesson from Helen on the names of the Greeks as they gaze down from the Trojan walls – reminisces to her how he once saw the *Amazones antianeirai* fighting on the Anatolian plains in his youth; later in the Trojan War, the same Amazons will be called in as a crack force to aid the cause of Troy against the Greeks.[7] In the Homeric world, Amazons are both adversaries and allies, both antagonists and heroes – albeit of a different kind.

But the Amazons have a much larger role to play in the Homeric story than a couple of throwaway comments suggest. To understand more about Homer's Amazons, I went to the British Library, just down the traffic-congested road from London's King's Cross station. The building might seem, at first glance, an unprepossessing portal into the past – all blocks of modern orange brick, square angles and glaring red gutters. But step inside and you're in a maze of history just waiting to transport you back in time. A tower of glass thrusts through the entrance showcasing thousands of ancient books, patinated red and muted brown, once collected by an eighteenth-century king. To one side, a velvet-dark gallery is filled with the library's greatest treasures – thick manuscripts, yellowed maps and handwritten notebooks, all of them landmarks in the history of words. An ornately illustrated medieval copy of the biblical gospels that survived a bloody Viking raid. A first edition of Shakespeare's plays, printed in 1623. A handwritten letter by the eighteenth-century intellectual and anti-slavery campaigner Charles Ignatius Sancho – first person of African descent to vote in a British election. Beatles lyrics worked out on scrap pieces of paper in scratchy, crossed-out ink.

It was another collection of words that brought me here, however – held, not in the Treasures gallery, but tucked away in the stacks and brought out for me to examine in the Manuscripts Reading Room, where readers confer in hushed voices over the rustle and flick of pages. Known as the Townley Homer (after its eighteenth-century owner, Charles Townley), it is at first sight a rather non-descript and bulky bound tome, with the faintly vanilla aroma of old book.[8] But what I was holding in my hands is actually an incredible antique: a manuscript that's nearly a thousand years old, and one of the most important surviving versions of Homer's *Iliad*. The yellowed parchment pages are criss-crossed in minuscule Greek script like cobwebs. At the centre of each page, in larger handwriting, is the text of the *Iliad*, laboriously copied out line by line by a scribe around 1059 CE (probably working in the cosmopolitan, Greek-speaking cultural capital of Constantinople). Surrounding it are tiny scribbles, known as 'scholia' (from Greek *scholion*, 'interpretation'), that record centuries of Homeric scholarship going all the way back to the venerable critics of the Library of Alexandria. These little notes helpfully offer synonyms for unfamiliar words; unpack obscure or ambiguous phrases; point to connections to other Homeric passages; recommend the removal of lines that (according to the ancient scholars) didn't belong to the 'original' Homeric text; or colourfully interpret literary undertones and themes. As I carefully turned the pages, the sheer volume of the centuries of Homeric learning presented here seemed to gleam under my fingertips like a veritable treasure trove of ideas.

But I was looking for a particular comment, on a particular line, at the very end of the *Iliad* – and so I began searching in the final book, at the doodled line that the scribe used to mark the opening of Book 24. I scanned over Thetis' visit to Achilles, veiled in black, with her final instructions to ransom Hector's corpse. I read again the night-time assignation as King Priam slips out of Troy, guided by the god Hermes, to enter Achilles' hut and force himself to make that most awful supplication – to kiss the hands of his son's killer – in a father's desperate plea to hold his son's body again. I saw Hector's body being returned to Troy: Cassandra shouting out when she sees her father and dead brother rattling towards the city on the cart, and the last laments by Hector's mother, sister-in-law and wife for the man they have lost. And then I reached the final, famous line: *hōs hoi g' amphiepon taphon Hektoros hippodamoio* – 'and so they held the funeral for horse-lord Hector'.[9]

But in this manuscript – in contrast to others, which are content to finish here – something different, and entirely unexpected, happens. The scholiast has scribbled in the margin, in fading age-spotted ink, an alternative ending: 'some people write: "and so they buried Hector. And then the Amazon came, daughter of brave Ares, slayer of men." '[10]

We have always known that the *Iliad* was not the end of the story. The poem only tells a small slice of the action (under two months) in the epic ten-year siege of Troy; it doesn't record the fall of the city when the Greeks penetrate the walls with the trick of the Wooden Horse, or even the death of Achilles, felled by an arrow to the heel. This last was left to the next instalment following on from the *Iliad* in the series of the Epic Cycle (the group of now-lost archaic narrative poems that told the story of the Trojan War): the *Aethiopis*, named after one of the epic's protagonists, an Ethiopian warrior called Memnon. If the *Iliad*'s job was to tell the story of Achilles' withdrawal from and return to the war, the *Aethiopis* took up the ensuing episode – the arrival of Troy's allies to bolster the Trojan side after the loss of Hector. These were the Ethiopians, led by Memnon, and the Amazons, led by their queen, who we know from later testimonies to the *Aethiopis* was called Penthesilea. A remarkable scene painted on a sixth-century BCE Greek vase, held at the British Museum, shows the legendary duel between Penthesilea and Achilles that was to come: Achilles driving his spear into Penthesilea's neck, her weapon held suspended, their eyes meeting at the moment of the death blow in a frisson of erotic, tragic power.

The narrative connection between the end of Homer's *Iliad* and the start of the *Aethiopis* is so tightly entwined that this particular scholiast, scrawling in the margins of the manuscript I was lucky enough to handle, suggests that one epic ran directly into the other: that the death of Hector in the *Iliad*, dispatched at the hands of Achilles, led immediately into the arrival of another warrior to take his place and challenge the best of the Greeks. In fact, the scholiast of the Townley manuscript suggests that, according to some, the *Iliad* of Homer *actually ended* with the entrance of Penthesilea: that its final words were about a warrior, a substitute for the prince of Troy, who was, quite extraordinarily, a woman. Contrary to everything we've learned about Homer's women so far (Andromache's battle advice ignored; Briseis and Chryseis traded like pawns in the game of war; Thetis doomed to lose a soldier son), here is a woman who can be not only a warrior in her own right, but a general: a woman whom Homer, as well as the poets of the Epic Cycle, saw as fit to lead, and to fight, in the Trojan War. As I looked again at these possible candidates for the final, closing words of the *Iliad*, glowing in the modern strip lighting of the British Library, crammed into the edge of a medieval page – 'And then the Amazon came' – it seemed astonishing, and infuriating, that the tale of this outstanding woman fighter and her troops has been pushed quite literally to the margins in the stories we tell about Homer's heroes: about Achilles, about Hector. Why is it, I wanted to ask, that I was always told that the battles of the Trojan War were all about men? Why wasn't I taught about Penthesilea and the Amazons when I learned about the *Iliad* and the warriors who fought at Troy?

In Search of the Amazons

The answer lies in the history of the Amazons' story, and the way that tale was interpreted (and misinterpreted) by later generations – from the classical Greeks who came after Homer, all the way to the male European scholars of the nineteenth and twentieth centuries who collected and curated the study of the ancient world.[11] To these intellectuals, brought up on Greek at boys' schools and fed on a diet of Homeric masculinity, it was patently obvious that Homer's Amazons existed only to tell them about the legends that came to define and exalt the Greek male, rather than any historical truth about women warriors. (It's striking to note the similarity to the comparable objections raised, in the late nineteenth century, against the reality of Troy.) Wasn't the fact that Greek writers placed them all over the ancient world – from Thrace to Anatolia to the Black Sea to the Caucasus – proof, they argued, that the Amazons were purely imaginary beings set in various mythical borderlands? Hundreds of years of gender stereotypes – that women couldn't possibly fight like men; that women were better seen and not heard; that women's bodies needed controlling by men (prone as they were to 'the hysterical', when the womb (*hystera*) was imagined to go for a wander); that women naturally belonged in the domestic sphere – only seemed to shore up their arguments.[12] The Amazons could only be, as one German scholar put it in 1825, 'mythological creatures'.[13]

It didn't help that many of the misogynistic gender stereotypes that underpinned this approach originated in another Greek locale: the grandiloquent texts and the marble-clad art of classical (fifth-century BCE) Athens. By the nineteenth century, classical Greece had already held pride of place for hundreds of years as the perceived origin and arbiter of the social and cultural values of Western civilization, such that modern classical scholars were all too happy to agree with the gender stories told by the ancient Athenians, and, in turn, (anachronistically) to project them back on to Homer and the Amazons. Much of the propaganda writ large across the Parthenon – that monument to the classical Athenian project, completed on the Acropolis of Athens in 432 BCE – rests on a billboard-like advertisement of the binary opposition of gender that elevates the classical Greek man by his subjection of the uncivilized, barbarian woman 'other', focused, above all, on the attention-grabbing, bare-breasted figures of the Amazons.

The facade of this monumental temple to power, soaring above the marble columns that circle the inner sanctum, carries a double layer of deeply significant decoration in stone: on the outer colonnade, a series of square slabs sculpted in high relief, celebrating legendary battles from myth; on the inner temple, a wrap-around frieze carved with contemporary scenes from the Great Panathenaic procession. The peaceful realm of the frieze makes a stark contrast to the slab reliefs (known as metopes), with their contorted bodies wrestling in mythical battles – including, on the west side, the invasion of Athens by the warrior-women Amazons, rampaging across the city and razing the Acropolis (the very outcrop of rock where the Parthenon now stands). These terrifying images of foreign conquest at the site of the crime – spear-wielding 'eastern' Amazons on rearing horses stabbing Greeks to the ground – would have provided a forceful reminder to fifth-century BCE viewers of the dangers of defeat by barbarians. But it would also have been a calculated echo of the terrible recent wars against the Persians (who, in 480 BCE, had advanced into Athens like the Amazons to burn the Acropolis), and the against-all-odds victory that had heralded the decades of Athenian hegemony. For the men who conceived the Parthenon (the leader Pericles, the sculptor Pheidias), the Amazons were the ideal myth to warn against the dangers of barbaric, effeminate outsiders, and, in turn, to promote the achievements of the Greek male.

But is this culturally loaded, Hellenocentric version of the story of the Amazons the only one? Were the Amazons just an imaginary prop for the self-fashioning of Athenian men? Or is it possible that these ancient myths extended beyond the boundaries of the classical Greek imagination, that they were seeded around a kernel of historical truth – that the Amazons were, in fact, real?

The answer is a resounding yes. The last decade or so has seen the emergence of astonishing archaeological evidence for real-life Amazons – or Amazon-like women – who fought in battle, who lived around the Black Sea (where the Greeks said they did) in the vast region known to later Greeks as Scythia, who lived as nomads and rode on horseback across the wilds of the steppes. The revolution in the re-evaluation of these ancient figures has been driven by advances in bioarchaeological techniques and DNA analysis, which, just like the female burials at Mycenae and Aidonia, and the Peristeria Penelope, have allowed archaeologists to move beyond the traditional sexing of burials by gender-binary interpretations of grave goods – swords and daggers belong to men, necklaces and jewellery to women – and instead, to let the bones speak for themselves. Warrior grave mounds (known as *kurgans*), like the one uncovered by Georgij Nioradze – filled with skeletons mutilated by gory battle wounds and laid to rest in military gear with swords, arrowheads and spears – had been dug up for decades, since the 1870s, all around the Black Sea: and they had always been labelled by archaeologists (less attentive than Nioradze) as the burials of warrior men.[14] Nioradze was very much ahead of his time when – at the extraordinary Late Bronze Age warrior burial at Zemo Avchala near Tbilisi in Georgia – he thought to sex the skeleton he had discovered based on osteological evidence, which included analysis of dental and craniometric traits. (Paradoxically for the warrior burial, however, in his 1931 excavation report Nioradze also draws on the traditional approach, using the 'feminine' grave goods – bracelets, rings and necklace beads – to back up his interpretation of the female gender of the grave's occupant, while conveniently ignoring the sword lying across her knees.)[15] If some of the hundreds of warrior graves found around the Black Sea could belong to women, modern archaeologists began to say, what would happen if they went back to the record and looked more closely at the others that had been assumed to be those of men?

This realization has led to some of the most dramatic sex reversals in the history of ancient archaeology – comparable to the 2017 genetic re-analysis of the Viking Birka warrior as a woman, which created such a sensation across the global media.[16] Two splendid burial mounds of warriors in ancient Thrace (modern Romania and Bulgaria), dating to the fourth century BCE and filled to the brim with skeletons accompanied by silver helmets and greaves, arrowheads and the bones of kitted-out horses, were originally – on their excavation in the mid twentieth century – thought to contain warrior chieftains and their wives. But in 2010, skeletal analysis revealed that all the bodies – all the warriors – were, in fact, women: female fighters, who had been buried with their weapons and their steeds.[17] On the opposite coast of the Black Sea, south of Tbilisi in Ordubad, Azerbaijan, a necropolis of warriors' graves excavated in 1926 (and assumed to belong to men) was shown in 2004 to contain at least one grave of a warrior woman, buried with her helmet, quiver and arrows.[18] Further south, near Tabriz in north-western Iran, DNA analysis of a 'broad-framed skeleton' buried with a sword amid 109 graves of weapon-carrying skeletons revealed two X chromosomes – a biologically female warrior.[19] And, in 2020, the partly mummified skeleton of a young Scythian warrior in Siberia from the seventh to sixth century BCE, discovered in 1988, buried with an axe, a one-metre bow and a quiver with ten arrows, underwent palaeogenetic testing – and was revealed to be that of a thirteen-year-old girl.[20]

Other discoveries continue to follow the same remarkable pattern: showing an unprecedented number of women fighters, not separated as in the legendary all-female society of the Amazons, but rooted in their communities, buried alongside the graves of children and male warriors – not only around the Black Sea, where the burials are most numerous, but across the Eurasian Steppe, from the western Black Sea all the way to Mongolia.[21] This new evidence has allowed us to go back and read ancient Greek testimonies to the Amazons' many homelands, not as a product of the haphazard mapping of myth as was once thought, but as an actual historical record of these women warriors as a part of the roving, nomadic populations that inhabited (and continue to populate) the steppe, moving with the seasons and living – and fighting – on the horses they domesticated. In some of these cemeteries, it's been discovered that female warriors represented as many as 37 per cent of the burials. More than 112 graves of women warriors from the fifth and fourth centuries BCE have been found in the ancient regions of Thrace and Scythia (to the north of the Black Sea), with another 130 in southern Ukraine and 40 further east towards the Caspian Sea. In the northern Black Sea area, in particular, it's been estimated that as many as 20 per cent of all fifth- and fourth-century BCE graves containing weapons belong to women.[22] Amid these wide-ranging nomadic cultures, spreading across a vast geographical area and over a period of more than a thousand years, the numbers of women buried with weapons (at least 25 per cent of all female burials in Scythia) suggest that a quarter of women could expect to become a warrior.[23] Some critics have pointed out that burial with weapons doesn't necessarily mean engagement in warfare (though one wonders whether the same argument would be made for a man buried with a sword): however, many female skeletons – just like the Zemo Avchala warrior – exhibit evidence of battle wounds. Sometimes weapons are even embedded in the bones, such as a metal arrowhead found in the skull of another woman buried not far from the

Zemo Avchala warrior – telling evidence that speaks to women's hands-on experience of war.

It's an undeniable fact that most of the warrior-women burials spread across the region of the steppe are from a much later period than we've been looking at: Nioradze's Late Bronze Age find is an outlier, and most graves clustered around the Black Sea belong to the flourishing of Scythian culture, from around the seventh century BCE onwards. But other, older warrior-women burials are found dispersed across the swathe of territories containing the graves of fighting women: including a burial from northern China from around 1200 BCE, replete with 130 weapons and honouring – not a man – but a celebrated warrior queen, Fu Hao.[24] And the graves of later women warriors show a marked continuity with their earlier sisters, hinting at a shared culture, not only in their practices of warfare, but also in the weapons used (such as the sharp-pointed Scythian axe, the *sagaris*, as well as bows and arrows, spears and javelins, swords, daggers and knives), a life spent on horseback, and related customs of burial. Nioradze's discovery provides a suggestive clue to the beginnings of a widespread way of life, centred around the Black Sea territories, that enabled women to be fighters who wielded swords and daggers like the Zemo Avchala warrior, who fired arrows from a bow, and who dealt (and succumbed to) blows from the deadly *sagaris*, which – as we know from later evidence – dangled from a hook on a wide weapon belt.[25] It's likely that these terrifying war belts were the source of the Greek myth about one of the Labours of Hercules, who was sent to recover the 'belt' of the Amazon queen Hippolyta – a legend which, along with other tales of the Amazons, I retold in my third novel, *For the Immortal* (2018). Hippolyta's 'belt' was, in all likelihood, one of these fearsome weapon carriers: a far cry from the Greek love belt of Aphrodite.

The archaeology of these women's graves gives us a sense of how such Amazon-like warriors would have fought: above all, on horseback – evidenced not only by their being buried alongside their horses, but also by the bowed legs exhibited by their skeletal remains, the bones bent out of shape from a lifetime of riding.[26] Some injuries suggest unpleasant falls – such as the claw-like hand of one female skeleton that bears witness to a badly healed and likely highly painful fracture.[27] And scientific analysis of the puncture wounds in skulls, like that of the Zemo Avchala warrior, enables us to conjure a graphic image of how such wounds would have been sustained: most head wounds would have been delivered by right-handed opponents wielding the *sagaris* in face-to-face combat, while slash wounds on left forearm bones suggest the left arm was used to ward off an attack.[28] It is possible that women fighters like these were observed by entrepreneurial early Greeks sailing along the Black Sea coast, since ancient myths hint at a possible early trade connection (and route for the exchange of stories). Colchis, in particular, an ancient kingdom in modern Georgia, lay at the heart of the age-old legend of the voyage of Jason on the *Argo* in search of the Golden Fleece (a tale that, intriguingly, is mentioned in Homer's *Odyssey*).[29] It's tempting, and not beyond the realms of possibility, to imagine that it was sensational tales such as these of a strikingly different culture, a different and unfamiliar role for women, brought back by those who had voyaged to the lands around the Black Sea, that – with the inevitable variations and embellishments of myth – found their way into the Greek tradition: that became the Amazons. Even the word 'Amazon' has its own fascinating history. An ancient tradition preserved in the Nart sagas – orally transmitted tales from the North Caucasus (between the Black and Caspian Seas, and in the heart of the old warrior-women homelands) that interweave Indo-European myths with local Caucasian fables – relates the story of a legendary warrior queen called Amezan who led her troops into battle: 'In that long ago age, women would saddle their horses, grab their lances, and ride forth with their men folk to meet the enemy in battle on the steppes.'[30] It's an intriguing possibility that the name of this heroic queen, Amezan, was heard by the Greeks and transferred into the Greek language as *Amazōn* – a loanword borrowed by the Greeks to describe a fierce warrior people with their extraordinary women fighters.

So when Priam reminisces about 'the Amazons, comparable to men', and – scribbled in the margin of a British Library manuscript – an *Amazōn* queen rides into battle at the *Iliad*'s close, it's possible that these are dim remembrances of real women warriors who inhabited the furthest reaches of the Greek world: women who once rode and fought on horseback across the Trojan plain and by the shores of the Black Sea, alongside their Amazon sisters. Perhaps it really was possible – as that note in the margin of the Townley Homer says it was – to be a woman in war.

Amazons in Mycenae

The Amazons may certainly have had a troubled afterlife, dogged by the combination of terror and fascination that marks the classical framing of their story. Another example – comparable to the take on the Amazons' tale in the iconography of the Parthenon – comes from classical Greece, but this time it is the product of a spot of false etymology. The Greek historian Hellanicus of Lesbos, writing in the mid fifth century BCE (contemporary with Herodotus), claimed – with the casual Hellenocentrism of many speakers of ancient Greek, that all words could be given a Greek origin – that *Amazones* must mean 'without breasts'. In Greek, *a-* at the start of a word means 'without', and *mazos* looks close enough (with a little squinting) to *mastos*, the Greek word for 'breast'.[31] The urban legend caught on, and the fantasy image of single-breasted Amazons – who, classical writers would assert with relish, cut or burned off one of their breasts with hot iron so that they could better use a bow – took hold.[32] Yet there is no evidence, either archaeological or iconographic (even in Greek paintings of Amazons), that supports this story: it's likely, as with the many other fantasies that have swirled around the Amazons, to be a toxic combination of restrictive, gender-binary assumptions about the limitations of the female body (women needing to self-mutilate to become more 'like men'), a pernicious xenophobia that, by a curious twist, uses an incorrect Greek etymology of a foreign word to denigrate non-Greek customs, and a deep-seated fear of unbridled feminine sexuality (Amazons are often depicted in Greek art with their breasts hanging dangerously and erotically loose).

The tight intertwining of eroticism and violence within the legend of the Amazons comes out in many of the major myths around Greek–Amazon encounters. The tradition of Penthesilea's death in the Trojan War at the hands of Achilles, as we have seen, has their eyes meeting in a doomed vignette of the ultimate enemies-to-lovers scenario, right at the moment of her death: as Achilles watches the life spill from her body – according to a version by Quintus of Smyrna, a Greek poet writing at the time of the Roman Empire – he falls tragically in love with the Amazon he has killed.[33] During Hercules' raid on the Amazon queen Hippolyta to steal her war belt as one of his Labours, Theseus (who was accompanying the band of heroes) is said to have snatched an Amazon sister, Antiope, and taken her with him back to Athens. It was this seizure (just like, rather ironically, the seizure of Helen of Sparta) that led the Amazons to ride on Athens and burn the Acropolis down to get her back. As the legend was transmitted over the centuries, however, historians and mythographers tended to mix up which Amazon was taken by Theseus – often naming Hippolyta, the Amazon queen, as his victim.[34] When Shakespeare decided to set A Midsummer Night's Dream (written around 1595–6) in the legendary world of Athens, he was drawing on a translation of an ancient Roman account that named Hippolyta as Theseus' bride, and centred his play on the upcoming nuptials between the Greek king and Amazon queen.[35] And so an Amazon – albeit a very different kind of Amazon from her Scythian forebears – made her way on to the Elizabethan stage.

While classical Greeks and later audiences alike may have approached the Amazons with a combination of titillation and terror, however, fascinating evidence is emerging from the older periods of Greek history that suggests that some ancient Greek women may – in fact – have been able to cross traditional gender boundaries: to fight and to hunt (the ultimate male activities), just like the Amazons. The trail begins in myth, with an exceptional woman who seems to echo the warrior spirit of the Amazons within the world of the Greeks: Atalanta.[36] Atalanta, so the legend goes, was abandoned by her father, King Iasos, who wanted a son and heir and had no time for a daughter – a common enough fate for infant girls in the male-dominated society of ancient Greece. Mortuary records from ancient Greek cemeteries, which show much higher numbers of male than female burials, seem to attest to this horrifying yet commonplace fact of ancient life: girls simply weren't wanted, and were often left to die on a mountainside where their bones would never be found.[37] Atalanta, however, survived: she learned to fend for herself, to hunt and wrestle and run faster than any man; and when Peleus – who had entrapped and raped Achilles' mother Thetis by grappling her to the ground – tried to wrestle with her, it was Atalanta who bested him. She was the only woman to take part in the hunt for the Calydonian Boar, a heroic quest for a rampaging monster that brought together all the greatest warriors of the age, including Peleus, Theseus, king of Athens, and Jason. Among all this masculine sinew, however, it was Atalanta – with her bow and arrow, just like an Amazon – who was the first to strike the boar. And one later compilation of ancient myths (probably from the Roman period) preserves a fascinating tradition in which Atalanta accompanies Jason and the Argonauts on the epic quest of the *Argo* for the Golden Fleece – a voyage which, the legends tell us, would have brought her into the heartlands of the Amazons themselves.[38]

Atalanta, a woman ahead of her time, an Amazon among the Greeks, has attracted the attention of contemporary writers seeking to reintegrate women into the Greek myths – including my own novel *For the Winner* (2017) and Jennifer Saint's *Atalanta* (2023), both of which put Atalanta at the forefront of her own story as a woman who refuses to play by the rules of her time, who forges a new place for women in the ranks of the legendary heroes of Greece. But archaeological evidence from the Bronze Age provides faint hints that it might have been possible – even within the boundaries of the Greek world – for Amazon-like Atalantas to exist. The Greeks certainly believed that Atalanta was real: the monstrous tusks of the Calydonian Boar were actually said to have been put on display as a tourist attraction at a temple at Tegea, Atalanta's birthplace. And when archaeologists uncovered the temple in the 1880s, they discovered real boars' tusks littering the altar – the tributes of generations of devout worshippers to Atalanta.[39] Other intriguing discoveries from across the Bronze Age Greek world hint at echoes of real-life Atalantas. A thirty-centimetre sculpture of a female body, excavated on the island of Keros in the Aegean Cyclades, shows a diagonal mark scratched across the torso that seems to be a hunter warrior's baldric.[40] A re-examination of a wall painting from the Late Bronze Age palace at Pylos, published in 2008, reveals the fragmentary remains of a painting of what is likely to be a female archer, drawing back her bow with a white-skinned arm – just like Atalanta at the Calydonian Boar hunt.[41] A fresco of a boar hunt from the palace at Tiryns, meanwhile, shows both red- and white-skinned hunters (red and white are by and large the generic colour code, borrowed from Egyptian art, for men and women respectively) setting out in chariots and chasing their prey, the 'women' clad in 'men's' hunting tunics.[42] And white-skinned (i.e. feminine-coded), muscled, male-clothed acrobats on the frescoes at Knossos, in Crete, engage in the dangerous sport of 'bull-leaping', hurling themselves into the air over the horns of bulls.[43] These are individuals who defy gender categorization, white-skinned 'women' wearing 'male' outfits and engaging – just like Atalanta – in the typically masculine activities of archery, hunting and sport: athletes, like Atalanta, who refuse to be limited by traditional gender stereotypes, and who transcend boundaries in all sorts of ways.[44]

But it's one find, in particular, that turns our expectations about women in war upside down: and it was found, not in the grass-covered burial mounds of the Black Sea, but in the gold-stuffed inner sanctum of Late Bronze Age Greece. We are back amid the dead at Grave Circle B at Mycenae – legendary ancient kingdom of Homer's Agamemnon, and archaeological beating heart of Schliemann's Mycenaean Greek culture. Olive groves and rustling vineyards slope away down the hillside, while above us loom the tumbling walls of the great citadel, towering on its rocky outcrop. And it is here, among the quiet dusty graves, in a grave labelled Γ, that we meet once again with a woman we have already come to know: Γ58, the woman whose skull was reconstructed through foren-sic techniques in the search for Helen's face; the woman whom DNA analysis has suggested was buried beside her brother, who earned her place through her high status as a daughter, like Chryseis; the woman, not the man, who may have been the only individual to be buried with that costliest of status symbols, an electrum death mask.

But she was buried with rather more than just a death mask. She was accompanied into the afterlife by a clutch of possessions that, extraordi-narily, has hardly ever been noticed: a warrior kit of weapons (two bronze swords and another sword with an ivory pommel).[45] Just like the death mask, they were immediately attributed – in spite of their position – not to her, but to the man lying beside her. And she isn't alone. It's a remark-able and little-known fact that half of all the female burials in Grave Circle B – this supposed monument to Mycenaean patriarchy, this seat of the lords of men, this stronghold of overweening Homeric kings and the legendary starting point of the armed Greek troops, led by Agamemnon, who were said to have left for the Trojan War – are associated with *weapons*.[46] The way this historical reality has been hidden in later testimonies and interpretations is illustrated by one particularly telling story. Georgios Mylonas, one of the archaeologists who excavated Grave Circle B in the 1950s – the one who had said that Γ58's swords must belong to a man – initially described the unearthing of one body that had been buried with a bronze 'sword'.[47] But, when an expert osteologist identified the bones as belonging to a woman, the archaeological report was rewritten: her sword became a *machairidion*, a diminutive knife, in Mylonas' final publication of his finds in 1973.[48] As always, this is as much a modern story as it is an ancient one; and perceptions about what a woman would (or should) carry meant that the traces of this woman and her weapon were almost edited out from the annals of history.

Which leaves us to wonder, with the hoofbeats of the Amazons drumming in our ears as the *Iliad*, the first Homeric epic, draws to a close – how many other ways were there of being a woman in the Late Bronze Age than we've always been told?

Odyssey

WOMEN AT HOME AND AWAY

'Her fame will never end:
the gods will make a song for men
of wise Penelope.'

AGAMEMNON ON PENELOPE – HOMER, *ODYSSEY*, 24.196–8

10

ATHENA

Shapeshifter

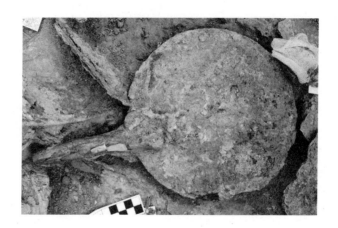

It's one of the things about being a deathless god, that she remembers being born. She remembers how it first began: a thickened seed of indeterminate jelly, swirling and electric in a mother's pink folds. She remembers the choking darkness, darker than night, in his belly when he swallowed them both – the tightness, like a squid caught in a net, all muscle and acid. She remembers the burst of white as the gaping hole tore open, remembers slithering damp and blinking into the daylight, remembers the father pronouncing the knot of limbs a 'she'. And the gods let loose a sigh when they heard it, like the wind that scrapes the mountain peaks. Zeus doesn't have a son, they said. It's a she. Just a she.

But that's not enough to say who or what she is. The grind of a blade's edge against bone, or the guttural screech of an owl – these are the sounds that echo her. Or her name. She prefers to speak her name, a flash like the glare off the surface of a mirror. More than god or goddess, expansive as the wild wide sea and strong and thick as an ox's tongue, the shout that cracks in a lightning voice around the reverberating skies.

I am: Athena.

Mirror, Mirror

The first sign is a flash of green in the soil, like Athena's eye.

It's 28 May 2015, rain drizzling in a haze over the Greek town of Pylos in the south-west Peloponnese, turning the curving sea the colour of iron. Drops patter on the leaves of the olive grove and the tarpaulin slung over the trench as the archaeologists lay out their trowels and buckets and set to work with their pickaxes amid the puddles. For days, the team – led by Sharon Stocker and Jack Davis of the University of Cincinnati – have been scraping back the soil here, in a grove at the foot of an olive tree.

They are working near the excavations Carl Blegen started in the 1930s, along the slope from the sprawling, low-walled ruins of the vast Mycenaean palace (now protected by a high-spec white metal roof). Blegen – with a Schliemann-like desire to connect his Mycenaean discovery with the heroes of Homer – had dramatically assigned his palace to the Homeric king of Pylos, Nestor, adviser to Agamemnon, who (the *Iliad* tells us) contributed ninety ships to the Greek war against Troy. Yet here beneath the olive tree, in the grounds that skirt the prehistoric palace and after days of labour, Davis and Stocker have only a stone slab, a deep shaft and piles of soil to show for their efforts. Perhaps they've found nothing more than a bog-standard ancient pit.

And then that flash of green. *Bronze*. The colour of tarnished, age-old copper, a key element in the defining metal alloy of the era, that means: *Bronze Age*.

As they continue to dig and the soil lifts, the green spreads into a pool of metal – and it's not just bronze, either.[1] Four spectacular gold signet rings. Hundreds of beads in amethyst, carnelian, amber and gold.

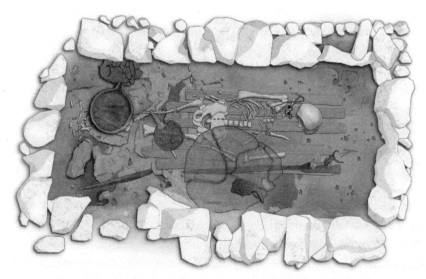

Treasure hoard: reconstruction of the grave of the Griffin Warrior (c.1500–1450 BCE). To the warrior's right lie a necklace and jug, with a mirror across the legs; to the left, a shield, sword and daggers.

Gold and silver cups. Dozens of seals intricately carved from precious stone. A bronze battle knife and metre-long sword with a gold-plated hilt. Boar's tusks from a helmet. Bronze basins, ivory combs, a bronze pitcher, a mirror of bronze with an ivory handle, and a gold-and-agate necklace. Over one and a half thousand objects in all – an unimaginable hoard that takes months to unearth and nearly finishes off the team in the process, that sends Stocker to a local clinic with heatstroke after weeks of work in the unforgiving Greek sun. And, beneath it all – nearly crushed by all this gleaming treasure – the grimy, mottled bones of a skeleton: the skull flattened and broken; a silver bowl placed over the ribs; and the corroded green-bronze mirror laid, like a looking glass into the past, across the leg bones.

Props of Power

Pottery from soil deposits around the grave suggest a burial date of around 1500–1450 BCE: the time of the first early burst of Mycenaean civilization on the Greek mainland, when the splendid royal complexes like that of Blegen's so-called Palace of Nestor nearby were built. Davis and Stocker named their discovery the tomb of the Griffin Warrior, after a griffin-decorated ivory plaque uncovered among the treasures, designed to accompany its occupant into the afterlife. But the riches here were more than gold deep. The bones of the grave's occupant – while they might seem mundane in comparison to the glittering metals that surrounded them – had several intriguing clues to reveal. From the skeletal remains, anthropologist Lynne Schepartz was able to estimate the individual's height – between 1.60 and 1.70 metres – as well as their age (around thirty to thirty-five years old).[2] Above all, by applying morphological analysis – mapping the shape of the skull, for instance, on a spectrum from minimal (female) to maximal (male) – Schepartz was able to confidently sex the skeleton as male: a result that was backed up genetically, in 2022, by a DNA sample taken from the petrous bone.[3] In 2016, with the help of a specialist in facial reconstruction, the Griffin Warrior was even (as far as is possible) brought back to life – the face reconstructed in layers of tissue built on a 3D-imaged scan of the skull, using the same method of tissue depth marking as the Manchester researchers did in their model of Γ58 at Mycenae.[4] As the spectacular discovery of the Griffin Warrior was splashed across the world's media, and his face popped up on everything from national spreads to news-feeds, journalists raced to reimagine him in their own colourful words: he was 'a handsome man' (according to Stacy Liberatore and Shivali Best in the *Daily Mail*) and even – because he was buried with a mirror and six combs – 'something of a dandy' (Nicholas Wade for the *New York Times*).[5]

Yet the gender-normative assumptions about the warrior's appar-ent concern for his appearance – as not conforming to mainstream masculinity – shows that there's a gaping hole in the leap from morpho-logical and genetic analysis to Griffin Warrior, and that's any discussion of gender. It might seem, at first, that concerns around gender – and, in particular, the notion of a differentiation between gender (as a spec-trum of identity, and/or a socially constructed category) and sex (as the characteristics of biology and physiology) – are a modern phenomenon. Certainly, gender and sexuality have been brought to the fore in the last few decades in an unparalleled way, making global headlines as defin-ing concerns that are being addressed in the ongoing campaign against discrimination and violence of any kind. The transgender rights movement continues to fight for the incorporation of trans rights (and protection against hate crimes) in state and national law, while in 2019 the word 'non-binary' was added to the *Collins English Dictionary* in recogni-tion of 'changes in how people relate to each other and define themselves'.[6]

But gender nonconformity and challenges to gender norms actually go back a long way, with deep roots into the history, as well as the myth-ology, of the Bronze Age world. Ancient Greek myth offers the trans, non-binary figure of the blind seer Tiresias, who was said – in one version of the legend – to have been born a man, become a woman and then (after seven years) turned back into a man. Another version of the myth, tellingly, invokes the power of Athena – describing how Tiresias came upon the virile virgin goddess while she bathed, and instantly lost his sight.[7] (Tiresias makes an important appearance in the *Odyssey* – as the blind seer in the Underworld who holds the key to the path of Odys-seus' voyage home.)[8] Enheduanna, the Mesopotamian priestess and earliest named author whom we met writing hymns of praise to Inanna (equivalent of Ishtar, the love goddess and goddess of war) in the late third millennium BCE, extolled the ability of the Mesopotamian goddess to transcend opposites, alongside her gender-transformative powers: 'To destroy, to create, to cut apart, to establish, Inanna, are yours. To turn a man into a woman and a woman into a man, Inanna, are yours.'[9] Inanna's priests and worshippers seem to have fully embraced this gender nonconformity: a fragment of a statue dating to 2000 BCE, held at the British Museum, gives the name and title of one 'Silimabzuta, person-man-woman (*lú-uš-sal*) of Inanna'; and Sumerian temple records, dating back to the middle of the third millennium BCE, give evidence of gender-nonconforming priests of Inanna called *gala* (who spoke using a female-only dialect and whose name was written with the signs for 'penis + anus').[10] Similar to this is a late third-millennium statue of a singer called Ur-Nanshe, from the Temple of Ninnizaza at Mari on the Euphrates, whose beardless face, long hair and delicate features perplexed the original excavators and suggest that the individual may have been an *assinu* – a singer who seemed to switch between male and female and performed in the cult of Ishtar (akin to the *gala*). In the New Kingdom of Egypt, on the other hand, in the mid fifteenth century BCE – right around the time that the Griffin Warrior was buried at Pylos – the female pharaoh Hatshepsut (who reigned *c.*1473–1458 BCE) gained unprecedented power as a woman ruler in the male-dominated structures of Egypt and notoriously presented herself in her statuary as male, adopting the sculpted masculine body, kilt, crown and false beard of kingly authority; she signed her statues with nonconforming feminine forms of the king's titles – akin, in English, to writing something like 'the king herself'. And over in Europe in the mid third millennium BCE, a grave uncovered in Prague in 2011 revealed a male skeleton buried according to all the conventions of a woman (including all the accoutrements, such as an egg-shaped container usually associated with females).[11]

What's interesting about the Prague burial, in particular, is the way that archaeologists were able to peer into the ground and see gender being – in modern terminology – *performed*. The way that the (male-sexed) body is laid to rest in a 'female' way (on their left side, not the typically 'male' right), and interacts with the (female-gendered) objects that accompany them, clearly acts out some kind of counter-story to the sex of the skeleton's bones. This way of thinking about the 'performance' of gender – first introduced by Judith Butler in the 1990s, as queer theory was beginning to gain ground in academic circles – suggests that the body isn't inherently 'male' or 'female': rather, it's the daily social performances we put on – the clothes we choose to wear, the objects we interact with, the gestures we make, the accessories we pick as ornaments – and the association of those performances with particular genders, that work to layer gender and sex (like a kind of costume we slip into) on to the surface of the body.

It might seem anachronistic to use modern words and concepts to interpret history. In instances like burials, we don't know if the non-binary gender identities staged by the objects that surround the dead represent real lived experiences: without access to textual records and individual testimonies, frustratingly, all we have to go on are the stories the artefacts tell. And yet the words that do crop up in the ancient texts, like the Sumerian 'person-man-woman' (*lú-uš-sal*) and *gala*, provide at least some evidence of an attempt to move towards a language that crossed gender binaries. (In a much later Greek text, the *Symposium* by Plato, the poet Aristophanes – who is imagined as one of the notable real-life guests in Plato's fictional banquet – comes up with a similar word in Greek, *androgynos* or 'man-woman', to describe his idea of intersex humans at the origin of the species; it's where the English 'androgyny' comes from.)[12] But we don't need the words we use to be the same to see that the Bronze Age world was a lot less binary than we might have thought. Words have a lot to tell us, but they are no substitute for hard material evidence, and burials also have a lot to say: through the way a person's body is presented with their treasured props and accoutrements, reflecting the diverse identities of a lifetime (and beyond). In the Prague burial, for instance, it's the skeleton's nonconforming, 'feminine'-associated position, and accompanying 'female' props, that seem to be trying to tell a life story that goes beyond binary gender.

All of which brings us back to the Griffin Warrior. Because, while some of the artefacts selected to accompany their owner into the afterlife were what archaeologists might traditionally (before the re-evaluation of Amazon and Mycenaean graves, anyway) have labelled as stereotypically masculine – sword, dagger, helmet – there were also, as we saw earlier, an abundance of treasures usually associated by archaeologists with women: a necklace, a bronze pitcher, six ivory combs, and an ivory-and-bronze mirror. In fact, as Sharon Stocker has pointed out, when it comes to the Griffin Warrior, neat categorization of male and female objects just isn't possible: everything in the burial challenges the traditional expectations about gender that archaeologists have had for decades. Meanwhile, although bronze mirrors are more often found with genetically female-sexed skeletons than male, when we zoom in on male graves containing mirrors, we almost always find them associated with warriors.[13] In other words, crucially, it's modern assumptions about binary gender and its expression that – faced with an ancient warrior buried with a mirror and comb – have led to the Griffin Warrior's gender-normative labelling (as in the *New York Times* coverage) as a 'dandy' who cares too much about his looks.

Burial artefacts can bear material witness to fluid gender, not just in their gender associations, but also in the intricate iconographies carved or painted on them. One of the objects buried with the Griffin Warrior – a precious sealstone – carries just such an image. On the gently curving surface of the gem, etched in shallow relief, it's just possible to make out a delicate engraving of two fantasy creatures rearing across the seal. Shrouded in scaly crocodile-like carapaces, skimmed by the rays of a brilliant sun, they toss their lion's heads while clutching cult jugs and burners in their claws.[14] To seasoned archaeologists like Stocker and Davis, they're instantly recognizable. These are so-called Minoan 'genii' – a modern classification (*genius* means 'guardian spirit' in Latin) that doesn't quite, I think, do justice to these extraordinary, category-defying, composite creatures of myth: local versions of the fabulous lion-hippopotamus-crocodile fertility goddess of Egypt, Taweret, that crop up in their dozens across Crete and the Greek mainland from the Middle to the Late Bronze Age. But what's particularly fascinating about them isn't their name; it's their gender. Egyptian Taweret (and her early descendants in the 'genii' of the Aegean) often hefts about a swollen pregnant belly, and a pendulous pair of breasts ripe for a spot of nursing. But, as time goes on, the iconography of Taweret imported into the rampant crocodile-lions

An agate sealstone with two 'genii' – fabulous mythical creatures that combine Egyptian and Greek, lion and crocodile, female and male.

of the Aegean world slowly takes on an identity of its own, until the creatures in question look much more like the pair we have here, in the Griffin Warrior's tomb: first dispensing with their breasts, then accessorizing with the tightly cinched waist-belt favoured by Mycenaean males. They're pregnant goddesses, in other words, who have become kings. They're animals who walk on two legs and carry water jugs like humans, icons that counter the division between female and male, lion and crocodile, Egyptian and Mycenaean – mythical beings that quite literally go beyond the binary, and point the way towards a world that exists beyond the confines of biological sex and monolithic identities.[15] They're visual incarnations of what appears to be a much more fluid, non-binary conception of gender in the world to which they belonged.

So there's a much bigger story being told here in the Griffin Warrior's burial – both in the types of objects chosen to accompany the body and the gender associations that they convey. When we look more closely, what we can see in the Griffin Warrior's tomb, just like in the Prague burial, is a tale of overlapping layers of gender and an expression of gender that goes beyond the binary. We don't have a written testimony of how the Griffin Warrior self-identified, or what objects such as the sealstone with its twin 'genii' meant to them. But two things make this grave unique (in comparison to other Mycenaean tombs, which were often used for the burial of multiple individuals and were, in many cases, subsequently looted). The first is the fact that it lay undisturbed since the day it was dug – giving us an unparalleled portal back into the past. And the second is that all the objects belong to (and so testify to the gender expression of) one individual.[16] Like Stocker and Davis, then, we can begin to excavate, to peel back the layers of gender enacted and expressed in the objects that clustered around this person for millennia, to reveal a stratigraphy of gender elements literally overlaying the Griffin Warrior's bones.

The combination of 'male'- and 'female'-gendered grave goods, and the clues contained in objects like the 'genii' sealstone, undoubtedly have something to tell us: and we can dig a little deeper into exactly what is going on when we start to investigate how all the artefacts have been put together – like a jigsaw puzzle that starts to make sense once you begin to assemble all the pieces. It becomes obvious, when you focus on the exact placement of the grave goods, that the piles of (masculine-coded) glittering weapons have been deliberately laid to the warrior's left, while the dazzling hoard of (feminine-coded) gold jewellery is to the right – with the body at the very heart, drawing them all together.[17] These seem to be an individual's personal belongings that proclaim, across the centuries, status, wealth and influence in a virtually unequalled display, and, at the same time, an ability to transcend gender associations in a unique and fluid way, with the body of the Griffin Warrior at their heart.

And the way these gender-crossing messages home in on the individual warrior is made clear, above all, by one of the most exquisite of all the treasures uncovered in the tomb. It's another agate sealstone, this one barely three and a half centimetres across, discovered close to the Griffin Warrior's right arm with a string hole drilled through the centre – likely worn as a bracelet.[18] Emerging from the soil as a small, knobbly bead thickly encrusted in lime, the excavators at first didn't pay it much attention. But as the team's conservator painstakingly cleaned up the stone, what began to emerge was nothing short of extraordinary: an astonishingly intricate miniature scene engraved in the minutest detail – hardly visible to the naked eye on the mottled surface of the agate – of a warrior in combat. It was only close-up photomicroscopy that revealed the full extent of the mastery on display – and gave Davis and Stocker the first hint that what they were looking at was not only one of the finest examples of engraving in the Aegean; it also had the potential to tell a story about the early beginnings of the legends that would make their way down to Homer's epics. The scene is that of a battle with a full-blown Bronze Age hero at its heart: a supple-bodied warrior, decked out in all the kit of an Aegean fighter, who stretches, hurricane-like, across the seal, toned muscles of belly and biceps taut as they thrust a sword into the neck of an opponent who crashes to their knees; beneath, draped across the ground, lies the collapsed body of an already-slain victim. The whole scene indisputably calls to mind the dynamics of Homeric warfare: the conquering Greek champion, the glory-bringing hand-to-hand duel, the sword splintering into the neck (reminiscent of many a gory Homeric description), the vanquished body spreadeagled in the 'beautiful death'. Are vignettes like this one, perhaps, what would become a dimly remembered antecedent of the tales of heroic battles, like the legendary duel between Achilles and Hector, that would hundreds of

The original Homeric hero? Scenes of warriors in hand-to-hand duels, like this one from the grave of the Griffin Warrior, may show the early myths that would later come to inspire Homer's epics.

years later form the stock-in-trade of the *Iliad*? It's a tantalizing, almost impossibly thrilling idea that what we might have here is an early representation of the real Late Bronze Age heroes whose myths would eventually become those of the fabled warriors of Homeric epic.

Yet Stocker and Davis have argued that there might also have been a much more personal, individual meaning to this scene. There are clear parallels between the powerful fighter depicted on the sealstone and the remains of the Griffin Warrior. The sword lying alongside the vanquished enemy on the ground, as well as the one being wielded by the victor, both bear a marked resemblance to the sword with the gold-plated hilt found next to the Griffin Warrior. The lustrous rippling locks of the central hero seem to evoke the combs discovered nearby in the tomb. Most excitingly of all, the conquering hero on the sealstone wears a bracelet with an engraved seal on it (could it be this one?), as well as a necklace with several minutely detailed beads that stream out behind the nape of the neck – remarkably similar to the gold and agate beaded necklace found just centimetres away, draped near the skeleton's neck, in the Griffin Warrior's tomb. These parallels lock together and point to the intriguing suggestion that this might, in fact, be a miraculously preserved representation of its original owner, dressed up in all the props that would ultimately accompany them to the grave, from millennia ago: either a bespoke commissioned portrait, or a treasured heirloom on which the Griffin Warrior consciously modelled themselves.[19]

Necklace-wearing, hair-flying, sword-wielding warrior: this very personal seal seems effortlessly to bring together the disparately gendered objects into one beautiful, wealthy, fluid body. It's possible that, in the grave array of the Griffin Warrior's tomb, the intersection between sword and mirror, knife and necklace, dagger and comb is simply an expression of that same image spread across the agate seal – a way to proclaim this warrior's empowered status by drawing on different prestige symbols. Or perhaps the gender associations are all our own, and there was, in fact, nothing particularly controversial or gendered to a Bronze Age eye about a warrior who wore a necklace and owned a mirror.[20] We just don't know. On this fluctuating stage, the Griffin Warrior is a kind of ancient shapeshifter, surrounded by the props of wealth and power and able to move flexibly between a whole spectrum of different identities, different genders – as they take up the gold-embossed sword, or the bejewelled necklace. In the eloquent, multi-layered objects gathered together in the Griffin Warrior's tomb, we appear to have echoes of a world – drawing together the gender-crossing statues of an Egyptian pharaoh and a pregnant lion-crocodile goddess from Egypt dressed as a Mycenaean king, the non-binary priests of the Mesopotamian Ishtar and the gender-fluid seer of ancient Greek myth – where a range of layered gender identities could be expressed, where they seem to have held valid and even empowered representation within the numinous spheres of the warrior, the god and even the king herself.

Robe Off, Armour On

In the Homeric epics, we come across someone very like the Griffin Warrior: someone who moves between different gender identities, who can carry both a man's spear and a woman's water jug – and that's Athena. The second epic traditionally assigned to Homer, the *Odyssey* – the poem that tells the tale of the Greek hero Odysseus' fantastical voyage home to Ithaca after the Trojan War – begins with a punchy programmatic word: 'man', or *andra* in Greek. 'Sing to me, Muse, of a man' (*andra moi ennepe, Mousa*), the epic begins: calling on the female goddess of song to tell the story of 'the man' Odysseus.[21] And yet, when the stage is set and the plot of the *Odyssey* is set in motion, the story starts – just like the *Iliad* – with a woman. Two women, in fact. The first is Calypso, the immortal goddess who, we are told, is holding Odysseus in perennial sex-filled captivity somewhere between Troy and Ithaca on her lush, paradisical island. And the other is Athena.

But is Athena really a woman? On two counts maybe not. First, she's a god, and so inhabits the alternative realm of divinity that doesn't fit neatly into human gender categories. Second, she's notoriously gender fluid. Of all the Greek gods who make up the Olympian pantheon, Athena is perhaps the one who slips with the greatest ease between genders. The story of her gender nonconformity starts at birth. Hesiod, a contemporary of Homer's who wrote a vibrant epic account of the creation of the gods, describes how Zeus – anxious not to be caught up in a cosmic cycle of gods overthrown by their male progeny (and he should know: he had overthrown his father Cronus before him) – got around the pregnancy of his threateningly clever wife, Metis (her name means 'cunning intelligence' in Greek), who was destined to bear a son who would rule as king of the gods.[22] Just as in the case of Thetis and Achilles, who was prophesied to be greater than his father, Zeus can't allow any threat to his power through a woman's ability to give birth. And so, with extraordinary and guttural violence (and a pinch of the characteristic bizarreness of Greek myth), he swallows the pregnant Metis – then goes on to give birth to Athena himself by cutting open his head with an axe. Athena leaps out fully grown with a fearsome battle cry, clad in armour so terrifying that the earth and sky shudder, the sea tosses with foam and the sun stops in the sky. The gods halt in their tracks, convinced – by the masculine coding of her weaponry and her battle cry – that she must be the male-gender son of whom Zeus was so terrified. But when she strips off her armour, Zeus, so the ancient legend says, 'was glad' at what he saw.[23] Not the son he'd feared: just a woman.

Nearly-a-son but not, born from a male god through the swing of an axe, wearing the armour you'd expect of a man but with a woman's body underneath, Athena is a complex web of gender paradoxes. She is born a woman, but is a resolute virgin (which means she never submits to men in sex – a key aspect of feminine gendering in antiquity – and never engages in the socially expected role of a mother). She is the goddess of the stereotypically masculine realm of war, but is also patron of the peaceful 'feminine' craft of weaving. Just like the Mesopotamian war (and love) goddess Ishtar/Inanna, Athena transcends binary identification: she moves between female and male, creator and destroyer. Homer threads these dual aspects into the narrative fabric of the poems. It is Athena, after all, along with Hera, who fights tooth and nail throughout the *Iliad* to smash the ramparts of Troy; and it is she who – when she has left it smouldering – gains the gods' approval to ensure, in the *Odyssey*, her favoured hero Odysseus' return home to enforce the peace.[24]

The *Odyssey* begins, famously, *in medias res* (a Latin phrase for 'in the middle of the action'). Odysseus is stuck at the final hurdle, a hostage (we're told) on Calypso's island after facing many dangers (like the frightful one-eyed monster Cyclops), constant delay (like his crew's unfortunate opening of the bag of winds when they were nearly home) and frequent distraction (like his multi-year sexcapades with the powerful goddesses Circe and Calypso – to whom, it has to be said, he seems to have submitted very willingly, at least at first). Enter Athena, who storms into the council of the gods determined to get Odysseus home at last. This is not only a bid to return her favourite to his rightful place, but a manoeuvre aimed at restoring peace and harmony to the turbulent island of Ithaca, where the suitors of Odysseus' wife Penelope – vying for both Odysseus' kingdom and Penelope's hand – are causing uproar in the palace, upending the social order, eating the royals out of house and home, and threatening to overturn Odysseus' rule. The situation is particularly fraught and unstable because Odysseus and Penelope's teenage son, Telemachus, still wet behind the ears and not yet ready to reign, cannot step into his father's role. And so Athena, striding into the limelight as the *Odyssey*'s driving force, unfolds a double plan of attack: first, she engages Hermes to order Calypso to release Odysseus, on Zeus' orders; and second, she flits across the sea to Ithaca, intent on guiding Telemachus on a journey to Pylos and Sparta so that he can seek news of his father, meet a couple of the fabled Greek heroes, Nestor and Menelaus, and gain some of the glory of adventure for himself.[25]

In order to approach Odysseus' son, Athena makes good on her gender fluidity and becomes a man: first Mentes, a local island chief, then Mentor, an old friend of Odysseus' and (in his absence) wise adviser to Telemachus. (It's Mentor's advice to Telemachus that has led to the modern use of the word 'mentor' to mean an experienced counsellor.) In other words, the goddess that everyone wanted to be born female starts out in the *Odyssey* by becoming a man, right in the opening act. There's one aspect to Athena's gender-shapeshifting that I find particularly fascinating – one that recalls archaeological finds like the Griffin Warrior – and that's the way Athena uses props and objects to signal different genders. We've already seen this aspect of Athena in the *Iliad*. Twice in the epic, when she arms for battle, the poet describes her stripping off 'her silky-soft embroidered dress, which she had made herself' (a symbol of her association with the realm of feminine weaving), slipping instead into a male tunic that belongs to Zeus, and arming herself with formidable 'weapons fit for war'.[26] Athena's terrifying weapons were legendary: above all, the mystical, ferocious, protective *aegis* – which Homer vividly imagines crowned with Panic, embroiled with Conflict, Strength and blood-chilling Battle Tumult, with the grim head of the Gorgon (whose gaze was said to turn men to stone) fixed gorily at its centre. This *aegis* is the property of Zeus and Athena alone: a fierce shield-like device that can be wielded in an instant, which Athena uses in self-defence even against the other gods, and that enables her to drop her robe and step into armour – and even straight on to a battle chariot – at a moment's notice.[27]

But weapons don't just allow Athena to slip between the gendered polarities of weaving and war: they also adapt as she shifts shape into a mortal man. At the beginning of the *Odyssey*, when she first darts down from Mount Olympus to go to the aid of Telemachus in Ithaca, Homer describes her brandishing her massive bronze-tipped spear that, he says, 'the daughter of a mighty father' wields (with the terrible power of a divinity) to slay heroes.[28] This is transformed, as she waits for Telemachus at Odysseus' gate, into a humble human weapon that gets stacked alongside other men's spears in the palace, at exactly the same time as she changes into her male form as Mentes.[29] (It's no coincidence that Homer pulls out a gender-neutral pronoun in ancient Greek – *min* – right at the point of Athena's transformation. Telemachus clasps the stranger's hand – 'addressing *them* (*min*)' with 'winged words'. Homer could have used 'her' (*tēn*), but he doesn't.[30] Telemachus doesn't speak to *her*: he speaks to *them*.) After another identity change by Athena – into Mentor – Telemachus assembles a ship and sails with Mentor to Nestor's kingdom of Pylos. Their black-painted ship runs up at the shore beneath the Pylos palace: the legendary location where, at the site of the same name and centuries after Homer, Carl Blegen would unearth Mycenaean remains that he linked to Nestor's home; the same site that, in the last few years, has yielded the Griffin Warrior's tomb. Here, on the dunes of the shore, Telemachus and Mentor come across Nestor and his sons, along with hundreds of men, engaged in a sacrifice to Poseidon of several bulls and a meat-rich feast, the carcasses roasted on spits; Mentor is given a two-handled golden cup to make the prayer to the gods that begins the feast.[31] This is precisely the kind of male-only meat consumption that has been evidenced in the skeletal make-up of the actual male inhabitants of Mycenaean Pylos. And, in fact, tangible evidence has been uncovered at the archaeological site of the Palace of Nestor of exactly this kind of feasting behaviour, with the burnt bones of as many as ten butchered animals discovered in one room – enough to feed thousands of people (just as we see in the *Odyssey*) in a single sacrifice.[32] Mentor's identity as a man, then, is vouchsafed by a spear, a cup and participation in the prestigious, men-only feast.

What's particularly exciting about all this are the many correspondences between the finds made in the Griffin Warrior's tomb, the unique geography of the area and Homer's descriptions in the *Odyssey*. Pylos is frequently described as 'sandy' in Homer (its 'epithet', to use the technical term): the very first scene in which we meet Nestor and his sons shows them sitting on fleeces and having a barbecue on the beach. A stunning yellow-sanded cove, now known as Voidokilia, forms a curving ring of dunes just downhill from the ancient palace at Pylos – and could very well be the place where Homer once imagined Nestor welcoming Telemachus and Mentor.[33] The two-handled golden cup that Mentor accepts from Nestor's son seems strikingly evocative of the several gold cups buried beside the Griffin Warrior, only steps away from the beach. And one of the spectacular rings discovered in the Griffin Warrior's Pylian tomb even shows a minutely detailed scene of a religious celebration at a seaside shrine – just like the sacrifice to the gods undertaken by the Pylians in the *Odyssey* 'on the sand'.[34] The artist responsible for the ring (whoever they may have been) has taken great pains to represent the sand, in particular, in scrupulous detail – dozens of minuscule circles impressed along the metal of the shoreline like tiny grains. And the figure of a goddess even seems to have floated down from the skies to visit her worshippers at their ritual: taller than the others, she stands to the right among her acolytes with a sumptuous flounced skirt, breasts bared and wing-like protrusions extending from her shoulders. Is this the kind of Mycenaean prototype of a religious epiphany, buried in a grave at Pylos, that was perhaps echoed later in the *Odyssey* – a divine visit to a sacrifice, on Pylos' sandy shore?

Robe Back On

Athena is not gender fluid in one direction, though. Later in the *Odyssey*, as Odysseus stumbles on to his last stop before reaching home, Athena goes out to see him looking like a young virgin girl (so Homer tells us), carrying a pitcher of water.[35] I can't help but think of the bronze jug buried on the Griffin Warrior's right side, along with the necklace, beads and rings. Athena is, once again, taking up the props of gender to code her gender to Odysseus. Water collection and carrying was a decidedly female task in Bronze Age Greece: we see it, for example, on the Bronze Age Thera frescoes, where women crowd around a well to collect water in their jars. The combination of weapons and pitcher, breastplate and necklace, in the Griffin Warrior's tomb – a wealthy and powerful individual who used the language of objects to articulate that power – allows us to read Athena's dramatic appropriation of different objects as a way to articulate changing gender roles.

And just as Athena is gender-nonconforming in her toolkit of props, ranging from a male spear to a woman's water jug, so, too, by contrast, she has a side that speaks to an activity that was to become the defining attribute of women across the ancient world: weaving. The association between women, weaving and Athena goes back to the very beginning, when – according to myth – women were first created, as a punishment for men. Pandora, the first woman, was said to have been modelled from clay by the gods as a *kalon kakon* – a 'beautiful evil' – specifically engineered to make men's lives worse.[36] It was Athena who was said to have been responsible for dressing this 'beautiful evil' in a gorgeous silvery gown, belt and veil that would fit her out for her beguilement of men. Women's seductive appearance, above all, the ancient poets say, makes for men's ruin (and, of course, they don't hesitate for a moment in assuming this is all the women's fault). 'Don't let a woman with her curvy butt and tempting words get in your head: she just wants your barn', warns Hesiod; like a delicate horse that's pretty to look at but useless for anything else, writes another, she'll lie around all day beautifying herself and never get stuck into housework.[37] (The next god to give their gift is Hermes, who grants Pandora 'a bitch's mind and the character of a thief':

succinct words that sum up, bleakly, the Greeks' systematic misogyny.)[38] And it was Athena who was charged with endowing Pandora with the skill that, for ancient Greek men, would go on to typify women (and women's wiles) – the art of weaving richly worked cloth.[39] This web of associations, which links women's highly charged and dangerous beauty and potent temptation of men to Athena's powers of weaving, is picked up in Homer's *Iliad*: for, when Hera dresses for her seduction of Zeus, it is, as we saw earlier, a divine robe woven by the female Athena that she puts on, and the intricately woven images of Aphrodite's feminine love belt that imbue her with her irresistible sexual power – and the power to get what she wants, too.[40]

But it is, above all, in the *Odyssey* where the nexus that began with Pandora – connecting women's weaving with their seductive potential and the power to keep men under their control – comes to the fore. As Telemachus' ship sails from Pylos to Sparta in the continued search for his father, Athena bounds back to Olympus, demanding that it is now time for Hermes to be sent to Calypso's island: Odysseus, she says, is to be released from the goddess, who forces the Greek hero to stay by her side. With Zeus' backing, Hermes duly sets out, skimming the ocean like a cormorant searching for fish and wetting its wing tips in the salt sea. He emerges from the indigo water at Calypso's island, Ogygia, where the nymph lives in a cave burdened with lush overgrowth, alders and poplars and scented cypress trees, suffused by flickering springs and iris-dappled meadows where falcons and sea crows chatter. A fire in the cave sends the smoke of citrus and pine drifting across the island. And in the cavern's dark recesses – menacingly, potently – stands the nymph, Calypso: singing and working at her loom, weaving a mesh across Odysseus, who is held captive behind her – like a fly caught in a spider's web.[41]

The question is – it has always been, all the way back to Pandora: what is so powerful about the weaving of a woman?

11

CALYPSO

Weaver

OGYGIA

She likes to hunt at dawn, when the sun dyes the ocean a mottled violet and she wades ankle-deep in the shallows, trailing the sea snails that cluster on the rocks and tint the water indigo. Sweeping her fingers in the salt water and plucking, ignoring the flail of the suckers. Squeezing the wormy flesh, naked and vulnerable, between two fingertips, then pounding the shell to fragments on the rock. Watching the drop of purple-red dye coalesce, like blood.

She likes to boil at noon. Staining the thread, like a drowning man's hair, in the purplish water that simmers in the cauldron. Fumes of worm and wool drifting across the island that make the birds scatter from their nests in the pine trees.

She likes to weave at dusk, when the sun turns the sea crimson like her web and she can thread and sing and shape the world in knots of string. Like a body that she can feel, the tapestry seems to her to come alive in the shadows that flicker, and the threads throb under her fingers. That blood-red purple twine that makes her dream, sometimes, that she's weaving with the guts of men.

Sometimes she thinks she's been alone for too long.

Colouring In

The chromatogram that flickers up on the screen of the Museum of Cretan Ethnology's Shimadzu 5050A Gas Chromatograph–Mass Spectrometer is in high-contrast black and white. The line of the graph jitters up and down in peaks, like a monochrome heart rate monitor, with annotations that translate the chart into figures: *19.782. 23.794. 43.733.*[1]

It might look like nothing more than a greyscale graph, destined to furnish the pages of yet another black-and-white journal.

But look a little deeper, and it explodes into a vibrant story about colour.

To Andrew Koh, in particular, these numbers mean something special. Koh is Museum Scientist at the Yale Peabody Museum, and an expert in ceramic residue analysis: the study of the organic materials stored in ancient pots, where chemical traces absorbed by the porous clay can be recovered through modern scientific techniques. Chief among these is gas chromatography–mass spectrometry (or, more palatably, GC–MS): the process of soaking fragments of ancient pottery in gently heated solvents to extract samples of what they once contained, which can then be separated – via the GC–MS instrument – into their different molecular components. Each molecule has its own special signature and can be charted and compared to those of known compounds, making it possible to identify a molecule's origins: for example, wine (tartaric acid) or olive oil (oleic acid).

But what Koh is seeing emerging on the chromatogram, as he sits in the brightly lit back rooms of the museum, is something quite different. The samples have been extracted from pots uncovered at an archaeological site at Alatzomouri Pefka, on the northern Cretan coastline and a mile or so from a Minoan palatial complex at Gournia. The Alatzomouri Pefka site is an unusual one: discovered in 2007 when a bulldozer unearthed a Minoan burial, it turned out to be – not a series of tombs, as the archaeologists originally thought – but an odd collection of basin-like hollows that seemed to have been deliberately cut into the rocky hill. Dating to the late eighteenth century BCE, the basins – standing isolated on the side of the slope, on a broad terrace surrounded by pine trees – were littered with stone tools, terracotta loom weights, smashed seashells and hundreds of fragments of ancient pottery: from massive storage jars, to tripod vessels blackened by fire. So what were these rock-cut hollows, the excavators wondered, and why had they been so carefully carved into the cliffs of a remote pine-covered hillside, a good distance from the nearest ancient town?

Koh's chromatogram seems to be providing the answer: *colour*.

Each spike in the graph has a hidden code that reveals a molecule in the residue left behind on Alatzomouri Pefka's ancient pots – and, as the lines shoot up and down, Koh can see that they're mapping exactly on to the compounds that make up natural dyes. Dibromoindigo, revealed by the chromatograph, is a deep purplish violet that is produced by crushing and heating a species of murex sea snail, which secretes the dye substance from a special gland; this colour was so desirable – and so expensive – in the ancient world that, in the later Roman period, only emperors were allowed to wear it. (This earned it the nickname 'royal purple' – a designation that actually goes all the way back to Late Bronze Age Knossos, where purple is, remarkably, described the same way on the Linear B tablets.)[2] Also present are alizarin and purpurin, vivid red dyes derived from the roots of the madder plant, and luteolin, derived from weld, a plant that produces bright yellow dye.[3] And alongside all these were the marks of lanolin – the natural oil produced in sheep's wool, which needs to be removed before dyes are applied.

What these results were showing, in other words, were the traces of a vibrant, prehistoric dye workshop: colouring in the now-invisible dyes that would have once filled vats and jars with a vivid array of rainbow hues. (Incidentally, although GC–MS isn't always used to identify colours, the 'chromatography' part of the GC–MS method comes from the ancient Greek word for colour, *chrōma*: the technique was originally invented to separate plant pigments. I remember doing paper chromatography in science lessons at school, and watching with fascination as the ink-like colours blotted their way up my scrap of paper.) The Pefka workshop had been, in other words, a bustling ancient site for the production of natural dyes that would be applied to wool and then woven into the gloriously rich-hued robes and textiles that we see depicted on frescoes throughout the Bronze Age Aegean world. The vats and basins would have been dye baths, carefully separated to soak different dye substances in water, while the tripod cooking vessels with their flame-blackened bottoms were heated over fire to process the murex purple dye. Before the advent of scientific techniques like GC–MS, natural dyestuffs – which are organic and don't leave hard evidence (with the notable exception of the hard mineral exterior of the murex seashells) – simply couldn't be recovered from the archaeological record. Now, Koh and the team are able to say, without a doubt, that they've found one of the most important sites for the prehistory of dyeing in Minoan Crete.

But what's even more exciting about the dyes identified at Pefka – red, yellow and purple – is that they match up exactly with the colours we see saturating the clothes on wall paintings of the same time period. This means that we can begin to connect the dots: to trace the story of the dyes manufactured in workshops across the Bronze Age Aegean, through their laborious transformation into clothes, all the way to who was wearing them. In one fresco from Akrotiri, Thera, a young girl with a blue shaved head (similar to the young priestess from the West House) sports a sweeping yellow veil, dyed with weld or saffron; red-dyed bands of colour (likely a product of madder) run along her sleeves and back, while purple crocuses – barely visible now – are picked out in murex purple on the shoulder of her dress.[4] This is an ancient fashionista decked out in all the brightest and best colours the Minoan world had to offer – straight from a dye workshop, just like the one at Pefka.

One of the most stunning revelations of the discoveries of palaces like Knossos, and the buried city at Akrotiri – and now, the added discovery of the dye workshop in northern Crete – is the sheer amount of colour that suffused this previously hidden Bronze Age world: from the riotously jewel-bright paintings that adorned their walls, to the multicoloured houses they lived in, to the flashing necklaces, bracelets, headbands and vivid, flamboyant clothing that they wore. The idea (propounded above all by the so-called father of art history, the eighteenth-century German antiquarian Johann Joachim Winckelmann) that the ancient world was a white one – and classical Greece above all, with its supposedly austere statues and pristine marble temples – is one of the longest-held, and most damaging, misconceptions to dog Greek history. It was born of a fundamental mistake. Ancient marble sculptures and architecture, exposed to the elements, almost always lost their pigment over time; buried artefacts, whose paint stuck to the soil, had their colour acciden-tally (and sometimes not-so-accidentally) brushed off in the process of cleaning. But it was also the product of a Western, Enlightenment desire not to question that mistake: to equate whiteness with beauty, purity and the supposed superiority of a (fantasy) 'classical' world.[5] (The very real danger of not questioning these kinds of assumptions continues today: racist groups in recent years have once again picked up on the so-called whiteness of ancient marble statues as symbols of white nationalism.)[6] In museums, books and video games, it's up to this generation to stop perpetuating an eighteenth-century delusion that has endeavoured to whitewash the past, and instead to acknowledge and restore the poly-chromy of the ancient world. Modern techniques, in recent years, have enabled experts to recover traces of paint on statues that have survived in tiny cracks and recesses (nostrils, mouths, navels), or to use cameras that can detect the minutest remnants of invisible pigments. The Elgin Marbles of the Parthenon – often in the past, by romantic aesthetes like Winckelmann, held up as the ideal of classical purity – were scrubbed clean in the British Museum in the 1930s in an effort to remove their paint: now, scientists are using infrared cameras to detect traces of the bright Egyptian blue that once splashed across the statues.[7] Slowly but surely, the ancient world is starting to be coloured in again.

The ancient Greeks would have been appalled by the suggestion that their world was a white one – Homer above all.[8] Anyone who has read Homer knows that the epics are bursting at the seams with colour. Soil, skin, blood and wine are *melas* ('black'). Flowers, thread, blood (again – there's plenty of war, after all), blushing cheeks and rainbows are *porphyreos* (usually translated as 'purple'). Swallows' feathers, dark hair and clouds are *kuaneos* ('blue', the root of our 'cyan'). The sea, famously, is *oinops* – usually translated as 'wine-dark', but really 'wine-looking' – which could, in fact, mean any number of things: dark, lustrous, saturated, reflective, bubbly or even just liquid.[9] When, in the *Odyssey*, Athena transforms Odysseus back from his beggar disguise, 'he became black-skinned [*melagchroiēs*] again', Homer writes, and 'the beard hairs grew blue [*kuaneai*] on his chin'.[10] Did Odysseus really have blue hair? Probably not: more likely, it's a kind of glossy, dark-bluish black (the same word is used for thunderclouds: we can imagine the roiling grey-blue-black of a storm). And did he have black skin? Maybe – or maybe, if we look beyond modern concepts of racial colour (which don't map on to ancient ways of thinking), Homer is writing in gendered terms instead: using the normative colour split between 'white' women and 'dark' men that we've already seen in wall paintings to underline Odysseus' virile masculin-ity.[11] These problems of translation (and they're just scraping the surface) show how shifting and complicated colour as a concept is – particularly when we're looking into other cultures, other value systems and other languages. But what we can't ignore is that the ancient world – through the glittering Bronze Age into the multicoloured realm of the Homeric epics and all the way to classical Greece – was, unquestionably, a riot of colour. And although some of that colour derived from paint (how many modern visitors to the Acropolis of Athens realize that the Parthenon was once flamboyantly painted?), much of it came from the clothes people wore on their backs – from the robes draped on the goddesses of the Parthenon, to the veil sported by the girl in the fresco at Thera.

And this is where women come into the story. Because the vibrant, colourful textiles that formed much of the polychrome backdrop to the ancient world were created by women, whose job it was to dye, spin and weave wool. The application of colour was just one of many stages in the process of producing textiles that has taken up most of the lives of most women across history. In the *Iliad*, when Hecuba goes to fetch the robe to give to Athena, it's referred to as the 'work of women' – the Sidonian women who have been enslaved by Paris – woven in shining colours.[12] In the *Odyssey*, the sea around Calypso's island is said to be purple – glittering, perhaps, with the murex sea snails that she uses to dye her wool.[13] And when, in Helen's very first appearance in the *Iliad*, she is shown weaving a tapestry of the Trojan War – imitating the poet's own enterprise in woven form – she works with purple (*porphyreos*) thread.[14] If we're going to put colour back into the ancient world, then the clothing made by women's hands is a good place to start.

Clothes Make the Man, But Women Made the Clothes[15]

When Hermes arrives at Calypso's island, the goddess is weaving. Walking to and fro before the loom in her cave, Homer tells us, she is singing and weaving with a golden shuttle. Odysseus, however, is not to be found within this intimate, private scene of a woman's work: he is, instead, the poet says, sitting weeping on the shore, looking out to sea.[16]

The *Odyssey*'s hero is well and truly shipwrecked. For nearly ten years, he has wandered across the ocean on his journey back from Troy. He has escaped forgetfulness on the island of the Lotus Eaters, blinded the monstrous Cyclops, slept with Circe (another weaving goddess who, we're told, lured him in after turning his crew into pigs), plunged to the depths of the Underworld to meet the prophet Tiresias, resisted the Sirens' song, evaded the clutches of dog-headed Scylla and the sucking whirlpool Charybdis.[17] His crew have committed the ultimate transgression, slaughtering – though they were warned not to – the sacred cattle of the god of the sun; in retribution, Zeus sent a storm that tore apart Odysseus' last remaining ship and drowned all his crew. Odysseus alone survived, washed up on the shore of Calypso's island. For seven years he has been marooned here, longing for home (though he sleeps with Calypso, and she has offered to make him immortal), but unable to leave without a ship.

Now, as Hermes flits down from Olympus and transmits Zeus' orders (backed up by Athena), Calypso is commanded to give Odysseus the tools he needs (a sharp bronze axe, a carpenter's adze and augers for boring holes) to make a raft to cross the sea.

But she also gives him something else: bolts of cloth, to make a sail.[18]

Textiles might seem trivial, mundane, even disposable now, in a post-industrialized fast-fashion world where many of us take the work required and the cost of cloth for granted. But Odysseus' seven-year wait for a sail is a timely reminder that the interconnected Bronze Age Aegean world we've been exploring throughout this book simply couldn't have existed without them. Since the mechanization of the textile industry in the wake of the Industrial Revolution – and, above all, the invention of the 'spinning jenny' in 1764 – the Western world seems to have forgotten just how valuable textiles used to be, and how much time and labour went into their production. And, as voracious consumers of fashion, we have come to ignore the cost on the people – and often the women – who produce them.

The advent of global fast fashion over the last few decades has brought cheap clothing made in sweatshops in developing countries to high-street stores in a dizzying array of seemingly endless and highly affordable styles. Textile-making has always been a major industry. It's been estimated that one in six people alive today work in some area of fashion, making it the most labour-dependent industry on the planet; most of these are women – including the vast majority of garment factory workers (around 80 per cent globally).[19] Yet, as consumption has rocketed to unprecedented levels (we now buy 400 per cent more clothes than two decades ago) and the demand for ever-cheaper prices and ever-more profit has ground on, it's been the sweatshop labourers – particularly in manufacturing nations like Bangladesh, India and China, where almost all industry has been outsourced to maximize profit – who have had to bear the cost. Below-subsistence wages that don't even cover half of what a family needs to survive. Gruelling workdays of 13–14 hours, seven days a week.[20] Unsafe working conditions that have led to horrific disasters like the 2013 Rana Plaza collapse in Bangladesh, the deadliest tragedy in the garment industry history in which 1,134 people were killed (most of them women) and at least 2,000 injured when an unsound factory collapsed on its workers. (The year following the Rana Plaza disaster was the industry's most profitable of all time.)[21] Little to no legal protection, collective or trade union rights mean that there is barely any protection against frequent verbal and even physical abuse from managers.[22] Meanwhile, Western consumers turn a blind eye to the human cost of cheap clothes, treating them like disposable rubbish – sending a lorry-load of worn clothing (most of which is non-biodegradable) to be burnt or buried in landfill every second, and making fashion the second most polluting industry in the world after oil.[23]

This deliberate attitude of ignorance today towards the women who make our clothes goes beyond the way we consume them: for a long time, it was a hallmark of the way we thought about the ancient past, too. Because traditional fabrics are perishable and don't survive in the historical record (with a very few exceptions), and because they were woven by women – who weren't seen (by generations of male scholars who studied the past) as worthy of anything more than a footnote – textiles were largely ignored in the study of the ancient world. If they were taken into consideration at all, it was only to gain insight into elite fashions: not the day-to-day reality of women's work, the bedsheets, blankets, tablecloths, wedding veils, nappies and funeral shrouds that made up the gritty fabric of the Bronze Age world.

Yet women's weaving – consistently emphasized in Homer as the epitome of female work (we only have to think of Hector and Telemachus sending Andromache and Penelope, respectively, to 'go in and do your work, stick to the loom and distaff') – plays a crucial role in the *Odyssey*: from Calypso's woven sail that helps Odysseus get home, all the way to Penelope's famous weaving trick, the funeral cloth that she weaves during the day and unpicks at night to fend off her suitors and wait for Odysseus' return.[24] It's a fundamental paradox that, while denigrated as 'only' women's work, weaving – and the products of weaving – are also represented as possessing immense power in the Homeric epics, both symbolic and real. (I can't help but see a similar paradox in the modern billion-dollar global textile empire that rests on powerless and exploited women's work.) Not only does Odysseus rely on the product of Calypso's weaving to get back home; not only does Penelope need a loom to deceive the suitors clamouring at her doors, for three long years – it goes much deeper than that. Homer also makes a direct comparison between weaving cloth and weaving tales, which makes the poet, too, a weaver-of-sorts of text.[25] (The English word 'text' actually comes from Latin *textus*, which means 'woven texture'.) We only have to look at Helen, whose very first cameo in the *Iliad* is the scene where she weaves 'the many troubles, tests, and tribulations that Trojan horsemen and bronze-armoured Greeks suffered at Ares' hands because of her'.[26] That is to say: she crafts the same story as the *Iliad*. These women weavers lie at the core of what Homer is and does. In many ways, they're the unsung poets of the epics.

So if we're going to recover the lost textiles and hidden colours of the Late Bronze Age that were the products of so many women's hands, and that lay at the heart of some of Homer's – and women's – stories, we'll have to bring together a whole ream of evidence of different kinds: from the everyday grind that's visible in the wear and tear on women's skeletons to the bureaucratic records of Linear B, from glossy Bronze Age wall paintings to lumpy clay artefacts that excavators often used to throw away, from advances in experimental archaeology to the latest developments in scientific methods like GC–MS.

And if we do all this, perhaps we'll be able to stop discarding the textiles of the past, if not the present, too.

Not-So-Fast Fashion

On the opposite side of Crete from Alatzomouri Pefka, along the string of wind-whipped craggy southern beaches, lies Myrtos: a sleepy fishing village with white-painted houses spilling down cobbled streets and tavernas clustering along the seafront. Just along the coast, however, an intrepid visitor willing to brave the leg-scraping thorn bushes and scramble up the stony slope will be rewarded, as I was, with the ghost of its ancient twin: a prehistoric village of tiny jostling rooms interspersed with steep alleyways, tumbling down a cliff that overlooks the azure sea and was abandoned over four thousand years ago.[27] All that remains of the walls now are criss-crossing stumps, fenced off and overgrown with silvery-purple wild lavender and thyme that fill the air with their gorgeous aroma. But we can tell – from the heap of weaving-associated artefacts uncovered in excavations – that it was a hive of activity when the Minoans lived here, with a cluster of houses (each probably containing a different family) busily engaged in textile manufacture. This little prehistoric settlement, inhabited for only a couple of hundred years before it was abandoned, preserves a remarkable time capsule of all the different stages of working with textiles. And so we can begin to reconstruct what life must have been like for the women of this humble Cretan village – and to recover all the labour that would have gone into the gathering and processing of materials and the production of cloth: a day, if you like, in the life of a prehistoric garment worker.

The first, and most basic, thing you need to make cloth are the fibres that will form the bulk of the thread: wool, for instance, or flax (which makes linen). Sheep bones discovered at Myrtos show that the inhabitants were rearing sheep for wool: as the bones present a mixture of male and female adults, and males are well known for producing good wool but no milk and tough meat, we can tell that they were being used for their wool.[28] Next came washing, preparing and dyeing the wool. Large tubs with spouts and convenient run-off channels, found in several of the houses, are clearly the wash tubs needed to rinse wool: traces of animal fats (revealed through gas chromatography) suggest that sheep's wool would have been soaked here to remove its natural grease.[29] Perhaps the wool was also dyed at the same time – a nearby hollowed-out stone bowl might have been used for grinding dyestuffs. In fact, several oak trees that grow near Myrtos are host to a particular type of insect, known as kermes, of which the female produces a particularly brilliant red dye (it's the origin of our word 'crimson') – so it's possible that this was a local speciality.[30]

Once our women had their wool and washed and dyed it – perhaps in a locally produced deep crimson – they would move on to one of the most labour-intensive steps: spinning. Woollen fibres, in particular, are very short (only a couple of centimetres at best, if you think about a sheep's fleece). To make them longer, the fibres need to be spun together, overlapping one bundle of fibres with another, to create a continuous thread. The women at Myrtos would have had a couple of tools at their disposal: in one hand a distaff, a large wooden stick that held the prepared wool; in the other a spindle, a smaller stick with a clay weight on the bottom (called a spindle whorl) that the spinner could flick round in circles to twist the wool from the distaff into thread. Although the wood of the distaff and spindle degrades with time, the clay spindle whorls – unimpressive lumps of coarse brown clay, a couple of centimetres across – remain: and dozens of them were found scattered all over the site at Myrtos, as if the spinning women were busy making thread anywhere and everywhere they went.[31] Modern estimates suggest that, before the invention of the spinning wheel (which came to Europe, probably from the east, during the Middle Ages), it would have taken seven or eight hours to spin enough thread to be able to weave for an hour – meaning that spinning would have kept women occupied for most of the day, watching their children at the same time, perhaps, as they stocked up on thread before they could even begin to weave.[32] It's no coincidence that, in Homer, Telemachus tells Penelope, and Hector tells Andromache, to 'stick to the distaff': spinning would clearly have taken up most of women's time, and it's what they above all came to be associated with. (In the nineteenth century, this led to the term 'the distaff side', a collective phrase that sought to gather all women within the province of the distaff.) And, although we don't see Calypso spinning, when Odysseus is finally released from her island and makes his way to his next and penultimate destination, the fantastically idealized, peaceful and civilized island of the Phaeacians – from where he finally succeeds in getting transport back to Ithaca – he meets the powerful queen of the palace, Arete, seated with her enslaved women by the fireside and busily spinning purple wool.[33]

It's not just at Myrtos that we have evidence of spindle whorls, the tangible – if easily overlooked – link in the chain that leads us back to the very concrete world of women's weaving. They crop up all over the Bronze Age Aegean like tactile voices from the past, reminders of the all-too-invisible world of women's work – sometimes making up the most numerous finds discovered on a site. At the archaeological site of Troy, it's estimated that over ten thousand clay spindle whorls have been excavated from Troy II alone (this is the layer of the site where Schliemann found 'Helen's jewels', and that corresponds roughly to the date of ancient Myrtos, around the mid to latter half of the third millennium BCE).[34] These whorls – some of them decoratively incised with soaring arches and curving lines – would have been used day after day by real women in Troy: perhaps even a woman who might have inspired the pattern for Helen herself, who might have sat spinning the vibrant purple thread for her weaving with just such a clay spindle whorl. It's even possible, at Troy, to trace the origin of the purple dye that Homer imagines Helen using when she weaves her tapestry of the Trojan War: heaps of crushed murex shells, cousins of those found at Pefka in Crete, are deposited all over the city from Troy VI/VIIa (the layers usually associated with Homer's Troy) and indicate a major production of the prized purplish-blue-red murex dye at Troy (and probably a substantial

A spindle whorl from the historical site of Troy (third millennium BCE).
Could an early precursor of Helen of Troy have spun her thread with this?

textile industry too) in the Late Bronze Age.[35] When Homer imagines Helen spinning and weaving purple thread behind the Trojan walls, it's thus possible to resurrect the faint traces of the colours of a real world at Troy – a world that was spun with the clay whorls and dyed purple with the sea snails we find at Troy today, into a web like Helen's.

And this brings us to the central part of producing textiles: weaving. Helen's tapestry and the clothes of our Myrtos women – indeed, any textile in the Bronze Age Aegean world – would have been created on a warp-weighted loom: a wooden frame with threads (known as the warp) hanging vertically to the ground, pulled tight by heavy clay loom weights. The weaver's job was to use a shuttle to interlace a second set of threads, known as the weft (an Old English past tense of 'weave'), horizontally over and under the warp – so creating the intertwined weave of cloth. (The ancient Greek word for weaving, huphainō, is etymologically connected to 'weft/weave' – meaning that when we say 'weave' today, we're using a word that's actually related to Homer's.) At Myrtos, clay loom weights – all that usually survives of ancient looms – were discovered in two piles near the washing tubs: one had collapsed from the room above, where the loom had possibly been placed on the flat roof. Here, just like the women we see weaving together on later Greek vase paintings, we can imagine groups of women gathering in the sunshine on the roof of their homes, raised above the humdrum noise of the Cretan village and cooled by the sea breeze, taking turns on one of the two large looms that they shared between them.[36]

As vivid a picture as we are able to conjure from the archaeological remains, what we can't possibly recover is how much time all these steps in the wool-working process actually took. This is where experimental archaeology comes in. Expert modern textile workers can recreate the tools used by Bronze Age women, copying the exact shapes and weights of spindle whorls and loom weights, and thus reproduce the kinds of threads and cloth that ancient spinners and weavers could have made. By measuring the length of time taken to manufacture different types and sizes of cloth with ancient technologies, specialists in textile production have been able to estimate how long it would have taken to spin and weave – for instance – a sail. According to Marie-Louise Nosch, an expert in Mycenaean wool-work, it would have taken one woman, working seven-hour days, around four years to spin and weave enough fabric for a single ancient Greek sail.[37]

And it's not only sails. Following the same logic, Nosch has been able to show that simply to spin enough thread for a piece of cloth known as a *te-pa* – which we know from the Linear B tablets was annually mandated, as a kind of local tribute to be sent to the palace at Knossos – would have required over six months of ten-hour-a-day labour by one woman. To get their required tribute into the palace every year, then, it's likely that all the women in the Cretan households around Knossos (and probably the children, too) would have had to be mobilized into textile work to meet the substantial targets we find listed in the Linear B records.[38] Homer presents a bleak picture of what this might have looked like. In one of the epic's most powerful similes, we find a stalemate in the raucous, violent battle around Troy compared to a quiet domestic scene: 'still they held steady – as a careful woman, a worker skilful with her hands, holds steady a pair of scales and keeps the wool and weight evenly balanced on both sides'. But it's no easy life. In this rare glimpse into the lived reality of weaving women, we see the hand-to-mouth world of a working mother, who – the poet tells us – is pushing to spin as much as she can, 'to earn a pitiful allowance for her children'.[39] This is a woman textile worker, struggling for a menial wage to support her family: a scenario that, as we've seen, is desperately common in the modern global textile industry, too. And we can see the toll taken by this strenuous daily labour on ancient female skeletons: analysis of Bronze Age cemeteries across Greece shows that women often experienced trauma (broken bones and injuries) on their upper skeleton (chiefly hands and forearms), hinting at their day-to-day involvement – and the cost of that involvement – in labour relying on repeated stress on the upper body, as in food processing and craft production.[40]

And it is this that brings us from Crete all the way back to the fantasy island of Ogygia, and Calypso's sail – and enables us, perhaps, to shed some light on exactly why Odysseus remained there for so long. Perhaps the traditional way of looking at it is all wrong, picturing the goddess – as the male gods Zeus and Hermes do, as well as the poet Homer – as a wily weaving temptress who ensnares Odysseus in her web (like Pandora), a woman whose weaving powers are a dangerous net that catches men. As an isolated weaver, unlike all the other groups of women we have seen – the queens and their enslaved weaving and spinning attendants like Homer's Arete and Helen, the assembly-line crowds of captive women at Pylos, the community weavers in hilltop villages like Myrtos – Calypso lives alone, cut off from a sisterhood of weaving women.[41] When Odysseus arrives, she has to work to meet a man's textile demands entirely by herself – not only the sail he needs for his ship, but his clothes, too (Homer is careful to tell us that she sends him on his way with plenty of new garments to wear).[42] Collecting and preparing wool, washing, dyeing, spinning, weaving, stitching, would have been a taxing enough task to take up most of the hours in a woman's day, as we've seen – and that's with a group of weaving women around you, plugged into the local wool and trade economies, with a domestic stock of looms and sheep and dyes. So perhaps this isn't a story about a woman holding a man captive. Perhaps, instead, it's a story about a woman who's been given an impossibly large and lonely task, who's been held hostage by the demands of her labour.

Perhaps, if you lived all by yourself in the middle of the ocean, it would take seven years to make a sail.

The True Cost of Clothes

Calypso's isolation means that she is also cut off from the wider economy of international trade. As the Bronze Age wore on, after the weaving village at Myrtos was abandoned, and the early second millennium BCE dawned, ships started to ply their way east from Crete across the Aegean and south towards Egypt, carrying precious cargoes of purple-dyed textiles for export to the wealthy consumers of ancient Egypt, the Aegean islands and Anatolia. In Egypt, from around 2000 BCE onwards, we find the glorious colours and patterns of Cretan textiles copied in tomb paintings, hinting at an eager market for Minoan-produced tapestries. Meanwhile, wall paintings across Late Bronze Age Greece, from the labyrinthine court at Knossos to the gold-drenched palaces at Pylos, Tiryns and Mycenae and the bustling streets of Akrotiri on Thera, bear witness to the fashionable Mycenaean elite's love of the sumptuously dyed and patterned textiles that Crete was so famous for. Women, like the veiled girl on Thera, dance across the frescoes wearing flounced skirts, tassels, headbands, patterned belts, all in gorgeous shades of red, blue, purple, yellow and white, produced by the kinds of natural dyes that were recently identified at Pefka. With the rise of the Mycenaeans, both on the mainland and in Crete, formidable bureaucracies began to form in major administrative centres like those of the palaces of Pylos and Knossos. These flourished on the pay-offs of local fashion and international trade, and developed over the centuries into massive centralized economies. As profits swelled, textile production became one of the main occupations of these palaces, in order both to meet the ever-increasing needs of the local elites, and – it seems likely – to fulfil trade demands. And increasing demand meant one thing: more labour.

So it is that, by the Late Bronze Age, we're seeing – captured in the snapshot of the Linear B records, the last office accounts of the palace scribes before the palaces burned down at the collapse of the Bronze Age – truly vast operations of textile production, dependent on a huge amount of low-status, female labour. We've already met some of these captives and their children when we traced the journey of the seven women of Chios who were taken to Pylos and allotted rations, along with their allocated job: making o-nu-ka, a finely decorated kind of cloth border. But they are just the tip of the iceberg. The Linear B tablets give evidence of around two thousand low-status women workers; at Pylos, the majority of these are engaged in textile production, putting their number into the several hundreds, while at Knossos on Crete (the other major source of Linear B) every single woman whose work can be identified is assigned to textile labour – over a thousand women in total.[43] Most of these – especially at Pylos – seem to be dependent (probably enslaved) labour, with nearly 40 per cent of all the women workers at the Pylian palace brought in from abroad: we read of women displaced in droves from Miletus (70 from this settlement alone), Halicarnassus (26 women), Knidos (20), Chios (7) – all locations in the eastern Aegean and western Anatolia.[44] It's interesting to note that these kinds of numbers, and tasks, are echoed in the Homeric epics. On the supposedly peaceful island of the Phaeacians, the realm of the spinning queen Arete, for instance, we're told that the king has fifty enslaved women in the palace who are charged with grinding flour or – significantly – spinning and weaving the fabrics for the palace.[45] In other words, even though we're in a fantasy land in the *Odyssey*, we're seeing the same numbers of workers, and the same kinds of textile jobs being assigned to palace personnel, as those of the actual, historical enslaved weaving women recorded on the tablets at the Mycenaean palace of Pylos.

The foreign female populations at Pylos are disproportionately clustered into textile production – suggesting that they were deliberately being sought to make up the labour shortfall.[46] And what a shortfall it would have been. The Linear B tablets give us some idea of the sheer scale of textile production: at Knossos, for instance, in around 1350 BCE, we know that the palace controlled around a hundred thousand sheep – a testimony to the unimaginably vast amounts of wool being processed (equivalent, in one season, to making a hundred thousand bulky modern sweaters by hand), and the massive operation the palaces were trying to run.[47] Some of the women appear to have been sought for their expertise in a specific area of textile work, such as 'the spinning-women from Miletus', 'the linen-working women from Asia Minor' or 'the Chian *onuka*-makers'; others seem simply to fill a gap in the relentless assembly line that shunts wool from combers to spinners (*a-ra-ka-te-ja*, from Greek *ēlakatē*, 'distaff'), then along to dozens of nameless weavers, stitchers (*ra-pi-ti-ra*) and decorators.

The enslavement of women during raids is a practice, as we've seen, that is brutally written into the Homeric epics, and that lies at the very core of the *Iliad*'s narrative (as well as military) economy – from Briseis and Chryseis, within the Trojan War, to the forecasted fate of Andromache after Troy's fall. But Homer also makes sure to mention women who have explicitly been captured for their ability with textiles. We have already encountered some of them: the Sidonian women, who wove the robe that Hecuba offers to Athena in the *Iliad* – and who,

Homer tells us, were enslaved by Paris on his way back to Troy with Helen.[48] When Agamemnon, meanwhile, attempts to make an offer of recompense to Achilles for taking Briseis, he suggests – not only Briseis – but seven women, too, seized on the island of Lesbos, who are particularly prized for their weaving.[49] (Just like the seven real women weavers from Chios, another Aegean island down the coast from Lesbos, at the historical Mycenaean palace of Pylos.) And Hector predicts a lifetime of weaving at the loom for Andromache, enslaved in Greece – just like the real women from Anatolia brought into endless weaving jobs for the palace at Pylos – if he loses the war.[50] Women in this world, it seems, face the constant danger of being corralled into forced textile labour, whether they're on the fringes of conflict like the Sidonian women, or at the very centre of the war like Andromache – rounded up by men to fill the royals' devouring needs for more cloth, and more capital.

Even in the cursory record-holdings of the Linear B tablets at Pylos, it's easy to read between the lines to see that the kind of textile work women were being made to do within the Mycenaean palace would have made for a grim existence. List after list of jobs to be filled, and rations assigned to nameless hordes of women and children, shows that the women like the spinners from Miletus and the Chian *onuka*-makers are consigned to a life of never-ending labour, their children co-opted into working for the palace. They are entirely reliant for their food on bland and unvaried quotas of wheat and figs (or sometimes barley and olives) from the higher-ups; they have no money, no property, no pay.[51] They are kept under close supervision in the central palace (rather than the outlying villages), and are assigned to specialized tasks rather than the entire production chain – perhaps, it's been suggested, to give the central overseer more control, or so as not to threaten the economy if one group decided to revolt.[52] This dire fate, doled out by the patriarchal central palace administration, is consistently targeted at women. With palace-controlled tasks running on completely gender-segregated lines, men and women can be seen to have led very different lives: we see only female bath attendants and flour grinders (just like the Phaeacian enslaved women in Homer), for instance, and only male shepherds and bronze smiths; and there are far more low-status women workers than men (who mostly occupy the middle rank of independent crafts-men).[53] In the rare cases when men and women do share the same jobs, it is the women who are given the labour-intensive, repetitive, low-ranked occupations.[54] Men are never mentioned with children, so it seems clear that (as often across history) women had to undertake a double and uncounted labour, in the form of childcare, alongside their textile duties. Men, on the other hand, operate on a different scale of recompense altogether: in one instance, a man doing the same task as a woman receives *sixty times* her food rations (probably because, in contrast to the low-status groups of women who depended on the palace, he was an independent contractor running his own workshop).[55] All these women weavers' titles, ethnicities or jobs are scrawled by the scribes across the Linear B tablets with the accompanying ideogram of a woman: a cartoonish figure made up of nothing more than a head and sketched-out skirt. It must have seemed to these women, sometimes, that they were indeed nothing more than the fabrics they made; that their broken bones and empty stomachs embodied the true cost of the lavish, many-coloured clothes they laboured so hard to create – with the work of their hands.

The closest we can get to visualizing the community of Mycenaean Greek women: the signs for 'woman' in the Linear B tablets, with the women represented by heads, breasts and skirts. It was these kinds of skirts that the women would have made with their own hands.

At a Fair Price

One of the most striking things about the Mycenaean Linear B tablets is the connection between exploitation and textiles, and the systematic aiming of that exploitation at women. As we've seen, the Homeric epics, too, present a picture of a palace textile economy that relies on the labour of enslaved women, in the purportedly ideal realm of the Phaeacians – where fifty enslaved women have been brought in to generate the exquisite textiles, 'the work of women' (the poet says), for which the Phaeacians are said to be renowned.[56] It would be – and has been, for critics in the past – all too easy to skim over the monotonous, monochrome description of these silent makers, and concentrate instead on the technicolour account that surrounds them of the bronze-walled, blue-enamelled, golden-portalled royal palace: the jewel in the crown of the final fantasy land on Odysseus' grand tour.[57] Sometimes, when you start to fill the colour in again, it shows a different world than you thought. But it's essential that we open our eyes. We need to start taking notice of the work of women's hands, both in the ancient world of myth and history, and today – and the undeniable cost at which it comes, the immense labour and exploitation of women (as well as our planet) that goes on behind textiles. Women's work is the thread touched by human hands that connects us to the past, and weaves the fabric of our future. Let's not ignore it any longer.

If history provides us with a vivid and salutary warning, then it also – as so often – shows another way forward. If we cross to central Anatolia in the early second millennium BCE, to an ancient city known as Kanesh – just over a hundred miles south-east of Hattusa –we find ourselves in the midst of a bustling Assyrian trading post, or *karum*. This powerful and cosmopolitan trade colony was established in the twentieth century BCE by Assyrian merchants trekking huge distances by donkey caravan along the trade routes that criss-crossed from Mesopotamia into the Anatolian heartland. The more than twenty-two thousand clay cuneiform tablets unearthed here – baked in the fire that devastated the city around the mid nineteenth century BCE – give us a wealth of information about the merchants who operated in the Kanesh trading quarter: and they have an eye-opening story to tell about the role of women in Assyrian textile sales. Because, unlike the Linear B tablets in Greece, they contain not just figures, records and transactions, but also stacks of private letters, written between the merchant agents who lived and worked in Kanesh and their families – and wives – back home in the Assyrian capital, Assur.

These letters give a fascinating insight into the inner workings of Assyrian business between women and men. They show, remarkably, that the wives, sisters and daughters of the Kanesh merchants were not only weaving the cloth and organizing the supply of textiles that were traded by their menfolk: they were actually raking in a considerable private profit from their work, delivered into their own separate financial accounts to spend for their own purposes – whether that was running the household, lending credit to both men and women, or investing capital in raw materials for more textiles (or more enslaved workers) to grow the business.[58] One sister in particular, called Taram-Kubi – a sharp-eyed businesswoman, keenly aware of the value of her textiles on the Anatolian market – complains that her brother isn't representing her properly, and insists that he sell her work at a fair price: 'To whom else but me,' she declares, 'would you send only 1 mina, 10 shekels for 6 textiles? Now Kutallānum is bringing you 6 *kutānum*-textiles. If you are my brother, you should not send me less than ⅓ mina per textile!'[59] In a second letter, her only sign-off is to remind him not to forget the money he owes: 'Why don't you send to me the proceeds from my textiles?'[60] Another woman, Lamassi, makes twenty-five large woollen textiles every year in her household, selling twenty via her husband in Kanesh; it's been estimated that, after taxes and the cost of raw materials, her annual financial return would have been enough to buy a small house in Assur.[61] These were women weavers who were determined to get a fair wage, to reap profits from their work and to invest in ever-expanding ventures; not just sisters and wives, not just textile workers, but entrepreneurial and successful business partners, too.

Clothes were about more than business, though, in the ancient world – as important as that was. They were also a central tenet of property holding, dowry and inheritance. It's this underlying symbolism of clothes – as part of the property of the household, and the property of the bride – that we see being drawn on when Odysseus is given clothes by the next woman he meets on his travels: Nausicaa, daughter of Arete and princess of the Phaeacians. And so it's time to hoist Calypso's hard-spun sail and sally forth to the penultimate stop on Odysseus' travels: the fantastically rich, and fabulously urbane, legendary island of the Phaeacians.

12

NAUSICAA

Bride

ISLAND OF THE PHAEACIANS

She goes to her dowry chest when no one is watching. After their nurse has left them, snuffing out the lamp with a song and a prayer, she slips out of bed. Bare feet on the wooden floor, cold as the river that slides out to the sea. Nightdress rustling as she drops, cross-legged, to the floor. Lifting the lid of the chest, the dry scent of herbs meeting her in the darkness, and the oil the slave women worked into the threads of the folded robes. Just like she's done every night since she was a girl. In all the ways that matter, she still is.

She feels them out, one by one, all the goods that measure her. She cannot see them in the dark, but does not need to: they are an extension of her own expendable body, these goods that will be traded with her on her wedding day. Mottled purple robes that her mother wove, soft and supple, like her skin. Pale spindles with their brittle finials, like her fingerbones. Gemstones gleaming onyx, like her eyes. And she knows what her suitors will compete to offer her father in return, once she goes on the market. She has seen the hordes of oxen in the river valley, waiting to be bartered for her hand, their hides fire-branded so they can't be taken back.

Sometimes, when the nights wear on and the moon chariot mounts the sky and she can't sleep, she thinks she'll climb into the chest and pull the lid shut. She wonders if they'll notice that she's gone. She is, after all, just one of the costly gifts that her father will trade with all the fabrics and jewels to the highest bidder. Why shouldn't she be carried with the chest, too? The slaves would heave her on the back of the wedding cart, tie her down with leather straps, and she'd toss and sway as the mules pulled their load to her chosen suitor's house. Just another piece of cargo.

The Price of a Bride

The year is turning into 1902, a chill breeze sweeping across the exposed rocks of the upper city, blowing sand across the half-excavated remains of ancient Susa in south-west Iran. It is just over thirty years since Schliemann struck gold at Troy, and smuggled the so-called jewels of Helen to Germany. Two years since Evans, under a flagrant Union Jack, cut his spade on Knossos.

The French, led by archaeologist and prehistorian Jacques de Morgan, have managed by royal decree to secure an indefinite monopoly on excavations in Iran. As the jostling European powers stake out their archaeological kingdoms across the map of the ancient world, vying for their slice of the past, de Morgan must feel, now, that it is his turn.

The two-metre-tall black stone column emerges from the earth over the course of a couple of months, broken into three hacked-off pieces, like an ancient jigsaw puzzle. As the dirt is brushed off and the fragments gradually assembled, the Iranian workmen run their fingers over the archaic script carved into the surface – hundreds of lines of miniature cuneiform symbols across the front and back of the sleek black column, topped by a relief carving that gleams in the winter sunlight. On the right, the Mesopotamian god of justice, Shamash, sits enthroned, straight-backed and resplendent, as he hands, with godly dignity, the symbols of kingship (a rod and ring of rope) to another male figure: the king Hammurabi, one of the most formidable rulers of the Old Babylonian Empire, who built Babylon into a force to be reckoned with through brutal military conquest and legal reform. Hammurabi's collection of laws was renowned through the ancient world, an instant classic that was copied and commented on for hundreds of years, parcelled out as scribal exercises in Mesopotamia well into the first millennium BCE – even though the original had never been found.

Until now.

As Assyriologists rushed to translate the text wrapping around the mysterious black stone, the discovery grew into a worldwide sensation.

This was, indeed, Hammurabi's law code, in its original eighteenth-century BCE form – looted from the neighbouring Babylonian Empire hundreds of years after its creation, seized by an Elamite king of Susa with a certain fondness for antiques (proving that the market for antiquities is, itself, an ancient one). It is one of the oldest, and one of the most complete, sets of laws ever to survive from the ancient world; the French, following their Elamite predecessor's example, promptly carted it off to the Louvre where it can still be seen today (a copy resides in the United Nations headquarters, not far from the Qadesh peace treaty with Puduhepa's seal). Produced around the late 1750s BCE, the laws etched into the surface of the column, nearly three hundred in total, appear to cover every eventuality that might crop up in civil and criminal law: from what to do if a woman has an argument with her husband, to how to deal with a farmer who has flooded his neighbour's fields, to the handling of medical malpractice. They provide redress for crimes – murder, robbery, assault – and address inheritance rights, sale and rental of real estate, appropriate professional conduct, ownership of enslaved people, and the resolution of debts (in the most dire circumstances, the remedy is to sell yourself and your family into slavery).[1]

While the overarching aim is to conjure a picture of benevolent justice (and it's likely that much of the code was a pious demonstration of Hammurabi's righteous rule for the benefit of the gods, as much as anything else), one can't help but notice, now, that – in this undeniably patriarchal society – women are treated as little more than the property of men: they're either betrothed virgins waiting in their fathers' homes, or wives sitting in the households of their husbands.[2] There's a noticeable disparity between how men and women are treated by the law. A woman – but not a man – who tries to divorce her spouse and is seen to be 'disparaging' him can be bound and thrown in the river; a wife – but not a husband – who spends too much money and talks her husband down can be enslaved in the house, while her husband remarries; a woman who fails to provide her husband with children can be summarily divorced; a wife who is assaulted and raped has to share the blame with her attacker, and is drowned alongside him.[3] And it's women, and women only, who are subjected to the worst and most severely grotesque punishments – like the unspeakably gruesome penalty of being impaled on a stake.[4]

One of the major categories Hammurabi is concerned with is marriage – above all, the financial practicalities of arranging a union between bride and groom, the inheritance of property and the allocation of possessions on a marriage's end. This might make prehistoric marriage seem a rather bureaucratic, materially orientated affair, and in some ways it was. Several clauses in Hammurabi's laws mention a 'bride price' (*terhatu*) – a payment from the groom to the bride's father that served legally to secure betrothal (and the alliance between both sides of the family) before the actual marriage took place: a kind of deposit to confirm the groom's commitment and, in turn, to stake his claim to the bride. (Other ancient languages – Sumerian, Hebrew, Aramaic, Hittite, Greek – have technical legal words for this kind of bride price, and it crops up in the Bible, too.) The bride, in turn, brought with her a dowry: a non-compulsory gift from her father (ancient words for dowry come from the term 'gift' – as does modern English dowry, from Latin *dotare*, 'to endow') that was transferred upon marriage to the new husband's household and was managed (and spent) by him. In contrast to the bride price, this didn't constitute a legal bond between bride and groom; instead, it acted as a financial start-up fund, a contribution towards setting up the new household and, ultimately, a fall-back provision for the wife, should she lose her husband. This is made clear by the fact that Hammurabi's laws state plainly that the only occasion on which a wife might gain access to her dowry was if the marriage ended: either in divorce (provided, of course, she didn't have to jump in the river) or on the death of her husband.[5] A widow gains some protection in the laws, with an element of control over her dowry (until it passes into the management of her next husband) and, in certain legal texts, some choice in the matter of remarriage.[6] But to gain such independence, her husband first had to do the decent thing and die.

For a young woman starting on the long road of betrothal, then, as her suitors vied with gifts of silver and gold and her father bargained with her dowry, it must have seemed that it wasn't only men who paid the price for a bride.

Cowgirls

Back in the *Odyssey*, night has fallen on the isolated, god-chosen, myth-suffused island of the Phaeacians, and Nausicaa – princess of the land – is sleeping. But her rest is not undisturbed. She is visited by a dream: Athena, protector of Odysseus and inveterate shapeshifter, has floated into her chamber like a breath of wind, in the guise of Nausicaa's close female companion. 'Your marriage is coming,' the goddess whispers, her words seeming to drift through Nausicaa's dreams. 'You'll need to wear beautiful clothes, and provide robes for your retinue at your wedding. You have suitors across the land; you won't be a virgin much longer. Go, when dawn breaks, and wash your clothes, the belts and dresses and shining cloths, in the river – far from the city, where the washing places are.'7

Of course (and as we'd expect of the cunning-minded goddess), Athena has an ulterior motive in preying on this young girl's hopes for marriage and sending her off, dreamy with fantasies of suitors and weddings, to the coast where the river runs into the sea. Because, at that very moment – washed up on the shore, dirty, naked and covered in brine, battered by a twenty-day storm on the voyage from Calypso's island and sleeping under a bush beneath a scattering of leaves – is none other than the epic's own hero: Odysseus.

Thus the stage is set, and the drama masterfully orchestrated, for the scene in which the sexually charged young princess – her mind filled with marriage – encounters the naked hero on the beach, while conveniently preparing the robes that will be her wedding dress and dowry. It's no surprise that – after she's burst in on Odysseus in the bushes (genitals covered by an opportune leafy branch), and he's gone off to wash and put on some robes from the princess's trousseau – Nausicaa turns to the enslaved women who are accompanying her and coyly says she wouldn't mind a man like him for her husband. Odysseus – just as wily as Athena – has already hastened to allay any fears she and her women might have had around sexual violence, at the same time as whetting her bridal fantasies in his opening address: flattering the young girl with compliments about the many suitors who must be competing with gifts for her bride price, he slyly wishes her 'all your heart's desires, a home and husband'.[8] And this flirtatious semi-courtship between the two is brought uncomfortably (given that Odysseus is already married to Penelope) into the open once Odysseus has made himself decent and headed to the royal palace. Here, Alcinous (Nausicaa's father and the Phaeacian king), clearly impressed by what he sees as well as by Odysseus' judicious conduct, promptly offers his daughter to the stranger as his wife – along with a substantial dowry, including a house and all its furnishings.[9] Odysseus doesn't explicitly refuse, but he is quick to take Alcinous up on his next offer of conveyance back home to Ithaca on a Phaeacian ship (perhaps the king has realized he was a little overeager in his matchmaking efforts); Nausicaa, lingering by the doorpost, sends off her wished-for suitor with a wistful bid to 'remember me when you reach home'.[10] We don't know to what extent Odysseus complied with her request; when he recounts his adventures to his wife Penelope back on Ithaca, he chooses, noticeably, to omit Nausicaa (though not Calypso or Circe) from his heroic tale. Perhaps he didn't remember her after all – or perhaps it's an indication that this was a particularly near-miss marriage, and one his wife wouldn't be too pleased to hear about. And so the delicate dance of romance between the hero and the princess – the love match that never was – draws to a not-so-nostalgic close.

But while Nausicaa may have been disappointed, what's fascinating about these passages – from our point of view – is the intimate behind-the-scenes picture they give of the formalities imagined in a union between bride and groom. The practices of bride price (mentioned by Odysseus) and dowry (offered by Alcinous) that we see in Odysseus and Nausicaa's never realized courtship are in fact remarkably similar to those found in Hammurabi's Bronze Age law code, as well as other contemporary legal records from ancient Mesopotamia. Trying to recover the context of the laws behind marriage in Bronze Age Greece is a vexingly frustrating task: we have no legal texts from the Mycenaean period, no sources of Greek law in the Linear B tablets (and, as always, we're not using the Homeric epics as evidence) – certainly not enough to reconstruct the basis of a prehistoric Greek legal system. Yet there are hints that, in the deeply interconnected world of the Bronze Age, where Egyptians wore Minoan clothes and Mesopotamian love goddesses glided into the tales the Greeks told, the flourishing tradition of Meso-potamian law also penetrated into the Aegean world. As one expert in ancient law, Raymond Westbrook, puts it: 'the widespread ancient Near Eastern legal tradition did not stop dead at the shores of the Eastern Mediterranean'.[11] And although, when Hammurabi's laws were first discovered they weren't immediately appreciated for their insight into the lives of women (the male archaeologists and scholars who studied them were more intent on what they said about Hammurabi the king and law-giver), in recent decades the value of the laws for our understanding of ancient women – in particular, brides, wives and widows – has finally been recognized.

So, with the help of Hammurabi, we can take another look at Homer. The bride price, which forms the beginning of marital negotiations in Hammurabi's laws and which Odysseus claims Nausicaa's suitors will be vying with each other to proffer, is an integral feature of Homeric marriage, and – as in other ancient languages – has its own technical term in early Greek: *hedna*. In Homer, these *hedna* are presented as a kind of competitive gift-giving that secures the bride for the highest bidder: in fact, it's for this reason, we're told elsewhere, that the fabu-lously beautiful Helen married Menelaus – simply because he brought her the most gifts.[12] It's an illuminating insight into why she might not have been fully committed to the choice – and why Paris, when he came along with his combination of irresistible looks and untold riches, might have seemed a better bet.

A father (no doubt rubbing his hands gleefully as the bidding went up) could look to make a good profit from a host of eager suitors for his daughter's hand. Although *hedna* could take the form of gold and bronze, one of the most popular (and highly profitable) bride-price gifts was livestock – especially oxen. These could come in vast quantities. One particularly keen suitor in the *Iliad* is described as paying out a hundred oxen to his prospective father-in-law, followed by a promise of another thousand sheep and goats.[13] The connection between marriageable girls and their ability to bring in much-needed cattle to the family firm was so strong that, in one description of a courtship dance in Homer, the nubile girls are called 'cattle-bringing maidens' – or, if you like, cowgirls.[14]

Just as in Hammurabi's laws, the bride price paid down as surety by the groom goes hand in hand with the dowry doled out by the bride's father. Homeric scholars have puzzled for decades over how and why bride price and dowry coexist. But when we look east for Mesopotamian parallels, what Hammurabi's laws show is that, within a Bronze Age legal system, the two were not only compatible, but that they actually served distinct and important purposes: the bride price sealing the guarantee of the betrothal (the legal side of the venture); the dowry fitting out the new household and providing financial security (the economic aspect).[15] This first function of the dowry – contributions of gifts towards the couple's home – crops up in all kinds of Old Babylonian dowry lists, from palm fibres (useful for a comfy mattress stuffing) that one daughter was given by her father, to another's fifteen eating bowls (clearly a woman who liked to dine in style). Some Bronze Age women even took their spinning and weaving equipment with them, as we can tell from the chemical composition of the clay in the loom weights they left behind (in some cases across the southern Aegean, more than 15 per cent were made from non-local materials, suggesting they travelled with women moving households).[16] But the dowry's role in home furnishing is seen on most magnificent display in a grandiose diplomatic letter sent in the mid fourteenth century BCE by Tushratta, the king of Mittani (a kingdom just north of Babylonia), to accompany his daughter Tadu-hepa when she was sent to the Egyptian court to marry the pharaoh Amenhotep III.[17] Here, with a rhetorical flourish that is designed in no small part to display the sheer, almost unimaginable wealth and power of the king, Tushratta lists the opulent gifts he is showering on his daughter and her nearly three hundred 'dowry personnel' to equip her and her household. Full sets of fabulous lapis lazuli and gold jewellery and exquisitely dyed purple-blue skirts and blouses for the princess; silver ankle bracelets and earrings for a hundred female retainers; lapis necklaces and golden bracelets for her closest handmaids; boxwood chests laden with carnelian pomegranates, grapes of gold, malachite finger rings, golden sealstones – as well as all she'll need to start a home, including everything from fly whisks, mirrors, spoons and washbasins to furniture, bed linen and bolts of cloth in every hue. It is this (on a much less grand scale) that King Alcinous offers Odysseus for a fully equipped house, and it's what Princess Nausicaa is preparing with her collection of freshly washed clothes: not only for herself, but (just like Princess Tadu-hepa's 'dowry personnel') for all the retainers who will be incorporated within her new household.

This aligns with a fundamentally important conception of the home (or *oikos* in Greek) in Homer: not just a house, but all the property that belongs to it – land, material possessions, enslaved people, and livestock. As in the Babylonian laws, the bride's dowry (whether it's a house, bronze and gold treasures, enslaved attendants or lavish clothes like Nausicaa's) is subsumed into the wider *oikos*, and becomes the husband's to use and to spend.[18] In the *Iliad*, for instance, we see Priam, king of Troy, drawing on the dowry of his first wife (Hecuba's predecessor) to pay for his sons' ransom, when they get captured by the Greeks in the Trojan War.[19]

If a marriage is terminated, on the other hand, then the dowry is to be repaid – both in Hammurabi's laws and in Homer: we find Telemachus worrying about how he would pay back Penelope's father, Icarius, if he sends her away (thus formally declaring the end of her marriage to Odysseus), as well as how he'll supply Penelope with a new dowry if she chooses to marry again.[20] It seems that wives did sometimes have a few possessions of their own: in ancient south-west Asia, some limited possessions – mostly enslaved people – are allocated to the wife from the dowry.[21] We find this in Homer, too: Penelope mentions a couple of enslaved attendants her father gave her when she left as a bride.[22] And there are historical examples from Late Bronze Age Greece, in the Mycenaean Linear B tablets from Pylos, where we find one wife who seems (rather dismally) to own a pair of sandals (the other six wives listed in the tablets have no possessions at all).[23] Likewise, when women give gifts to each other in the Homeric poems, all they are able to give is textiles – the robes they've made with their own hands, such as Nausicaa's gift of clothing to Odysseus or Hecuba's gift of robes to the goddess Athena, the products of a woman's world; not the golden cups and silver bowls that men lavish on each other. Homer sums up the situation in a brisk and telling line: 'all the women now who have a household [*oikos*] under the control of their husbands'.[24] Most property, within the realm of the *oikos*, not to mention the wives as well, quite clearly belonged to the man of the house.

My Property, My Slaves, My High-Roofed House

Which brings us to a knotty problem that lies at the heart of the *Odyssey*, and that occupies Hammurabi, too: what happened when the husband of the house went missing in action? It was a question that would have been all too common among the warring Bronze Age empires. Who took over the rights to property when the man wasn't there – and what was the status of his wife? This crucial concern, and its repercussions, is in many ways the driving force behind the *Odyssey*'s plot: it propels much of the turmoil that happens behind the scenes on Ithaca during Odysseus' travels, stirs up the conflict around Penelope, and provides the critical impetus for the hero's return home even as he taps his fingers waiting for his convoy among the Phaeacians. Because, although the romantic dalliance with Nausicaa might display the sunny practices of bride price and dowry during peaceful courtship, in Ithaca, meanwhile, the marriage of Penelope and Odysseus shudders on the rocks of the Greek king's absence – and underlines the vast economic and social ramifications of the breakdown of a highly propertied marriage (and inheritance) that has been fractured by war. In Odysseus' decade-long crusade at Troy, with his status in the ten years following the war uncertain – missing in action? Remarried? Dead? – Penelope oscillates unpredictably (and dangerously) between marriageable bride, to be courted by eager suitors with their *hedna*; well-endowed widow, wielding her inheritance with an heir too young to assume the throne; and faithful wife, guarding her husband's possessions within the *oikos*. Her dubious status in Odysseus' absence means that she exemplifies – in one fell swoop – all the different ways a woman could interact with property through marriage, and that we see written out with legal precision in Hammurabi's law code.

Hammurabi's laws have an answer, as they so often do, to the problem of missing husbands and a wife's property rights. And it's one that, I think, serves to give a compelling historical background to Penelope's apparently contradictory actions in Homer that – for centuries – have vexed and confused scholars. The problem with Penelope has always been a simple one. If she's faithful to Odysseus and believes he still lives, then why doesn't she turn away the more than a hundred suitors who throng the halls of the palace at Ithaca, hoping for her hand in marriage (and, with it, the kingship of Ithaca)? And if she's not, and thinks he's dead, then why doesn't she choose a husband, and put an end to the drain on the palace's resources by the suitors with their constant feasting (not to mention their off-putting personalities)? Her actions – 'not refusing marriage, nor putting an end to it', as Telemachus complains – threaten to put Ithaca in a downward spiral to potential obliteration, as the suitors devour (through their constant feasting) all the livestock the palace owns.[25]

But it's possible that a Late Bronze Age wife may, in fact, have had little other choice. Hammurabi's laws make it clear that a woman's sole and imperative responsibility – if she doesn't want to get thrown in the river – is to stay by her husband's side and guard his possessions: otherwise, if she 'squanders her household possessions, and disparages her husband, they shall cast that woman into the water'.[26] A wife's loyalty to her husband and her duty to protect his property seem to be bound up in a package that required the utmost circumspection towards the household belongings (and the ultimate cost to be paid if she failed). At the same time, the laws provide some shaky reassurance for a woman whose husband has gone missing: 'If a man should be captured and there are not sufficient provisions in his house, his wife may enter another's house' – the choice of man seems, in this case, to be entirely hers, just as it is Penelope's.[27] (In fact, we're told that Odysseus even ordered Penelope before he left to choose her own husband if he didn't come back from Troy.)[28] But if 'her husband returns and gets back to his city' (the phrasing of Hammurabi's law is supremely close to the *Odyssey*'s plot), 'that woman shall return to her first husband'.[29] So while her husband is gone, she can live with another man; as soon as he returns, however, she defaults to her original husband – and all his lost property is (by the standards of the earlier clause) her responsibility. Such a wife would be trapped in a legal catch-22: expected by law to defend her husband's possessions, by necessity draining his resources as she strives to make ends meet and legally entertaining the suit of another man, yet knowing that her husband could return at any time – and, if he does, that the losses on his property will be set to her account.

It's this kind of impossible scenario in which Penelope finds herself.

Just as in Hammurabi's law code, the Homeric poems make clear that a core expectation of a wife is to act as steward to her husband's property: in particular, it is Penelope (or her female housekeeper, in her stead) who holds the key to the storeroom where all the valuables are kept; Telemachus, planning his voyage to Pylos and Sparta and needing to stock up on supplies, has to ask for it to be unlocked before he can go in.[30] In other words, Penelope is quite literally responsible for the household wealth – and, consequently, it is she who is held accountable for Odysseus' dwindling resources. But Penelope is not one to let herself be backed into a corner. She is known – as Odysseus is – for her cautious yet sharp intelligence: her epithet, *periphrōn*, means something along the lines (in Emily Wilson's brilliant translation) of 'circumspect'. And Hammurabi's laws show us a way in which Penelope's uncertain status also affords her particular advantages. There is a stipulation, in one of the laws, that a widow can choose not to leave her home after her husband has died (so enjoying the use of his estate alongside her dowry, which is to be returned to her); her children will have to pay a penalty if they try to pressure her to depart.[31] Similarly, Telemachus knows that his mother – by choosing to remain – has caught him in a stalemate. 'I cannot send her away if she does not want to go . . . I would have to pay a great price back to Icarius, if it's me who sends my mother away,' he says, appearing to refer to a comparable kind of penalty to that imposed in Hammurabi's laws.[32] By manipulating the loopholes that enable her to simultaneously take on the legal roles of property-protecting wife, dowered widow and bride-price-earner, Penelope is able, in fact, to engineer the ultimate coup: to elicit gifts from her suitors and incorporate them seamlessly into her husband's *oikos*, all the while keeping her options open to move in with another man (should resources run out) and simultaneously replenishing the pot with seemingly endless *hedna*.

At one point in the *Odyssey*, Penelope actually makes her strategy explicit. With a laugh, she decides (prompted by the ever-resourceful Athena) to appear before her suitors, in order – so she says – to fan the flames of their passion and extract gifts from them, so that she can be even more honoured by her husband and son (in an ancient economy where more goods mean more honour, this is clearly a key way for Penelope to win her husband's respect).[33] Descending from her chambers with beauty shed around her by the goddess, she rebukes them openly. In the past, she says, suitors for a rich noble's daughter used to compete with each other to bring the most oxen and sheep, to throw feasts for the bride's friends and to give her glorious gifts.[34] The suitors immediately run to fetch their offerings – sumptuous woven robes, golden brooches, amber necklaces and precious earrings.[35] And so Penelope draws on the impasse a little longer, and her husband's storerooms are replenished. She can even boast, a while later, that 'I protect it all: my property, my slaves, my high-roofed house. And I honour the bed of my husband.'[36]

Her proud pronouncement is almost a word-for-word manifesto for the good wife from Hammurabi's laws: protecting her husband's property, and showering him with respect. It's unlikely, by this measure, that she'll be due a dunking in the river any time soon. But does the sly 'my' that creeps into her legal defence ('my possessions') suggest she's enjoying her husband's absence from the marital property just a little more than she claims?

Heir to History

Two would-be brides in tandem, then, both angling for a husband and manipulating their property in different ways, within the confines of a patriarchal system, to get what they want: an unmarried virgin, gathering her dowry and putting it on the back of the man she wants to wed in the hope that she can bind him to her; a wife (also a potential bride-to-be and widow), spinning three property plates – bride price, dowry and husband's possessions – and all the while trying to balance the accounts until her husband returns. It's by setting women like Nausicaa and Penelope into a Bronze Age context that we can begin to understand the undercurrents of the laws concerning betrothal, marriage and property that would have directed the lives of so many women across the ancient world – and that set Homeric narratives into motion, such as Nausicaa's never-realized courtship with a bride price and dowry (reminiscent of the clauses in Hammurabi's legal code) and Penelope's property dilemma while her husband is away at war (for which Hammurabi specifically makes provision).

In saying this, I'm not by any means suggesting that Homer (or the many oral poets of the Greek tradition) necessarily knew of, or were thinking about, the ancient law code, written on stone by a Babylonian king and copied by scribes over the centuries, that was dug up at Susa in 1902; or that the poems' narrative is organized with an eye to Bronze Age legal constraints. This is, after all, first and foremost, an epic with a tangled history, not a cut-and-dried treatise on law. But I do think it's likely – with the swelling tide of evidence for the remarkable permeability of cultures and ideas in the Bronze Age from ancient Mesopotamia into the Eastern Mediterranean and across Anatolia into the Aegean – that there may have been a shared legal tradition that addressed the property rights of brides and wives, and that may have underpinned the stories of women like Nausicaa and Penelope in the *Odyssey*. It's by shining this kind of light on the ancient past that we can begin to understand better the women behind the myths. Like joining the fractured pieces of Hammurabi's law code back together, it's another piece of the past, another fragment of history that we can fit together to read the story that it tells.

But Nausicaa doesn't just interact with history as a bride commanding a bride price. Five years before the last missing piece of Hammurabi's laws was unearthed at Susa, she would enter the spotlight in a very different way. In 1897, Samuel Butler – eclectic English novelist, painter and critic – published a controversial book, *The Authoress of the Odyssey*. The claim: that the *Odyssey* was written by a woman – in fact, by none other than Nausicaa herself. For Butler, this was a clear and self-evident fact (built up on an edifice of his own assumptions about gender). The sheer quantity of female characters in the poem, he said – not only Nausicaa and Penelope, but also Calypso, Circe, Helen, Arete – and the sympathy with which they seem to be portrayed meant, to him, that it must have been written by a woman.[37] And not just any woman: this is a girl who is, apparently, 'young, headstrong, and unmarried' (young because – according to Butler – the author doesn't have a lot of sense, and is naive enough to believe that Odysseus would actually have wanted to leave Calypso to go back to a middle-aged wife(!); headstrong because she must have been used to getting her own way to be able to finish the epic; unmarried because otherwise she wouldn't have had the time), who writes, he says, with an 'instinctive house-wifely thrift'.[38] Only women can be interested in the trappings of women's affairs, says Butler: hence the *Odyssey*'s concerns with matters of the *oikos* and the representation of women's pursuits, such as Nausicaa's clothes-washing.[39] Besides, he asserts, women write in a particular way: the literary style of the *Odyssey* ('sweetness', 'charm') – as well as the 'mistakes' he claims to have identified in descriptions of the men-only pursuits of fighting and hunting – have, he says, a woman's authorship stamped all over them.[40]

Butler's arguments that women only write nicely (like the little girls made of sugar and spice in the nineteenth-century nursery rhyme), that they're only interested in certain things, and that they can be identified by what they get wrong, are, of course, both offensive and simplistic, based on generalized assumptions about the fixity and universality of gender; they tell us much more about Butler, and late-nineteenth-century ideas about Homer, gender and authorship, than about the ancient past. If Homer was a woman (and most critics tend nowadays to stress instead the long, multi-authored tradition that led to the patchwork formation of the epics, rather than Butler's idea of a lone individual genius – whatever their gender), then it certainly wasn't for Butler's reasons. But, in 1955, Robert Graves – author of the massively popular historical novel *I, Claudius* (1934) – was inspired by Butler's theory to pen a (much less successful) novel about Nausicaa, *Homer's Daughter*, that turns her into an energetic modern woman and satirical, emancipated poet of the *Odyssey*. (In one of his letters, Graves expresses his hope that 'every nice Vassar girl' will be able to imagine herself as the Nausicaa of his novel.)[41] Contemporary writers, too, view Nausicaa through a modern lens: the Greek poet Chloe Koutsoumbeli, in her 'Penelope III' (translated into English by A. E. Stallings in 2016), turns Nausicaa – 'some spoiled Nausicaa / hemmed into the wrong age / with white socks and school-girl skirts' – into a metaphor for the struggling Greek educational system, in the wake of the devastating 2008 financial crisis.[42]

Nausicaa as modern Greek schoolgirl, Nausicaa as Victorian bard, Nausicaa as Bronze Age bride: her many incarnations speak to the ever-changing interpretations of the Homeric texts, as they are read and reimagined over the years. But Nausicaa isn't the only, or the last, woman Odysseus interacts with on the Phaeacian isle. Her advice, when she clothes him in her dowry robes, centres on how to approach the most important person in the land: the woman who wove the very garments Odysseus wears, and who sits at the very heart of the king's court, spinning purple wool – Arete, the phenomenally powerful queen of the Phaeacians, who, we are told in the *Odyssey*, is treated as a goddess by her people, and dispenses justice to men and women alike.[43] It is on her, and her alone, that Odysseus' chances for hospitality at his final destination, and his hopes for procuring a ship onwards to Ithaca, depends. 'Walk straight past my father,' Nausicaa baldly instructs him, 'and throw your arms around my mother's knees: if you win her favour, you may hope to reach your home.'[44]

So how is it that the favour of a woman – even a queen – was able to decide the destiny of a man?

13

ARETE

Host

ISLAND OF THE PHAEACIANS

They tell her that she rules a perfect world. That her palace – bronze-clad, with doors of gold – was built by gods. That all year round, pomegranates droop, lush, like open mouths on the fruit trees in her orchard. That the ships sail without steering, light as thistledown, fast as thought: they say they cannot sink.

But then, she thinks: why does she have nightmares?

She's immersed beneath the ocean. It's quiet, beating on her eardrums, a flat fluorescent blue. Silent. Dead. She swims like a fish trapped in a net. The cliffs of the shore glitter underwater like crabs' eyes, watching her as she presses through the foaming dark, knowing what's there. Wanting to stop, to wake, but the dream pushing her on, a god's watery finger at her back.

And then it looms up before her. The ghostly prow from the seabed. The rigging slack and trailing, the sail yawning in the current like a white ray fish. The pallid keel driven into the sand, encrusted with limpets and seaweed like a rock.

And the bodies float around it, their eyes staring blank from the ship-wreck. And she wakes and runs screaming in the darkness from her bed, mouth buried in her blankets so the children don't hear her.

Because she knows that the perfect world is about to end – that, perhaps, it never was.

Age of Bronze

Forty metres underwater off the coast of south-western Turkey, and Faith Hentschel is doing the morning commute. The ocean above her is a haze of blue, and glassy fish flicker past, dashing like silver arrows through the columns of sunlight as she swims. She barely registers them:

her focus is ahead, past the bubbles blossoming from the regulator in her mouth and into the depths where it gets darker. She sinks further, finning as fast as her ears can clear, ignoring the water's chill on the neoprene of her wetsuit and the swirling intoxication of the gases from her tanks – compressed into a narcotic equivalent at this depth – that fills her brain.[1] All she wants is to get to work.

And then she reaches the ink-blue sea floor, where boulders covered in barnacles crouch like sea creatures and sand stretches into the gloom. She sees the stream of bubbles that means her diving partner, Cemal Pulak, has made it to the trench, too. Takes out her measuring tape, trowel, waterproof clipboard and pencil.

And so the work day begins.

In early July 1984, Hentschel was one of the first marine archaeologists on the excavation – led by George Bass and Cemal Pulak – of one of the most sensational Bronze Age finds ever to be made: the discovery, hundreds of feet under the surface of the Mediterranean Sea, of the world's oldest-known shipwreck. This was a merchant vessel that sank to the depths at Uluburun on the south-western tip of Turkey around the end of the fourteenth century BCE, along with its staggering cargo of stacks of copper and tin, a hundred and fifty storage jars filled with precious goods for export, and mounds of priceless ivory, ebony, gold, jewellery and swords: nearly seventeen tons in all. For the archaeological specialists who received the tip-off from a local sponge diver who first glimpsed the wreck, this was a once-in-a-lifetime find: 'an archaeologist's dream', as the excavation director George Bass put it – a time capsule from the Bronze Age.[2] The wreck was miraculously well preserved in the minutest detail – from a wooden writing board (the oldest ever found), probably used to list the ship's contents and discovered hidden in a storage pot; to oleander branches that were used as weather fencing around the deck to keep out the waves; to individual fibres from bolts of textiles dyed in murex purple; to the intricately crafted mortise-and-tenon joints of the hull. With more than fifteen thousand artefacts, it's one of the largest and richest hoards of Bronze Age goods ever to be found – and, more than that, the unusual combination of bulk raw materials and high-end elite products provides an unhoped-for window into its ancient world. Before advances in marine archaeology enabled the underwater

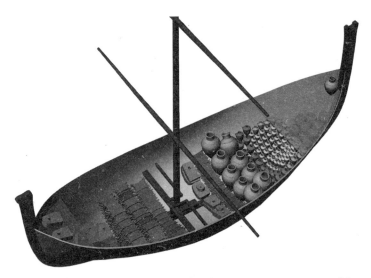

Bringing bronze to the bronze-clad Achaeans? Reconstruction of the Uluburun ship's cargo, with overlapping ingots of copper and tin, as it would have been before it sank (c.1320 BCE).

excavation of shipwrecks like the one at Uluburun, what little information we had about interregional trade and international connections had to be gleaned in large part from the hard-wearing artefacts that managed to make it through the mill of history – mostly pottery. Elite goods from the ancient world often crop up in contexts that tell us little about the objects' long histories. Meanwhile, costly raw materials like copper and tin simply don't tend to survive: they tend not to leave traces in the archaeological record, with the result that – although we knew they were *there* – the quantities, routes and methods of export have been, until now, well-nigh impossible to determine. And this is important, because tin and copper are the two key ingredients converted into that most highly sought alloy of the age, bronze: the remarkable metal that underpinned the technological and social revolution of the Bronze Age, and lent its name to Homer's 'bronze-clad Achaeans'.

In the last few decades, however, by piecing together the puzzle represented by the ship's cargo, applying new scientific methods and cross-referencing thousands-of-years-old texts, the unprecedented finds at

Uluburun have begun to unlock a fascinating story – not just about the goods the ship carried on the day it sank, but about the intricate economic and diplomatic networks that criss-crossed the Late Bronze Age Mediterranean, the complex social customs and lavish gifts, and the sheer range of goods generated by and underpinning ancient patterns of innovation, technology, diplomacy, war and trade. This was a world, it would seem, that transformed the kings, the merchants – and sometimes, in rare cases, as we will see, even the women – of the Late Bronze Age into players on a truly global stage.

The first piece in the puzzle – after the significant challenge of mapping, documenting and recovering each and every artefact at a record depth of 40–60 metres underwater, where dives were limited to a bottom time of only twenty minutes, and where rock-hard, concreted goods had tumbled hundreds of metres in every direction down the steep slope of the seabed as the hull disintegrated – was to understand what the ship was doing there at all. Years of day-in, day-out cutting-edge underwater excavation (resulting in a total of 22,500 dives across eleven seasons – all of which Hentschel participated in – logging a total of 6,613 hours underwater at the wreck site), as well as painstaking research in laboratories all over the world, have allowed scientists and archaeologists to begin to reconstruct the details of the ship's last fatal journey.[3] We are now able to estimate when it sailed, where it came from and where it might have been going – and even to gather evidence on some of the passengers who were travelling on board, from the food they were eating to the clothes they wore and the games they played. Combined dendrochronological analysis (tree-ring dating) and radiocarbon dating of remnants of the ship's keel, as well as fragments of the branches used to cushion the ship's cargo (the wood preserved in the toxic environment created by copper), reveal a date of around 1320 BCE, plus or minus fifteen years.[4] (This also matches up with the chronology suggested by artefacts on board: Bronze Age specialists are able to use changes in pottery styles, in particular, to assign dates with some accuracy.) That puts its final voyage in the last decades of the fourteenth century BCE: the period of the heyday of the Mycenaean palaces on the Greek mainland, the rule of the illness-stricken Hittite king Mursili II (father of Puduhepa's husband, Hattusili III) and the gold-lavished reign of Tutankhamun in Egypt.

But it appears that this vessel didn't start out from the bustling stately centres and thriving ports of Greece, Anatolia or Egypt. With no written evidence on board (or elsewhere) to tell them where it sailed from, scientists turned their attention instead to the ship's functional equipment: its anchors (twenty-four of them), service storage jars, the lamps used by the sailors for light at night (still blackened with soot where the wick had burnt), and even the galley wares that they ate from. These, it seems reasonable to assume, would likely have been made at (or near) the ship's origin port (in contrast to high-value goods for trade, which would have been circulated and stockpiled in entrepôts).[5] By examining the stones, sand and clay used to furnish the Uluburun ship's basic equipment under the microscope, and comparing them to the make-up of modern rock samples, researchers have been able to pinpoint a location for the source of the ship's outfit – from just north of the Carmel coast of Israel. Perhaps this means that its home port may even have been the ancient port city of Tell Abu Hawam (modern Haifa).[6] This would make the Uluburun ship Canaanite – a general term used to denote the Semitic-speaking peoples who lived in the second millennium BCE along the Levantine coast, the strip of the east Mediterranean shore that was crucial in controlling overland trade routes between Egypt in the south, Mesopotamia to the east and the Hittite Empire to the north, and whose ports were a hub for trade to Cyprus, Crete and beyond.[7] (It's fascinating corroborating evidence that we find paintings of Syro-Canaanite ships,

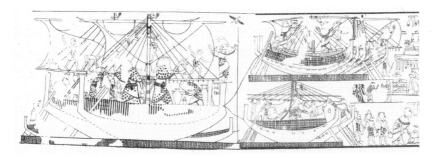

Syro-Canaanite ships in an Egyptian tomb, from the same date as the Uluburun ship (14th century BCE). Canaanite storage jars and weather fencing, just like those shown here, were found in the shipwreck.

weighed down with cargoes of distinctive Canaanite storage jars – just like those found on the Uluburun ship – in Egyptian tombs of the same period.) And it's a location that is confirmed, strangely enough, by some of the smallest and most obscure finds that the archaeologists managed to extract from the wreck: snails. These minuscule land snails were accidentally preserved, trapped in tree resin that, at half a ton, was one of the ship's main consignments (probably for export for use in perfume or incense: the amount matches quantities in Egyptian and Mycenaean accounts of bulk imports). The snails have been identified as local to the northern Dead Sea region, in ancient Canaan – where the resin would have been collected (along with the unfortunate gastropods) and transported to the coast for shipping.[8]

So it would have been here, along the eastern Mediterranean coast at one of the busy harbour towns filled with merchant traders and hawking travellers, that our ship would have loaded up. Goods didn't just come from nearby, though. Lead isotope analysis at the University of Oxford's Isotrace Laboratory has shown that the enormous quantity of copper carried on the Uluburun ship – ten tons of it, still stacked in neat overlapping rows like metal tiles, just as they were when the ship sank – was mined from Cyprus (in fact, it can even be traced to a specific region on the island).[9] In a way this isn't a surprise: Cyprus came to be renowned for its rich copper ores in the metal-greedy Bronze Age, and our word for copper actually comes from the island's name (copper, in later Latin, was *aes Cyprium* or 'Cypriot bronze', shortened to *cuprum* – hence *Cu* for copper in the modern periodic table). But if copper came in from the Mediterranean island to the north-west (it may have been stockpiled in the Levantine ports for outward trade), the tin had an altogether different provenance. A study published in 2022 conducted geochemical analysis on the staggering one ton of tin held on the Uluburun ship (the largest quantity of ancient tin ever found), and discovered – extraordinarily – that a third of it contains the chemical fingerprints of tin from prehistoric mines in Tajikistan and Uzbekistan: around two thousand miles east of its final resting place.[10] Other cargo is just as multicultural. More than forty beads of amber discovered in the wreck have been identified by infrared spectroscopy as from the Baltic, far away in northern Europe. There are over a hundred immaculate ceramic vessels from Cyprus; hundreds of kilograms of cobalt-coloured blue glass ingots (probably used as a cheaper lapis lazuli substitute) and thousands of faience beads from Egypt; three ostrich eggshells from the eastern Mediterranean or north Africa for transformation into exotic vases; dozens of logs of African blackwood, known as *hbny* in Egyptian (the root of our 'ebony'), imported from eastern Africa; unworked elephant tusk and hippopotamus teeth from Syria. Raw materials and luxury goods of at least ten different ancient cultures in all are represented, spread over a geographical area of thousands of miles from the northern limits of Europe to central Asia.

It wasn't just the cargo that was international, though. Since it's possible to differentiate between the mass produce collected for trade (in superlative quantities and pristine condition) and the scattered, well-worn items that could only have been personal possessions, archaeologists have been able to narrow down not only the number of people on board, but even where they came from. The presence of three or four sets of personal balance weights in the Syro-Canaanite system – used for weighing out items on board and at the destination port, some with pieces missing and replaced with homemade additions – along with one sword and three daggers in a Canaanite style, indicates four Syro-Canaanite merchants: probably three traders and their captain, who directed the ship. Then there would have been the crew, probably also Canaanite to guess from the source of the bowls they ate from and the lamps they used; we even have the knucklebones they played with, not knowing it was their last game before the ship went down.[11] But it also seems – intriguingly, for our search for the Late Bronze Age Aegean – that two Mycenaeans were on board. A handful of Mycenaean objects were found in tantalizing pairs: two high-status bronze Mycenaean swords; two Mycenaean drinking sets; two knives; two elite-style glass-bead necklaces; two personal seals. The massive size, diversity and cost of the consignment on the ship has already led scholars to argue that it must have been paid for by a king, or at the very least a member of the elite, who would be able to shoulder the significant risks of long-distance trade and control the palatial structures that could absorb such valuable, high-end materials – let alone command the capital to procure such a quantity of goods in the first place. (By way of comparison, the purchasing

Shut up and weave: the Odyssey's *Penelope sits before her famously unfinished weaving, in a pose of despondent silence, while her son Telemachus looks on. From a late fifth-century BCE Greek vase.*

Grave goods of a real bronze-clad Achaean (note the bronze sword with golden hilt), in the tomb of the Griffin Warrior, Pylos (1500–1450 BCE).

The original Homeric
hero? This stunning example
of Late Bronze Age craftsmanship – featuring
a scene of a hero in combat carved in miniature
on an agate sealstone – was found in the grave
of the Griffin Warrior at Pylos in 2014; it's over
three and a half thousand years old. It may have
been images of heroes like these that inspired
Homeric poetry.

'The king herself':
the female pharaoh
of Egypt, Hatshepsut
(reigned c.1473–1458
BCE), as a male ruler.

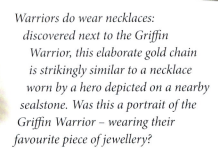

Warriors do wear necklaces:
discovered next to the Griffin
Warrior, this elaborate gold chain
is strikingly similar to a necklace
worn by a hero depicted on a nearby
sealstone. Was this a portrait of the
Griffin Warrior – wearing their
favourite piece of jewellery?

A goddess descends
to her worshippers on the
sandy shore (note the tiny grains
of sand) on a ring from the Griffin
Warrior's tomb at Pylos – just as
Athena visits Nestor in 'sandy Pylos'
in Homer's Odyssey.

Putting the colour into a woman's
world: a girl from Akrotiri, Thera,
sports a vibrant yellow-dyed veil
with dots of red and bands of blue
and purple flowers embroidered on
her skirt and bodice – all the work
of women's hands.

The entire weaving process, from
an archaic Greek vase (c.550 BCE).
A community of women works
together to spin with a distaff and
spindle (left), weave on the warp-
weighted loom (middle), and fold
the finished cloth (right).

A reconstruction of the world's oldest shipwreck, as it would have looked after it sank: the Uluburun ship, which vanished off the coast of Turkey over three millennia ago.

A diver holds a copper 'oxhide' ingot, excavated from the Uluburun ship's vast cargo of ten tons of copper and a ton of tin. The overlapping of the ingots (seen below the diver's feet) enabled archaeologists to reconstruct the shape of the ship's hull.

Paintings in Egyptian tombs, from the same time period as the Uluburun ship, show men in Minoan dress called Keftiu (likely 'Cretans' or 'Aegeans') – carrying metal ingots, just like those found at Uluburun.

Circe turns Odysseus' men into pigs by mixing up a well-chosen charm, on this fifth-century BCE vase.

The spice of life: women gather saffron, a powerful gynaecological drug, on a wall painting from Akrotiri (c.1600 BCE).

Taking a bath: a real Late Bronze Age bath from the Palace of Nestor at Pylos. In Homer's Odyssey, *the poet imagines Telemachus sinking into a bath (perhaps this one?) in this very palace – washed by Nestor's daughter, Polycaste.*

On Cephalonia, seismic activity can detach whole mountainsides – as here, at Myrtos beach, when I visited in 2014. Could it have been an earthquake that buried the secret of the location of Penelope's island, Ithaca? Was this the reality of the anger of Poseidon – god of earthquakes – against Odysseus?

Circe turns Odysseus' men into pigs by mixing up a well-chosen charm, on this fifth-century BCE vase.

The spice of life: women gather saffron, a powerful gynaecological drug, on a wall painting from Akrotiri (c.1600 BCE).

Taking a bath: a real Late Bronze Age bath from the Palace of Nestor at Pylos. In Homer's Odyssey, *the poet imagines Telemachus sinking into a bath (perhaps this one?) in this very palace – washed by Nestor's daughter, Polycaste.*

On Cephalonia, seismic activity can detach whole mountainsides – as here, at Myrtos beach, when I visited in 2014. Could it have been an earthquake that buried the secret of the location of Penelope's island, Ithaca? Was this the reality of the anger of Poseidon – god of earthquakes – against Odysseus?

An early Circe? Powerful Mistresses of Animals, like this one from Çatalhöyük, Turkey (c.6000 BCE), are found throughout the ancient world. Here she is grasping a pair of lionesses.

The return to Penelope: Odysseus, disguised as a beggar, draws near to Penelope – who still sits with her head in her hands – signalling the approaching end of the Odyssey. This relief, from the fifth century BCE, shows the enduring popularity of Homer's epics.

The Western canon, immortalized in Raphael's Parnassus: *in the centre, the blind bard Homer, flanked by the Roman poet Virgil (right) and Florentine writer Dante (left) – (male) poets who built on Homer's legacy. The foot of the Muse of epic poetry, Calliope, to the right is a reminder of the goddesses who inspired it all.*

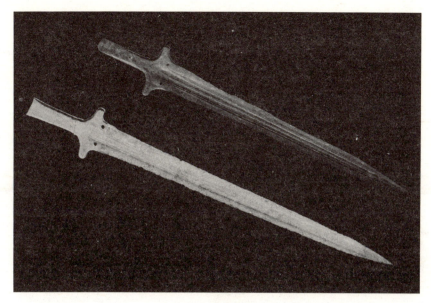

Detective work: Mycenaean possessions in sets of two, including these bronze swords, suggest there were two Mycenaean Greeks on board the Uluburun ship when it sank. They were likely royal envoys.

power of the copper and tin on board alone was equivalent to the entire annual tribute of a vassal king to his Hittite imperial overlord.)[12] It seems likely, then, that these two high-status Mycenaean individuals – marked out as elite by their clutch of prestigious possessions – were emissaries representing the elite or royal interests of the purchasers, sent to oversee the contingent of hugely valuable goods and present them personally at their final destination.[13]

And it's this that gives us the final clue as to where the ship was going: because the presence of these two foreign envoys points to who the Uluburun ship's recipients might have been. Examples matching the ship's other precious cargo – ivory from Syrian hippopotamus teeth, faience and blue glass from Egypt, ostrich eggs from the eastern Mediterranean and north Africa, pottery from Cyprus, amber from the Baltic – have all been discovered as imports on the Mycenaean Greek mainland.[14] Some are even mentioned in the palace records of the Late Bronze Age Linear B tablets – like *ku-wa-no*, for instance, probably an imported loanword

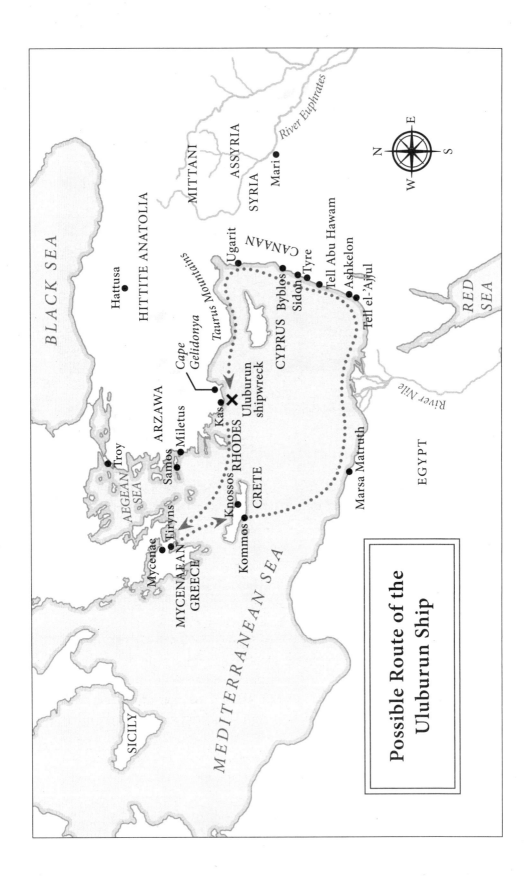

Possible Route of the
Uluburun Ship

from Hittite for blue glass, and the source of Homer's *kuaneos*, 'blue' (Homer even tells us that Agamemnon wears a breastplate, a gift from a king of Cyprus, which is decorated with *kuanos* or blue glass).[15] Mycenae, in particular – a hugely wealthy palatial centre, associated in Homer with Agamemnon, and (to judge from the richness and unusual multicultural diversity of the archaeological finds) one of the few places that the Uluburun excavators believe would have been capable of absorbing such a quantity of luxury goods – has revealed over a hundred eastern-imported materials, more than almost any other site in Greece (including blue glass, hippopotamus and elephant ivory, and ostrich eggshells), as well as nine Canaanite storage jars, just like those used for transport on the Uluburun ship; at Mycenae's port, Tiryns, archaeologists discovered large amounts of Cypriot pottery (another of the Uluburun ship's exports).[16] Following the prevailing winds and currents of the summer sailing season, then, our ship would probably have set off from the Carmel coast of Israel with its cargo of local Canaanite pottery and Dead Sea snails, then headed north with a brief stop at the ancient port city of Ugarit in northern Syria (a Syrian house mouse came aboard here: its jawbone has been identified).[17] The vessel then skirted west, hugging the coast of southern Anatolia where – if it hadn't met its end – it would have crossed into the Aegean Sea, and finally headed for safe harbour in Greece: possibly even dispatching its precious load into the port of Tiryns and on into the heart of golden Mycenae itself. This is a ship that attests to a truly international world – that blows out of the water the assumptions that used to be made about an isolated ancient landscape, and a lack of contact between ancient south-west Asia and the Aegean.

It wasn't just the Uluburun ship's treasures of ivory, gold, pottery and glass that the Mycenaeans would have wanted to get their hands on, though. We know from archaeological discoveries – like that of the Griffin Warrior at Pylos – that the Mycenaeans, with their warrior armies devouring quantities of bronze for their sharp-tipped spears, swords, shields and helmets, were a major consumer of the metal. In many ways, the Uluburun shipwreck makes clear that it was the quest for raw materials – and the constituents of bronze, above all – that was one of the major factors driving the boom in long-distance intercultural trade and communication (and so, too, the exchange of ideas and technologies, and the onset of wars as resource-hungry empires clashed) across the Mediterranean in the Late Bronze Age. The Uluburun ship carries (probably not coincidentally) the ideal 10:1 ratio of copper (ten tons) to tin (one ton), sufficient to produce high-quality bronze: eleven metric tons of it – enough, in fact, to equip an army of nearly five thousand Bronze Age warriors with swords.[18] In the *Iliad*, when Homer describes the grand fleet of Greek ships sailing out to the Trojan War, Agamemnon – king of Mycenae – is said to lead a hundred vessels across the sea against Troy, carrying 'by far the largest, finest army, and with pride he dressed himself in shining bronze'.[19] A hundred of Agamemnon's ships, each (from what Homer says elsewhere) with an average of fifty men, makes five thousand.[20] Five thousand men to be kitted out with 'gleaming bronze' swords: exactly (in a staggering coincidence) the amount carried on the Uluburun ship. Is it possible that this vessel that met its end as its prow foamed into the Aegean, taking down with it two Mycenaean envoys and the luxury cargo of a king, was bringing the mass of metals needed by a Mycenaean ruler like Agamemnon – to prepare for a war like that against Troy?

Social Network

There's another legendary Greek king, though, who is now on his way back from the Trojan War and in desperate need of a boat: and he happens to have washed up in the *Odyssey* in a fantasy land, ruled by Queen Arete and populated by the mythical Phaeacians, which is famed, above all, for its ships. Not only are the Phaeacians of the *Odyssey* said to 'have special talent for launching ships to sea'; their vessels are apparently propelled by magic, needing no pilots or steering oars, speeding across the ocean as quick as a thought. Above all (and Odysseus would have been in a mind to appreciate this), they're said to be unsinkable.[21] Obviously, it's one of these fabulous mythical ships that Odysseus needs if he's going to get back to Ithaca, and avoid the fate met by so many unfortunate vessels from the real world, like the Uluburun craft. But it's made clear to him by Nausicaa (even as she hands over the clothes he'll need to preserve his modesty) that – if he stands any chance of getting home – he needs to win over, not the king, but the Phaeacian queen. Arete – the woman – is the key. Arete is not just a fantastically powerful queen with a resumé that any ruler would give their eye teeth for: 'we look at her,' Athena (disguised as a girl carrying a water pitcher) tells Odysseus, 'as if she were a goddess, and point her out when she walks through our town. She is extremely clever and perceptive; she solves disputes to help the men she likes.'[22] But Arete also, interestingly, encompasses several of the themes we've seen recent scientific discoveries uncovering in powerful women in the Late Bronze Age: both endogamy (she's married to her uncle, and that links into the latest aDNA study showing evidence for Bronze Age cousin marriage) and matriliny. The Phaeacian line of succession detailed in the *Odyssey*, fascinatingly, similarly to the three-generation female burial at Aidonia, goes through her (via her great-grandmother). She doesn't just call the shots among the Phaeacians, then: it's her bloodline on which their royalty rests.

And so, in search of this all-powerful queen, the Greek hero wends his way through the Phaeacian city as evening falls, past the harbour thronging with ships, to the palace. Its walls are made from sheets of bronze, decorated with costly strips of *kuanos* (blue glass), the doors of pure gold set within a silver frame, the seats within covered in a gorgeous soft fabric dripping oil, 'the work of women', Homer tells us.[23] (These are the fifty enslaved women we met before, who have been made to weave in the royal palace.) Through the chambers goes Odysseus, to the centre of the royal hall where Arete sits by her husband Alcinous, spinning purple wool. Throwing his arms around her knees, Odysseus (the consummate courtier, always with a way with words) issues a brief but effective supplication – wishing her, her husband, and all her people and children health and prosperity, and asking her for what he needs above all: a ship home.

Without being asked who he is, the stranger is promptly given food and wine (his demeanour and honeyed tongue, perhaps, winning him the queen's tacit approval), and is promised protection and safe conveyance back to Ithaca the next day. A bed is made up for him with purple blankets and soft fleeces, and sumptuous gifts prepared – nuggets of gold and newly washed garments from all the Phaeacian leaders, as well as the gift of King Alcinous' own gold-wrought cup.[24] And it's Arete, the queen, who personally fetches a handsome treasure chest from the royal storerooms, and loads it up with everything that's being given to the stranger – all the clothing, the gold bullion, her husband's golden goblet, and even her own personal present of a tunic and cloak.[25]

It might seem strange, even arrogant, to us, that Odysseus thrusts himself into the centre of the court and asks such a substantial favour of a queen, a woman he has never met – without so much as giving his name, or offering anything in return. It might seem even odder that he is so successful in getting his way, and at such an absurd profit, too. But the rituals Arete and Odysseus are participating in, like a sort of dance where both partners know the moves, take place within a key framework that has a specific name in Homer, and forms the social glue that holds much of the *Odyssey* together: *xenia* in ancient Greek, or 'guest friendship'. In an ancient world where social networks were welded, not by likes or viewing numbers on online media platforms, but by the links of reciprocity forged by real gift-giving, the rituals that governed the exchange of favours and gifts were both elaborate and complex. Under the auspices of *xenia* as we see it in Homer (and we've already come across it in Telemachus' visits to Pylos and Sparta), a stranger might ask for hospitality at anyone's house. The host was bound, by the rules of the gods (*xenia* was governed by no less a deity than Zeus), to offer food, and not to ask their guest's identity until they had eaten. The guest might stay as long as they wished, and, when they chose to leave, the host was obliged to help them on their way, sending them off with a shower of gifts that cemented the relationship they had established. Such gifts – the higher the status of the visitor, the more precious they would be (and once the Phaeacians realize who Odysseus actually is, they add more gold to the booty heap) – might be kept and handed down the generations, remembered through the tales passed from mother to daughter, father to son (as well as the tradition of sung poems, permeated by recollection of the legends of the past, of which the Homeric epics formed a part).[26] They could even be weaponized as diplomatic links that created deep-rooted alliances. In the *Iliad*, for instance, when the Greek warrior Diomedes and a Trojan ally from Lycia, Glaucus, meet on the battlefield and stop to chat, they realize that they share a relationship of guest friendship, sealed by gifts. Diomedes recalls a stunning two-handled

golden cup which stands in his palace at home, that Glaucus' grandfather gave his father's father after claiming his hospitality in Greece.
The two warriors then refuse to fight each other – *xenia* is a powerful
political tool, more powerful, apparently, than the dues they owe their
own armies – and further consolidate the bond between them by swap-
ping armour on the battlefield (even if Diomedes does end up with the
better end of the bargain, when he exchanges his own bronze for Glaucus' much more valuable solid gold).[27]

Homeric *xenia* is thus not simply a hospitality code designed to protect
the needs of guests: it is a vibrant, full-scale ancient social network,
played out in the metals and fabrics of the material world. The more gifts
you are able to display in your treasure rooms or, even better, on your
person (and the costlier they are), the more social capital you are able
to wield – and the more powerful and internationally connected you
become. When Agamemnon in the *Iliad* straps on a breastplate made of
precious tin and gold and studded with blue glass, sent direct to Troy as
a guest gift by the king of Cyprus, it's a palpable and swaggering declaration of the support he commands from foreign royalty in his campaign
against Troy (as well as the trade networks, from tin to blue glass, that
he can control). And when, at the end of the *Odyssey*, Penelope sallies
into Odysseus' storeroom – packed with the goods she's worked so hard
to protect – and fetches his famously hard-to-string bow for the final
marriage contest, it's no coincidence that this powerful weapon was a
guest gift presented by a distinguished ally of her husband's (one of the
famed Argonauts, no less). The bow becomes a concrete and salient
reminder that – just like Agamemnon's political clout that wins the day
at Troy – it is the Ithacan king's social status, his inviolable identity as
host, and his formidable gift network, as much as his physical prowess,
that Penelope's suitors will fatally fail to challenge.[28]

And this brings us back, once again, to the historical Uluburun ship.
By focusing on the massive consignment of copper and tin, we've set the
shipwreck in the framework of east–west trade and the frenzied search
for bronze that drove so many Late Bronze Age ships across the Mediterranean. But if we switch our focus to some of the other priceless treasures
found on the wreck – the blue glass and tin, the purple-dyed fabric,
ivory tusks, boxwood containers, gold and silver ornaments, precious

beads and ostrich eggshells – we can start to see another layer of the story the Uluburun ship is telling us: and that's the intriguing evidence for prestigious, high-end Bronze Age gift exchange. It's been suggested that a stunning single chalice of solid gold found in the wreck, probably of Levantine make, may have been an example of this kind of high-status gift. Its unique prestige, with hammered gold bands encircling the bowl, and markedly high value would have set it apart from the bulk goods for export (as well as, of course, the coarse galley wares knocking about for the vessel's crew), reserved for elite gift-giving at the ship's destination – just like Alcinous' cup of gold gifted to Odysseus, or Diomedes' golden cup brought into Greece from Lycia. (Incidentally, Lycia was the ancient country occupying the coast of south-eastern Turkey, near where the Uluburun ship met its end.) In its inclusion of both utilitarian raw materials for export (ten tons of copper) and possible elite gifts (a single golden cup), the Uluburun shipwreck provides suggestive evidence for a fluid mode of trade and exchange in the Bronze Age: where the boundaries between gifts and commodities were blurred, and where, perhaps, a royal purchaser or host like Arete might expect to profit from (and ultimately reciprocate) high-status gifts that were added to a bulk shipment, both as a sign of goodwill and as a seal on a long-term relationship.

The gold cups presented as guest gifts by Alcinous to Odysseus, and the grandfather of a Lycian soldier to a Greek, represent a fascinating (if tentative) link to the Uluburun wreck's golden chalice. But we don't need to lean on Homer to find evidence for luxury gift exchanges between queens and kings in the Late Bronze Age world. We have hundreds of ancient letters providing ample evidence of large-scale elite gift-giving in the Late Bronze Age, in a remarkable cache of diplomatic correspondence – written and sent in exactly the period when the Uluburun ship sank – unearthed by chance over a century ago in an Egyptian field. It's in the tablets of this extraordinary archive that we are able to summon up the silenced voices of the real historical princesses and queens who stood – like Arete – behind the trail of gift exchange in the Late Bronze Age world, and whose hands reached deep into the social network.

My Messenger Has Brought Coloured Cloth

Which brings us to one of the most recognizable female players in Late Bronze Age history: the powerful, and proverbially beautiful, queen and Great Royal Wife of the court of Egypt, Nefertiti. Nefertiti's face is known across the world as one of the most iconic pieces of ancient art: the stunningly lifelike bust with its serene gaze and *Mona Lisa*-esque half-smile. Until her portrait was discovered in 1912 lying in the ruins of the ancient city of Akhetaten (modern Tell el-Amarna, or Amarna) in Egypt, however, Nefertiti was all but forgotten – not because of the vagaries of time or the gradual crumbling of ancient monuments, but through a very deliberate act of forgetting in which she and her husband, the pharaoh Akhenaten (ruler of Egypt in the latter half of the fourteenth century BCE), were quite literally erased from the records of history. The reason: their radical attempt to turn their backs on the Egyptian polytheistic religion and divert worship instead to Akhenaten's sole chosen god, the sun deity Aten. Later, as Egypt reverted to the old gods and Akhenaten and Nefertiti were denounced as heretics, the purpose-built shiny new capital they had built at Amarna in honour of Aten was abandoned. Their temples and their statues were brutally smashed; their names excised from the official lists of Egyptian rulers. Nefertiti's name, like her husband's, was chipped out of the annals of history, the golden seals bearing her title – symbols of the power she once wielded alongside Akhenaten – now nothing more than scrap to be melted down for their weight in metal. It's hugely telling that one of Nefertiti's official seals – a scarab of solid gold stamped with her name, and the first artefact ever to be found in Asia Minor or the Aegean naming either Akhenaten or his wife – was found on the Uluburun shipwreck, scrambled in a miscellaneous heap of crumpled bracelets and fragments of cut metal, probably stored in a bag at the ship's stern ready to be melted into bullion for the crew. By the late fourteenth century BCE, when the Uluburun ship sank – only a few decades after the deaths of Nefertiti and Akhenaten – Canaanite merchants were already peddling the official seal of the late Egyptian queen for gold: a sign of just how far Nefertiti had fallen.

But the desertion of Amarna – engineered by Nefertiti's stepson
Tutankhamun as a deliberate rejection of the monotheistic heresy it
represented – was, paradoxically, exactly what allowed its preservation.
In 1887, a Bedouin woman working in a field on the eastern bank of the
Nile, around two hundred miles south of modern-day Cairo, stumbled
across a stash of nearly four hundred clay tablets covered in cuneiform
writing. When they were translated from Akkadian, the lingua franca of
the day, these turned out to be a unique collection of diplomatic letters
between the Egyptian pharaohs and the neighbouring great powers,
including the kings of the Hittite, Babylonian and Assyrian empires: a
perfectly preserved portrait of the inner workings of the Egyptian court
and Late Bronze Age international relations during the mid fourteenth
century BCE when the court was based at Amarna.

What's particularly remarkable about the Amarna letters (as they're
now known) is the insight they give us into the complex, and hugely
lavish, practice of gift exchange between the Great Kings of the age. It
becomes clear that letters among the big-league imperial powers were
being sent largely for diplomatic purposes – declarations of friendship, requests for shipments of goods, negotiations of international
marriages to seal alliances, and so on – and it's luxury gifts that lie at
the heart of this correspondence. In fact, when you flick through the
letters, it's remarkable just how many of them are occupied with the
exchange of *stuff*: praising gifts that have arrived, enumerating gifts
being sent in return, or expressing ill-concealed disappointment at
gifts that didn't live up to expectations (or, worse, that haven't come
at all). The king of Assyria sends a couple of royal chariots, two finely
bred white horses (Assyrian horses were particularly prized) and a
lapis lazuli seal, in the hope that the Egyptian pharaoh will send back
gold (which, the Assyrian king claims, is as common as dirt in Egypt)
to help him build a new palace he's embarked on.[29] The king of Mittani,
Tushratta (Tadu-hepa's father, who gave her such a splendid dowry
when she went to marry the Egyptian ruler), dispatches five chariots,
five teams of horses, and a male and female attendant taken as captives
in war – I can't help but think of Homer's Briseis and Chryseis – plus,
in a second letter, a fabulous golden cup inset with lapis lazuli.[30] Meanwhile, the pharaoh writes to a vassal king ruling in Canaan – not far

from the home port of the Uluburun ship – ordering that he send over forty 'extremely beautiful female cupbearers' (enslaved women) 'in whom there is no defect', in return for linen garments, an ebony chair and forty pieces of silver per enslaved woman.[31] Women traded to a pharaoh for chairs, clothes and money. The traffic in women – just like the captive Chian textile workers in the Linear B tablets at Pylos, in the same period – is clearly going strong.

It's hard to miss, when you read through the Amarna letters, that some of the transfers that are going on between the kings bear a remarkable resemblance to the Uluburun cargo. One in particular that stands out is the shipment from the king of Cyprus (called Alashiya in the letter), who sends massive quantities of copper (we know the Uluburun copper came from Cyprus), on a similar scale to Uluburun (200 ingots of copper in one letter, 500 in another; Uluburun has 354), and probably on a similar kind of boat.[32] This boatload is shipped off in exchange for Egyptian ebony, gold, horses and linen textiles. It seems, then, that what we're finding in the textual archives of the mid fourteenth century BCE – and backed up by the remains of the Uluburun shipwreck – is a sort of palace-directed trade disguised as reciprocal gift-giving, where the great powers are circling each other in a tit-for-tat bid for the resources they need: copper-rich Cyprus and Babylon, with its eastern-imported lapis lazuli, bargaining in thinly veiled negotiations with the gold-wealthy Egyptian kings.[33] Interestingly, the Mycenaeans don't crop up in the corpus of the Amarna letters; but this may just be an anomaly due to the haphazard nature of the archive, transported from its original storerooms to the new capital, and the manner of its discovery. A comparable letter found at Hattusa, the Hittite capital, certainly sees the Hittite king Hattusili III – Puduhepa's husband – addressing the ruler of the Ahhiyawans/Achaeans as 'my brother' and 'Great King', and planning to redeploy to the Ahhiyawan king a gift earmarked for the pharaoh of Egypt.[34] Mycenaean ceramics – prestige gifts and containers for the import of olive oil – are found everywhere in the abandoned city of Amarna.[35] Meanwhile, the Linear B tablets at Pylos and Knossos make several references to *ke-se-nu-wi-ja*, or *xenia* – gift exchange within guest friendship, in relation to the export of cloth and olive oil (using the same word, as we saw above, that would later be used in

Homer to describe Odysseus' gift shower from Arete).³⁶ And multiple Egyptian tombs from the period show images of men from Keftiu – most likely Crete – gorgeously apparelled in Aegean style as they carry ceramics for trade with the pharaoh under the guise of gift exchange: one even shoulders an ingot of copper, instantly recognizable from the metal cargo carried by the Uluburun ship.

Crucially, however, this isn't just about bartering material wealth: the kings who are writing to each other with the details of the shipments of goods also, on a more lofty level, employ gift-swapping as a vital marker of and direct corollary to the alliances they share. As King Burna-Buriash II of Babylon pontificates in a letter to Akhenaten: 'between kings there is brotherhood, alliance, peace, and good words if there is an abundance of [precious] stones, silver, and gold'.³⁷ Rulers, in the Amarna letters, frequently write to each other as 'brothers', and the Babylonian king is particularly clear about the way in which these political alliances are tangibly cemented across the generations, just like the decades-old guest friendship between Diomedes and Glaucus in Homer: 'from the time my ancestors and your ancestors made a mutual declaration of friend-ship,' he writes in another missive, 'they sen[t] beautiful greeting-gifts to each other, and refused no request for anything beautiful.'³⁸

Now, there's no doubt that this is mostly a masculine world – and strikingly similar, at that, to the swaggeringly male world we see in the Homeric epics, where a king of Cyprus (just like the real Cypriot king who writes with a consignment of copper in the Amarna letters) can send the Greek king Agamemnon rare tin and blue glass as a guest gift – both of which were found on the Uluburun ship. In the *Odyssey*, Menelaus remembers visiting Thebes in Egypt – a real historical city, a few hundred miles upriver from Amarna – and being given two silver bathtubs, two tripods and ten ingots of gold by the Egyptian king; while, when he hosts Telemachus, the Spartan king offers him a chariot and three horses (the same gift as the actual king of Assyria to the Egyp-tian pharaoh).³⁹ And, in Homer, just as in the Amarna letters, this is a world where women are treated as the consummate commodity. When Agamemnon is trying to persuade Achilles to return to war in the *Iliad*, he rattles off a list of heaps of gold ingots, swift horses and enslaved weaving women from Lesbos that he's willing to give him – just like the forty 'extremely beautiful female cupbearers' we saw above, ordered by the historical Egyptian king from Canaan.[40] And it's not just enslaved women that Agamemnon offers Achilles; he also sweetens the deal with marriage to one of his three daughters back in Greece: 'you can choose one of them and take her back without a bride-price to your father's house. And he will give you lavish wedding gifts, such as no father ever gave his daughter.'[41] Daughters are often similarly traded in the Amarna letters – along with fabulous dowries, like that of the Mittanian princess Tadu-hepa – in the game of diplomatic marriage, like so many ingots of metal: 'if you send the gold I wrote you about, I will give you my daughter,' runs one particularly unfatherly dispatch, from a Babylonian king to the Egyptian pharaoh.[42] (The pharaoh writes back with a brilliant retort: 'is it nice that you give your daughters away in order to obtain the gift of your neighbours?')[43] And yet these real women who were traded in marriage – historical precursors of the trade in enslaved women and brides in Homer – also make themselves heard in a few fascinating passages in the Amarna letters, where we not only see them being bartered back and forth by men – we also get a glimpse of women sending gifts, and fostering diplomatic relationships, of their own.

One of the most interesting examples is a letter penned by a royal wife of Akhenaten – not Nefertiti, who was Akhenaten's chief consort, but another of his wives, or rather, brides-to-be, who would have joined Nefertiti in the pharaoh's harem: the daughter of Burna-Buriash II, the bombastic king of Babylon who had spent so much time lecturing Akhenaten on the importance of gifts. Burna-Buriash's daughter – who does not give her name in the correspondence – seems to have taken her father's lessons very much to heart. Writing, most likely, from Babylonia (given what can be discerned from the nature of the script), she takes it upon herself to make contact with her future husband, appearing to understand perfectly the diplomatic nature of her marriage, and the international alliances between men that are at stake in her union. With daughterly piety, she expresses a wish that her father's gods look favourably on her husband, and conveys her hopes for the pharaoh's success in his current military campaign. Above all, she shows how seamlessly she has absorbed the royal etiquette of prestigious gift exchange, learned at her father's knee, by sealing her letter to her husband-to-be with a gift

that is not only precious but appropriately gender-coded: 'my messenger,' she writes, 'brings (you) coloured cloth'.[44] We've already seen how
the dyeing of cloth was an important prestige marker in the Late Bronze
Age, particularly in the case of the vivid purple murex dye, as well as
how the longstanding history of spinning and weaving as women's work
would have marked this as an explicitly feminine-gendered artefact. It
seems likely, then, that the princess's choice was a highly conscious one:
a beautiful and expensive cloth, that articulates her subordinate role to
her future husband in a world dominated by opulent and overweening
kings – and, at the same time, asserts her participation as a Babylonian
princess and future ally in the network of diplomatic gift exchanges
across the power-hungry empires of the Bronze Age.

But women didn't only write to men: they also wrote to each other,
engaging in a form of exchange that worked seamlessly in tandem with
that of their husbands. One royal letter in the Amarna archive hints at
a parallel messenger system between royal queens, where wives' envoys
travelled with those of their husbands to carry messages between the
women, just like those of the men: 'may your own messengers go
regularly with the messengers of [the pharaoh] to my wife,' the king
of Mittani writes to the Egyptian dowager queen, 'and may my wife's
messengers go regularly to you'.[45] And one such correspondence between
Late Bronze Age queens is actually preserved – not in the collection of
Amarna letters, but in the copious Hittite archives unearthed at the
capital of Hattusa, and dating to a few decades later. This missive from
Queen Nefertari of Egypt (Great Royal Wife of Ramesses II) to Queen
Puduhepa of Hatti – the Hittite queen whose seal marks the peace treaty
following the Battle of Qadesh – seeks, by forging links between these
two powerful queens, to further shore up the peace established between
the empires of the Egyptians and Hittites in the wake of the great battle
of 1274 BCE. The Egyptian queen addresses her Hittite counterpart as
'sister', and even underlines the parallel relationship to their husbands
by adopting the language of brotherhood wielded so effectively in the
Amarna letters by the kings: wishing for 'good brotherhood forever
between the Great King, the King of Egypt, and the Great King, the King
of Hatti, his brother', Nefertari claims that 'I am likewise in a condition
of peace and brotherhood with you, my sister'.[46] Just like the lavish gift

exchanges between kings in the Amarna letters, Nefertari, too, shows that she is intimately acquainted with the rules of the gift game – and, just like the Babylonian princess sending cloth to her husband-to-be, she demonstrates the efficacy of a well-placed, gender-coded present, selecting textiles for all but one of the gifts to her 'sister': twelve dyed linen garments (the Egyptian queen is careful to specify the total), including a particularly fine cloak and several coloured tunics. If men sent cups and chariots to forge alliances, it seems that Late Bronze Age women did their diplomacy through clothes.

Which brings us back to the bottom of the seabed off the coast at Uluburun. Because the ship that met its end here, bearing Nefertiti's seal, wasn't only carrying a consignment of copper and tin sufficient to equip an Agamemnon-sized army. It wasn't only loaded with elite gifts, like the goblets of gold given by the king of Mittani to the Egyptian pharaoh (in the Amarna letters), or Alcinous to Odysseus (in Homer). It also contained faint traces of cloth, preserved underwater for thousands of years in the sediment of some of the storage jars – coloured blue and purple with (almost certainly) the highly valued murex dye. It's impossible to say for sure what these textiles were doing there. Were they bolts of cloth intended for trade? Garments worn by the elite Mycenaean messengers? Or were they prestigious gifts intended for exchange – like Nefertari's fine-dyed cloaks and tunics – between the rulers of the luxury-devouring, power-jostling coastal empires that this ship visited? Were they, perhaps, the final remnants of the priceless coloured cloth once sent by an envoy, on the orders of an Egyptian queen or a Babylonian princess?

Networking Women

And so, from the diplomatic correspondence of a Babylonian princess in a ruined Egyptian city to an octopus-infested Mediterranean shipwreck, the picture of the gifts Arete gives to Odysseus on his travels in the *Odyssey* starts to fall into place. A tunic and a cloak: exactly the greeting gifts selected by Queen Nefertari of Egypt for her 'sister' Puduhepa – a woman's woven gifts, in other words. Meanwhile, the cup of gold given by her husband Alcinous fits into the pattern of precious-metal presents sent between the Great Kings of the Late Bronze Age, like the lapis-encrusted golden goblet dispatched to Egypt by the king of Mittani. The Amarna letters and the shipment of luxury goods in the Uluburun wreck, including dyed cloths and a gold chalice, allow us to peer into an ancient diplomatic gift world, at the highest echelons, that enabled some ancient queens to reach into the international networks that crossed all the way from the banks of the Nile to the fringes of the Euphrates, and to circulate goods and letters of their own – even if the system was, at the same time, critically divided along the lines of gender. Here, it seems, kings and queens across the empires of the Late Bronze Age sent each other lavish presents that worked both to secure their gendered networks and to cement their separate and binary roles: a kings' club forged in golden chariots, cups and battle alliances; a coalition of queens woven out of exchange in coloured garments, personal envoys and (like Akhenaten's Babylonian bride) marriage bonds.

This seems to be precisely what we're seeing in the carefully orchestrated exchange – garments from Arete, goblet from Alcinous – that sends Odysseus on his way from the Phaeacian court. But it's not the only instance in Homer of these kinds of parallel, but complementary, gendered guest gifts. We've already come across the sumptuous presents of silver bathtubs, tripods and gold said to have been showered on the Spartan king Menelaus by an Egyptian ruler, when he stopped off on his way back from the Trojan War. Menelaus' wife, Helen, however, is not left out of the giving spree. We are told by Homer that she is said to have received her own special gifts from the Egyptian queen Alcandre: specifically, a golden distaff and a silver wool-basket on wheels.[47] When we see her in the *Odyssey*, during Telemachus' visit to the Spartan court, Helen has settled herself in her chair, her distaff already loaded with purple wool ready to be turned into finely spun thread, just as we see Arete spinning at the Phaeacian palace (acting out, in Helen's case, with perhaps a little too much conviction for a woman recently returned from Troy, the part of the perfect wife). These presents from an Egyptian queen to the Spartan beauty are not only symbolic gifts: they are a demarcation of women's expected role as textile workers, in a way that crosses international barriers and power structures, and demonstrates the longstanding connections women could make with each other through the tangible implements of the labour they shared. The idea of spinning with a golden distaff might seem the stuff of fabulous legend. But similar high-end precious weaving artefacts made of silver and gold have actually been found in elite women's burials of the Bronze Age – like a woman entombed at the Early Bronze Age site of Alacahöyük in central Turkey, her body swathed in precious jewellery, and a gold and silver spindle laid carefully beside her now-skeletal hands.[48]

It's not just the tools, but also the products, of weaving that connect powerful queens in Homer. Menelaus and Helen send Telemachus off, not with the chariot and horses that Menelaus originally offered, but (at Telemachus' own request) a two-handled cup, plus a silver bowl that we're told the Spartan king picked up as a guest gift along the Levantine coast (perhaps somewhere near the home port of the historical Uluburun ship).[49] Helen, however, decides to add a present of her own. Going into the palace storerooms, she selects the most stunningly woven of all the robes she has made – presumably with wool spun from the golden distaff we saw her with earlier – and gives it to Telemachus with the explicit instructions that it must be entrusted to the care of his mother Penelope until it can be worn by his bride on their wedding day. 'This,' she says, proffering the gift, 'will be a monument to Helen's hands.'[50] Similar to the gift of textiles shipped by a Babylonian princess to her husband-to-be, Helen selects a garment as an appropriately gender-coded wedding present – but, in Helen's case, this is to go directly into a woman's world, to be kept by Penelope, and handed on to Telemachus' future bride. (One wonders how Telemachus' newly-wed would react to a good-luck gift from Greece's most renowned homewrecker.) Her gift enters a circulation pattern that operates between women: queen to queen, mother to bride. And, as a 'monument to Helen's hands', her sumptuous weaving is a unique means for Helen to broadcast her own work, her own name, her own glory, across the Greek isles. By weaponizing the socially accepted channel of gift-giving and the socially mandated role of women as weavers, Helen is able to make gift exchange work, uniquely, in her favour – as a means to preserve her memory abroad, and to send her

own story (just like the tapestry she wove at Troy, giving her version of
the Trojan War) out into the world.[51]

The dichotomy of gift-giving we see in Homer – kings exchanging
with kings, queens with queens (and occasionally kings) – and the
division of luxury goods (above all, weaving paraphernalia and textiles
for women) thus seem to match up with the patterns of gendered gift
exchange that are displayed in the Late Bronze Age correspondence at
Amarna, as well as the prestige goods loaded on to the Uluburun ship.
By combining the evidence of these millennia-old letters with a real
Bronze Age shipwreck, we can begin to understand what's going on in
the complex gift-exchange networks between Homer's women – and the
ways in which a few elite females, in Homer, are able to lay claim to
a name for themselves, through the power of a web of gifts. Powerful
international links are established through tunics and cloaks woven by
queens like Arete and handed out to well-connected foreigners; precious
distaffs exchanged between female rulers of far-distant countries, like
Alcandre of Egypt and Helen of Sparta; and gorgeous robes sent as part
of a circuit of women's diplomatic gifts, splashing women's names and
memories far across the sea, and into the pages of legend.

Shipwreck

The sea, however, is a dangerous place. The Phaeacians might be said to
live in a perfect world of peace, giving safe convoy to all men in magical
ships that never sink; but they do have one thing to fear. Their flawless
seamanship, the way they offer passage within their vessels to all, has
(so Homer says) angered the god of the ocean, Poseidon. The father of
King Alcinous once apparently pronounced a prophecy that one day, as
a Phaeacian ship returned from its convoy over the misty sea, Poseidon
would strike it, turning it to stone, and pile a mountain of rock over their
fair city.[52] Tragically for the Phaeacians, who duly set Odysseus aboard
one of their ships and escort him to Ithaca, the prophecy is finally ful-
filled. Having dropped off Odysseus and winging its way back towards
the Phaeacian harbour, the ship is suddenly struck by an incensed
Poseidon (who smites it with the flat of his hand) and anchored at the

bottom of the ocean as a rock.[53] And Poseidon has good reason to be annoyed: his hatred of Odysseus (born of an implacable grudge after Odysseus' blinding of his son, the one-eyed Cyclops Polyphemus), and determination to thwart him on his journey home, has coursed through the *Odyssey* with predictable and tragic consequences. It was Poseidon, for instance, who sent the storm that wrecked Odysseus on the Phaeacian isle in the first place. Now one of the unsinkable, swift-as-thought Phaeacian ships has not only chauffeured the Greek hero safely back to Ithaca; it's also disgorged a treasure trove of gifts to shower on Poseidon's enemy. No wonder, perhaps, that the sea god resorts to turning it to stone. The petrified ship of the Phaeacians has been identified, over the years, in many real geographical locations – but above all in the coastal outcrops of rock around the island of Corfu, which was (even in ancient Greek times) associated with the mythical isle of the Phaeacians. One rock in particular, known as Kolovri, with its flattened side emerging from the enamel-blue waves and its curving outline resembling a sail, seems to bear an uncanny resemblance to the stone-frozen ship of legend – a monument to the final journey of the mythical ship that could never sink.

Real ships from the ancient past, however, *did* sink, and, as we've seen, can be discovered – even as they require immense archaeological expertise to be recovered at such challenging depths, and in the face of the inevitable decay wreaked by the passing of the centuries. The ship that descended to the seabed off Uluburun in the late fourteenth century BCE, although incredibly well preserved in the integrity of its cargo, had disintegrated substantially over the thousands of years since it last sailed – its wood, in particular, riddled with holes bored through by shipworms. The archaeologists who excavated it were keen to replay exactly how this process of decomposition happened. So in 2006, a full-scale, fifteen-metre-long replica of the Uluburun ship, *Uluburun III*, was purposely built and sunk not far from the original location, off the south-western Turkish coast. This site – known as the Kaş Archaeopark – enabled scientists to track the vessel's deterioration (over the course of about two years) via modern scientific methods including photogrammetry and 3D-modelling. It's also used as an underwater training ground for the next generation of marine archaeologists who will, hopefully, go on to make even more extraordinary discoveries and continue refining our picture of Late Bronze Age trade – as well as a recreational spot for tourists, and a way of raising public awareness of the astonishing finds at the Uluburun wreck.

In the *Odyssey*, Arete and Alcinous are punished by Poseidon, in the end, for the hospitality they give Odysseus. But they do get one thing in return before he leaves. After the customary feasting, bathing, clothing and all the rites of hospitality, on the eve before his departure from the glimmering island, King Alcinous at last asks who Odysseus is. The Greek king has just revealed something about himself, weeping at the story of the capture and fall of Troy told by the Phaeacian bard. Now, Alcinous demands, is the time not only to tell them his name and where he comes from, but the adventures that brought him here. 'Tell us,' says the king, 'where you wandered, what lands you came to, the cities and the people – both the savage and unjust, and the ones who know the laws of *xenia*.'[54] He wants, in other words, what we might call the original performance of the *Odyssey* – a first-hand rendering of the adventures of the hero's homecoming, the near-misses with open-mawed monsters, the dangerous liaisons with spellbinding nymphs and witches, the descent to the gaping caverns of the Underworld, that would make Odysseus (and his prototypical odyssey) famous.

And so Odysseus, the *Odyssey*'s hero, clears his throat – and the most famous act of the epic, the tale of his wanderings that has captured the imaginations of audiences across millennia, finally begins.

14

CIRCE

Witch

They say she likes to turn men into pigs. She says: the men do it themselves. All she does is slip the skin off, like a knife paring an apple, to show the boorish truth.

Sometimes she can't tell them apart – the men she's not yet changed, and the ones she has. Jostling about her, snouts at her skirts. Grunting and rolling their corpulent bellies. She tosses them slops in pots of clay: chunks of cheese, barley swill, handfuls of tree nuts. They set to it hungrily, muzzles wet, and before they've lifted their snouts, they've become what they already are. Her magic – drops of root sap, bitter-smelling plant stems snapped into the scourings – is the flick of her power, like a sword drawn, the twist that drives the blade home: the meal does the rest.

She likes the efficiency of it. Quick and clean. Dinner served, the dregs scrapped up, the sties filled with round pink pork.

Eat up, she tells them. Eat up.

What Pigs Eat

Kim Shelton, Berkeley professor and Director of the Nemea Center for Classical Archaeology, is looking at a graph of pig swill. Her practised eyes skim the flickering screen as she taps out codes in rhythm, translating the symbols like a magician unravelling a spell charted in chalk across a blackboard. Dots litter the grid, circles and triangles, numbers labelled with chemical elements, percentages and occult Greek signs that climb the y-axis – $\delta^{13}C_{co}$, $\delta^{15}N$, $\delta^{18}O$. Latin captions complete the *Da Vinci Code*-style cipher: *Bos. Capra. Ovis. Sus.*[1]

It might seem a long way off from a bucket of slops, but Shelton's cryptic numbers – ground out from bits of Bronze Age pig bone, now gleaming on a Californian computer screen – actually have a weird and wonderful story to tell about the world of pigs. And they bring us to one of the most complex, and misunderstood, women of the *Odyssey*, the first witch in Western literature – a woman, like Shelton, who knew a lot about pigs.

If Circe was a witch, however, Kim Shelton is an archaeologist.

Shelton has many responsibilities, but one of her main roles is to direct the excavations at a Late Bronze Age site located just beyond the fortification walls of the citadel at Mycenae on mainland Greece – made famous, above all, by the imposing Lion Gate, surmounted by two stone-carved rampant lionesses: the epitome of ancient power and might, and an unmissable statement of Mycenae's clout to the many ambassadors, traders and kings who would have passed beneath. Mycenae's proud lionesses loomed above the ruins for centuries, long after the city was abandoned: Roman travellers described them with awe, and it was these that clinched the identification with ancient Mycenae when the site was eventually rediscovered in the early eighteenth century. It's also cuttingly symbolic of our hunt for Late Bronze Age women that the eponymous lions of the Lion Gate have been systematically misgendered as male – when they're actually a fierce and gorgeous pair of female lions. (If you visit Mycenae, I encourage you to annoy as many people as you can by pointing out that this is, in fact, the 'Lioness Gate'.)[2]

But Shelton is focusing on two very different spots on the site. One is a religious complex high up on the citadel, known as the Cult Centre, that would have served the rarefied ritual needs of the royal Mycenaean palace. The other lies in the sprawling residential–industrial districts downslope of the Mycenaean palace – a motley collection of stone-walled buildings that are all that remains of an ancient pottery workshop-cum-multi-generational home, now known as Petsas House. (Here, she's pinpointed a handy well that was filled up with animal carcasses at about the time the building was destroyed, c.1320 BCE – right around the period that the Uluburun ship sank.) Over five summers, between 2010 and 2014, she and her team have painstakingly gathered and analysed ancient animal bones from both the Cult Centre and Petsas House, aiming to garner more information about the down-to-earth, bog-standard animals – the pigs, cows, goats and sheep – that made up the animal population of Late

Bronze Age Mycenae. These were the household flocks whose bleating and lowing, as they grazed nearby or scrapped for peelings in the courtyard, were the sounds of everyday life; the fattened livestock whose flesh was butchered and stewed to make family meals; the carefully selected victims whose bones were scraped clean for sacrifice.

Now, nearly a hundred animal bones have been sampled by bioarchaeologist Dr Gypsy Price and zooarchaeologist Dr Jackie Meier, two specialists in isotope analysis and ancient animal domestication who are working alongside Shelton to unlock the secrets of Mycenae's sheep, goats and pigs. The bones have been ground into a powder, rinsed, soaked, centrifuged and passed through an isotope ratio mass spectrometer, a machine that's able to take a sample and identify the various kinds (and relative abundance) of isotopes, or different versions of the same element. Shelton is particularly curious about what these isotopes might have to tell us about Mycenaean animals' diet – because, just like strontium in our teeth, the particular mix of isotopes (particularly carbon and nitrogen) that are written into our bones contain, locked into the chemistry of our tissues, the unique signatures of what we eat. All plants, for example, absorb nitrogen, but in recognizably different ways and (therefore) amounts: legumes, for instance (such as beans, peas, chickpeas, lentils, clover and bitter vetch), have noticeably lower levels of a particular stable isotope of nitrogen known as ^{15}N. Because we are what we eat, animals that consume plants low in ^{15}N will have a correspondingly reduced level of the isotope laid down in their bone tissue, which means we can work out approximately what they were eating. But it also means we can gain important clues as to whether, and in what ways, they might have come into contact with humans, since legumes like chickpeas and beans, as well as purpose-grown fodder like vetch, are commonly used as feed for domesticated animals (and it's likely they were in the Late Bronze Age, too). Later classical sources – no less an authority than the philosopher Aristotle – recommend, for the best and most succulent pork, fattening your pigs on a strict regimen of figs and chickpeas.[3] So a pig bone displaying a low ^{15}N value will not only point to a pig that lived on a diet of chickpeas or beans; it will suggest a highly domesticated and strictly managed animal – a pig whose diet was being purposely modified by humans.

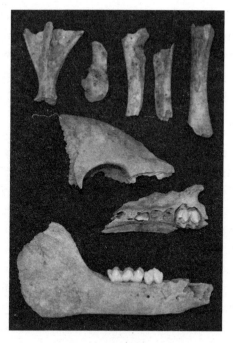

Pork on the menu: Late Bronze Age pig bones recovered from Petsas House in Mycenae.

Which brings us back to Shelton and her graph. The results fed back by the mass spectrometer – the circles on the chart labelled *Sus* (Homeric Greek, as well as Latin, for 'pig') – show that Mycenae's pigs have a fascinating story to tell. The pigs slaughtered at the Cult Centre, which ended their lives butchered on the altars of the palace temple, exhibited lower ^{15}N values and isotopic signatures that point towards legume- and grain-based fodder: pigs, in other words, that have been fed a controlled diet, purposely aimed at fattening them up for a particularly plump and juicy sacrifice.[4] It may be that these pigs were reared in the rolling grain-rich farmland that surrounded the Mycenaean capital, and levied by the state as a form of taxation: terms for 'fattened pigs' and swineherds crop up in the Linear B administrative tablets of the palace, with specific allocations to royal banquets, feasts and sacrificial offerings.[5]

Animal sacrifice – the slash of a knife through flesh, the gush of blood – was the pulsating heart of ancient Greek religion. An animal was butchered as a ceremonial offering to the gods; its flesh was roasted and eaten in a ritual meat feast that brought the (male) community together, and the bones were offered up to the gods, as well as the fatty smoke that rose up to the sky. Victims could be anything from bulls to sheep, goats and – importantly – pigs. The antiquity of these kinds of customs, stretching right back into the Bronze Age, is backed up by recent discoveries of burnt pig bones, slashed with cut marks, heaped up in Late Bronze Age palaces like Pylos and religious sanctuaries (one not far from Mycenae) – as well as, tellingly, in the heart of the Cult Centre at Mycenae itself.[6] The practice, it seems, would have been to spit and roast the pig's carcass, strip the flesh to provide a satisfying human feast – hence the cut marks – and then throw the bones on the fire for the gods. Thus communal feasting, set at the heart of the palatial complex and linked into the world of conspicuous consumption and resource control that the Late Bronze Age palaces stood for, neatly aligns with religious requirements – a state banquet, a tax levy and a temple sacrifice, all rolled into one convenient pig-shaped package.

If pigs were being fattened for sacrifice up at the palace, however, down in the town a pig's life would have looked altogether different. At Petsas House, the team discovered that the pigs' bones displayed much higher values of ^{15}N – suggesting that, in contrast to their porcine relatives in the citadel, these pigs were grazing on an enriched diet of the waste produced by humans: the familiar scenario of the family pig in the courtyard, grubbing around among the vegetable peelings, leftover meals and general rubbish.[7] But pigs would still have held a special place, even here – above all, on Late Bronze Age plates. Of all the animal bones recovered by Shelton and her team from the ancient house, pig bones constituted far and away the largest proportion: over 40 per cent, almost half the total, with a particular concentration of young pigs.[8] This abundance of pigs in the archaeological record matches recent statistics from other important centres in Mycenaean Greece, such as Pylos and Tiryns.[9] The reason this is surprising is because pig bones weren't found in large numbers before the last few decades, when archaeologists focused more on elite sites and concerns (why would the swashbuckling Schliemann, obsessing over the jewels of Helen, have interested himself in pigs?), and didn't have access to scientific techniques of analysis like the isotope ratio studies led by Price. This caused some archaeologists to suggest that there was even a taboo against pigs – condemnation of pigs' scavenging and uncleanliness, along the lines of the banning of pork in both the Torah and the Quran – across early state societies.[10] Yet, from the pile of piglet bones in Petsas House, it seems pork was very much on the menu in Late Bronze Age Mycenae, at least. The new evidence in fact suggests that home cooking, in Greece in the fourteenth century BCE, would have commonly featured locally, even domestically, produced pork – with pigs (cheap to keep, quick to breed) as an ideal resource for an independent household looking to provide food for themselves.[11] This is backed up by the finds of pig skeletons buried in the ash at Akrotiri on Thera: in the West House alone, for instance (home of the adolescent priest girl), as many as ten pigs were discovered – the family herd of a well-to-do household.[12]

This model of two-tier pork consumption – elite sacrifice and feasting on fattened full-grown swine, versus domestic husbandry focused on piglet-based meals – matches up neatly with the picture we're given in Homer's *Odyssey*. When Odysseus returns to Ithaca and stumbles up the path from the harbour, his first port of call is the hut of a loyal swineherd, Eumaeus. Eumaeus lives on the scrubby hillside near the palace next to the pigsties he's built himself; his job is to fatten the pigs (nearly a thousand of them) and send the very largest and fattest of the swine up to the Ithacan palace for Penelope's ever-hungry suitors.[13] He's got a careful diet worked out to feed the animals, we're told: 'good nutritious acorns, which fatten pigs'.[14] But this kind of specially curated pork isn't for everyone: when, following the rules of *xenia*, the faithful old swineherd ushers into his home a disguised Odysseus – lately returned from his travels and transformed into a beggar by a tap of Athena's magic wand – it is two young piglets (not the best of the bunch, he says; the suitors have eaten the rest) that Eumaeus plucks out to slaughter and barbecue for their evening meal.[15] The division is clear: juicy acorn-fattened pigs are sent up to the palace for the nobles' feasts; enslaved people, and those who can't afford better, eat piglets reared within the home.

What pigs eat, and what pigs get eaten: the evidence from the ancient bones at Mycenae give us a story that moves from slops to roasting

spit, and that reflects – through the secrets locked in the bones of the
meat it consumed – a society that sacrificed pigs on smoking altars in
the temple, feasted on them in the palace, and herded and butchered
them within the humble home. It's intriguing that it was pigs, above
all – beyond cows, goats or sheep – that displayed these dietary differences in Shelton's study, suggesting that the specific management practices, foddering restrictions and fattening regimes were aimed mostly
at pigs: giving them a central role in Mycenae's meat market, as well
as its ritual palette of religious offerings to the gods.[16] Analysing the
chemical composition of these ancient pig bones enables us to gain key
insights into the inner social, economic and religious workings of one
of the most important Late Bronze Age palace states – that can only be
glimpsed at the margins of the Linear B tablets, and that seem to gleam,
half remembered, in the barbecue hog roast that awaits Odysseus when
he at last returns to his home.

But that's only part of why we should care about pigs, and what pigs
eat.

The other, and more important, reason to care about pigs is because
Circe does.

Potions and Pig Swill

Circe: the woman who would come to be known as the first-ever witch
in the West. But, although she was later canonized as the prototypical
witch, it's important to note that Homer never actually says she is one.
What she is, in Homer, is *polypharmakos*: 'an expert in many kinds of
drugs' (*pharmaka* are various kinds of plant-based potions and drugs –
ranging from harmful toxins to helpful medicines – hence the English
word 'pharmacy').[17] She carries a magic wand, which she uses to strike
her victims like a switch against swine; she slips men potions, brewed
from herbs, and smears them with charmed ointments. She is halfway
between goddess and woman: a deity who, paradoxically, uses human
speech (Homer calls her 'the beautiful, dreadful goddess Circe, who
speaks in human languages').[18] She is a goddess of power, yet she speaks

like a human and lives, not on Olympus with the other divinities, but alone on a far-distant island called Aeaea.

And what does she do, all by herself on her island? The thing she is most famous for: she turns men into pigs. This is the story Odysseus relays to the Phaeacians, as he relates the tales of his marvellous travels at Arete and Alcinous' hearth. We are halfway through the epic recitation of Odysseus' adventures: the hero, we are told, has just put in his ship at the brush-covered island of Aeaea. Of the scouting party he sent, only one man has returned, panting with terror, gasping out his news of a dreadful enchantress within her halls, her gates guarded by lions and mountain wolves drugged by her baneful charms. The sound of her voice, her song reeling them in like a magic spell, as she weaves at her loom. The Greek men stepping through the doors, entranced; the goddess coolly lacing their honeyed wine with a magical potion that turns them into pigs. The pigs stumbling, squawking and screeching, into their sties.

Odysseus, being Odysseus, sets out at once, not only to recover his men, but also to experience this for himself (he is not the epic's titular character for nothing). On his way, he is visited by a god, Hermes, who offers the Greek hero *pharmaka* of his own. This comes in the form of a magical plant which – Hermes says – the gods call moly, with black roots and a milk-white flower. (Possibly Homer is thinking of garlic, said in antiquity to be a protective charm against their equivalent of vampires.)[19] Odysseus duly accepts the messenger god's help, and, when he drinks Circe's potion, remains unchanged; having rushed on Circe with his sword drawn, as Hermes advised him, he readily complies with Circe's counter-offer to go with her to bed. And off the hero trots. He'll end up spending a year wallowing in sexual paradise: and it's his crew who will have to remind him about getting back home.[20]

Hermes' prophylactic plant tells us a lot about Circe's own magic. Above all, it confirms that to be *polypharmakos* is to have an expert knowledge of plants – the potent leaves and roots, brought forth by the grain-giving earth, that are seen to possess formidable magical powers.[21] This accounts for the way Circe prepares her charm, mixing her *pharmaka* into a thick drink made up of barley, cheese, honey and wine.[22]

And her ingredients are carefully calculated: barley, in particular, is another ancient pig-fattener attested on the Linear B tablets.[23] Perhaps Circe is feeding up her victims in anticipation of eating them later: after all, when she turns around and offers Odysseus a meal, his initial demand is that she first change his companions back again – worried, perhaps, that she's about to roast them on a spit for dinner. Or perhaps it's precisely barley's nature as pig fodder that is imagined, by a sort of associative property, to turn men into pigs.

Pharmaka, then, can be helpful (like Hermes') or harmful (like Circe's) – as with any potent drug. We have some rare evidence from the Linear B tablets at the Late Bronze Age palace at Pylos that backs up the identification of *pharmaka* as powerful plants. In this case, their power is beneficial: we find a record of either tree mallow or hibiscus being specially brought into the palace as a *pa-ma-ko* (that is, a *pharmakon*, or healing drug).[24] Mallow extract – also found in the archaeological record – is a known anti-inflammatory and can be combined with water to make a soothing gel: the ideal good kind of drug.

So if Circe's *pharmaka* are powerful plants (albeit on the dangerous end of the spectrum), then it makes perfect sense that Odysseus' moly is the only match for her charms. Yet the idea of women possessed with an extensive knowledge of *pharmaka* probably has its origins in a much less arcane realm: their role as medicinal-plant gatherers and experts in herbal lore.[25] Women (ever at the margins) don't seem to be listed explicitly as healers in the Linear B tablets, but we see the intimate connection between women and plants represented time and time again in the visual repertoire of Late Bronze Age Greece.[26] Hordes of naked, plant-picking women with riotous hair gyrate across the ornate golden signet rings of the Minoan and Mycenaean world, tugging at plants and shrubs in a clear effort to pluck them from the ground – possible early reflections of Bronze Age women's rituals around plant-gathering. Many of these rituals seem to be accompanied by ecstatic, even orgiastic dancing, and appear to take place at night, as indicated by the presence of stars, moon and even the Milky Way scattered across the skies. Similarly, this time adorning the walls of one of the houses in Thera's Akrotiri, we find the painting of the saffron gatherers (all women), who are shown in their dazzlingly dyed robes bending to pluck the crimson stamens of

A real magic wand: part of a midwife's birth kit from Egypt
(early second millennium BCE).

the saffron crocus. This fragrant spice was also used as a therapeutic drug in antiquity, particularly for women – known for its ability to help bring on labour, to stimulate menstrual bleeding and as a pain-killer during both menstruation and birth. We have already seen, on the peak of Mount Petsophas in Crete, how the collection of women's votive offerings hinted at a medical midwifery tradition that included weasels, tortoises and puppies; it's been suggested, too, that on Thera the frescoes of saffron pickers are celebrating the role of women in herbal medicine and in its regulation of a girl's first menses.[27] Meanwhile, some Bronze Age midwives carried real magic wands – just like Circe's – in their birth kits, aimed at warding off harm from newborns. One stunning example from Egypt in the early second millennium BCE, made from a hippopotamus tooth, features incised images carved into the surface including the goddess of childbirth Taweret – the lion-hippopotamus with a crocodile backpack – swallowing a snake. So perhaps it was an early kind of midwife or wise woman, kitted out with her plants and her magic wand, who became absorbed into the figure of Circe: a blurring of the boundaries between magic and medicine, where women's skill in healing drugs set them apart.

It's easy to see how these kinds of historically attested, highly female-gendered activities – engaged in only by women, underscored by the healing power of herbal medicine and laced with the esoteric associations of female bleeding and childbirth – might have been transformed into the misogynistic fantasy of witchcraft that would dog women for centuries. And it's in the stories men tell – in literature, above all, from the Homeric epics onwards – that these powerful witch figures, with their intimate knowledge of plants, start to bloom into their full and most fantastical forms. Circe with her many *pharmaka*, with her drugged wine and her charmed ointments that turn men into pigs and back again, is only the beginning of the tale. Medea – the enchantress of Colchis, and (incidentally) Circe's niece, whose magical herbs and charms helped Jason to win the Golden Fleece – is said (in classical Greek tragedy) to uproot plants while naked, letting the root sap drip into her collection phials. The efficacy of her herbal lore is made clear in the myth: she uses her knowledge of plants to rejuvenate her father-in-law, Aeson, and even cures the hero Hercules of madness.[28] What can help can also harm, though; and it's toxic *pharmaka* daubed on gifts to Jason's new bride that help Medea to murder her rival and give rise to her reputation for demonic violence (at least they're the start).[29] By the time we get to the Roman period, we find witches like Erictho, a hideous Thessalian crone who is said to lurk in graveyards and fill corpses with the most noxious plants, in order to perform a necromantic oracle for the son of the Roman general Pompey.[30]

These nightmare figures born from the imaginations of much later (male) writers are a far cry from Circe, and, above all, from how she's represented in Homer. To understand Homer's Circe, we have to forget later fantasies of witchcraft, and focus on the real female plant experts of the Late Bronze Age: from the saffron gatherers on Thera to the pharmacists of the Linear B tablets, to the plant-uprooting figures engraved on golden rings: the first true *polypharmakoi*. These were the women who gathered herbs to make remedies, who administered cures (likely focused around menstruation and childbirth) and may have practised some of the earliest folk-medicinal healing. These were the women whose skilled knowledge and practice of a female tradition of herbal lore came to be twisted into that millennia-old word of fear and fantasy: *witch*.

The question, however, remains: why pigs?

Why Pigs?

In her modern retelling of Circe's story, Madeline Miller's Odysseus asks the goddess: 'Why pigs?' Circe doesn't, at the time, give an answer. 'Sometimes you must be content with ignorance', is all she says.[31] But ancient philosophers and moralists, like Odysseus, were obsessed with the question of *why pigs*. Heraclitus, an early Greek thinker writing around 500 BCE, pronounced that it's because Circe – a woman who lives by herself and is empowered enough to ask a man to have sex with her: always a danger sign in the eyes of men – is meant to be the ultimate emblem of wanton luxury in Homer. The men's transformation into pigs, for Heraclitus, is symbolic of their surrender to bestial pleasures; Odysseus alone, the wise man and rational leader, is able to resist. And it wasn't just Heraclitus who was keen to praise Odysseus: Athens' best-known philosopher, Socrates, took the same approach. Circe didn't turn men into pigs, Socrates pontificates to his friends while at a dinner party; they *became* pigs because they were gluttons (one imagines his fellow diners slowly putting down their plates and shuffling away from the buffet). Meanwhile, Odysseus is apparently saved because of 'his own self-control and avoidance of overindulgence' in merely sipping at Circe's potion. (We're then blessed with Socrates' two most fun tips: don't eat if you're not hungry, and don't have sex with good-looking people.)[32] All this manly moralizing seems rather ironic, given that Odysseus does, in fact, down Circe's concoction just like the rest of his crew. It's Hermes' magical moly, not Odysseus' so-called self-control, that saves him. And it's even more ironic, given that it's Odysseus' men who have to remind him, after a year of non-stop sex with Circe, that he was actually meant to be on his way back home.

But there's another way forward. Once we take up the investigative tools of history, it's actually possible to begin to uncover the factors, within the context of Late Bronze Age Greece, that could have forged such a suggestive link between women, swine and herbal magic – in a way that might have turned Homer's Circe into an enchantress of pigs. The first step on the trail is the Bronze Age trope of goddesses as

Mistress of Animals: the Mesopotamian goddess Ishtar, wearing a helmet and weapons, tramples a lion on a leash (from an Akkadian seal, late third millennium BCE).

legendary animal tamers, the so-called 'Mistress of Animals' (*potnia thērōn*) motif – an instantly recognizable iconography of goddesses that is found in a great swathe throughout ancient Mediterranean and south-west Asian art, showing a human-like divine female grasping (or being fawned upon by) two animals, one on each side. The earliest-known example goes all the way back to around 6000 BCE, from the site of Çatalhöyük in southern Turkey, with a clay sculpture of a corpulent woman with pendulous breasts seizing a pair of lionesses. Other examples are strewn across ancient cultures: from the great Mesopotamian warrior goddess Ishtar, who tramples a lion on a leash with magnificent self-composure, to the Egyptian Qetesh – naked, sensual and dangerously magical atop her lion steed (spear and snake in one hand, plants in the other) – to the wild Anatolian, lion-riding mountain mother Cybele. And the Mistress of Animals also makes an appearance in Bronze Age Greece. A fabulously fierce female is found on a Minoan seal from Knossos: staff or spear outstretched like a wand, power-posing on a mountaintop with a palace behind her and flanked by two rampant lionesses; to the right, a man gazes up at her, arm raised in obeisance. Linear B tablets, also from Knossos, make mention of a goddess called *qe-ra-si-ja*, or 'Mistress of Wild Beasts'.[33] And the snake-wrangling goddesses of the Knossos palace, with their symmetric serpents gripped one in each hand, fit neatly into this pattern, too. All these potent animal-tamers are also, like Circe, sexually charged: mistresses of animals, dangerous and powerful as they are, often flirt with taking mortal lovers in the ancient myths (who frequently run into trouble through their association with these redoubtable women). Aphrodite, in a hymn attributed in antiquity to Homer, wanders on to a mountainside near Troy looking for her mortal lover, Anchises, and is immediately encircled by fawning wolves, lions, leopards and bears; another of her mortal fancies, Adonis, is gored to death by a boar.[34] Meanwhile, the goddess Ishtar, who tries to seduce the mortal Gilgamesh in the Babylonian epic of the same name from the second millennium BCE, is rejected by the hero as he reminds her what she did to her other mortal lovers: striking them and turning them into wolves.[35] The parallel with Homer's Circe is unmissable.

But even if Circe fits the role of the lion- and wolf-taming goddess who transforms her lovers into beasts, where do pigs come from? We know, from the work that's being done by archaeologists such as Shelton to explore the role of pigs in Late Bronze Age Greek society and economy,

An early Circe? On a mountaintop (a palace stands to her left), a woman power poses with staff (or wand) outstretched and lionesses at her sides; a man cowers before her.

that they were important for survival. So Circe's pig husbandry might be a purely practical choice, as a Late Bronze Age economic move for a woman living in the middle of nowhere on a resource-limited island: an upward conversion of her assets in a one-woman landholding, from vegetarian and pig-fattening barley (in the potion) and acorns (tossed to the pigs) into succulent meat. Homer is careful to tell us that Circe has pigsties built next to her palace – suggesting that Odysseus' visit isn't the first time she's plumped for pigs.[36] And yet there are hints that this is about more than just practicality. Pig sacrifice, in particular, lay at the heart of several occult magico-religious rituals across the ancient world connecting women and women's sacred and magical cults, above all, with themes of sexuality, fertility, death and rebirth. One of the most widespread and mysterious women-only cults of ancient Greece – which seems to have had deep prehistoric roots – was the Thesmophoria: a three-day female festival celebrating Demeter, goddess of the earth and the harvest, and her daughter Persephone, who was raped as she picked flowers by the god of the Underworld, Hades, when the death god burst with his chariot out of a yawning chasm in the earth.

The Thesmophoria festival's main event was, crucially, the slaughter of piglets, which were killed at night and tossed into a pit to decay – commemorating, so it was said, a local swineherd's pigs that fell into the earthen chasm along with Persephone.[37] In this annual re-enactment ceremony, performed by women in the dark to much chanting and flickering of torches, the pigs' limp corpses were imagined as substitute humans – replacements for Persephone's assaulted and victimized female body, descending underground into the pit. But it also celebrated Persephone's ultimate return to the world (in the myth, for six months of the year, bringing with her spring's natural bounty and the summer ripening of crops): the Thesmophoric pigs were eventually brought up by the worshippers, to be placed on the altar of the mother goddess Demeter to ensure the burgeoning sexual fertility of the women at the festival, and the flourishing of the harvest in general.

It's difficult to find specific evidence for the Thesmophoria in the Bronze Age, which – as a women-only, highly secretive cult – is hard enough to uncover even in the later periods of history (although some burnt Mycenaean pig bones have been found at Eleusis, another ancient

Greek site with strong links to Demeter and Persephone).[38] But there's
evidence that the association between pigs and harvest was an age-old
one, going all the way back to the Stone Age (to judge from prehistoric
clay figurines of pigs, some of them imprinted with grains of corn).[39]
And other rites, from elsewhere in the Bronze Age world, hint suggestively at a similar occult nexus between pigs, women, fertility, rebirth,
substitution rituals, the Underworld – and even magic. At a Hittite sanctuary at Yazılıkaya (in modern-day Turkey), a couple of cave chambers
in a craggy outcrop a stone's throw from the capital at Hattusa stand
open to the skies, millennia-old relics of a holy site of the ancient
Hittites. It's still possible to visit these extraordinary open-air temples –
royal tombs mingling with places of sacred worship, their walls carved
with statuesque reliefs of the cosmic gods. In one cave, however, right
beside the funerary chamber of a Hittite king, archaeologists digging at
the site uncovered a particularly gruesome burial: a pig foetus, its tiny
bones nailed into the ground with ten bronze pins. Its position next to
the burial chamber – marked out by the image of the Death-god carved
into its wall, in the form of a dagger – hints that this nailed-down piglet
was perhaps a magico-religious totem, sacrificed in association with the
death of the king.[40]

This theory is supported by a ritual recipe written by a Hittite Old
Woman called Tunnawiya – one of the best-known female ritual experts
from the Hittite Empire, who authored as many as five surviving ritual
texts in the cuneiform tablets. One of her prescriptions, known as the
'Ritual of the Ox' and probably written around the fifteenth century BCE,
recommends a cure for a royal couple who are under threat of death.
Aside from dismembered bits of a sheep (which are to be carefully laid
on the corresponding parts of the royal patient), the key ingredients are
two piglets: one living and one (bizarrely) made of dough. The live piglet
is to be waved around at a distance from the king and queen under their
mantle of disarticulated sheep, while the dough pig is held close to the
patient as the Old Woman recites her incantations, calling on the Death-
god to retreat from his victim and take the piglet as a substitute. The live
pig is then almost certainly slaughtered, thus finally – by providing the
Death-god with the life he wanted – removing the threat of death hanging over the royal couple.[41] A similar remedy, this time prescribed by a

different wise woman, Hantitassu, orders the applicant to dig a pit, kill a piglet and stick it downwards into the hole so the blood flows into the ground – then pray to the queen of the Underworld.[42]

As in the case of the piglet sacrifice at the Greek Thesmophoria, it's not only death that pigs are connected to in the Hittite rites conducted by Tunnawiya and Hantitassu – there's also a clear link between the slaughter of a pig and the promise of health and vitality that it brings to the world of humans. (Another of Tunnawiya's rituals, this time a fertility booster, has a male or female piglet to be waggled around and then sacrificed – depending on the sex of the person who is having trouble conceiving.)[43] Death and life are perceived as different sides of the same coin – and pigs have an important role to play in both.

In all these instances, we can see how pigs are demonstrably being cast in the role of human substitutes: explicitly in the Hittite pig-surrogate rituals, implicitly in the journey of the slaughtered piglets into the 'Underworld' pit and back again during the clandestine female rites of the Thesmophoria. It's possible that the idea of pigs as substitute humans suggested the fantasy of a transformation the other way – men into pigs.[44] But it's also suggestive that, in both cases, these pig-centred rituals – sprinkled with not a little of the spice of secrecy and magic – are performed by powerful women: the esoteric rituals of the Old Woman practitioner Tunnawiya, and the women of the Thesmophoria re-enacting the rape and redelivery of Persephone to the upper world. In these transformative rituals that promised the heady and powerful experiences of death and rebirth, sacrifice and healing, through women's access to the potency of pigs as surrogate humans, we might be getting a glimpse into yet another strand of Circe's history: a wise woman who knows the precise and terrible power of a pig.

In Our Heads Forever

So if we bring it all together – the early women *polypharmakoi* collecting herbs, the lion-taming goddesses brandishing their staffs, the secret female-only rituals that incorporated pigs into a subversive story of rape, death and rebirth, and the wise women with their substitute swine and their spells of renewal – we find an image refracted back at us of Circe: a unique blend of Greek, Egyptian, Hittite and Mesopotamian mythologies that tangle together to create a powerful herbalist, lover, animal tamer, pig witch, and goddess of sex and death. Sex, because it is Circe, after all (at least in Odysseus' version of the tale), who invites Odysseus into her bed for a year of erotic pleasure. Death, because when Odysseus' crew (turned back into men) at last manage to get him to leave, it is she who sends him on his way with the detailed instructions he needs to reach the Underworld ('the sacred groves of Persephone', she calls it), to speak to the seer Tiresias and get directions back to Ithaca.[45] With an intimate knowledge of pit-sacrifice rituals that suggests parallels with both the pig burial of the Thesmophoria and the spells of the Hittite wise women, Circe tells him exactly how to perform the necromantic pit sacrifice that he'll need to summon the dead, specifying particularly that the blood of his animal victims needs to drain down into the pit to the spirits of Hades – just, in fact, like Hantitassu's slaughtered piglets.

It may not be incidental that Circe has such an intricate knowledge of the paths to Persephone's underground realm. If Persephone's story is linked with pigs just as much as Circe's, then there are other, intimate connections between the two goddesses: both of them notorious plant pickers (Persephone is gathering flowers in a meadow when Hades assaults her – among them, roses and crocus, two gynaecological plants; we're reminded of women's roles as harvesters of medicinal herbs); and both, crucially, endangered by men who encroach violently and sexually on their female world.[46] Madeline Miller picks up on this resonance to answer Odysseus' question 'Why pigs?' – rewriting Circe's story as a response, like Persephone's, to a brutal and traumatic rape, a righting of the wrongs done against her body. For Miller, the reason Circe lights on pigs seems to be their squealing in the sties as she was raped: the pigs' cries allow her to express her own trauma, and to afflict an assault on her attackers in return.[47]

The difficulty in retelling Circe's tale is that the story of the *Odyssey* is quite simply all about Odysseus. The Circe episode, in Homer, is all about proving the cleverness of the Greek hero in evading her magical charms, his self-restraint (as expounded by the philosophers), his conquest of yet another feminine obstacle (in a line-up that includes

Calypso, Nausicaa and Arete, as well as Scylla and the Sirens) as he beds
the goddess and then extracts from her the information he needs. It's
no coincidence that all this is told from Odysseus' point of view, by a
very biased narrator intent on telling his version of the tale. Influential
narratives like the *Odyssey* have, as we've seen throughout this book,
undeniably constructed the way we talk about women, the way we think
about witchcraft, and – of course – the way we understand Circe. New
Circes respond to the *Odyssey*'s male-centrism by claiming a voice that
speaks out in overt criticism of the epics: a poem by Margaret Atwood,
for instance, has Circe hurl at Odysseus, 'you leave in the story and the
story is ruthless'.[48] Nikita Gill has Circe reject the story outright and build
a new story for herself: 'Why be a half-finished poem in some forgotten
poet's story, when one can be an odyssey in and of herself?'[49] Meanwhile
Toni Morrison, in her *Odyssey*-inspired *Song of Solomon* (1977) – a novel
that earned her the first-ever Nobel Prize in Literature to be awarded to a
black woman – transforms Circe into a black midwife of the same name.
Her Circe's combination of ancient power (she protects the protagonist,
embraces her sexual allure, commands a throng of dogs and gives the
hero the instructions he needs to complete his voyage) and marginality,
both in story and society, works to construct a pointed commentary on
the intrinsic racial and gender discrimination built into the narrative of
the hero's journey.[50]

If Circe is made to stand in the background of both the *Odyssey* and
(in a critically feminist and intersectional way) the *Song of Solomon*,
however, there is one way in which she does, in fact, reach out beyond
the confines of Odysseus' extended sojourn on her island: and that's in
the way she's remembered. We, as Homer's audience, know this to be
true: Odysseus is telling Circe's tale to the Phaeacians in the *Odyssey*,
thus preserving both her story and her name (albeit embedded in his
own narrative). But Odysseus also carries her memory with him. As
he's packing up the costly guest gifts for his final departure from fantasy
land – the tunics, cloaks and gold heaped up for him by Arete – he
fastens the chest securely by tying it with a knot 'that he had learned
from Circe'.[51] Odysseus clearly hasn't forgotten his Aeaean queen. In fact,
we might remember the love knots from the Assyrian tablet: perhaps
this is yet another of Circe's magic charms – a way of eternally binding

Odysseus to her narrative, and winding hers into his. A poem by Louise Glück – in which an uncompromising Circe tells Odysseus what to say to his wife when he reaches home – picks up on this enduring power of Circe's tale:

> When
> you see her again, tell her
> this is how a god says goodbye:
> if I am in her head forever
> I am in your life forever.[52]

Even as Odysseus' ship slides over the horizon, prow pointed towards Ithaca, Circe's story lives on.

But not all women have a name. Not all women are left to witness how the tale ends. There are some women – twelve women, unnamed and enslaved – who end their lives as the *Odyssey* comes to a close strung up by their necks in the Ithacan palace courtyard, feet twitching as they gag at the noose.

Not all women get to be remembered.

15

EURYCLEIA

Handmaid

ITHACA, GREECE

Water is what she knows. She can get a grip on water. Some might think it rarefied, pure – but they've never had to wash bloodstains out of paving stones, and water does the job well enough then. Water is there when the mess comes: and it always comes. It grounds her, even when the world slips out of focus. And it does that more than ever as the years go by.

When she was little more than a girl, nursing the young master, it was the damp round her nipples on the sheets that reminded her what she had been bought for. A fleshy pair of breasts swollen with milk, traded off for twenty oxen, so the lady didn't have to bother with the dark stickiness of feeding.

When she was a woman, it was the bathwater that slid from jug to tub and bloomed across her apron as she rubbed the master's back. Other things, too, in the greasy wetness of the bath, though he told his wife otherwise and it wasn't like she had a choice. There's a reason they only wanted women slaves to wash them.

When she was a matron, it was the flack-flack of the tunics as they beat them on the river rocks, the drops of filth spattering her skin like freckles. They went together to the river's edge, she and all the slave girls – most whose names she didn't know. Names don't matter when you're up to your elbows in the master's baby's dung-stained linen, trying not to scrape your nails in the muck. They are all in the grip of a name that is much more powerful than their own.

Now that she's old and no longer comely, the girls go without her to the shore, and the men don't want her at their baths any more. Wash the floor, Eurycleia, the mistress says. It's not clean: wash it again.

She says nothing. But she knows whose fault it is that the stones are never clean.

Why Water Matters

Out in the Ionian Sea, around one hundred and fifty miles west from where Eurycleia was said to have bathed the newly returned Odysseus, a ship floats on the horizon. But this is no Bronze Age craft with black-painted hull. It's a fully fitted-out German research vessel – steel blue and almost a hundred metres long, with twenty on-board scientific laboratories, winches and cables of up to eleven thousand metres, and loaded with a deep-sea piston corer. RV *Meteor* is on a months-long international research trip, bound from the port of Malaga in Spain, skirting the north African coast past Sicily, circling Crete, Cyprus and the Levantine coast, then across the Aegean past Greece towards what's known by scientists as the Calypso Deep – the deepest trench in the Mediterranean Sea, over five kilometres from surface to seabed, and an Ionian Sea landmark.[1] If it weren't for the conspicuous lack of bird-bodied Sirens, dog-headed Scyllas, potion-brewing witches and sultry nymphs, this might make for a veritable odyssey of its own.

At this moment in the summer of 1993, though, the *Meteor* is in the clear waters of the Ionian, poised to release the piston corer from a fluorescent orange crane arm on the ship's aft. The hi-vis-jacketed technicians and engineers, overseen by expert geologist Jörg Keller, have linked up the corer, checked the cables and secured the bolts, and now signal to the control deck. In one slick motion, the 18-metre-long steel tube is upended, held steady by the crane above the waves, then the cables spool out and, like a whale slipping underwater, it slides down beneath the surface.

Piston coring is one of the staples of oceanography. It enables marine scientists to plunge the weighted metal tube of a corer thousands of metres down to the seabed and extract cookie-cutter sections of the ocean floor, sometimes dozens of metres long. In this case, length really does matter: just like on land, sediment gradually builds up on the seabed over time, which means that the deeper we can cut through the ocean floor, the further back we go – over hundreds of thousands of years, in fact. The sea floor is a unique resource for studying the climate patterns of the past, like a locked-in time capsule, because – unlike on land – the sediment here is (almost always) undisturbed by the human activities of digging and building. And if we can use modern scientific methods to interpret the information sealed within the sand and clay, it's possible to find a wealth of history stored in these underwater chronicles.

One of the many fascinating narratives is locked into the chemistry of some of the tiniest, yet most important, plants on the planet: phytoplankton (an ancient Greek-derived word that means 'wandering [*plankton*] plant [*phyton*]'). These microscopic itinerant plants float around in water like a miniature forest, using sunlight to generate energy via photosynthesis (the process that converts carbon dioxide and water into oxygen). Phytoplankton thus produce about half of all the oxygen on earth, more than all the tropical rainforests on land combined – although they make up only around one per cent of the global plant biomass. When these powerful little drifters die, they fall to the seabed and, in some cases, their shells turn into fossils in the ocean-floor sediment – and their chemical make-up contains a detailed record of the environment when the plankton were alive. In particular, it's possible to detect changes in water temperature from alterations in the proportions of different chemicals present in the fossils. By measuring the chemical composition of these temperature-sensitive molecules, we can estimate the temperature of the water at the time each specific organism was drifting in the ocean current.

What's particularly fascinating about the sediment cores extracted by the team from the Ionian seabed is what the fossils have to tell us about ocean temperatures at the end of the Bronze Age, when real Mycenaean ships (the patterns of Odysseus' craft) might have been forging through the waves. At around 1000 BCE, it's possible to see the plankton responding to a sharp drop in sea surface temperature – a fall of 3–4°C, meaning that the sea reached its coldest point in the last twelve thousand years.[2] This kind of temperature decline would have had a critical effect on the basic functioning of the water cycle – the natural system that transfers water from the ocean back into the atmosphere and on to the earth through rain. Cooler seas lead to less water evaporating from the oceans, which means less rainfall on land – and, consequently, drought.[3]

We've already seen the evidence from the Hittite capital of Hattusa of a centuries-long dry period, captured in the tree rings, accentuated by an extreme arid period of three years in the early twelfth century BCE. The additional evidence provided by the Ionian Sea sediment cores adds another piece to the puzzle. Not only does it show that this megadrought extended over the entire Aegean and eastern Mediterranean (that is, far beyond Hattusa); it also demonstrates that this cool, dry period was a climatic effect that persisted over hundreds of years – that was still being felt in, and after, the first millennium BCE. (The climate wouldn't recover until the Roman period, around 350 BCE.)

The findings made by Keller and the team on the RV *Meteor* have recently been backed up by multiple ancient-climate studies, across a whole range of almost mind-bogglingly varied evidence that fits together to create a unified picture of climate change – and, above all, drought – at the close of the Late Bronze Age, in a massive sweep that extends from the Mediterranean into south-west Asia. Sediment cores from across the Aegean and Adriatic confirm a decline in sea temperature at the end of the Late Bronze Age and into the Early Iron Age.[4] Stable isotope data from mineral deposits in Soreq Cave (northern Israel) and the Mavri Trypa Cave (just off the coast of Pylos, Greece) records rapidly diminished rainfall, attesting to low annual precipitation over the centuries of the Late Bronze Age–Early Iron Age transition.[5] And pollen records from Syria to Egypt, Cyprus to Israel to Greece – the minuscule pollen grains preserved as fossils in the silt at the bottom of lakes and rivers – tell the same story: a prolonged and widespread drought, lasting from around 1200 to 850 BCE, with its devastating peak during the twelfth century BCE.[6]

All this had a catastrophic – and visible – effect on the people of the Late Bronze Age. With less rainfall, fewer crops would have survived, resulting, critically, in less food. We can actually watch this happening in the climatic record: by measuring the relative amounts and types of pollen preserved in samples of sediment taken from lake and river beds, we're able to trace a significant drop in cultivated crop production over exactly the same period. As the drought dragged on, there was less and less food to fill the storerooms and the coffers of the palatial bureaucracies, and the international trade that had sent ships winging between the great ports and cities dried up. The complex palace-centred economies – like a tree that depended on the roots of agriculture to sustain the burgeoning urban populations and the interconnected networks of far-flung commerce – simply toppled. Invaders, sensing an opportunity, gave a final push to the teetering trunks of power. Rebellions flared. One after another, like fiery beacons lighting up the coast, the great bronze-burnished cities from Mycenae in Greece to Knossos on Crete, Troy to Hattusa, from Ugarit in Syria to Canaanite Megiddo (the Armageddon of the Bible), burned and fell.

Over the course of around a hundred and fifty years, the old world was reduced to ashes.

And it all began with water.

Handmaids and Hand-Washing

Women in the ancient world knew about water: enslaved women above all.[7] When, in the *Iliad*, Hector pictures Andromache's life in slavery, he imagines her being forced to fetch water from a spring for her Greek masters. When Nausicaa goes to the river to wash her dowry clothes, it's her enslaved girls (the Homeric word is *amphipoloi*) she takes with her to do her laundry. And when Odysseus – transported back to Ithaca by his Phaeacian convoy, magically disguised by Athena as a beggar and now wandering about the Ithacan palace, observing the havoc wrought by Penelope's suitors – is offered a foot bath by Penelope, it's Eurycleia, the old enslaved nurse, who is assigned the task of washing the beggar's feet.[8]

Eurycleia – which means 'wide fame' in ancient Greek – is given a name, and a backstory, that many of the unnamed enslaved women in Odysseus' palace do not get. Her lot in life is, by now, a depressingly familiar one for a Late Bronze Age woman: sold as a young girl for the extraordinarily high price of twenty oxen, she was enslaved to Laertes, Odysseus' father.[9] (This shows Homer constructing a world with a booming market in enslaved women: they're not just captured in war, like Briseis, but also traded for large sums in peacetime.) Homer tells us that Laertes treated her like a second wife, but didn't have sex with her because his actual wife – Anticleia, whose name means 'anti-fame' – would be angry: which goes to suggest that *not* being raped as an enslaved woman was the exception, rather than the norm.[10] Eurycleia, we are told, breastfed both Odysseus and then his son, Telemachus; when Odysseus returns, she plays a pivotal role in bringing him back into the household, acknowledging him with the instinctive recognition that only a mother(-figure) can provide. In a dramatic recognition scene that forms one of the most iconic moments of the *Odyssey*, as the old nurse takes up her master's feet, she sees a scar shearing up his thigh: a wound from a boar hunt that Odysseus sustained as a younger man.[11] She drops his leg into the basin, spilling water across the ground, and cries out with tear-filled eyes and broken voice: 'You are Odysseus! My darling child! My master!'[12] As a narrative device, Eurycleia's response is a key moment in the chain of suspense-ridden instances of recognition towards the end of the *Odyssey* that gradually re-establish Odysseus in his place as rightful master of the household: from Eumaeus to Telemachus, Eurycleia, and ultimately Penelope.[13]

There is actual evidence from the Late Bronze Age for the role of baths and women's washing of men, that gives historical context to the female activities that lay behind Eurycleia's foot bath. A terracotta sculpture from Cyprus, dating to the Late Bronze Age, depicts a three-dimensional scene of a young woman bathing a man sitting in a tub.[14] Meanwhile, the Linear B tablets at Pylos label a large group of women workers as *re-wo-to-ro-ko-wo* – probably equivalent to the later Greek word (also used in Homer) *loetrochooi*, 'bath pourers' (a term that's used in the *Odyssey* specifically for the enslaved women who drew water for the bath).[15] There's even, incredibly, evidence for what this kind of bath might have looked like: during the excavations of the Late Bronze Age palace at Pylos – dubbed 'Nestor's palace' by Carl Blegen – archaeologists uncovered a perfectly preserved bathtub, surprisingly recognizable and almost modern in shape, made of terracotta and painted with dancing spirals. It's hard not to think of the moment in the *Odyssey*, during Telemachus' visit to Nestor's palace at Pylos and as a part of the typical guest rituals, when Homer describes the young Ithacan prince being bathed by one of the king's daughters, Polycaste.[16] We hear how he sinks into the bathtub, how she washes and rubs his skin with oil, then swathes him in a tunic and cloak. (It's worth noting that it's more commonly enslaved women who are tasked with bathing duties, though members of the household like Polycaste do sometimes get involved too.) It's a thrilling possibility that the Late Bronze Age terracotta bathtub preserved at Pylos might have been the prototype for Homer's imagining of the bath in Nestor's palace – where Odysseus' son was once said to have been bathed by a king's daughter.

There is one more essential water-supply task, in addition to laundry and bathing, that we find enslaved women undertaking in the *Odyssey* – and that's washing the floors. Once Eurycleia has been brought into the fold of supporters who can be relied on in Odysseus' quest for vengeance, Penelope – who is still, as far as we know, in the dark about the beggar's identity – announces, rather abruptly, that she will set a contest to determine at last which of the suitors will become her husband. In this ancient Greek version of Cinderella's shoe, she declares that whoever can string Odysseus' famed bow and shoot an arrow through twelve axes in a row (there's a lot of controversy about how exactly this might have worked) will win her hand.[17] After all the suitors have failed, it is time for Odysseus at last, with spectacular showmanship, to step forward: stringing the bow with the ease of a hero, he drives the arrow through the axes, establishing himself once again as both Penelope's husband and the king of Ithaca. But if this feels a bit too fairytale, there's one more thing to be done that grounds us grimly in Homer's world. Odysseus gives a nod to his son, who moves to stand beside him, armed and ready; the father takes aim and shoots one suitor gorily through the throat, while the son hurls his bronze-tipped spear between another's shoulder blades, tunnelling through his chest. A hideous massacre ensues: Odysseus, Telemachus and the enslaved men on Odysseus' side viciously chop their way through more than a hundred suitors, till the halls of the palace run with blood.

And this is where it's time to call on the nameless enslaved women. As Odysseus surveys the corpse-littered hall, bodies piled one on top of the other, oozing gore, he orders Eurycleia to select – out of the fifty enslaved women he owns – those who 'made those treasonous plots while I was gone'.[18] The allegation against them is made clear in Odysseus' ensuing orders. First, they are to drag out the corpses and mop up the blood with water and sponges – then, once they have done their cleaning job, they're to be summarily murdered. 'Eradicate all life from them,' he tells

Telemachus. 'They will forget the things the suitors made them do with them in secret, through Aphrodite' (a euphemism for sex).[19] He's already spelled out his certainty that this was sexual assault by the suitors: 'you raped my slave girls,' he hurls at the men (before he slaughters them). In other words, the enslaved women of the palace are going to be killed by their master, not because they willingly engaged in sex with his opponents, but because they couldn't protect themselves from being raped.[20]

For thousands of years, Odysseus' twelve enslaved women were forgotten, or – if they were remembered at all – labelled as disloyal servants and criminals who were justly executed in Odysseus' righteous anger: their fate justified because they should, as enslaved women, somehow have had better control over the bodies they did not own, their gruesome punishment warranted because they were women. Their lack of agency as enslaved people is frequently eclipsed in modern translations and commentaries, which often flatten them euphemistically into 'maids' or 'servants'.[21] Levels of misogyny that aren't present in the Greek have been imported to shame their sexuality: Alexander Pope's 1725 translation renders them as 'nightly prostitutes to shame', while Robert Fagles' 2006 version, as Emily Wilson points out, delivers 'sluts' and 'whores'.[22] (The Greek has none of this.) By contrast, Wilson's new 2018 translation is emphatic in drawing attention to them as enslaved people; she and other critics are working to bring the enslaved women to the fore, prompting readers to think critically about their rape, their enslavement and the way they've been ignored – as sexual assault victims, as enslaved people, as women. And it's a conversation that fiction, too, has pioneered. Margaret Atwood's 2005 novel *The Penelopiad* arose from a driving sense that 'the hanging of the 12 "maids" – slaves, really – at the end of *The Odyssey* seemed to me unfair'.[23] Atwood's *Penelopiad* gives the hanged women of the *Odyssey* a voice once again, and allows them to tell their side of the tale: investigating what is, perhaps, one of the *Odyssey*'s darkest moments, and bringing their murderers to a chilly reckoning.

The abruptness by which Odysseus, the supposed 'hero' of the *Odyssey*, turns to the murder of the suitors and orders the slaughter of his enslaved women begs the question as to exactly why his ferocious attack is aimed so explicitly at these seeming side characters. How do we go from Odysseus' happy homecoming to the gruesome group hanging that

Telemachus commits in the courtyard, looping a ship's cable around the necks of the twelve enslaved women and stringing them up in a row, like slaughtered birds? As Homer describes it: 'As doves or thrushes spread their wings to fly home to their nests, but someone sets a trap – they crash into a net, a bitter bedtime; just so the girls, their heads all in a row, were strung up with the noose around their necks to make their death an agony.'[24] In part, it seems to be a way of wiping the slate clean: the neatly symbolic cleaning up of the bloodstains by the enslaved floor washers, seconds before their murder, makes this absolutely clear. Those who remember a regime without Odysseus are summarily disposed of; meanwhile, Telemachus can inflict his humiliation at the years of his suitor-induced impotence and emasculation, during Odysseus' absence, on the women who (he says) 'poured down shame' on him and his nascent rule.[25]

Telemachus' accusation is subtly adjusted from Odysseus', who earlier presented the enslaved women as victims of rape. Telemachus – psyching himself up, perhaps, for the horrific deed he's about to perform – turns the focus on to the effect *on him* of their sleeping with the suitors. And this brings us to another, much deeper-running, anxiety that lies behind the hanging of the enslaved women in the *Odyssey*: the threat that these women represent to the male slaveowner. The poem hints, at points, that the enslaved women might actually have had some agency in their collusion with the suitors.[26] One enslaved woman, who does get a name – Melantho – speaks out and turns her biting criticism twice against Odysseus in his disguise as a beggar, thus aligning her with the suitors' discrediting of the master of the house.[27] And Odysseus, as we saw, when he orders Eurycleia to summon the twelve enslaved women who slept with the suitors, claims that 'the women . . . made those treasonous plots while I was gone.'[28]

And although some of this is probably a rhetorical flourish designed to justify the massacre of all Odysseus' enemies, there's also a glimmer of visceral fear in the picture it paints of a world fallen apart, in the eyes of the Greek king: rival males occupying the seat of his power, consuming his possessions and competing for his wife; enslaved women transformed into potential rebels, who have their own bodies and their own sexual desires, who have the power to ally themselves with male challengers to the throne, and who might, even, desire an autonomy of their own.[29] But in a deeply and systematically unequal society that pits rulers against the ruled, men against women, slaveowners against slaves – in a narrative that only has space for Odysseus – this is a zero-sum game. For the *Odyssey* to end with the triumph of a man, for Odysseus' story to win out, he and his son must silence the enslaved women who might try to make their own stories heard.

The *Odyssey*, then, is not simply about Odysseus coming back because he wants to see his wife, or because he misses his home. The stakes are altogether higher than that. Odysseus has to return to Ithaca because the elite, aristocratic social order of the slave-owning man is quite literally falling apart at the seams, challenged by the threat posed – at least in part – by the enslaved women he owns. So when Odysseus steps out of the scrubbed halls to wash his hands of blood and go to face Penelope, the feet of the enslaved women still twitching in the courtyard behind him, and we're told that the king is back on the throne and all is well again, we should ask if this really is the happy ending we've been taught to see it as. We should ask whether it really does feel – as the *Odyssey* presents it – like anarchy righted. 'Whose anarchy?' we might ask. 'Whose happy ending?' For the male slaveowner, his elite family and select aides like Eurycleia, it's a happy-ever-after of sorts, to be sure. But the price of the story of Odysseus' restoration is the bodies and the lives of his enemies – and the twelve enslaved women, who only wanted to fly.[30]

Perfect Storm

But Odysseus isn't the only one to be facing up to a crisis; and the enslaved women aren't the only ones to die. If we return to the discoveries made on RV *Meteor* in the Ionian Sea, and advances in ancient-climate analysis in the last few decades, we're able to unpack a crisis in the making, and one of the biggest historical mysteries of the Late Bronze Age: the sudden, dramatic fall, around 1200 BCE, of cities in huge swathes, and the virtual disappearance of entire civilizations across the Mediterranean, known as the Late Bronze Age collapse. Across Mycenaean Greece, the great royal palaces went up in flames. The concept of the chief ruler, the *wanax*, which we find on the Linear B tablets and in Homer, vanished from Greek political vocabulary as the axes of power shifted.[31] Writing disappeared (not to emerge again until hundreds of years later when the alphabet was imported, and the Homeric epics written down), when the bureaucratic systems that supported the complex palaces collapsed, and historical records melted away (leaving the so-called 'Dark Age'). So it's time now – as King Odysseus butchers his way through the opposition and Ithaca bubbles with turmoil – to move from the world of fiction and into a major historical phenomenon that will bring us back one last time, not only to the fire-scarred ruins of Troy that sparked the stories of the Homeric epics, but also to many of the cities and sites we have already visited in the Late Bronze Age world – from Mycenae to Pylos, from Ugarit (stop-off port of the Uluburun ship) to Babylon and Hattusa, capital of the Hittites.

We've already seen how the fear of a world unable to cope with human habitation any more may have sparked the original legend of the Trojan War – Zeus' attempt to depopulate a groaning and overburdened earth: making the *Iliad*, in part, an epic about climate disaster.[32] We've seen already how drought, captured in the record of the tree rings at Gordion, was a critical factor in the collapse of the sprawling Hittite Empire just after 1200 BCE – hinted at in the Hittite queen Puduhepa's early warnings of famine ('I have no grain in my lands'). We've followed the burgeoning swell of modern scientific evidence – from pollen records extending from Syria to Egypt and Greece, mineral deposits in Greek and Israeli caves, and sediment cores from the Mediterranean – that shows that the drought wasn't localized to the Hittites, but was instead a centuries-long, widespread climate crisis that led to cooling seas and a prolonged decrease in rainfall, in a monumental dry wipe that crossed the eastern Mediterranean and south-west Asia. Yet it begs the question whether drought alone would really have been sufficient, by itself, to cause the kinds of devastation revealed in the archaeological record. The Late Bronze Age collapse was an astonishingly globalized event, running like a seismic fault across a vast geographic area from Greece to Syria and from Turkey to Egypt, witnessing the rapid disintegration of civilizations from the Mycenaeans and Minoans to the Hittites, Babylonians, Assyrians, Mittanians, Cypriots and Canaanites. We can see, in the

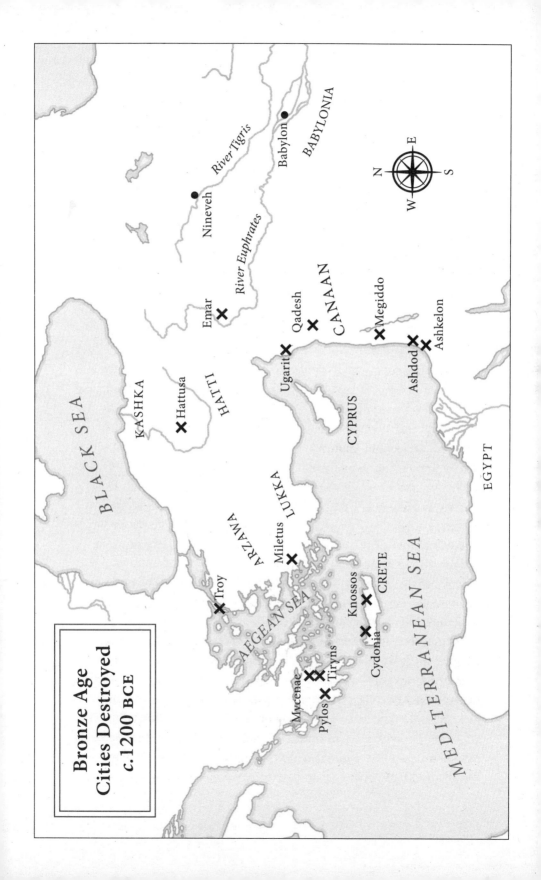

Bronze Age
Cities Destroyed
c.1200 BCE

archaeology, like mines detonating across a battlefield, dozens of palatial cities and their empires, hundreds of miles apart, going up in flames one after another, over the course of about a hundred and fifty years. This had to be a disaster that was big, and lethal, enough to hamstring some of the most powerful civilizations of the ancient world, and leave many of them unable to clamber back up for hundreds of years, if at all. There must have been more than one culprit in this perfect storm of calamities that blasted some of the greatest imperial players off their pedestals and eroded the foundations of history.

And it seems – from what scattered references in contemporary ancient sources appear to indicate – that there was. If the oceans were cooling, then there was another, very different, danger making its way over the horizon from the sea, white sails fluttering, oars quivering to the beat of the war drum. 'No land could stand before their arms . . . They desolated its people, and its land was like that which has never come into being.'[33] So wrote the Egyptian pharaoh, Ramesses III, at his temple at Medinet Habu, chronicling the world-changing events of the year 1177 BCE – when an unknown group of disparate attackers now called 'the Sea Peoples' (though this name was never used in antiquity) swarmed across the Mediterranean Sea like ancient Vikings, leaving a bloody mess in their wake. Ramesses details six tribes in particular: the Peleset, Tjekker, Shekelesh, Shardana, Danuna and Weshesh. After a ferocious sea battle off Egypt (or series of battles: no one's quite sure), the pharaoh's forces dispatched them with cold-blooded efficiency. 'They were dragged in,' Ramesses says, captioning a newspaper-cartoon-style panorama of the hideous chaos of the battle – arrow-ridden soldiers collapsing on deck and men floating, drowned, in the water – 'enclosed, and prostrated on the beach, killed, and made into heaps from tail to head.'[34]

But not every imperial power was as successful at deterring the Sea Peoples. These ruthless invaders, Ramesses goes on to report (with no little pride at Egypt's status as sole conquerors), cut a swathe of brutal devastation across the eastern Mediterranean and beyond, tearing down Egypt's most powerful neighbouring empires and cities – including what we believe to be the realm of the Hittites, Arzawa in western Anatolia (south of Troy) and the island of Cyprus.[35] Other places seem to have been hit, too. In cosmopolitan Late Bronze Age Ugarit, the Syro-Canaanite

Invaders in 1177 BCE: the Egyptian pharaoh (right) battles the swarming
Sea Peoples, at Ramesses III's temple at Medinet Habu.

city where the Uluburun ship put in to port, the destroyed remains of
the city – sacked and burnt around 1190 BCE – contained, hidden in the
rubble, copies of the last desperate letters sent before the enemy came.
'My father, now the ships of the enemy have come,' reads one distraught
missive.[36] Another (published as recently as 2016) shows the last king of
Ugarit pleading with the Hittites for help: the invaders, we are told, have
reached a nearby city and are already on their way to Ugarit. 'Now may
my lord send me forces and chariots to save me and may my lord save
me from the forces of this enemy!'[37] In one particular letter, the invaders are even given a name, Shikila, which can be connected with one of
the bands of Sea People invaders, labelled in the Egyptian records as
Shekelesh.[38]

But if the Sea Peoples did indeed destroy Ugarit, both the archaeological
record and the city's extraordinary archive of letters show that this wasn't
the only calamity this once-flourishing trade hub suffered, as the turbulent thirteenth century wore on into the twelfth. In around 1250 BCE, or a
little thereafter (so around seventy years before the Sea Peoples attacked),
an earthquake shuddered through the town, knocking solid stone walls
out of kilter (we can see signs both of the damage and the inhabitants'
subsequent efforts at repair).[39] Seismic activity – shockwaves from the
Dead Sea fault radiating down the Levantine coast – was then followed

by a deadly famine (likely a result of crop failures from the megadrought that started around 1200 BCE). In another recently published letter, sent by a local official to the king of Ugarit, the citizens plead desperately for more food: 'grain staples from you are not to be had! (The people of) the household of your servant will die of hunger! Give grain staples to your servant!' The king duly sends a frantic call for relief out to the Egyptian pharaoh (Ramesses II's predecessor, Merneptah, who ruled from 1213 to 1203 BCE): '[In] the land of Ugarit there is a severe hunger: May my lord save [the land of Ugarit], and may the king give grain to save my life . . . and to save the citizens of the land of Ugarit.' The pharaoh sent a shipment of gold, textiles and seven thousand dried fish in response, but it wasn't enough. As one major international player after another succumbed to grain shortages, famine ricocheted across the closely linked network of trade routes of the eastern Mediterranean: Egypt was soon sending out relief efforts, not just to Ugarit, but also to the Hittites. Merneptah writes that he has 'caused grain to be taken in ships, to keep alive this land of Hatti', and the Hittite king sends a panicked missive down to Ugarit, asking where a massive 450-ton shipment of grain has gone, declaring dramatically, 'It is a matter of life or death!'[40]

And it was into this febrile, unstable atmosphere – the palaces and temples rent by earthquakes, the grain stores emptied, the wells dried up – that the invasions and unrest represented by the Sea Peoples entered the historical stage. Around 1190 BCE, the city of Ugarit burns, arrow-heads scattered throughout its ruins, valuables buried as the terrified citizens flee the devastation. One of the last letters sent from the city before it fell bears witness to the terror as people watched their world fall apart: 'the army was humiliated and the city was sacked. Our food in the threshing floors was burnt and the vineyards were also destroyed. Our city is sacked. May you know it! May you know it!'[41] It must have felt like a curse laid upon the people of Ugarit: earthquake, drought, famine and war, all in the space of fifty-odd years. No wonder they never returned to their city again – and Ugarit was abandoned for millennia, until its accidental discovery a hundred years ago: an empty skeleton, a stripped-to-the-bone victim of this perfect storm of calamities.

Ugarit's fate – natural disasters, climate change leading to water scar-city and a food-production crisis, a collapse in trade, and social unrest with invasions, migrations and potentially even internal rebellion – illustrates the successive acts of the drama, one following another with the awful inevitability of a Greek tragedy, that played out not just in one city but across the Late Bronze Age stage in the late thirteenth and early twelfth century BCE. Hattusa, capital of the Hittite Empire, experienced decades of famine and trade difficulties (witness the letter to the king of Ugarit, urgently pressing for the 450 tons of grain) before it was abandoned and violently destroyed. We're not sure whether this is to be attributed to the Sea Peoples, other more local enemies or internal revolt: many scholars think it's unlikely that the Sea Peoples were to blame, as most of the sites in Anatolia were simply abandoned, and it seems more likely that the Hittite Empire was instead fatally weakened by drought, famine, disruption of the trade routes and mass migration.[42]

Troy, meanwhile, was devastated by an earthquake around 1300 BCE, and then, about a hundred years later – after the city had patched itself up – was attacked and destroyed around 1190–80 BCE. There's evidence of a raging fire that tore through both upper and lower cities, arrowheads embedded in walls and sling bullets in heaps, unburied bodies lying in the streets. One of the excavators, Manfred Korfmann, describes the hideous discovery of a sixteen- or seventeen-year-old girl (perhaps the same age as Homer's Chryseis or Briseis), her feet burnt by fire, her body only half buried before her corpse was hastily abandoned.[43] The clues that this was a city that fell in war seem to fit together (the presence of weapons, especially arrowheads in walls, being a key indicator that this was a human, rather than a natural, catastrophe this time around).[44] But, crucially, we don't know *who* the attackers were. Sea Peoples? Hittites?

Or was it, perhaps, the Mycenaean Greeks, as the *Iliad* says? One of the problems with positing the Mycenaeans as the invaders of Troy (aside from the obvious fallacy of using fiction as evidence for fact) is that, as we've seen, the palaces of the Mycenaean mainland were, themselves, undergoing a similarly catastrophic collapse at exactly the same time. Mycenae – supposed in Homer to be the thriving kingdom of Agamemnon, capable of sending a hundred ships against Troy – suffered a major earthquake in 1250 BCE followed by crippling destruction around 1190 BCE: excavations show a massive terrace wall contorted by the heat of a huge blaze that transformed it to the consistency of concrete and

Arrows at Troy.

carbonized beams of wood.[45] The palace at Pylos bears witness to a
similar fire around 1180 BCE that fused walls to shapeless lumps and
disintegrated bricks to piles of dust, melted gold and, as we saw above,
fortuitously fired the clay tablets of the archives at kiln-like temperatures
(the only reason they came to survive the ensuing millennia).[46] We also
know, from the stable isotope data analysed in 2017 from the Mavri Trypa
cave just off Pylos, that Mycenaean Greece experienced a debilitating
dry period, with a dramatic onset around 1200 BCE and dragging on over
the next two hundred years – that would have undoubtedly destabilized,
if not destroyed, the palatial centres with their high dependency on agri-
cultural productivity.[47] But here in Late Bronze Age Greece, there's no
indication whether these raging fires were caused by invaders (and even
if they were, it's unlikely to have been the Sea Peoples), internal rebellion or earthquakes; they may even have been accidents. All we can tell
is that there was a period of intense drought coinciding with a swathe
of massive fiery destruction that engulfed the palaces of Mycenaean

Greece, one after another, between around 1225 and 1190 BCE – burning down Mycenae, rich in gold, and turning Pylos into a heap of rubble and embers. If Troy really was being sacked by the Mycenaeans – and Homer is the only shaky testament to this – then they would have had an unwelcome surprise, to say the least, on their return home.

So not all cities were razed at the same time, and not all of them by the Sea Peoples. Some fell to earthquakes, some to fire, and some were simply abandoned. Some were cut down with the sword, others were settled in peace. We know that some of the newcomers to Canaan, on the Levantine coast, brought with them a new species of pig and several different kinds of plants – no doubt Circe would have approved – which hints at a decidedly non-violent form of immigration.[48] Some were attacked from without, others may have rebelled from within. Over the course of around a century, as drought swept across the land and crops dried up, as earthquakes shook the foundations of the earth and the grain-filled ships melted away from the harbours, as migrants fled across the seas looking for new homes and invaders put cities to the torch, the complex, interlinked civilizations of the Late Bronze Age were thrown into chaos. This was, as historian Eric Cline has argued, a large-scale systems collapse: the multiple interactions of many different stressors working on a complex society, breaking down networks, lynching trade, sparking migration, like a juggernaut spiralling out of control.[49] Climate change. Earthquake storms. Water shortages. Food scarcity. All these – combined with the concentration of power in the elite hands of the Bronze Age palaces, and the international web of trade networks that bound one civilization to another over vast distances – meant that when one cog in the globalized machine went down, the whole thing did.

And if it all sounds scarily familiar, that's because it is. Cline, writing in 2020 (in the midst of the global pandemic), identified multiple eerie similarities between the emergencies facing us today and those of 1177 BCE.[50] We, too, are confronted by climate change and devastating extremes of weather across the globe. We, too, are faced with critically low water supplies, with roughly half of the world's population experiencing severe water scarcity for at least part of the year. We, too, are in the grip of a global food crisis, with more than 345 million people facing high levels of food insecurity in 2023 – over double (200 million more) than before the pandemic hit.[51] 'It's a matter,' Cline writes, 'of not *if* but *when*' the same kind of global collapse, recorded in the Late Bronze Age and remembered in the legend of Troy, happens again.[52]

The question is, now, whether we're capable of learning from the past.

End of an Era

The widespread collapse of Late Bronze Age cities around 1200 BCE bears urgent lessons for our own global society and the climate emergency we're facing. But it also gives us a way of looking at the *Odyssey* anew. If we take in the combined picture that the latest evidence for the collapse is showing us – simultaneous city destructions, collapsing palatial structures and possible unrest due to invasion or rebellion, threatened food supplies due to drought, devastating earthquakes – then we have an interesting new lens through which to magnify the tensions and the threats that lie latent behind the *Odyssey*. In the Homeric epic, Ithaca is under threat from internal pressures due to Odysseus' absence in the Trojan War. If the latest dating of the destruction of Troy VIIa is correct, and Troy was burnt to the ground around the same time as Mycenae and the other Greek palatial centres were razed, then the confluence we see in Homer between unrest at home and conflict abroad might be seen to map on to a memory of a historical pattern of simultaneous discord and destruction. It's been suggested, in particular, that the fall of the Mycenaean palaces in Greece may have been caused by rebellion along class lines, or that the Bronze Age palaces collapsed (and their collapse was magnified) because of the concentration of the economy in the hands of a small but powerful elite.[53] The *Odyssey* is, as we've seen, an epic that is centrally concerned with the reinstatement of the economic and social power of the king – his restoration to the treasures and food supplies that are his, and his reclamation of power over his overweening subject kings (the suitors, who have stepped out of line and are now trying to grab the kingship of Ithaca for themselves) and his enslaved workers. The suitors, in particular, are blamed throughout the poem for the depletion of food resources – a scarcity of supplies that we've seen worries everyone from Penelope to Telemachus to Eurycleia. Seen in this context, perhaps the brutal punishment meted out to the consummate scapegoats of the enslaved women represents an attempt to bat away the terrifying spectres that were to become the hallmarks of the end of the Bronze Age (and that Homer's audiences, over the centuries, would have known only too well): unrest and attack, the draining of food resources and the irreversible collapse of palatial authority. The *Odyssey*, concerned as it is with narrative happy endings and the restitution of the hero, allows the king to return, his enemies to be slaughtered and balance to be restored – at least for now. But the ghosts of the enslaved women, and the flapping of their feet like the butterflies' wings that bring the hurricane, hint darkly that there is much more still to come.

There is, however, one more ancient disaster that took down many a Late Bronze Age city, from Mycenae to Ugarit to Troy: earthquakes. And it is the earthquakes, creeping along the cracks of the seismic fault beneath the Ionian islands, that will lead us into one of the most intriguing mysteries of the *Odyssey* – the location of Ithaca itself.

16

PENELOPE

The End

ITHACA, GREECE

Waiting. Who wants to be famous for that? First prize for doing nothing. First prize for not being gone when he comes home. First prize for not having had the courage to leave.

And it's not even a prize, just a sentence suspended. She watched the slave girls. She saw the way their throats gulped when her son – the boy who'd slipped between her own legs, damp and unshelled – hung them out to dry.

Yet there's a part of her, now, after all these years, that has learned to relish the wait. That feeling of slowing down time. Burying yourself in the fabric of your body. Sinking into the time-worn web of flesh and bone. And she's clever enough to know that – when he was gone, and she hardened herself to stone – was when she was the most free. Now he's home, and she yearns for those times of waiting. The weathered thread between each finger, thick and real. The cracks in the clay around the olive tree. The silence in the wrinkles of her skin.

But that's the burden women have to bear. To grind away each day at who you are and not to disappear. To live a life that's measured by when his exploits come to an end. To be the ending to his story. Before he came back, she let herself wonder – weaving at her loom in the days, unpicking at nights – what her ending might have been.

But if her power is in waiting, then she'll wait. Take the old and brittle parts of her and make them new. Build up layers of rock and lie in wait, like a woman turning into stone: a rock the sea rakes but never moves.

And perhaps then she'll have an ending of her own.

Earth Shaker

It's June 2014, a searingly hot day on the Greek island of Cephalonia (of *Captain Corelli's Mandolin* fame), and I'm on the last steps of the trail in search of Penelope and Homer's Ithaca. I've driven around the zigzagging hairpin bends of this verdant, wild, mountainous island, breathing in the scents of Mediterranean summer – wild thyme and pine – and stopping for a herd of goats to amble across the road, bleating with the clanging of their bells. The panorama that spreads out before me, as I turn to reach the summit, is nothing short of breathtaking. Rocky tree-covered slopes tumbling down into sparkling turquoise waters. Terracotta roofs gleaming amid the blue and green, the tiny fishing village of Assos far below, nestled around its curving harbour. The low-lying peninsula of Paliki shimmering on the horizon in a grey-blue mist. As I dip down towards the sea, the colourful houses of the Assos waterfront pop up, covered with blooms in cascades of bright purple and pink. Umbrellas flutter along the harbour edge, where the beach slips into the glittering water, and I sit for a moment to sip a drink at one of the local tavernas and take in the view.

And then it happens. My chair starts rattling along the floor. It's like a high-speed freight train thundering through a tunnel cut underground along the shoreline, and I can feel the vibrations thrumming through the ground and up my legs.[1] It's utterly silent, though, just a shaking that doesn't feel like shaking at all, because it's the floor that's moving, not me. Then it's over, as fast as it came. The earth stands still again. We all look at each other across the taverna, exchange a couple of nervous laughs. Slowly, conversation breaks out again, and as we fidget with our drinks, everyone is muttering the same thing: *Earthquake.*

What I experienced that June day was, in fact, just one of thousands of minor aftershocks, the tail end of two strong earthquakes that had rocked Paliki (the large peninsula jutting out to the west of Cephalonia, joined to the main island by a narrow neck of land) earlier that year. In January and February 2014, Cephalonia was hit by a pair of earthquakes of a magnitude 6.1 and 6.0 on the Richter scale. That's equivalent (in terms of the energy released) to detonating 2.4 million tons of TNT high explosive over the course of just over a week – putting them among Cephalonia's strongest recorded earthquakes, and producing the largest ground-motion values ever documented in Greece.[2] Rockfalls and landslides were triggered across the island, with massive boulders breaking off the mountains and thundering down across roads and into the sea. One of the major coastal routes leading from the capital of Argostoli around to Paliki collapsed, caving in from underneath (it was still blocked off when I visited in June). Most bizarrely of all, perhaps – to those of us who aren't used to living in one of the most seismically active places on earth – the entire peninsula was actually lifted out of the ocean by the violent upthrust of the earthquake, its landmass raised by as much as fifteen centimetres: so much so that, as you drive round the shoreline today, you can see new beaches that have formed along the coast. (In one such location, an enterprising taverna has made the most of the geological novelty, offering its guests a hearty meal of local fish and a lounge on water-surrounded sunbeds planted in the shallow sea.)

As my week in Cephalonia wore on, and I explored more of the island, the devastating after-effects of the 2014 earthquakes became visible everywhere. Perhaps most dramatic of all was Myrtos beach – a stunning crescent of white sand tumbling into azure sea and edged by tree-covered mountains that's gained a global reputation as one of the most beautiful beaches in the world. But when I tried to make my way down the winding cliff path to Myrtos, I found the entrance blocked by colossal sheared-off lumps of rock, some of them the size of cars, that had clearly plummeted in an avalanche from the surrounding crags. As I retreated and took in the view to the beach from the mountain above, the full spectacle of the story was dramatically revealed: the whole face of the mountain had slipped down, leaving the white rock fresh as a new scar and littered with scree.

It's all very dramatic, and Cephalonia – teetering at the edge of a major tectonic fault, where the Eurasian plate crashes into the African one – is a fascinating (and terrifying) living case study for anyone who's interested in the cataclysmic growing pains of our earth's crust. But the question remains: what does all this have to do with Homeric Ithaca? And why am I standing on a Cephalonian beach, searching for traces of Homer's Penelope amid the rockfall, when there's another island that's actually *called* Ithaca, just one short hop across the Ionian Sea?

Furthest Out to Sea

The search for Ithaca isn't just about the narrow view of Odysseus' quest to return home. The hunt for the location of Homer's Ithaca has occupied antiquarians and amateurs alike for centuries – all the way back to the ancient world itself, where it was a popular game among the Greek and Roman literati to pair up Odysseus' destinations with real place names, and young schoolboys were trained to copy out passages from the *Odyssey*, detailing the idiosyncratic geographic features of (for example) the Cyclops' island. The problem with Ithaca, in particular, is that – unlike the fantasy isle of the Cyclops – it's located by the poet in a very real, very human world. It's given a specific geographical location in Homer, without any one-eyed monsters, magical nymphs or bewitched ships, and its rulers interact with places that we know, from the archaeological record, *did* exist as major political players in the Late Bronze Age – like Pylos and Sparta on the mainland, or even Troy (which, before Schliemann, everyone thought was just a legend). So is it possible that we might actually be able to find the Ithaca of Penelope, or even the palace where the later poet imagined her waiting twenty years for her husband to return – just like the windswept ruins that were to become the Homeric Helen's Troy?

The complications begin with the fact that, as we've seen above, there is an actual island that's called Ithaca today, and has been for hundreds of years. (I'll refer to this island as Ithaki, its modern Greek name, to avoid confusion with Homer's Ithaca.) The issue is that Ithaki doesn't match up to Homer's description of Ithaca at all. The major passage detailing Odysseus' homeland comes, in the *Odyssey*, at the dramatic moment where, at the request of his Phaeacian hosts, the hero at last reveals who he is:

I am Odysseus, Laertes' son, known to all
for my tricks, and my fame goes to the sky.
I live in Ithaca, where leaves rustle on
high Mount Neriton, and nearby
lie many islands, close to each other:
Doulichion and Same and Zacynthos with its woods.
Ithaca lies low, furthest out to sea
towards the dark; the rest face dawn and sun.[3]

So we have three clues to help us on our way.[4] First, Ithaca is one among a group of islands called Doulichion, Same and Zacynthos. Second, it is low-lying (apart from one conspicuous peak, it's not particularly mountainous). And third, it's furthest to the west ('towards the dark' means, quite simply, in the direction towards sunset). The problem is that modern Ithaki doesn't fit this description at all. Although it's got the modern island of Zakinthos nearby, and Cephalonia (to the west of Ithaki) can reasonably be identified with Same – there's a town on the island of that name – there's no sign of Doulichion. Meanwhile, as we've already seen, Ithaki isn't furthest to the west: Cephalonia is. In fact, Ithaki is furthest *east*. Nor is it low-lying (which is the best translation of Homer's *chthamalē*, often used of something set low to the earth – *chthōn* in Greek).[5] Ithaki is mountainous, with, on occasion, steep cliffs that plunge near-vertically into the sea – the antithesis of *chthamalē*. East and high, not west and low. And we're still missing an island.

For thousands of years, learned academicians and amateur Homerists have wrestled over the problem, a copy of the *Odyssey* in one hand and a map in the other. Illustrious archaeologists like Wilhelm Dörpfeld – Schliemann's successor at Troy – became obsessed with identifying their own version of Homer's Ithaca; this ended up, in Dörpfeld's case, requiring some pretty tortuous linguistic gymnastics (to turn Lefkas, an island to the north of Ithaki, into Homer's Ithaca, Dörpfeld had to resort to twisting the compass of Homer's 'west' into 'north').[6] A couple of locals suggested Cephalonia as a possible candidate – but they were unable to explain where the missing islands of Doulichion and Same had gone. Even the British prime minister William Gladstone tried his hand at finding Odysseus' home.[7] The hunt for Ithaca was on.

Endgame

At this point, before we try to approach the shores of Ithaca, we need to look for Penelope – because the search for Penelope, which we started all the way back at the beginning with the Peristeria Penelope, isn't just the endgame of this book; it's also the endgame of the *Odyssey*.[8] Odysseus' search for Ithaca is, in many ways, the search for Penelope. When Odysseus, trying to get directions back home from the dead seer Tiresias in the Underworld, comes across the ghost of his dead mother, she reminds him bluntly of the two goals he's yet to achieve: 'Have you not yet arrived in Ithaca, nor seen your wife at home?'[9] And as a bloodthirsty Odysseus later exults over the suitors in the palace massacre, he imagines what it was they were all hoping for: 'you must have often prayed here in my hall that I would not regain the joys of home, and that my wife would marry you instead'.[10] Everyone is clear that being back in Ithaca means being with Penelope. The aim of the epic – the aim of Odysseus – is to find Ithaca, and to find his wife. Just as the drama of the Trojan War (and the premise of the *Iliad*) opens with Helen launching the ships against Troy, Penelope (and Ithaca) is Homer's final destination – calling the Greeks back home, completing the narrative circle and translating women's roles from bringers of war into the guarantors of peace. It's no coincidence that Penelope's recognition of her husband – and thus his final reintegration into the Ithacan household – is drawn out until (almost) the last possible moment of the epic.[11] The *Odyssey*'s ending, with the Greek hero recognized and restored to his rightful place as king and husband to the queen, hangs on Penelope's endgame.

But Penelope – just like Ithaca – is difficult to pin down. We've already seen how she manages to slip between roles and so achieve the near-impossible, balancing – at the same time – the identities of property-protecting wife, dowered widow and gift-earning bride. (This is a form of disguise analogous to Odysseus' compulsive lying about his name and identity – and makes clever Penelope the perfect match for the Ithacan king.) She is also cunning enough to come up with the famous weaving trick: making her many pressing suitors wait until she has finished a funerary cloth for her father-in-law and then – so she

tells Odysseus-the-beggar, with unmissable pride – unpicking it every
night for three years.[12] As a simple repetitive pattern would never take
this long to weave, and the suitors would never have believed her otherwise, it's been suggested that Penelope's web would perhaps have been a
kind of 'story cloth' (much like the later Bayeux Tapestry): a beautifully
wrought textile work of art, taking years to complete, with figures woven
into it depicting an important myth or history – just like Helen's weaving
of the scenes of the Trojan War in the *Iliad*.[13] We know these elaborate
story cloths, depicting myths and local history, existed in antiquity – the
most famous being the enormous classical *peplos*, with its woven frieze
of the battle of the gods and the giants, which took four Athenian girls a

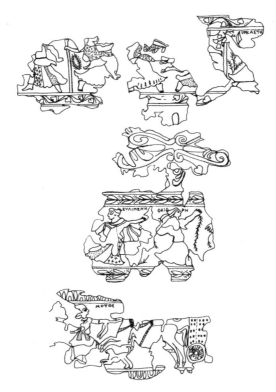

*Story cloth (4th century BCE), showing cartoon-strip-like images of
women from Greek myth. Is this what Penelope's web might have
looked like?*

whole year to weave in celebration of Athena for the Great Panathenaia; and ancient story cloths have actually been discovered in fragments from the Black Sea region in the fourth century BCE. But we're never told what's on Penelope's web. Is she, like Homer, weaving the story of the *Odyssey* – just as Helen weaves an analogue for the *Iliad*, with her own tapestry version of the Trojan War? Are we seeing Penelope taking on the role of poet, recording the myths and legends of her land? Or is she even, perhaps, trying to tell her *own* story?

There's a lot more we don't know about Penelope than what she was weaving, however. Homer doesn't explicitly say, for instance, whether or not she slept with any of the suitors during her husband's twenty-year absence. Nor are we actually told whether Penelope realizes that the rag-covered beggar is, in fact, her husband before the official moment of recognition. She certainly makes some pretty telling comments that suggest she may have more of an idea of the beggar's real identity than she lets on (my favourite is her pointed remark to Eurycleia on how similar his hands and feet are to Odysseus'); and modern novelists, like Margaret Atwood in *The Penelopiad* (2005), have imagined the elaborate dance of disguise between Penelope and Odysseus, these two consummate tale-tellers, each believing they have the other fooled.[14] But Homer doesn't make it clear either way. Not knowing, in Penelope's case, just as in Odysseus' – the multiple layers that you have to peel back to get at the truth – is part of the point.

And this understanding that the truth isn't always what it seems – that part of her character that's just like Odysseus, distrusting, relying on her cunning to get by, unwilling to lean on anybody else – means that Penelope is determined to make Odysseus reveal himself on her terms, not his. When Odysseus finally sends Eurycleia to tell his wife that he has returned – that he's strung the bow, and murdered all her suitors – Penelope comes cautiously downstairs, and sits apart from her husband, watching him carefully. And when she speaks at last, it's to compel him to show her who he is, in the way she wants to recognize him (and wants him to recognize her). As her final test, she orders Eurycleia to move the marriage bed from their chambers for the guest to sleep on. Odysseus instantly goes on the attack. 'Who moved my bed?' he demands. It cannot, he claims, be moved: he made it himself, carving it into the trunk of an olive tree that grows through the palace. His conclusion is a bitter one: 'I do not know if someone – a man – has cut the olive trunk and moved my bed.'[15] It's no coincidence that Penelope's neatly calculated test revolves around the place where she and her husband used to have sex: tying in her recognition to a patent demonstration that their bed is where it was all along (a literal sign that she hasn't been sleeping around, in other words) is an ingenious way of publicly broadcasting her sexual submission to Odysseus.[16]

And so, having spelled out to her husband both her marital fidelity and her sharp wits, Penelope at last allows herself to be convinced. The couple fall into each other's arms, head to bed, and the endgame is complete: although there's so much to catch up on that Athena keeps the sun from rising for a while, so they can get to talking about (almost) all that's happened. And if Odysseus doesn't mention that he spent eight years having sex with two of the women in his tale, and if we never know how faithful Penelope really was, then maybe – as much for the sake of our protagonists' circumspection as the need for happy endings – Homer lets it lie.

So Odysseus is home at last, back in Ithaca, back with Penelope. In the *Odyssey* at least, both Ithaca and Penelope have been found. But there's one more thing about Penelope that makes her not so easy to uncover. Whenever she appears, throughout the poem, shuttling between her chambers and the great hall (in contrast to Odysseus, she never leaves the confines of the palace), she's always conspicuously covered: 'holding a gauzy veil before her face', Homer says.[17] And when Odysseus first lands back on Ithaca and stumbles up the bay, Athena obscures everything in mist, so that, to him, 'the friendly harbours and the winding paths and leafy trees were all quite unfamiliar'.[18] In this way, too, looking for Penelope is like looking for Ithaca: always hidden in plain sight.

Hidden in Plain Sight

And so we come at last to one of the newest, and most tantalizing, theories to shake the Homeric world in recent years. It started in February 2003, when the British businessman Robert Bittlestone was reading up before a planned summer holiday to the modern island of Ithaki. Bittlestone was struck, as generations of readers of the *Odyssey* had been before him, by the poor match between modern Ithaki and Homer's Ithaca. But rather than trying to force the Greek to mean something it doesn't or assuming that Homer was geographically illiterate, Bittlestone sat down with a translation of the *Odyssey* and decided to take the poet at his word. He collated a group of four key clues about the Ithaca that's described in the *Odyssey*: not only its position (furthest to the west of a group of islands called Ithaca, Same, Doulichion and Zacynthos) and topography (low-lying to the sea), but also its specific features – like, for instance, the bay with distinctive jutting headlands to which the Phaeacian ship sails to deliver Odysseus back to Ithaca. He noticed – as several local residents had already independently done – that there was a distinct and curious correspondence between these features and those of Paliki, the peninsula on the western side of Cephalonia. Not only does it have a harbour (to the north, called Atheras Bay) with very pronounced projecting headlands, but, crucially, it's the bit of land furthest to the west of the Ionian isles, and – apart from two or three peaks – has a much lower elevation than the surrounding islands. But this still didn't explain why Homer said it was a separate island of its own – when the peninsula is very clearly joined to Cephalonia by a several-miles-long neck of land, known as the Thinia valley, made up of hundreds of acres of woodland and undulating hills.

And then Bittlestone had a simple idea. What if Paliki was, in fact, once a separate island? What if it actually was once cut off by the sea? If this were the case, then Paliki would become Ithaca, Cephalonia would be Same, modern Ithaki would be Doulichion (there's actually evidence it was called this from antiquity to medieval times) and Zacynthos would match its ancient namesake. We'd have all our islands back again – with ancient Ithaca low-lying to the sea and the furthest to the west.

What if Penelope's Ithaca had simply been lying hidden in plain sight all along, disguised beneath a veil of geological rock, and a different name?

What's so enticing about the Schizocephalonia hypothesis (a term Bittlestone later coined, from ancient Greek *schizō* or 'split') is not only that it can be tested by modern geoscientific techniques – it's actually backed up by ancient evidence. Early in the first century CE, a Greek intellectual called Strabo living in the Roman Empire wrote a virtuosic *Geography* in seventeen books – a hugely ambitious compendium of the entire geography of the then-known world, drawing together sources and observations from earlier writers with his own deductions and eye-witness accounts. Strabo, Bittlestone discovered (with mounting antici-pation), had written in his account of Cephalonia that 'where the island is narrowest it forms an isthmus so low-lying that it is often submerged from sea to sea'.[19] The ancient geographer, with characteristic precision, even identifies the towns lying either side of the narrow neck of land – so we can tell he was referring to the Thinia valley. This means that, either in Strabo's day or (perhaps) in the earlier sources he was consulting, there was a sea channel sometimes, but not always, separating Paliki from the Cephalonian mainland. They were once, indeed, two separate islands.

For Bittlestone's theory, this was something of a windfall. But until it's possible to show *how* and *when* the separation between the islands happened, and to prove that the channel was wide enough in the Late Bronze Age to be navigable (and thus to truly split the islands), the link between Paliki and Homer's Ithaca remains nothing but a theory. And this is where geology comes in. Bittlestone immediately contacted John Underhill, a professor of geoscience and expert in the geology of Cepha-lonia. In Underhill's eyes, if the amount of land now filling the hypothetical sea channel had built up in the relatively short period, geologically, of three thousand years, it would have had to have been shifted there by one or more catastrophic earthquakes. Only this could have caused the kind of major landslide necessary to detach colossal faces of the adja-cent mountains and drop them into the putative sea channel at a stroke. When Underhill came to make a geological map of the Thinia valley, he discovered a pattern that suggested exactly that: a veritable geological mess, with a jigsaw puzzle of rocks of different ages lying next to one another – a key indicator that some of the older material had crashed down from the surrounding mountains.[20] And he was, in fact, able to identify a vast area of land-slipped material, bedding down into the valley and potentially filling in any channel that might have been there.

If this was going to happen anywhere, then Cephalonia – and the Thinia valley above all – is, it has to be said, an outstanding candidate.

Cephalonia, as I experienced myself in 2014, is one of the most seismically active areas not only in Europe, but in the world: it stands at the very
edge of the continental plate where Europe collides with Africa, along
what is known as the Hellenic Trench, a feature that runs south of Crete
and across to Rhodes. (In fact, if you chart the fault line from its western
end under Cephalonia all the way along its arc to the east, it comes out
in southern-central Turkey, where the deadly 7.8-magnitude earthquake
of February 2023 caused so many fatalities.) The same boundary makes
a right-angle bend to the south-west of the island and is marked by a
massive underwater fault line – the Cephalonia Transform Fault – that
runs under the ocean along the western coast of Cephalonia (in other
words, Paliki's western shore), where these two gigantic fragments of
the earth's crust slip past one another. One of the older tectonic structures, known as the Ainos thrust line, traverses the sidewall of the eastern
slopes of Strabo's channel: the millennia-long mountain-building here
has led to an oversteepening of the bedrock, which makes the Thinia
valley particularly susceptible to landslides and rockfalls during an
earthquake.[21] Cephalonia has suffered major earthquakes throughout
recorded history – the most severe recent catastrophe (before the 2014
disaster) being in 1953, when a 7.2-magnitude earthquake devastated
the island (destroying 80 per cent of the houses, with entire villages
swallowed by the crumbling fissures), triggered massive rockfall and
landslides, sending whole neighbourhoods tumbling into the sea, and
tilted and uplifted the island by as much as sixty centimetres in the space
of a few seconds.[22] Rocks sticking out of the sea around the island bear
witness to this earth-shifting event: it's possible to see, with the naked
eye, bands of different-coloured rock that show where the sea level once
was, before the land was thrust violently upwards. One rock, in particular, near Poros on the south-east coast of Cephalonia, displays a whole
catalogue of different notches that bear witness to uplifts going way back
into the past – and possibly captures a record of similarly, or even more,
violent earthquakes throughout the timeline of Cephalonia's history.

So Cephalonia is a potential candidate for an earthquake gigantic
enough to cause the catastrophic volumes of landslide that are reflected
in the geological record of the Thinia valley. Two vital questions, however,
remain: when the landslip that affected the area happened, and whether

there was indeed a sea channel there before. The existence of a sea channel seems now to have much evidence in its favour. There certainly was a channel in the Thinia valley 400,000 years ago, according to geological studies – just as the ancient geographer Strabo said there was. Recently drilled boreholes have identified massive amounts of fractured rocky material in the valley that would be typical of landslips; another borehole has identified marine sands at sea level underneath landslip material, and yet another has brought up marine microfossils, fossils of minuscule sea dwellers that could only have appeared there if the region was once covered by sea. These findings have been backed up in other ways, too, using techniques such as electrical resistivity tomography (ERT) – which injects current into the ground to obtain a picture of what lies under it by measuring subtle changes in the electric field – that confirm that the valley sub-surface contains massive amounts of loose material and is riven by fault lines. ERT, together with ground-penetrating radar and electromagnetic surveys, has also revealed that a flat marshy area some distance west of the Thinia valley was once not just under the sea, but that it was buffeted by five major radiocarbon-datable tsunamis over the last eight thousand years or so (two of them post-Homeric), washing sediment nearly a kilometre inland: clear scientific evidence for the kinds of major historical earthquakes that could have triggered both tsunamis and massive landslides, and might have caused the sea channel to be translated, uplifted and eroded in the Thinia valley.[23] It's even been suggested that the curving, sheltered bay that would once have lain in the area that is now silted-up marsh might formerly have been a Bronze Age harbour.[24]

The next steps to be taken – and the focus of research in the past few years – are to pin down the date that the channel was blocked off and seawater stopped flowing between Paliki and Cephalonia. Ongoing work is looking at dating the landslide on the channel's western edge – trying to work out when the terrain now covered by a landslide that thundered down the mountain was last exposed to sunlight (using a method called OSL, or optically stimulated luminescence, dating), which would tell us when the landslide happened. Did it take place one thousand, two thousand or even five thousand years ago? The answer will be crucial to the chronology of the Homeric hypothesis – because if the sea channel was infilled after the Late Bronze Age, then it would endow Paliki with all the major identifying features of Homer's Ithaca: it would make it a low-lying island, which faces the dusk.

Bittlestone's hypothesis is an astonishingly neat suggestion, and allows us, perhaps for the first time, to visualize the place where the *Odyssey* imagines Penelope waiting as her husband fights at Troy and makes his decade-long return; the island which was said to have drawn suitors from Same, Doulichion and Zacynthos; the palace where she supposedly wove her fabled story cloth. And it's this that has brought me, in the summer of 2014, to Cephalonia – to follow in Bittlestone's footsteps, and visit for myself the possible location of Penelope's island. I drive up to Atheras Bay, in the north, with its two crouching headlands, shimmering waters and sandy beach, where Odysseus might once have returned from his travels.[25] I circle past the jutting scrub-covered hilltop, with its commanding view down the gulf, that's still known by locals as Kastelli – 'castle' – and that Bittlestone and his team think might be the possible location of a Mycenaean palace.[26] I drop down to the spreading flash-flooded area of the marsh beneath it, which has now been shown to have been under the sea and was, perhaps, once, the ancient city's harbour.

And yet, as I scramble up hills and splash through impossibly clear bays, as I follow the route of what was once an ocean channel from one curving shore to another and begin to imagine the sea-girt island where Penelope might once have stood, I have to remind myself that it's all too easy to get carried away. If we want to commit ourselves to uncovering the facts of history, if we want to pay attention to the story that the past is actually telling us, rather than the narratives of fiction, then – as I outlined at the very beginning of this book – we have to be rigorous in working from actual, historical, archaeological and scientific evidence out towards Homer, and not the other way around. Bittlestone's hypothesis is an example of the latter, where Homer has provided the starting point. And so we have to tread exceptionally carefully, bearing in mind the cautions laid out about the very specific interweaving of fact and fiction, past and present, that makes up the complex fabric of the Homeric epics. As with any premise that uses an epic poem as the basis for historical fact (let alone an epic that stirs up so much emotion and has had such a high cultural currency) there's a risk of a certain bias towards the evidence that fits, to which Bittlestone (like many Homeric enthusiasts, Schliemann being the most prominent example) was sometimes prone. (To the credit of Bittlestone and his team, however, and in contrast to Schliemann, they have been putting on hold archaeological excavation at possible Homeric sites on Paliki, in association with the local Ephorate of Antiquities, until the geological timescales have been confirmed.) It's not that there can't be some portion of truth preserved in the epics; simply that we cannot rely on the epics alone to make leaps of logic. Ithaca is a case in point: the hypothesis accords (broadly speaking) with the Homeric text, but Homer alone isn't enough to prove the geology. Until the date of the rockfall in the Thinia valley is known, we won't be able to go any further. What we do know is that the channel was definitely under the sea at some point; we know where it was, and we know why and how it was covered. We just don't yet know the final crucial piece in the puzzle: when.

But that doesn't take away from the tantalizing fact that we will, at some point, find out whether the latest Ithaca theory is right or not – nor the excitement of the way in which the real world veiled behind ancient myth is still being uncovered, with new discoveries being made every day, and more to come. On Paliki, new technologies and new questions are driving the search for the land that the real Penelopes of the Late Bronze Age called home. Deep under the Ionian Sea, sediment cores are providing evidence for the ancient climate change that may have ended their world. New archaeological digs are uncovering the remains of infants they were forced to bury. New scientific methods are revealing the DNA that gives an intricate microscopic view of their genetic make-up, while recently developed techniques of mass spectrometry allow us to see the rainbow of textile dyes they used to drape themselves in colour. Such discoveries never cease to surprise us, in all their complexity, variety, urgency, relevance – opening up a window on to everything from fast fashion to climate change to the battle for equality, and, above all, bringing the real women behind Homer's world, the warriors, the enslaved captives, the weavers, the mothers and the queens, to the fore.

There's always more to find. And that's worth waiting for.

Coda

AEGEA

A New History

The Power of a Name

I was always taught that the Aegean Sea was named after a white man. 'The Aegean', that catch-all word for Greece and the islands scattered between it and the western coast of Turkey, united by the expanse of blue that gleams between them. Aegeus, I was told, leapt to his death from the Athenian rocks into the sea, when he thought his son Theseus had been killed by the Minotaur – and so gave his name to the ocean in which he drowned.[1]

But as I was writing this book, I unearthed another name: *Aegea*. According to the ancient historical sources I uncovered, Aegea was an Amazon, and she was an African (from Libya). She was a great warrior and queen who sailed the seas with her Amazons to fight at Troy. She ransacked the cities of Anatolia and the windy heights of Troy, took plunder from King Priam or his father Laomedon (long before the Greeks even came), and voyaged back with her army to her Libyan home. But on the way – on this odyssey of her own – her ship sank, taking her and her army to a watery grave. And so, according to one particular Roman historian from the second century CE, the Aegean was actually named after *her*.[2]

So why don't we know her story? Why is the story of the Aegean made out to be the legend of a white Greek man, rather than the tale of an African woman who fought her way to the top? Her history is relegated to two lines in a little-known treatise on Latin grammar; she's not the subject of the top-spot sweeping epics, like Homer's, that have passed down the tales of men over the centuries. (We might be reminded of another Amazon who fought at Troy, Penthesilea, whose story was confined to the margins of a medieval manuscript as an alternative ending to Homer's *Iliad* – and then forgotten.) History is about which facts we choose to recall. It's not that women weren't there in the historical record, or that they weren't making a name for themselves. It's simply that, in the past, women weren't chosen to be remembered. And their stories, like Aegea's, eventually were lost.

It's been the aim of this book to find them again – to search for them in the record, and to restore them to their rightful place both in their own legends and in the history books. It's a hugely exciting time to be looking back into the ancient past, as we're starting to tap into the bits of history that have been forgotten and uncover the stories we thought were lost. Advances in archaeology, as we've seen, are allowing us to recover the intricate details of women's lives (that used to be deemed irrecoverable) in ways we'd never have imagined: to reconstruct their faces with 3D modelling, to map their genetic make-up, to scan the geological contours of the places they lived in. Recent developments in the study of the ancient world mean that we're finally focusing on the women that crowd the pages of the Homeric epics, and showing how central they are to driving the narratives of the *Iliad* and *Odyssey*. At the same time, modern movements like #MeToo, Black Lives Matter and the campaign for transgender rights show that giving suppressed voices a chance to speak is a battle we're still fighting. And that's reinvigorating historians and writers alike, who are turning back to the ancient myths and stories to engage with them in new ways: both to uncover new records and evidence for the real people of the ancient world, in all their complexity and diversity, and to allow their once-silenced voices to speak again.

In all this conversation around who gets a voice – who gets to land on the right side of history – there's never been a more important time to ask ourselves to be rigorous in distinguishing between *historical events* (the objective facts of what happens at any given time) and *history*: the canonical version that certain actors, with certain agendas, decide to pass on, and that certain cultural commentators (with ideologies of their own) enshrine as the definitive story.[3] Think of the difference between the *historical event* of the destruction of a city called Taruisa or Wilusa in north-west Anatolia around the early twelfth century BCE, and the *history* whereby later classical chroniclers elevated the Trojan War and its overweening male heroes to a major place in the story of Greece. We may remember how Herodotus, the so-called 'father of history', posited classical Athens' victory in the fifth century BCE against the Persians as a natural continuation of the Greek defeat of Troy – making Troy into an origin point for his own tale of Greece's rise. These histories – so often disguised as a factual account without an agenda – say a lot about the historians themselves, and the people who read their work, and what they care about. It also has a lot to say about the stories – like Aegea's, like so many of the women in this book, real and imagined – that *weren't* told, that got erased from the archives of history. If we want to aim for more equality now, then we need to keep interacting with and interrogating the tales that have been told about the past based on the new evidence being unearthed, in order to understand the processes of oppression and exclusion that have taken place across the centuries, and retrieve the lost or silenced voices that history forgot.

History, as Herodotus' rewriting of the Trojan War shows, is always being rewritten. And nowhere is this more true than in the case of Homer, whose epic poems were the product of a centuries-long process of recomposing and repurposing, adapted and translated with a new spin in each individual bard's composition that eventually came to be written down as the *Iliad* and *Odyssey* in the versions we know today. The rewriting (or reworking) of Homer has been in business since the beginning: the potential for adaptation, the foregrounding of different voices and characters, is central to the epics' very nature. In fact, it seems to me that it's this inextricable element of mutability that makes the *Iliad* and the *Odyssey* what they are, and allows for reinterpretations that are continually relevant, that help to keep the life blood of these ever-growing, ever-mutating poems pumping through the centuries. Not only are they extraordinary epic tales, offering defining moments of love, loss, glory, bravery, death – stories that defy irrelevance, stories that you already know and yet you read again and again as if for the first time.[4] They also thrive on change. They need to be commented on, reacted to, translated, modified, adapted, according to what each generation wants to say, and who they want to include.

In uncovering the women of the past and of Homer's stories and giving them a voice, my account is inevitably subject to the same interpretative bias as any other history, and any other story. This new counter-history – of an Aegea, not an Aegean – searches for the experiences of women in the Late Bronze Age and the tales that have been told about them, bringing to the fore the stories of the captives and daughters and warriors who have been forgotten, thus casting a new light on the ancient past. In so doing, I've been astonished not only by the extraordinary women I've come face to face with, but also by the sheer diversity and interconnectedness of the ancient world – from the Aegean to the banks of the Tigris in Mesopotamia and from the Hittite Empire to the Egyptian Nile, from international dynastic marriages to borrowed gods, from stories shared between cultures thousands of miles apart to goods shipped from one end of the Mediterranean to the other. Nor does gender stand alone. Issues of marginalization intersect across racial, class and gender divides, as well as gender identities. To talk about Athena is not just to talk about a woman or a goddess, but to delve into what gender (and the construction of the gender binary) means; to talk about Nausicaa and her Babylonian legal models is to challenge a straightforward narrative of Western history; to talk about Briseis or Eurycleia is to embrace all the enslaved people who were hidden and silenced in the ancient world, and beyond.

And so this book encourages you, the reader, to be discerning about this and all the other histories that are offered up to you. It attempts to show how we might critically examine the facts, texts and stories we tell about ourselves and each other, based on a thorough analysis of the evidence, in order to improve the way we interpret the world. Above all, I hope that it will encourage you not to be afraid to be challenged to think in new ways. History is a conversation we are all part of, and we need to keep having that conversation, critiquing it, debating it. This is just one voice among many. We all have a part to play in thinking about how we remember the past – and how we write the future.

LIST OF CHARACTERS AND GLOSSARY

Here you will find a useful list of the many figures from myth and ancient history who crop up in *Mythica*, as well as a guide to archaeological and other specialist terms. Cross-references to other entries are highlighted in bold.

ACHAEA Region of ancient Greece (hence Homer's term for the Greeks as **Achaeans**), likely to be synonymous with Hittite **Ahhiyawa**.

ACHAEANS The name in the Homeric epics for the Greeks (also Argives or Danaans), and likely to be what the Late Bronze Age **Mycenaeans** called themselves.

ACHILLES (*Myth*) Son of the goddess **Thetis** and captor-owner of the enslaved Trojan woman **Briseis**; his wrath at the loss of Briseis to the Greek king, **Agamemnon**, is told in Homer's epic the *Iliad*.

ADNA Short for 'ancient DNA': DNA recovered from archaeological samples.

AEAEA (*Myth*) Island home of the goddess **Circe**; appears in the *Odyssey*.

AEGEA (*Myth*) **Amazon** queen of Libya who led troops to plunder **Troy**; her ship sank on her return, giving an etymology for the Aegean Sea.

AEGIS (*Myth*) **Athena**'s battle weapon (shared by **Zeus**), crowned with the head of the **Gorgon**.

AETHIOPIS, THE One of the lost epics that made up the Epic Cycle, a group of narrative poems about the Trojan War; it made up the next in the series of events following the *Iliad*, with the arrival of the **Amazons** led by **Penthesilea**. See also the *Cypria*.

AGAMEMNON (*Myth*) Husband of **Clytemnestra**, brother-in-law of **Helen of Sparta/Troy** (via his brother **Menelaus**) and owner of the enslaved Trojan woman **Chryseis**; king of the Greeks, who led the Greek forces against **Troy**. Appears in the *Iliad* and (as a ghost) the *Odyssey*.

AHHIYAWA   Kingdom named several times in the **Hittite** archives, likely referring to **Achaea** or Greece.

AhT 20   **Hittite** oracle tablet of the late fourteenth–early thirteenth century BCE (aimed at curing the Hittite king **Mursili II**) that mentions female ritual practitioners and the Hittite princess **Massannauzzi**.

AKHENATEN   Husband of **Nefertiti** and others, including the daughter of **Burna-Buriash II**; pharaoh of Egypt (*c.*1353–36 BCE). Originally known as Amenhotep IV, he changed his name to foreground his worship of the sun god Aten.

AKHETATEN   New capital of **Nefertiti** and **Akhenaten** (modern Tell el-Amarna) on the east bank of the Nile in Egypt.

AKKADIAN   A language, written in **cuneiform** and spoken in ancient Mesopotamia, that was the lingua franca of ancient south-west Asia.

AKROTIRI   The site of a Cycladic Bronze Age settlement on Thera (Santorini).

ALAKSANDU   Thirteenth-century BCE king of **Wilusa**, named in the **Hittite** archives in a treaty with the Hittite king.

ALATZOMOURI PEFKA   The site of a late eighteenth-century BCE **Minoan** dye workshop on Crete.

ALCINOUS   (*Myth*) Husband of **Arete**, father of **Nausicaa**; king of the **Phaeacians**. Visited by **Odysseus** in the *Odyssey* on his return journey from **Troy**.

AMARNA   Modern name for the site of ancient **Akhetaten**.

AMAZONS   (*Myth*) Fierce women warriors who were said to live around and beyond the Black Sea, and whose tales are told in multiple ancient Greek myths. See **Hippolyta** and **Penthesilea**.

AMENHOTEP III   Husband of **Tadu-hepa**, princess of **Mittani**; pharaoh of Egypt (*c.*1390–53 BCE).

ANDRA   Ancient Greek word for 'man' (nominative *anēr*); the first word of the *Odyssey*.

ANDROMACHE   (*Myth*) Princess of Thebe who came to **Troy** when she married **Hector**, and mother of **Astyanax**; appears in several books of the *Iliad*.

APHRODITE   (*Myth*) Ancient Greek goddess of love and sex.

APOLLO   (*Myth*) Ancient Greek god of archery, prophecy, healing and the sun; twin of **Artemis**. A **Wilusan** god (who may be a west Anatolian version) has the name Apaliuna; the **Hittite** sources give Apaluwa.

APSU   (*Myth*) Mesopotamian river god and husband of **Tiamat**, the sea goddess; conceived in the Babylonian epic *Enuma Elish* as the primeval parent (with Tiamat) of all the gods.

ARES   (*Myth*) Ancient Greek god of war.

ARETE   (*Myth*) Queen of the **Phaeacians**, mother of **Nausicaa**. The key to **Odysseus'** return in the *Odyssey*, whom he has to supplicate to get a ship back to **Ithaca**.

ARGONAUTS   (*Myth*) Warriors who sailed on the fabled *Argo* with **Jason** to steal the Golden Fleece from Colchis.

ARIADNE   (*Myth*) Princess of Crete who rescued **Theseus** from the **Minotaur** in the labyrinth; she was abandoned by him on Naxos and became the consort of the Greek god **Dionysus**.

ARTEMIS   (*Myth*) Ancient Greek goddess of the hunt; twin of **Apollo**.

ASHUR   The capital city of ancient Assyria in Mesopotamia.

ASTYANAX   (*Myth*) Son of **Andromache** and **Hector**.

ATALANTA   (*Myth*) A woman hunter and warrior who could run faster than any man, wrestled **Peleus** and won, was first to strike the Calydonian Boar, and may have voyaged with **Jason** and the **Argonauts**.

ATHENA   (*Myth*) Ancient Greek goddess of wisdom, craft and war.

ATRAHASIS, THE   **Akkadian** epic including Babylonian creation and flood myths.

ATREUS   (*Myth*) King of **Mycenae**, father of **Agamemnon** and **Menelaus**.

BATTLE OF QADESH   See **Qadesh, Battle of**.

BOĞAZKALE   The site (in modern Turkey) of the ancient capital **Hattusa**.

BRISEIS   (*Myth*) Trojan enslaved woman whose trafficking between **Achilles** and **Agamemnon** initiates the plot of the *Iliad*, along with the release of **Chryseis**.

BURNA-BURIASH II   Father of the unnamed princess of Babylon who writes to **Akhenaten**; king of Babylon (*c*.1360–33 BCE).

CALYPSO   (*Myth*) Nymph who lives on the mythical island of **Ogygia**; the *Odyssey* opens with **Odysseus** on her island, where he stays for seven years of his voyage back to **Ithaca**; she provides him with the raft-building instructions, sail and clothes he needs to return home.

CANAAN   Bronze Age historical civilization and ancient region along the eastern Mediterranean coast.

CASSANDRA   (*Myth*) Prophet who predicts the sack of **Troy** but is cursed by **Apollo** never to be believed; daughter of **Hecuba** and **Priam**, queen and king of Troy.

CHARYBDIS   (*Myth*) Mythical whirlpool in the straits opposite **Scylla**'s cave; **Circe** warns **Odysseus** to choose to pass Scylla rather than Charybdis.

CHRYSEIS   (*Myth*) Trojan enslaved woman whose release from **Agamemnon**, along with the trafficking of **Briseis**, initiates the plot of the *Iliad*.

CHRYSES   (*Myth*) Father of **Chryseis** and priest of **Apollo**.

CIRCE   (*Myth*) Goddess and witch who lives on the mythical island of **Aeaea**; **Odysseus** stays with her for a year on his voyage home, and she provides him with the crucial information he needs to return.

CLYTEMNESTRA   (*Myth*) Queen of **Mycenae** after marriage to **Agamemnon**; sister of **Helen of Sparta/Troy**. The *Odyssey* alludes to the story of **Clytemnestra**'s murder of **Agamemnon** on his return to Greece.

CUNEIFORM   Writing system of wedge-shaped marks on clay tablets used in ancient south-west Asia.

CYCLOPS   (*Myth*) One-eyed giant called Polyphemus, encountered – and blinded, after a violation of *xenia* – by **Odysseus** on his voyage home. He lays a curse on Odysseus through his father **Poseidon**, who causes many of the setbacks on Odysseus' voyage.

CYDONIA   Ancient city in north-west Crete (modern Chania).

CYPRIA, THE   One of the lost epics that made up the Epic Cycle, a group of narrative poems about the Trojan War; it narrated the series of events leading up to the *Iliad*, including **Helen**'s departure from **Sparta**, **Cassandra**'s prophecy of the sack of **Troy**, the sacrifice of **Clytemnestra**'s daughter Iphigenia at Aulis, and the enslavement of **Briseis** and **Chryseis**.

DAPHNE   Female oracle at Delphi, likely mythical, who was said to have composed outstanding verses of poetry, and from whom Homer was said to have stolen his poetry.

DEMETER   (*Myth*) Ancient Greek goddess of the harvest and mother of **Persephone**, both of whom were worshipped in the **Thesmophoria**.

DEMODOCUS (*Myth*) Bard of the **Phaeacians**.

DIOMEDES (*Myth*) Greek warrior whose climactic moment (*aristeia*) in the Trojan War is described in Book 5 of the *Iliad*; guest friend of **Glaucus**, with whom he exchanges armour in Book 6.

DIONYSUS (*Myth*) Ancient Greek god of wine, theatre and religious ecstasy.

DISTAFF Tool used for spinning wool into thread: the wool is gathered on the distaff, a tall (usually wooden) stick that acts as the holder from which the wool is drawn for spinning.

EIDŌLON Ancient Greek word for 'likeness' or 'phantom'; used of the alternative story (most famously told by **Euripides**) of **Helen of Sparta/ Troy**'s phantom going to Troy instead of her.

EILEITHYIA (*Myth*) Ancient Greek goddess of childbirth and labour, with her cult centre at the cave at Amnisos in Crete.

ENHEDUANNA First named author in the world: a Sumerian priestess of the twenty-third century BCE who wrote hymns for the goddess **Inanna**.

ENUMA ELISH **Akkadian** epic of the Babylonian creation myth.

ERITHA Priestess of **Pylos** mentioned by name on the **Linear B** tablets.

EUMAEUS (*Myth*) Enslaved swineherd of **Odysseus** on **Ithaca**; appears in the *Odyssey*.

EURIPIDES Classical Athenian dramatist (*c*.480–407/6 BCE) who wrote many tragedies reworking the myths of the women of the Trojan War.

EUROPA (*Myth*) **Phoenician** princess abducted by **Zeus** in the form of a bull and raped; mother of **Minos**, legendary king of **Knossos**.

EURYCLEIA (*Myth*) Enslaved nurse of **Odysseus** on **Ithaca**; has a key role to play in the *Odyssey* when she recognizes Odysseus by his scar.

FAIENCE Glass-like coloured glazed quartz, used for modelling small objects and figurines in ancient south-west Asia.

Γ55 Male skeleton from grave Γ (grave gamma) in **Grave Circle B**, **Mycenae**, dating to the seventeenth–sixteenth century BCE: almost certainly the brother of **Γ58**.

Γ58 Female skeleton from grave Γ (grave gamma) in **Grave Circle B**, **Mycenae**, dating to the seventeenth–sixteenth century BCE: almost certainly the sister of Γ55, and buried with a warrior kit of weapons and a precious electrum death mask. Her face has been reconstructed.

GALA   Sumerian gender-nonconforming priests of **Inanna**, who spoke a female-only dialect and whose name was written as 'penis + anus'.

GC-MS   Abbreviation for gas chromatography–mass spectrometry, the scientific method of extracting, separating and identifying the molecular components of ancient residues.

GENII   (*Myth*) Modern (Latinate) term (singular: *genius*) for the composite mythical figures often represented in **Minoan** and **Mycenaean** art, derived from the Egyptian fertility goddess **Taweret**.

GERAS   Ancient Greek word, often used in Homeric epic, of a prize of honour won in battle.

GILGAMESH, EPIC OF   **Akkadian** epic of the heroic saga of Gilgamesh.

GLAUCUS   (*Myth*) Lycian warrior fighting as an ally of the Trojans in the Trojan War; guest friend of **Diomedes**, with whom he exchanges armour in Book 6 of the *Iliad*.

GORGON/MEDUSA   (*Myth*) According to the canonical version of the myth, Medusa is one of three Gorgon sisters, whose gaze turns men to stone; she is raped by **Poseidon** and decapitated by Perseus, and her head affixed on **Athena**'s *aegis*.

GÖZLÜKULE   The site (in modern Turkey) of ancient **Tarsus**.

GRAVE CIRCLES A/B   Two Late Bronze Age royal cemeteries in **Mycenae**, with burials from the seventeenth and sixteenth centuries BCE.

GREAT PANATHENAIA, THE   The major festival of classical Athens involving the procession to and robing (with the *peplos*) of the statue of **Athena** Parthenos in the **Parthenon**.

HADES   (*Myth*) Ancient Greek god of the Underworld who raped **Persephone**; the name is also used eponymously of the Underworld.

HAMMURABI   King of Babylon (*c.*1792–50 BCE) and author of one of the oldest law codes in human history.

HATSHEPSUT   Pharaoh of Egypt (*c.*1473–58 BCE) who had unprecedented power as a woman ruler.

HATTUSA   The capital city of the **Hittite** Empire in central Anatolia (modern **Boğazkale**, Turkey).

HATTUSILI III   Husband of **Puduhepa**; Great King of the **Hittites** (*c*.1267–37 BCE) and co-signatory of the Qadesh peace treaty after the **Battle of Qadesh** in 1274 BCE.

HEBAT   (*Myth*) Hurrian goddess and Queen of Heaven; **Puduhepa** was instrumental in assimilating her into the **Hittite** religion.

HECTOR   (*Myth*) Husband of **Andromache**, father of **Astyanax**; prince of **Troy** and leader of the Trojan troops in the *Iliad*.

HECUBA   (*Myth*) Queen of **Troy**, mother of **Hector**, **Paris**, **Cassandra** and others; appears in several books of the *Iliad*.

HEDNA   Ancient Greek word for 'bride price', the sum of money (or goods) paid as surety for the bride's hand by the groom.

HELEN OF SPARTA/TROY   (*Myth*) Originally Helen of **Sparta**; daughter of Leda, who was raped by **Zeus** in the form of a swan. She was given by **Aphrodite** as the prize to **Paris**, prince of **Troy**, when he selected the goddess in the Judgement of the golden apple as the most beautiful among Aphrodite, **Hera** and **Athena**; his seizure of Helen caused the Trojan War.

HELENUS   (*Myth*) Twin brother of **Cassandra**; seer.

HEPHAESTUS   (*Myth*) Ancient Greek god of craftsmen and blacksmiths; husband of **Aphrodite**.

HERA   (*Myth*) Ancient Greek queen of the gods; goddess of women, marriage and childbirth.

HERCULES   (*Myth*) Ancient Greek warrior who performed the legendary Twelve Labours and was the first to sack **Troy**.

HERMES   (*Myth*) Ancient Greek messenger god and guide of the dead to the Underworld.

HERMIONE   (*Myth*) Daughter of **Helen of Sparta/Troy** and **Menelaus**.

HERODOTUS   Classical Greek historian from Halicarnassus (*c*.484–*c*.425 BCE) who wrote the first extant history of the Persian Wars.

HESIOD   Archaic Greek epic poet (likely late eighth–early seventh century BCE), author of the *Theogony* (an epic of the birth of the gods) and the *Works and Days* (a didactic epic), as well as the *Catalogue of Women* (a list of heroines and their heroic sons).

HIPPOLYTA   (*Myth*) Queen of the **Amazons**, owner of the belt which **Hercules** stole as one of his Labours, and (in some versions) abducted by **Theseus** to Athens.

HISARLIK   The site (in modern north-west Turkey) of ancient **Troy**.

HITTITES   Bronze Age historical civilization and major imperial power in central Anatolia; one of the dominant forces in ancient south-west Asia.

ICARIUS   (*Myth*) Father of **Penelope**, brother of Tyndareus (the husband of Leda): thus uncle of **Helen of Sparta/Troy**.

ILIOS/ILION/ILIUM   Variant terms in the Homeric epics (and later Latin) for **Troy**.

INANNA   (*Myth*) **Sumerian** goddess of love and war, equivalent to **Ishtar**.

ISHTAR   (*Myth*) **Akkadian** goddess of love and war, equivalent to **Inanna**.

ISIS   (*Myth*) One of the most important ancient Egyptian goddesses, goddess of life and death, magic and the cosmos.

ITHACA   (*Myth*) Island of **Penelope** and **Odysseus** in the Ionian Sea.

JASON   (*Myth*) Leader of the **Argonauts** on the voyage for the Golden Fleece.

JEWELS OF HELEN   Erroneously named hoard of gold discovered by Heinrich Schliemann at **Troy** in 1873, that dates to *c*.2400 BCE. See also **Priam's Treasure**.

KANESH   Assyrian trading post in central Anatolia (modern Turkey).

KIZZUWATNA   Region in south-east Anatolia (modern Turkey); birthplace of **Puduhepa**.

KLEOS   Ancient Greek word for 'glory'.

KNOSSOS   (*Myth*) Seat of the legendary King **Minos** of Crete – father of **Ariadne** – and mythical location of the labyrinth and **Minotaur**. A historical Bronze Age palace was discovered here by Minos Kalokairinos (in 1878) and Sir Arthur Evans, during excavations between 1900 and 1931.

LAERTES   (*Myth*) Father of **Odysseus**.

LETO   (*Myth*) Ancient Greek goddess, mother of **Artemis** and **Apollo**.

LINEAR A   Undeciphered script used by the **Minoans** on Crete.

LINEAR B   Script used by the Late Bronze Age **Mycenaeans**; deciphered by Michael Ventris, building on important work by Alice Kober, in 1952.

LOOM WEIGHTS   Large clay weights used to keep the vertical threads (warp) of the loom taut.

LUWIAN   Ancient Anatolian language.

LYCIA Ancient region along the south-western Anatolian coast (modern Turkey).

MASSANNAUZZI Princess of the **Hittites** mentioned in the oracle tablet *AhT* 20 who may have been responsible for forging connections between Greeks and **Hittites**; daughter of **Mursili II**.

MEDEA (*Myth*) Princess of Colchis and witch, whose magical skills secure **Jason** the Golden Fleece; niece of **Circe**.

MEDUSA See **Gorgon/Medusa**.

MELANTHO (*Myth*) Enslaved woman of **Penelope** and **Odysseus** in **Ithaca**.

MEMNON (*Myth*) Son of the goddess Dawn, king of the Ethiopians; the tale of his duel with **Achilles** in the Trojan War forms the narrative of the lost epic the *Aethiopis*.

MENELAUS (*Myth*) Husband of **Helen of Sparta/Troy**, father of **Hermione**; king of **Sparta** through Helen.

MĒNIS Ancient Greek word for 'divine wrath'; the first word of the *Iliad*.

MENTES (*Myth*) First disguise of **Athena** in Book 1 of the *Odyssey*; king of the Taphians.

MENTOR (*Myth*) Second disguise of **Athena** in Book 2 of the *Odyssey*; friend of **Odysseus** and guardian of **Telemachus**.

MINOAN A modern term (derived from the mythical King **Minos** of Crete) for the historical Bronze Age civilization of Crete.

MINOS (*Myth*) Father of **Ariadne**, husband of **Pasiphae**; legendary king of **Knossos** and father of the **Minotaur**.

MINOTAUR, THE (*Myth*) Half man, half bull, born of **Pasiphae** when **Poseidon** cursed her to have sex with a bull.

MITTANI Ancient Late Bronze Age empire in northern Mesopotamia.

MOIRAI, THE (*Myth*) The Fates, who portion out the allotted span of mortals' lives.

MOLY (*Myth*) Mythical plant given by **Hermes** to **Odysseus** as protection against **Circe's** spells.

MTDNA Mitochondrial DNA: this genetic material is passed down solely through the maternal line.

MUREX Type of sea snail whose hypobranchial gland produces a compound that was used to make purple dye.

MURSILI II   Father of **Massannauzzi** and probably the target of the oracle tablet *AhT* 20; king of the **Hittites** (*c.*1321–1295 BCE).

MUSES, THE   (*Myth*) Ancient Greek goddesses of poetry, song, music, history and dance who inspired poets and were said to know everything.

MYCENAE/MYCENAEANS   Mycenae is the site of a Late Bronze Age palace and fortified citadel located in the north-eastern Peloponnese in Greece; (*myth*) ruled by King **Agamemnon**. 'Mycenaean' is a modern term for the Late Bronze Age civilization of mainland Greece.

MYC2/III   Female skeleton from grave III in **Grave Circle A**, **Mycenae**, dating to the sixteenth century BCE and buried with the remains of a baby on her chest.

MYRTOS   The site (in Crete) of a prehistoric **Minoan** village.

NAUSICAA   (*Myth*) Princess of the **Phaeacians**, daughter of **Arete**; she is instrumental in **Odysseus'** return in the *Odyssey*, as she guides him to supplicate her mother for a ship to take him back to **Ithaca**.

NEFERTARI   Egyptian queen and correspondent of **Puduhepa**; Great Royal Wife of **Ramesses II**.

NEFERTITI   Egyptian queen and Great Royal Wife of **Akhenaten**; she may have ruled alone as pharaoh after his death.

NEREUS   (*Myth*) Ancient Greek god of the sea (called 'Old Man of the Sea' by Homer) and father of **Thetis**.

NESTOR   (*Myth*) King of **Pylos** who advises the Greek troops in the *Iliad*, and entertains **Athena** (disguised as **Mentor**) and **Telemachus** in Book 3 of the *Odyssey*.

OCEANUS   (*Myth*) Ancient Greek god of the great river that encompasses the earth, and husband of **Tethys**; conceived in Homer as the primeval parent (with Tethys) of all the gods.

ODYSSEUS   (*Myth*) Husband of **Penelope** and slaveowner of **Eurycleia**, king of **Ithaca** and one of the Greeks to fight at **Troy**; his journey home after the Trojan War, and encounters with **Calypso**, **Nausicaa**, **Arete** and **Circe**, is narrated in Homer's epic the *Odyssey*.

OGYGIA   (*Myth*) Island home of the goddess **Calypso**; appears in the *Odyssey*.

OIKOS   Ancient Greek word for 'house' and 'home', and also for all the property within a household.

ONUKA   **Mycenaean Linear B** term for a finely ornamented cloth border.

OSTEOLOGY   The scientific study of bones (from ancient Greek *osteon*, 'bone').

PANDORA   (*Myth*) The first woman according to Greek myth, created as a punishment for men.

PARIS   (*Myth*) Son of **Hecuba** and **Priam**, prince of **Troy**; after choosing **Aphrodite** in the Judgement of the golden apple (over **Hera** and **Athena**) and with **Helen of Sparta** (later Troy) awarded as his prize, he sailed to **Sparta** to take her back to Troy, thus initiating the Trojan War. He is also known by the Greek name *Alexandros* (Alexander).

PARTHENON   Classical Greek monument on the acropolis of Athens with substantial sculptural decoration on the pediments, metopes and frieze, completed in 432 BCE.

PASIPHAE   (*Myth*) Mother of **Ariadne** and the **Minotaur** (when she was cursed by **Poseidon** to have sex with a bull); sister of **Circe**; legendary queen of **Knossos**, Crete.

PATROCLUS   (*Myth*) Ancient Greek warrior at **Troy** and close companion of **Achilles**; Homer is unclear whether they were lovers, but the later Greek tradition made it clear that they were seen as such. Patroclus' death in the *Iliad* at the hands of **Hector** is the turning point of the epic and the motivation for Achilles' return to battle.

PELEUS   (*Myth*) Raped **Thetis** and so father of **Achilles**; beaten by **Atalanta** in a wrestling match. King of Phthia.

PENELOPE   (*Myth*) Queen of **Ithaca** and mother of **Telemachus**; the tale of her attempts to push back against the 108 suitors besieging her in Ithaca (particularly her unweaving trick) forms one of the central narratives of Homer's epic the *Odyssey*, and the lynchpin of the plot.

PENTHESILEA   (*Myth*) Queen of the **Amazons**, who led the Amazon troops to aid the Trojans after **Hector**'s death; the tale of her duel with **Achilles** in the Trojan War forms the narrative of the lost epic the ***Aethiopis***.

PEPLOS   Woven robe worn by classical Greek women; a special *peplos* dedicated to the goddess **Athena** was presented to the goddess in the festival of the **Great Panathenaia**.

PERICLES   Leading statesman of Athens (*c.*495–29 BCE) and proponent (in Thucydides' version of one of his speeches) of women's silencing.

PERISTERIA   The site (in mainland Greece) of a Bronze Age settlement and royal **Mycenaean** chamber tombs, containing the remains of a Mycenaean woman.

PERSEPHONE   (*Myth*) Daughter of **Demeter** and queen of the Underworld after she was raped by **Hades**.

PETSAS HOUSE   **Mycenaean** pottery workshop and residence in Late Bronze Age **Mycenae**, dating to the fourteenth century BCE.

PETSOPHAS   **Minoan** peak sanctuary in Late Bronze Age Crete, with clay figurine offerings dating to the nineteenth to eighteenth century BCE.

PHAEACIANS   (*Myth*) Legendary islanders ruled by Queen **Arete**, visited on **Odysseus'** final stop on his voyage home in the *Odyssey*. The island of the Phaeacians is called *Scheriē* in Homer; I have called it 'the island of the Phaeacians' to avoid confusion.

PHARMAKA   Ancient Greek word for 'drugs', both healing and harmful.

PHOENICIANS   Ancient people who lived and traded along the eastern Mediterranean coast (modern Syria and Lebanon to Galilee), organized around city kingdoms including **Sidon** and Tyre.

PHRYGIA   Iron Age civilization and region in western-central Anatolia (modern Turkey).

PIYAMARADU   **Hittite** renegade of the thirteenth century BCE who was involved with the **Ahhiyawans**; **Puduhepa** prays for his destruction.

POLYPHARMAKOS   Ancient Greek word meaning 'expert in many kinds of drugs', used in the *Odyssey* of **Circe**.

POLYPHEMUS   See **Cyclops**.

POSEIDON   (*Myth*) Ancient Greek god of the sea; key divine antagonist of **Odysseus** on his return in the *Odyssey*, after he blinds Poseidon's son (the **Cyclops Polyphemus**).

POTNIA   Ancient Greek word for 'lady' or 'mistress'; appears in the **Linear B** tablets as *po-ti-ni-ja*. Also *potnia thērōn*, 'Mistress of Animals', the title used of **Artemis** and other goddesses who could tame wild beasts.

PRIAM   (*Myth*) Husband of **Hecuba**, father of **Hector**, **Paris**, **Cassandra** and others; king of **Troy** in the *Iliad*.

PRIAM'S TREASURE Erroneously named hoard of gold discovered by Heinrich Schliemann at **Troy** in 1873, that dates to *c.*2400 BCE; includes the so-called **jewels of Helen**.

PUDUHEPA Great Queen of the **Hittites** (*c.*1267–37 BCE) and wife of **Hattusili III**; co-signatory of the Qadesh peace treaty after the **Battle of Qadesh** in 1274 BCE.

PYLOS The site (in mainland Greece) of a **Mycenaean** palace, destroyed by fire around 1200 BCE; in myth, the seat of King **Nestor**.

PYTHIA, THE Title of the female oracle of the temple of **Apollo** at Delphi.

QADESH, BATTLE OF Battle between **Ramesses II** and the **Hittite** king Muwattalli II (brother of **Hattusili III**) in 1274 BCE.

RAMESSES II Husband of **Nefertari**; pharaoh of Egypt (*c.*1279–13 BCE). Fought the **Battle of Qadesh** against the **Hittites** and drew up the Qadesh peace treaty with **Puduhepa** and **Hattusili III**.

RAMESSES III Pharaoh of Egypt (*c.*1184–53 BCE) who chronicled the 1177 BCE attack of the **Sea Peoples**.

SAPPHO First extant woman poet of ancient Greece (fl. *c.*600 BCE), from Lesbos.

SCAEAN GATES (*Myth*) Main gates of **Troy** in the *Iliad*.

SCYLLA (*Myth*) Mythical dog-like monster with six heads, in the caves in the straits opposite **Charybdis**, who seizes **Odysseus**' crew on his return; later (post-Homeric) tradition has her as a nymph transformed by **Circe**.

SCYTHIA Iron Age (and later) region and kingdom in the northern Black Sea area (modern Ukraine and Russia).

SEA PEOPLES Modern term for the groups of invaders who attacked Egypt in 1177 BCE, and may have contributed to the Late Bronze Age collapse.

SIDON City-kingdom in **Phoenicia**, on the eastern coast of the Mediterranean (modern Lebanon); used in Homer for Phoenicia as a whole.

SIRENS (*Myth*) Mythical bird-women who sing epic poetry that enchants sailors; **Circe** tells **Odysseus** how to hear it, instructing him to bind himself to the mast of his ship in the *Odyssey*.

SPARTA The site (in mainland Greece) of an archaic and classical Greek city state, with remains nearby of a Bronze Age settlement and site of worship of **Helen of Sparta/Troy** and **Menelaus**; in myth, the seat of Helen of **Sparta** (later of **Troy**) and Menelaus, who ruled through marriage to Helen.

SPINDLE   Tool used for spinning wool into thread: the wool is drawn down from the **distaff** on to the spindle, which is spun in circles (hence 'spindle') to twist the wool into thread.

SPINDLE WHORL   A heavy clay disc on the bottom of a **spindle** that helps the spindle to spin.

STRABO   Ancient Asiatic Greek geographer (*c.*64 BCE–21 CE) who wrote a monumental *Geography* in seventeen books.

SUMERIA   Region of ancient city states in the southern part of Mesopotamia (modern Iraq).

TADU-HEPA   Princess of **Mittani**, sent with an enormous dowry by her father King **Tushratta** to marry the Egyptian pharaoh **Amenhotep III** in the mid fourteenth century BCE.

TARSUS   Ancient city in south-central Anatolia (modern **Gözlükule**, Turkey).

TARUISA   A place located in north-western Anatolia (modern Turkey), identified in the **Hittite** records next to Wilusiya (**Wilusa**); these names have been connected to the names in Greek for **Troy** and **Ilios**.

TAWERET   (*Myth*) Ancient Egyptian goddess of fertility and childbirth, depicted as a hippopotamus with limbs of a lion and a crocodile carapace.

TELEMACHUS   (*Myth*) Son of **Penelope** and **Odysseus** who silences Penelope at the opening of the *Odyssey* and hangs the enslaved women at the end; his travels in search of his father make up the first four books of the *Odyssey*.

TELL EL-AMARNA   See **Amarna**.

TETHYS   (*Myth*) Ancient Greek mother goddess and wife of **Oceanus**; conceived in Homer as the primeval parent (with Oceanus) of all the gods.

THEANO   (*Myth*) Priestess of **Troy** in the *Iliad*.

THESEUS   (*Myth*) Raped **Helen of Sparta/Troy** and the **Amazon Antiope** (sometimes known as **Hippolyta**); with **Ariadne**'s help, escaped the **Minotaur** and then abandoned her on Naxos. King of Athens.

THESMOPHORIA   Women-only festival celebrating **Demeter** and **Persephone**.

THETIS (*Myth*) Goddess and sea nymph; mother of **Achilles** after she was raped by **Peleus**.

THUCYDIDES Classical Athenian historian (*c*.455–*c*.400 BCE) who wrote the *History of the Peloponnesian War*.

TIAMAT (*Myth*) Mesopotamian sea goddess and wife of **Apsu**, the river god; conceived in the Babylonian epic ***Enuma Elish*** as the primeval parent (with Apsu) of all the gods.

TIRESIAS (*Myth*) Blind seer who transitioned between being a man and a woman, before living as a man; visited by **Odysseus** in the Underworld in the *Odyssey*, and gives him directions back to **Ithaca**.

TROY The site at **Hisarlik** of an ancient city, destroyed by fire and (potentially) invaders in the Late Bronze Age around 1190–80 BCE, and generally identified with **Troy**; in myth, the seat of Queen **Hecuba** and King **Priam**, and location of the ten-year Trojan War.

TUDHALIYA IV Son of **Puduhepa** and **Hattusili III**; king of the **Hittites** (*c*.1237–1209 BCE).

TUNNAWIYA **Hittite** 'Old Woman', or female ritual practitioner, and author of ritual texts in the fifteenth century BCE.

TUSHRATTA Father of **Tadu-hepa**; king of **Mittani** in the mid fourteenth century BCE.

ULUBURUN The site (in modern Turkey) of a Late Bronze Age shipwreck.

WANAX **Mycenaean Linear B** term for 'ruler' or 'high king'; in Homer's ancient Greek, this is *anax*.

WILUSA A place located in north-western Anatolia (modern Turkey), identified in the **Hittite** records as the site of hostility between **Ahhiyawans** and Hittites; likely to be the Hittite name for **Troy** (Greek *Ilios*).

XENIA Ancient Greek word for 'guest friendship'; a key theme of the *Odyssey*.

ZEUS (*Myth*) Husband of **Hera**; ancient Greek king of the gods.

NOTES

INTRODUCTION

1 Homer, *Odyssey*, 1.356–9.
2 Mary Beard, *Women and Power: A Manifesto* (Profile Books and London Review of Books, 2017), p. 3.
3 Homer, *Iliad*, 1.565.
4 Homer, *Odyssey*, 1.1; my translation.
5 Iosif Lazaridis et al., 'Genetic Origins of the Minoans and Mycenaeans', *Nature*, vol. 548, no. 7666 (2017), p. 214; Supplementary Information 1, p. 13.
6 Women had a rich vein of song traditions – washing and weaving songs, lullabies – that have been lost to history: see Andromache Karanika, *Voices at Work: Women, Performance, and Labor in Ancient Greece* (Johns Hopkins University Press, 2014).
7 See Eric H. Cline, *After 1177 B.C.: The Survival of Civilizations* (Princeton University Press, 2024), pp. 4–6, 195–9.
8 Thucydides, *The Peloponnesian War*, 2.45.2; Euripides, *Children of Hercules*, 476–7; Sophocles, *Ajax*, 293 (all my translations).
9 Semonides 7.16–18 (translated by Diane Arnson Svarlien).
10 Hilary Mantel, 'The Reith Lectures 1: The Day is for the Living' (BBC Radio 4, 2017).
11 Friedrich Nietzsche, *Beyond Good and Evil*, translated by R. J. Hollingdale (Harmondsworth, 1990), p. 167; Ioannis Kakridis, 'The Role of the Woman in the *Iliad*', *Eranos*, vol. 54 (1956), p. 27.
12 As reported in Donna Zuckerberg, *Not All Dead White Men: Classics and Misogyny in the Digital Age* (Harvard University Press, 2018), p. 28 with n. 32.
13 The post continues: 'Things are improving dramatically at New College of Florida.' Christopher F. Rufo, 22 September 2023, https://twitter.com/realchrisrufo/status/1705248085763346661.
14 Saidiya Hartman, *Wayward Lives, Beautiful Experiments: Intimate Histories of Social Upheaval* (W. W. Norton, 2019), p. 42.
15 Johanna Hanink, 'It's Time to Embrace Critical Classical Reception', *Eidolon*, 1 May 2017, https://eidolon.pub/its-time-to-embrace-critical-classical-reception-d3491a40eec3.
16 There are ancient precedents: Sappho's rewriting of Helen in fr. 16, Euripides' *Trojan Women* and Ovid's *Heroides* are perhaps the most notable examples.
17 Gregory Nagy, *Poetry as Performance: Homer and Beyond* (Cambridge University Press, 1996), pp. 110–14.
18 Andrew Ford, *Homer: The Poetry of the Past* (Cornell University Press, 1992).
19 Moses I. Finley, 'The Trojan War', *Journal of Hellenic Studies*, vol. 84 (1964), p. 9.

20   Homer, *Iliad*, 2.389, 12.402, 20.281: see Martin Litchfield West, 'The Rise of the
     Greek Epic', *Journal of Hellenic Studies*, vol. 108 (1988), pp. 156–7.

21   Richard Seaford, *Reciprocity and Ritual: Homer and Tragedy in the Developing
     City-State* (Clarendon Press, 1994), p. xvii; Oliver Dickinson, 'Homer, the Poet of
     the Dark Age', *Greece & Rome*, vol. 33, no. 1, (1986), p. 24.

22   Moses I. Finley, *The World of Odysseus*, 2nd edition (Penguin, [1954] 1979), p. 20.

23   Ian Rutherford, 'Diplomatic Marriage as an Engine for Religious Change: The
     Case of Assuwa and Ahhiyawa', in *Linguistic and Cultural Interactions Between
     Greece and Anatolia: In Search of the Golden Fleece*, edited by Michele Bianconi
     (Brill, 2021), pp. 167–81.

24   Homer, *Iliad*, 6.168–9.

25   This is the Uluburun shipwreck: see Chapter 13.

1. HELEN: THE FACE

1   Ernst Meyer (ed.), *Briefe von Heinrich Schliemann* (Walter de Gruyter, 1936), p.
     132 (original emphasis), as quoted in D. F. Easton, 'Priam's Gold: The Full Story',
     Anatolian Studies, vol. 44 (1994), p. 224.

2   Easton, 'Priam's Gold', pp. 225, 227, 233.

3   Homer, *Iliad*, 3.243–4; my translation.

4   Ibid., 3.406–9.

5   Ibid., 3.428–9.

6   Ibid., 3.442; my translation.

7   Ibid., 6.344 and 356; my translation.

8   Homer, *Iliad*, 6.356; my translation.

9   Ibid., 6.357–8; my translation.

10   Homer, *Odyssey*, 4.266; my translation.

11   Homer, *Iliad*, 16.702–3; my translation.

12   Richard Claverhouse Jebb, 'Homeric Troy', *Fortnightly Review* NS 35.208 (1884),
     p. 446.

13   Gregory Nagy, 'Observations on Greek Dialects in the Late Second Millennium
     BCE', *Proceedings of the Academy of Athens*, vol. 86, no. 2 (2011), p. 83.

14   Hector W. Catling and Helen Cavanagh, 'Two Inscribed Bronzes from the
     Menelaion, Sparta', *Kadmos*, vol. 15, no. 2 (1976), fig. 1.

15   Theocritus, *Idylls*, 18: see Bettany Hughes, *Helen of Troy: Goddess, Princess,
     Whore* (Jonathan Cape, 2005), pp. 81–3.

16   Danae Coulmas, *Schliemann und Sophia: Eine Liebesgeschichte* (Piper, 2002), p. 8.

17   Matthew Gumpert, *Grafting Helen: The Abduction of the Classical Past*
     (University of Wisconsin Press, 2001).

18   Herodotus, *Histories*, 1.3.1–2.

19   Ovid, *Heroides*, 16–17; *Metamorphoses*, 15.232–3.

20   Laurie Maguire, *Shakespeare's Names* (Oxford University Press, 2007), p. 77.

21   Sappho fr. 16.1–2; my translation.

22   Rhina Espaillat, 'On the Walls', in *Gods and Mortals: Modern Poems on Classical
     Myths*, edited by Nina Kossman (Oxford University Press, 2001), p. 219.

23   Cicero, *On Invention*, 2.1.1–3; Pliny, *Natural History*, 35.64.

24 Hughes, *Helen of Troy*, pp. 25–6.

25 Homer, *Iliad*, 3.121.

26 Bridget M. Thomas, 'Constraints and Contradictions: Whiteness and Femininity in Ancient Greece', in *Women's Dress in the Ancient Greek World*, edited by Lloyd Llewellyn-Jones (Classical Press of Wales, 2002), pp. 5–7, 11.

27 Sappho fr. 23.5, Euripides, *Helen*, 1224.

28 As speculated in Hughes, *Helen of Troy*, p. 65.

29 Jonathan H. Musgrave et al. 'Seven Faces from Grave Circle B at Mycenae', *Annual of the British School at Athens*, vol. 90 (1995), pp. 107–36.

30 Louise Schofield, *The Mycenaeans* (British Museum Press, 2007), p. 35.

31 Andreas Vesalius, *De humani corporis fabrica libri septem* (1543), Book 1.1.

32 Musgrave et al., 'Seven Faces from Grave Circle B at Mycenae', p. 111.

33 Easton, 'Priam's Gold', pp. 233–4.

34 'Ukraine Emergency', https://www.unrefugees.org/emergencies/ukraine/ (last accessed 27 August 2024); 'Ukraine war: UN General Assembly condemns Russia annexation', 13 October 2022, https://www.bbc.co.uk/news/world-63237669 (last accessed 20 January 2024).

35 Homer, *Iliad*, 6.454–5.

2. BRISEIS: SLAVE

1 Margalit Fox, *The Riddle of the Labyrinth: The Quest to Crack an Ancient Code and the Uncovering of a Lost Civilisation* (Profile Books, 2013), pp. 132, 184.

2 The crossword analogy is Michael Ventris's, from his 1 July 1952 BBC radio broadcast announcement of his solution of Linear B: see Michael G. F. Ventris, *Work Notes on Minoan Language Research and Other Unedited Papers* (*Incunabula Graeca*, vol. 90), edited by A. Sacconi (Edizioni dell'Ateneo, 1988), pp. 363–7.

3 Alice E. Kober, ' "Total" in Minoan (Linear Class B)', *Archiv Orientální*, vol. 17 (1949), pp. 386–98.

4 Fox, *The Riddle of the Labyrinth*, p. 305; note that he did not acknowledge Kober in his original BBC broadcast in 1952, only in a lecture in 1954 (as Fox writes, 'too little, too late').

5 See, for example, the documentary *A Very English Genius*, BBC Four, 22 July 2002.

6 Fox, *The Riddle of the Labyrinth*, p. 18.

7 Transcription and translation is from Barbara Ann Olsen, *Women in Mycenaean Greece: The Linear B Tablets from Pylos and Knossos* (Routledge, 2014), p. 121, n. 135.

8 Olsen, *Women in Mycenaean Greece*, p. 67.

9 John Chadwick, 'The Women of Pylos', in *Texts, Tablets and Scribes: Studies in Mycenaean Epigraphy and Economy Offered to Emmett L. Bennett, Jr.*, edited by J.-P. Olivier and T. G. Palaima (Ediciones Universidad de Salamanca, 1988), p. 81.

10 Ibid., pp. 72–3; Olsen, *Women in Mycenaean Greece*, pp. 73, 77.

11 Homer, *Iliad*, 24.675–6.

12 Briseis: Homer, *Iliad*, 19.287–300; Achilles' talking horse (Xanthus): Homer, *Iliad*, 19.408–17.

13   Homer, *Iliad*, 2.689–93.

14   Ibid., 20.191–4; my translation.

15   Homer, *Iliad*, 1.348: see *Homer: The Iliad*, translated by Emily Wilson
     (W. W. Norton, 2023), p. xlviii.

16   Homer, *Iliad*, 6.414–28.

17   Ibid., 6.454–8; see Barbara Graziosi and Johannes Haubold (eds), *Homer:
     Iliad VI* (Cambridge University Press, 2010), p. 46.

18   Homer, *Odyssey*, 8.523–30.

19   Homer, *Iliad*, 2.354–6.

20   Homer, *Iliad*, 9.337–9.

21   Her subsequent fate, as an enslaved woman to Achilles' son Neoptolemus, is told
     in Euripides' tragedy *Andromache* (mid 420s BCE).

22   PY Ep 705: see Kalliopi Efkleidou, 'The Status of "Outsiders" within Mycenaean
     Pylos: Issues of Ethnic Identity, Incorporation and Marginality', *Minos*, vol.
     37 (2002), pp. 277–8, who argues that she is of the higher-status dependent
     personnel.

23   Olsen, *Women in Mycenaean Greece*, pp. 28–9, 109, 111–13.

24   Ibid., pp. 40–41.

25   Efkleidou, 'The Status of "Outsiders" within Mycenaean Pylos', p. 285; Olsen,
     Women in Mycenaean Greece, pp. 78, 86, 109.

26   Chadwick, 'The Women of Pylos', pp. 83, 91–2.

27   Emily Hauser, 'Women in Homer', in *The Cambridge Companion to Greek Epic*,
     edited by Emma Greensmith (Cambridge University Press, 2024), pp. 274–94;
     Nancy Felson and Laura M. Slatkin, 'Gender and Homeric Epic', in *The Cambridge
     Companion to Homer*, edited by Robert Fowler (Cambridge University Press,
     2005), pp. 91–114.

28   Homer, *Iliad*, 22.154–6.

29   The island of Melos; this act of Athenian realpolitik is famously dramatized
     in Thucydides' Melian dialogue (Thucydides, *History of the Peloponnesian
     War*, 5.84–116).

30   Dares Phrygius, *De excidio Troiae historia*; Dictys Cretensis, *Ephemeridos belli
     Troiani libri sex*.

3. CHRYSEIS: DAUGHTER

1   Emily Townsend Vermeule, 'The Promise of Thera: A Bronze Age Pompeii',
     The Atlantic, December 1967, https://www.theatlantic.com/magazine/
     archive/1967/12/the-promise-of-thera/303778/.

2   Spyridon Marinatos, *Excavations at Thera, I–III: 1967–1969 Seasons*, 2nd edition
     (Archaeological Society of Athens, 1999), p. 14.

3   Vermeule, 'The Promise of Thera'.

4   The dating of the Thera eruption has caused much controversy, between those
     who favour an earlier date (around 1600 BCE) based on radiocarbon dating,
     and those who put it around 1500 BCE by connecting extensive comparative
     pottery chronologies to dates in Egyptian history. For an accessible summary,

see Michael Balter, 'New Carbon Dates Support Revised History of Ancient Mediterranean', *Science*, vol. 312 (2006), pp. 508–9.

5 Lyvia Morgan, *The Miniature Wall Paintings of Thera: A Study in Aegean Culture and Iconography* (Cambridge University Press, 1988), p. 4.

6 Homer, *Iliad*, 1.1.

7 Ibid., 1.115.

8 Sara Immerwahr, 'The People in the Frescoes', in *Minoan Society: Proceedings of the Cambridge Colloquium*, edited by O. Krzyszkowska and L. Nixon (Bristol Classical Press, 1983), pp. 143–53.

9 Christos G. Doumas, *Prehistoric Thera* (John S. Latsis Public Benefit Foundation, 2016), pp. 43–8.

10 Nanno Marinatos, 'The West House at Akrotiri as a Cult Center', *Mitteilungen des Deutschen Archäologischen Instituts, Athenische Abteilung*, vol. 98 (1983), pp. 1–19.

11 Marianna Nikolaidou, 'Looking for Minoan and Mycenaean Women: Paths of Feminist Scholarship Towards the Aegean Bronze Age', in *A Companion to Women in the Ancient World*, edited by Sharon L. James and Sheila Dillon (Wiley-Blackwell, 2012), p. 52.

12 Doumas, *Prehistoric Thera*, p. 264.

13 Louise Hitchcock, 'Entangled Threads: Who Owned the West House at Akrotiri?', *Journal of Prehistoric Religion*, vol. 25 (2016), pp. 25–9.

14 Sarah P. Morris, 'A Tale of Two Cities: The Miniature Frescoes from Thera and the Origins of Greek Poetry', *The American Journal of Archaeology*, vol. 93, no. 4 (1989), pp. 522–3.

15 Homer, *Iliad*, 22.154–6.

16 Ibid., 6.457.

17 Boar's-tusk helmet: Homer, *Iliad*, 10.261–71; body shield: ibid., 2.389, 12.402, 20.281.

18 Morris, 'A Tale of Two Cities', pp. 511–35.

19 Martin Litchfield West, 'The Rise of the Greek Epic', *Journal of Hellenic Studies*, vol. 108 (1988), pp. 156–9; Joachim Latacz, *Troy and Homer: Towards a Solution of an Old Mystery*, translated by Kevin Windle and Rosh Ireland (Oxford University Press, 2004), pp. 267–74.

20 Thomas F. Strasser and Anne P. Chapin, 'Geological Formations in the Flotilla Fresco from Akrotiri', in *Physis: l'environnement naturel et la relation homme-milieu dans le monde égéen protohistorique*, edited by Gilles Touchais et al. (Peeters, 2014), pp. 57–66.

21 Note the alternative tradition (not mentioned in Homer) at Pausanias, *Description of Greece*, 3.20.10–11, that Icarius tried unsuccessfully to persuade Odysseus to settle in Sparta; Penelope chose to leave with her husband.

22 PY An 654.8–9.

23 Jonathan H. Musgrave et al. 'Seven Faces from Grave Circle B at Mycenae', *Annual of the British School at Athens*, vol. 90 (1995), p. 111.

24 Ibid., pp. 119–21; Schliemann's famous so-called 'Mask of Agamemnon' (too early to really be Agamemnon's, just like 'Helen's' so-called jewels) was discovered in Grave Circle A.

25   Abigail S. Bouwman et al., 'Kinship between Burials from Grave Circle B at
     Mycenae Revealed by Ancient DNA Typing', *Journal of Archaeological Science*,
     vol. 35, no. 9 (2008), p. 2583.

26   Although it's most likely that they're siblings, they could also be first or second
     cousins, but still through the maternal line: Abigail S. Bouwman et al., 'Kinship
     in Aegean Prehistory? Ancient DNA in Human Bones from Mainland Greece
     and Crete', *Annual of the British School at Athens*, vol. 104 (2009), p. 306.

27   Eirini Skourtanioti et al., 'Ancient DNA Reveals Admixture History and
     Endogamy in the Prehistoric Aegean', *Nature Ecology & Evolution*, vol. 7 (2023),
     pp. 290–303.

28   Ibid., Supplementary Information 1, pp. 39–41, individuals with IDs AID012,
     AID014, AID017.

29   Kalliopi Efkleidou, 'Looking for Houses in the Tombs: The Evidence for House
     Societies in the Mycenaean Argolid', in *Oikos: Archaeological Approaches to
     House Societies in the Bronze Age Aegean*, edited by Maria Relaki and Jan
     Driessen (Presses universitaires de Louvain, 2020), p. 299.

30   Margalit Finkelberg, 'Royal Succession in Heroic Greece', *Classical Quarterly*,
     vol. 41, no. 2 (1991), pp. 305–6.

31   Oliver Dickinson et al., 'Mycenae Revisited Part 4: Assessing the New Data',
     Annual of the British School at Athens, vol. 107 (2012), p. 177.

32   Paul Rehak, 'Crocus Costumes in Aegean Art', in *Hesperia Supplements*, vol. 33:
     XAPIΣ: Essays in Honor of Sara A. Immerwahr (American School of Classical
     Studies at Athens, 2004), pp. 85–100.

33   Gregory Nagy, 'Homeric Poetry and Problems of Multiformity: The
     "Panathenaic Bottleneck" ', *Classical Philology*, vol. 96, no. 2 (2001), pp. 109–19.

34   Gregory Nagy, *Homer the Classic* (Center for Hellenic Studies, 2009), p. 450.

35   Francesca Schironi, *The Best of the Grammarians: Aristarchus of Samothrace on
     the Iliad* (University of Michigan Press, 2018), p. 607.

4. HECUBA: QUEEN

1   Machteld J. Mellink and Kathleen M. Quinn, 'Hetty Goldman (1881–1972)', in
     Breaking Ground: Pioneering Women Archaeologists, edited by Getzel M. Cohen
     and Martha Sharp Joukowsky (University of Michigan Press, 2004), p. 321.

2   Hetty Goldman, 'Preliminary Expedition to Cilicia, 1934, and Excavations at
     Gözlü Kule, Tarsus, 1935', *American Journal of Archaeology*, vol. 39, no. 4 (1935),
     p. 527.

3   Hetty Goldman, 'Excavations at Gözlü Kule, Tarsus, 1936', *American Journal of
     Archaeology*, vol. 41, no. 2 (1937), p. 267.

4   Known as Luwian hieroglyphs, after the Anatolian people whose language was
     spoken by the majority of the Hittite Empire during the Hittite New Kingdom.

5   Homer, *Iliad*, 16.719; my translation.

6   Ibid., 6.242–50.

7   Ibid., 11.101–2, 21.84–5, 22.46–8, 24.496.

8   Ibid., 6.289–92.

9   Ibid., 6.286–311.

10   Hilda L. Lorimer, *Homer and the Monuments* (Macmillan, 1950), p. 445.

11   Mary Bachvarova, *From Hittite to Homer: The Anatolian Background of Ancient Greek Epic* (Cambridge University Press, 2016), pp. 199–265.

12   Jan Paul Crielaard, 'Basileis at Sea: Elites and External Contacts in the Euboean Gulf Region from the End of the Bronze Age to the Beginning of the Iron Age', in *Ancient Greece: From the Mycenaean Palaces to the Age of Homer*, edited by S. Deger-Jalkotsy and I. S. Lemos, Edinburgh Leventis Studies 3 (Edinburgh University Press, 2006), pp. 286–7.

13   Martin Litchfield West, *The East Face of Helicon: West Asiatic Elements in Greek Poetry and Myth* (Oxford University Press, 1997); Johannes Haubold, *Greece and Mesopotamia: Dialogues in Literature* (Cambridge University Press, 2013), pp. 18–72.

14   Bachvarova, *From Hittite to Homer*, pp. 166–98.

15   West, *The East Face of Helicon*, p. viii.

16   Bachvarova, *From Hittite to Homer*, pp. 234–65.

17   The title of this section ('Then the Ships Came') is a quote from a Hittite letter mentioning a journey to Ahhiyawa, *AhT* 25 = *CTH* 581: see Gary M. Beckman et al., *The Ahhiyawa Texts* (Society of Biblical Literature, 2011), p. 247.

18   Trevor Bryce, 'The Role and Status of Women in Hittite Society', in *Women in Antiquity: Real Women Across the Ancient World*, edited by Stephanie Lynn Budin and Jean Macintosh Turfa (Routledge, 2016), p. 306.

19   *AhT* 26 = *CTH* 590: text and commentary are in Beckman et al., *The Ahhiyawa Texts*, pp. 248–52.

20   The text that provides evidence for this is known as the Tawagalawa letter (*AhT* 4 = *CTH* 181): see Beckman et al., *The Ahhiyawa Texts*, pp. 101–22, especially pp. 115–17.

21   *AhT* 4 §12: see Beckman et al., *The Ahhiyawa Texts*, p. 115.

22   This is the so-called 'Ahhiyawa question', first initiated by Emil Forrer in 1924. On 'Achaean' as the likely term used by the Mycenaeans, see Gregory Nagy, 'Observations on Greek Dialects in the Late Second Millennium BCE', *Proceedings of the Academy of Athens*, vol. 86, no. 2 (2011), p. 85.

23   Stephen Scully, *Homer and the Sacred City* (Cornell University Press, 1994), pp. 7–8: note also *Pergamon*, for the walled citadel, and *Ilion*, used once in Homer, *Iliad*, 15.70–71 (hence Latin *Ilium*).

24   Trevor Bryce, *The Routledge Handbook of the Peoples and Places of Ancient Western Asia: From the Early Bronze Age to the Fall of the Persian Empire* (Routledge, 2009), pp. 692–3.

25   Homer, *Odyssey*, 11.521; Paul Kretschmer, 'Der Name der Lykier und andere kleinasiatische Völkernamen', *Kleinasiatische Forschungen*, vol. 1 (1930), p. 8.

26   Most scholars associate Tawagalawa (the name of the brother of the Ahhiyawan king) with the Greek name Eteocles, Linear B *E-te-wo-ke-le-we*: see Beckman et al., *The Ahhiyawa Texts*, p. 120.

27   Nikoletta Kanavou, *The Names of Homeric Heroes: Problems and Interpretations* (Walter de Gruyter, 2015), pp. 83–6. On 'Paris' and 'Priam' as apparently Luwian names in origin, see Calvert Watkins, 'The Language of the Trojans', in *Troy and the Trojan War: A Symposium Held at Bryn Mawr College, October 1984*,

edited by Machteld Johanna Mellink (Bryn Mawr Commentaries, 1986), pp. 56–8.

28 Sarah Morris, 'From Kizzuwatna to Troy: Puduhepa, Piyamaradu, and Anatolian Ritual in Homer', in *Proceedings of the 24th Annual UCLA Indo-European Conference*, edited by Stephanie W. Jamison et al. (Hempen, 2013), pp. 151–67.

29 Duane Roller, 'When is a Queen Truly a Queen: The Term *Basileia* in Greek Literature', *Society for Classical Studies 149*, 5 January 2018, https://classicalstudies.org/when-queen-truly-queen-term-basileia-greek-literature.

30 On the Mycenaean 'glass ceiling', see Cynthia W. Shelmerdine, 'Women in the Mycenaean Economy', in *Women in Antiquity: Real Women Across the Ancient World*, edited by Stephanie Lynn Budin and Jean MacIntosh Turfa (Routledge, 2016), pp. 618, 632.

31 PY Ep 704: see Shelmerdine, 'Women in the Mycenaean Economy', pp. 619–20.

32 Morris, 'From Kizzuwatna to Troy', p. 153.

33 Homer, *Iliad*, 6.299: see Morris, 'From Kizzuwatna to Troy', p. 155.

34 Hans G. Güterbock, 'Observations on the Tarsus Seal of Puduhepa, Queen of Ḫatti', *Journal of the American Oriental Society*, vol. 117, no. 1 (1997), p. 144.

35 Morris, 'From Kizzuwatna to Troy', p. 156.

36 On Kubaba and Hecuba, see Rostislav Oreshko, 'In Search of the Holy Cube Roots: Kubaba – Kubeleya – Κύβεβος – Kufaws and the Problem of Ethnocultural Contact in Early Iron Age Anatolia', in *Linguistic and Cultural Interactions Between Greece and Anatolia: In Search of the Golden Fleece*, edited by Michele Bianconi (Brill, 2021), p. 152; on Puduhepa and Hebat, see Stefano de Martino, 'Hurrian Theophoric Names in the Documents from the Hittite Kingdom', in *Theonyms, Panthea and Syncretisms in Hittite Anatolia and Northern Syria: Proceedings of the TeAI Workshop Held in Verona, March 25–26, 2022*, edited by Livio Warbinek and Federico Giusfredi (Firenze University Press, 2023), p. 92.

37 Homer, *Iliad*, 6.311.

38 *CTH* 772.1 = *KBo* 4.ll, 45–6; *KUB* XXXV.I02(+)I03 III.11. The translations are from Watkins, 'The Language of the Trojans', pp. 58 and 60.

39 Six times in the *Iliad*: 2.811, 6.327, 11.181, 11.711, 13.773, 15.71.

40 Bachvarova, *From Hittite to Homer*, pp. 418–57.

41 Watkins, 'The Language of the Trojans', p. 59.

42 Beckman et al., *The Ahhiyawa Texts*, p. 279.

43 'Replica of Peace Treaty between Hattusilis and Ramses II', https://www.un.org/ungifts/replica-peace-treaty-between-hattusilis-and-ramses-ii.

5. ANDROMACHE: WIFE

1 Now the Max Planck Institute for Geoanthropology.

2 Eirini Skourtanioti et al., 'Ancient DNA Reveals Admixture History and Endogamy in the Prehistoric Aegean', *Nature Ecology & Evolution*, vol. 7 (2023), p. 291.

3 Ibid., pp. 296–7.

4 Iosif Lazaridis et al., 'The Genetic History of the Southern Arc: A Bridge

between West Asia and Europe', in *Science*, vol. 377, no. 6609 (2022), Supplementary Information, p. 137.

5   T. Matney et al., 'Understanding Early Bronze Age Social Structure through Mortuary Remains: A Pilot aDNA Study from Titriş Höyük, Southeastern Turkey', *International Journal of Osteoarchaeology*, vol. 22, no. 3 (2012), pp. 338–51.

6   Homer, *Odyssey*, 10.11–12.

7   Ibid., 7.63–6.

8   Argyro Nafplioti, 'Mycenae Revisited Part 2. Exploring the Local Versus Non-Local Geographical Origin of the Individuals from Grave Circle A: Evidence from Strontium Isotope Ratio ($^{87}Sr/^{86}Sr$) Analysis', *Annual of the British School at Athens*, vol. 104 (2009), pp. 279–91.

9   Oliver Dickinson et al., 'Mycenae Revisited Part 4: Assessing the New Data', *Annual of the British School at Athens*, vol. 107 (2012), pp. 181–3.

10 PY Vn34 + 1191 + 1006 + fr.: see Barbara Ann Olsen, *Women in Mycenaean Greece: The Linear B Tablets from Pylos and Knossos* (Routledge, 2014), pp. 150–53.

11 Homer, *Iliad*, 6.396–7.

12 I am indebted for these readings to Marylin B. Arthur, 'The Divided World of *Iliad* VI', *Women's Studies*, vol. 8, nos. 1–2 (1981), pp. 32–7, and Barbara Graziosi and Johannes Haubold (eds), *Homer: Iliad VI* (Cambridge University Press, 2010), pp. 44–7.

13 Wine: Homer, *Iliad*, 6.264–5; blood: 6.266–8; spear: 6.319–20.

14 Homer, *Iliad*, 6.370–80.

15 Ibid., 6.429–30.

16 Homer, *Odyssey*, 6.182–4.

17 Hector does return to Troy at *Iliad*, 7.307–10, but nothing is said of Andromache, so this is effectively their final parting.

18 Homer, *Iliad*, 6.490–3.

19 Emma Bridges, *Warriors' Wives: Ancient Greek Myth and Modern Experience* (Oxford University Press, 2023), pp. 24–31.

20 As later recounted in Euripides, *Trojan Women*, 712–79.

21 Homer, *Iliad*, 6.357–8; my translation.

22 Sappho fr. 44 L-P.

23 Melissa Mueller, *Sappho and Homer: A Reparative Reading* (Cambridge University Press, 2023), pp. 132–53.

24 Euripides, *Andromache* (mid 420s BCE) and *Trojan Women* (415 BCE).

25 Jean Racine, *Andromaque* (performed 1667, published 1668).

26 Plutarch, *Brutus*, 994d-e.

6. CASSANDRA: PROPHET

1   Constantine Bida, *Lesya Ukrainka: Life and Work*, translated by Vera Rich (University of Toronto Press, 1968), pp. 11–12.

2   See 'Do Moho Fortepyano' ('To My Piano'): ibid., p. 8.

3   Lesia Ukrainka, *Cassandra*, translated by Nina Murray (Harvard University Press, 2024), p. 145.

4   Ibid., p. 105.

5   Hugo Winckler, 'Die im Sommer 1906 in Kleinasien ausgeführten Ausgrabungen', *Orientalistische Literaturzeitung*, vol. 9, no. 1–6 (1906), p. 626.

6   Homer, *Iliad*, 13.365–6, 24.697–706.

7   Aeschylus' *Agamemnon* (458 BCE) and Euripides' *Trojan Women* (415 BCE), as well as Euripides' lost *Alexander* (also 415 BCE).

8   Aeschylus, *Agamemnon*, 1202–13: later authors follow this story.

9   Pindar, *Paean* 8a (P. Oxy. 52i(A)).

10 *TrGF* 5 F41a-63.

11 Virgil, *Aeneid*, 2.246–7.

12 This is relayed in the lost *Iliou Persis*, summarized by Proclus.

13 Euripides, *Trojan Women*, 308–461.

14 Aeschylus, *Agamemnon*, 1072–1330.

15 Ibid., 1212.

16 Diodorus Siculus, *Library of History*, 4.66.5f; Pliny, *Natural History*, 7.56.205; Plutarch, *On the Oracles of the Pythia*, 402d; Pausanias, *Description of Greece*, 10.5.7; *Sibylline Oracles*, 3.419–25.

17 Virginia Woolf, *A Room of One's Own and Three Guineas*, edited by Anna Snaith (Oxford University Press, [1929] 2015), p. 38.

18 Diodorus Siculus, *Library of History*, 4.66.5f.

19 For another ancient theory around Homer's plagiarism of a woman – this time a female poet called Phantasia – see Daisy Dunn, *The Missing Thread: A New History of the Ancient World Through the Women Who Shaped It* (Weidenfeld & Nicolson, 2024), pp. 9–11.

20 Pindar, *Pythian Odes*, 3.29; my translation.

21 Homer, *Iliad*, 2.485; my translation.

22 See Homer, *Odyssey*, 22.347–8 (on the poet Phemius) and 17.382–5 (on the poet as craftsman).

23 Hesiod, *Theogony*, 217–19.

24 Homer, *Iliad*, 22.209–13; cf. 24.527–33.

25 The *Moirai* only occur once in Homer in the plural, at *Iliad* 24.49.

26 Homer, *Iliad*, 1.566–7.

27 Ibid., 9.412–16.

28 Ibid., 18.114–25.

29 *AhT* 20 = *KUB* 5.6 = *Bo* 2044 + 7094-1: for the text, see Gary M. Beckman et al. (eds), *The Ahhiyawa Texts* (Society of Biblical Literature, 2011), pp. 183–209.

30 For the date, see Beckman et al., *The Ahhiyawa Texts*, pp. 209, 272, 287.

31 Trevor Bryce, 'The Role and Status of Women in Hittite Society', in *Women in Antiquity: Real Women across the Ancient World*, edited by Stephanie Lynn Budin and Jean Macintosh Turfa (Routledge, 2016), p. 316.

32 Sarah Morris, 'From Kizzuwatna to Troy: Puduhepa, Piyamaradu, and Anatolian Ritual in Homer', in *Proceedings of the 24th Annual UCLA Indo-European Conference*, edited by Stephanie W. Jamison et al. (Hempen, 2013), pp. 156–7.

33 Where she is called Matanazi: see Beckman et al., *The Ahhiyawa Texts*, p. 209.

34 *AhT* 20 §24, translation from Ian Rutherford, *Hittite Texts and Greek*

Religion: Contact, Interaction, and Comparison (Oxford University Press, 2020), p. 106.

35   Alfonso Archi, 'Aštata: A Case of Hittite Imperial Religious Policy', *Journal of Ancient Near Eastern Religions*, vol. 14, no. 2 (2014), p. 146.

36   Rutherford, *Hittite Texts and Greek Religion*, pp. 133–5.

37   Homer, *Iliad*, 1.62–3.

38   *Cypria* fr. 1 West; my translation.

39   *Homer: The Iliad*, translated by Emily Wilson (W. W. Norton, 2023), p. lix; Natalie Haynes and Emily Wilson, 'The *Iliad*: How Modern Readers Get This Epic Wrong', *BBC Culture*, 5 October 2023, https://www.bbc.com/culture/article/20231004-the-iliad-the-ultimate-story-about-war.

40   Jürgen Seeher, 'After the Empire: Observations on the Early Iron Age in Central Anatolia', in *Ipamati kistamati pari tumatimis: Luwian and Hittite Studies Presented to J. David Hawkins on the Occasion of His 70th Birthday*, edited by Itamar Singer (Institute of Archaeology, Tel Aviv University, 2010), pp. 220–21.

41   Sturt W. Manning et al., 'Severe Multi-Year Drought Coincident with Hittite Collapse around 1198–1196 BC', *Nature*, vol. 614 (2023), pp. 719–24.

42   Eric H. Cline, *1177 BC: The Year Civilization Collapsed*, 2nd edition (Princeton University Press, 2021), pp. 157–66.

43   *KUB* 21.38 obv. 17f.

44   The 'perfect storm' theory: see Cline, *1177 BC*, pp. 162–4.

45   Doris Lessing, *The Wind Blows Away Our Words* (Picador, 1987), p. 16.

46   Nancy Sorkin Rabinowitz, 'Christa Wolf's *Cassandra*: Different Times, Different Views', in *Homer's Daughters: Women's Responses to Homer in the Twentieth Century and Beyond*, edited by Fiona Cox and Elena Theodorakopoulos (Oxford University Press, 2019), p. 85.

47   See Ukrainka's letter to Olga Kobylyanska dated 27 March 1903, https://www.l-ukrainka.name/uk/Dramas/Kassandra.html, explaining why she chose to write about Cassandra: 'She knows that her beloved Troy will perish, along with her family and everything dear to her. She must speak the truth aloud because it is true' (translated by Yuliya Kostyuk). See also Olesya Khromeychuk and Sasha Dovzhyk, 'Ukrainian Cassandras', *London Ukrainian Review*, vol. 2 (August 2022), https://www.londonukrainianreview.org/posts/editorial.

48   Lesia Ukrainka, *Cassandra*, translated by Nina Murray (Harvard University Press, 2024), p. 39.

49   Ibid., p. 189.

7. APHRODITE AND HERA: SEDUCER AND MATRIARCH

1   Cathy Gere, *Knossos and the Prophets of Modernism* (University of Chicago Press, 2009), p. 76.

2   Joan Evans, *Time and Chance: The Story of Arthur Evans and His Forebears* (Longmans, Green, 1943), p. 312.

3   In his diary entry for 21 March 1894, after being shown around Kalokairinos's excavations, Evans wrote, 'I see no reason for not thinking that the mysterious

complication of passages is the Labyrinth': see Ann Brown and Keith Bennett (eds), *Arthur Evans's Travels in Crete: 1894-1899* (BAR Publishing, 2001), p. 12.

4   J. Lesley Fitton, *The Discovery of the Greek Bronze Age* (British Museum Press, 1995), p. 134.

5   On snakes, see Daniel Ogden, *Drakōn: Dragon Myth and Serpent Cult in the Greek and Roman Worlds* (Oxford University Press, 2013), pp. 8-9.

6   Arthur J. Evans, *The Palace of Minos at Knossos*, 4 vols (Macmillan, 1921-35), vol. 2, p. 277.

7   Evans, *The Palace of Minos at Knossos*, vol. 1, pp. 430-35.

8   Goddess and priestess: Evans, *The Palace of Minos at Knossos*, vol. 1, pp. 500-504. Both priestesses: Friedrich Matz, *Göttererscheinung und Kultbild im minoischen Kreta* (Wiesbaden, 1958), ch. 2.

9   Gere, *Knossos and the Prophets of Modernism*, pp. 106-11; though note, for a positive view, Nanno Marinatos, *Sir Arthur Evans and Minoan Crete: Creating the Vision of Knossos* (I. B. Tauris, 2015), pp. 107-26.

10 Evans, *The Palace of Minos at Knossos*, vol. 3, p. 457.

11 Cynthia Eller, 'Two Knights and a Goddess: Sir Arthur Evans, Sir James George Frazer, and the Invention of Minoan Religion', *Journal of Mediterranean Archaeology*, vol. 25, no. 1 (2012), pp. 88-95; Gere, *Knossos and the Prophets of Modernism*, pp. 77-80, 86-9.

12 On the forgeries, see Kenneth Lapatin, *Mysteries of the Snake Goddess: Art, Desire, and the Forging of History* (Da Capo Press, 2002), pp. 153-75, also pp. 67-73.

13 Evans, *The Palace of Minos at Knossos*, vol. 1, p. 503; vol. 3, pp. 444-8; vol. 4, pp. 31-3. See John G. Younger, 'Waist Compression in the Aegean Late Bronze Age', *Archaeological News*, vol. 23 (1998-2000), pp. 1-9.

14 Homer, *Odyssey*, 8.266-366.

15 Ibid., 8.274-5.

16 Homer, *Iliad*, 14.166-86.

17 Ibid., 14.214-17. 'Decorated belt' is my own translation.

18 Lilah Grace Canevaro, *Women of Substance in Homeric Epic: Objects, Gender, Agency* (Oxford University Press, 2018), p. 217.

19 Homer, *Iliad*, 14.175.

20 Homer, *Iliad*, 14.315-17, 321-2.

21 Homer, *Iliad*, 14.219, 223: see Christopher A. Faraone, 'Aphrodite's ΚΕΣΤΟΣ and Apples for Atalanta: Aphrodisiacs in Early Greek Myth and Ritual', *Phoenix*, vol. 44, no. 3 (1990), pp. 220-21.

22 Robert Arnott, 'Healing and Medicine in the Aegean Bronze Age', *Journal of the Royal Society of Medicine*, vol. 89, no. 5 (1996), p. 267.

23 Homer, *Iliad*, 21.470. See Sarah Morris, 'Potnia Aswiya: Anatolian Contributions to Greek Religion', in *Potnia: Deities and Religion in the Aegean Bronze Age*, edited by Robert Laffineur and Robin Hägg (Université de Liège, 2001), pp. 423-34.

24 Trevor Bryce, *The Kingdom of the Hittites* (Oxford University Press, 2005), pp. 124-7.

25 Ian Rutherford, *Hittite Texts and Greek Religion: Contact, Interaction, and Comparison* (Oxford University Press, 2020), pp. 109–13.

26 Syncretism is a word that actually has a connection to Crete. It was first used by the ancient historian Plutarch, to describe a federation of Cretans – from *sun-* = 'together' and *Krētes* = 'Cretans': Plutarch, *On Brotherly Love*, 19.

27 Charles Halton and Saana Svärd (eds), *Women's Writing of Ancient Mesopotamia: An Anthology of the Earliest Female Authors* (Cambridge University Press, 2018), p. 64 = *ETCSL* 4.80.1, lines 198–209; p. 80 = *ETCSL* 4.07.3, lines 1–38.

28 The Old Babylonian Ammiditana hymn: the translation is from Martin Litchfield West, *The East Face of Helicon: West Asiatic Elements in Greek Poetry and Myth* (Oxford University Press, 1997), p. 384.

29 Translation in Christopher A. Faraone, *Ancient Greek Love Magic* (Harvard University Press, 1999), p. 101.

30 Known as *egalkura* spells: Faraone, 'Aphrodite's ΚΕΣΤΟΣ and Apples for Atalanta', pp. 223–4.

31 Homer, *Iliad*, 18.395–405, *Homeric Hymn to Apollo*, 316–20. See also the alternative version where he is thrown by Zeus: Homer, *Iliad*, 1.590–94.

32 Canevaro, *Women of Substance in Homeric Epic*, p. 110.

33 Homer, *Odyssey*, 8.447–8 (barely a hundred lines after the story of Hephaestus and Aphrodite, and also a *desmos*).

34 Evans, *The Palace of Minos at Knossos*, vol. 1, p. 434.

35 Stylianos Alexiou, 'Contribution to the Study of the Minoan "Sacred Knot"', in *Studien zur Geschichte und Epigraphik der Frühen Aegaeis: Festschrift für Ernst Grumach*, edited by William C. Brice (Walter de Gruyter, 1967), p. 4.

36 Bizarrely, this resemblance was first noted by a Victorian prime minister of the United Kingdom, William Gladstone; see West, *The East Face of Helicon*, pp. 147, 383.

37 West, *The East Face of Helicon*, p. 147.

38 Evans, *The Palace of Minos at Knossos*, vol. 1, p. 500.

39 See Robert Graves, *The White Goddess: A Historical Grammar of Poetic Myth*, 6th edition (Farrar, Straus and Giroux, [1948] 1973), pp. 99–107.

40 Fiona Benson, *Ephemeron* (Jonathan Cape, 2022), pp. 53–97.

41 Ibid., pp. 114–15.

42 Ibid., p. 67.

43 Jennifer Saint, *Ariadne* (Wildfire, 2021), pp. 18–19.

44 PY Un 443 + 998 (*po-re-no-zo-te-ri-ja*): see Roger D. Woodard, 'Linear B *po-re-na, po-re-si, and po-re-no-*', *Classical Inquiries*, 4 February 2018, https://classical-inquiries.chs.harvard.edu/linear-b-po-re-na-po-re-si-and-po-re-no/.

8. THETIS: MOTHER

1 Erik Hallager and Maria Andreadaki-Vlazaki, 'The Greek-Swedish-Danish Excavations 2014: A Preliminary Report', *Proceedings of the Danish Institute at Athens*, vol. 8 (2017), pp. 287–91.

2 Photini J. P. McGeorge, 'The Pit L Baby Burial – Hermeneutics: Implications for

Immigration into Kydonia in MMIII/LMI', *Proceedings of the Danish Institute at Athens*, vol. 8 (2017), pp. 294, 296, 298.

3   Photini J. P. McGeorge, 'Intramural Infant Burials in the Aegean Bronze Age: Reflections on Symbolism and Eschatology with Particular Reference to Crete', in *Le mort dans la ville: pratiques, contextes et impacts des inhumations intramuros en Anatolie, du début de l'Âge du Bronze à l'époque romaine*, edited by Olivier Henry (Institut français d'études anatoliennes, 2013), p. 4.

4   Maria Andreadaki-Vlazaki, 'The Arrival of the Mycenaeans at Kydonia: Ancient Tradition and Archaeological Evidence', in *One State, Many Worlds: Crete in the Late Minoan II–IIIA2 Early Period. Proceedings of the International Conference Held at Khania, Μεγάλο Αρσενάλι, 21st–23rd November 2019*, edited by Anna Lucia D'Agata et al. (Edizioni Quasar, 2022), pp. 193–212.

5   Eirini Skourtanioti et al., 'Ancient DNA Reveals Admixture History and Endogamy in the Prehistoric Aegean', *Nature Ecology & Evolution*, vol. 7 (2023), pp. 294, 297.

6   Güllog Nordquist and Anne Ingvarsson-Sundström, 'Live Hard, Die Young: Mortuary Remains of Middle and Early Late Helladic Children from the Argolid in Social Context', in *Autochthon: Papers Presented to O. T. P. K. Dickinson on the Occasion of His Retirement*, edited by Anastasia Dakouri-Hild and Susan Sherratt, British Archaeological Reports International Series 1432 (BAR Publishing, 2005), p. 162.

7   McGeorge, 'The Pit L Baby Burial', p. 298.

8   Homer, *Iliad*, 24. 93–4, 105; my translation (the Greek phrase is *penthos alaston*).

9   Ibid., 18.432–4; my translation.

10 Pindar, *Isthmian Odes*, 8.26–48.

11 Pindar, *Nemean Odes*, 3.35–6; 4.61–5; Ovid, *Metamorphoses*, 11.221–65.

12 Homer, *Iliad*, 1.414; the first question is my translation, the second is Wilson's.

13 Ibid., 18.54; my translation.

14 Homer, *Iliad*, 1.418, 18.56.

15 Homer, *Iliad*, 9.412–16.

16 Ibid., 1.495–533.

17 Ibid., 1.528–30: for the reminder about Achilles' mortality (a direct consequence of Zeus keeping a hold on power and Achilles not being his son), see 1.505–6; and 1.396–405, for the remarkable story of how Thetis freed Zeus.

18 Laura M. Slatkin, *The Power of Thetis and Selected Essays* (Center for Hellenic Studies, 2011), p. 31.

19 Homer, *Iliad*, 8.370.

20 Homer, *Iliad*, 18.457–61. The falcon simile in Homer is on Thetis' return: 18.616–17.

21 Ibid., 24.131–2.

22 Gregory Nagy, *The Best of the Achaeans: Concepts of the Hero in Archaic Greek Poetry*, 2nd edition (Johns Hopkins University Press, [1979] 1999), pp. 16–18.

23 Ibid., p. 94.

24 Slatkin, *The Power of Thetis*, p. 47.

25 Homer, *Iliad*, 16.440–57.

26 Ibid., 5.311–45.

27 Zeus doesn't experience labour, but he does 'give birth' in a sense, in the myth of the birth of Athena from his head: see Chapter 10, and Hesiod, *Theogony*, 886–900; fr. 343 M-W.

28 *Homeric Hymn to Apollo*, 91–119.

29 Homer, *Iliad*, 11.269–70.

30 Homer, *Odyssey*, 19.188.

31 KN Gg 705.

32 Margalit Fox, *The Riddle of the Labyrinth: The Quest to Crack an Ancient Code and the Uncovering of a Lost Civilisation* (Profile Books, 2013), pp. 268–80.

33 Pausanias, *Description of Greece*, 1.18.5.

34 Carl Kerényi, *Dionysos: Archetypal Image of Indestructible Life*, translated by Ralph Manheim (Princeton University Press, 1977), fig. 6.

35 Simone Zimmermann Kuoni, 'The Obstetric Connection: Midwives and Weasels Within and Beyond Minoan Crete', *Religions*, vol. 12 (2021), pp. 1–30.

36 Pliny, *Natural History*, 30.43.14. Oxytocin is used for the same purpose today, though in the form of a synthetic medication, not weasel secretion!

37 Kuoni, 'The Obstetric Connection', pp. 7, 11.

38 Birgitta P. Hallager and Photini J. P. McGeorge, *Late Minoan III Burials at Khania: The Tombs, Finds and Deceased in Odos Palama* (Paul Åström, 1992), pp. 37–8.

39 Ibid., pp. 32, 37.

40 Lynne A. Schepartz et al., 'No Seat at the Table? Mycenaean Women's Diet and Health in Pylos, Greece', in *Anthropology à la Carte: The Evolution and Diversity of Human Diet*, edited by Lynne A. Schepartz (Cognella, 2011), pp. 359–74.

41 Susan Sherratt, 'Feasting in Homeric Epic', *Hesperia*, vol. 73, no. 2 (2004), p. 304.

42 Hallager and McGeorge, *Late Minoan III Burials at Khania*, p. 38.

43 Lynne A. Schepartz et al., 'Mycenaean Hierarchy and Gender Roles: Diet and Health Inequalities in Late Bronze Age Pylos, Greece', in *Bones of Complexity: Bioarchaeological Case Studies of Social Organization and Skeletal Biology*, edited by Haagen D. Klaus et al. (University Press of Florida, 2017), pp. 164–7.

44 Nordquist and Ingvarsson-Sundström, 'Live Hard, Die Young', pp. 163–4.

45 Stephanie Lynn Budin, 'Maternity in the Bronze Age Aegean', in *Women in Antiquity: Real Women across the Ancient World*, edited by Stephanie Lynn Budin and Jean Macintosh Turfa (Routledge, 2016), p. 599.

46 Anne Ingvarsson-Sundström, *Asine III: Children Lost and Found: A Bioarchaeological Study of Middle Helladic Children in Asine with a Comparison to Lerna* (Swedish Institute at Athens, 2008), p. 95.

47 Carina Iezzi, 'Regional Differences in the Health Status of the Mycenaean Women of East Lokris', in *New Directions in the Skeletal Biology of Greece*, edited by Lynne A. Schepartz et al. (American School of Classical Studies, 2009), pp. 185–6.

48 Budin, 'Maternity in the Bronze Age Aegean', pp. 595, 599.

49 Ibid., p. 599.

50 Nordquist and Ingvarsson-Sundström, 'Live Hard, Die Young', pp. 161–2.

51   Ibid., p. 162.

52   Hallager and McGeorge, *Late Minoan III Burials at Khania*, pp. 45–6.

53   Photini J. P. McGeorge, 'Health and Diet in Minoan Times', in *New Aspects of Archaeological Science in Greece. Proceedings of a Meeting Held at the British School at Athens, January 1987*, edited by Richard E. Jones and Hector W. Catling (British School at Athens, 1988), p. 48.

54   McGeorge, 'Intramural Infant Burials in the Aegean Bronze Age', p. 2.

55   Budin, 'Maternity in the Bronze Age Aegean', p. 596.

56   Nordquist and Ingvarsson-Sundström, 'Live Hard, Die Young', pp. 163–4.

57   Yannis Tzedakis and Holley Martlew, *Minoans and Mycenaeans: Flavours of Their Time. National Archaeological Museum, 12 July–27 November 1999* (Kapon Editions, 1999), p. 158.

58   Kim Shelton, 'Petsas House, Pottery Production, and the Mycenaean People in LH IIIA2', in *RA-PI-NE-U: Studies on the Mycenaean World Offered to Robert Laffineur for His 70th Birthday*, edited by Jan Driessen (Presses universitaires de Louvain, 2016), pp. 322–4. I owe the 'trainer/sippy cup' formulation to Kim Shelton (in a personal communication).

59   Though note a small number of scenes representing lamenting men, as pointed out in Margaretha Kramer-Hajos, 'Mourning on the Larnakes at Tanagra: Gender and Agency in Late Bronze Age Greece', *Hesperia*, vol. 84, no. 4 (2015), p. 634.

60   Homer, *Iliad*, 24.719–76: see Emily Hauser, *How Women Became Poets: A Gender History of Greek Literature* (Princeton University Press, 2023), pp. 36–40.

61   Though Homer also, gruesomely, points to the latter: as Agamemnon exhorts Menelaus to war in the *Iliad*, he shouts, 'Let none of [the Trojans] escape the massacre dealt by our deadly hands, not even one! Even the little babies not yet born, whose mothers carry them inside their bellies, will not escape' (Homer, *Iliad*, 6.57–9).

62   Homer, *Iliad*, 1.505–6, 352, 417–18.

63   The cauldron: scholiast on Apollonius of Rhodes, *Argonautica*, 4.816 = Hesiod fr. 300 M-W. The fire: Apollonius of Rhodes, *Argonautica*, 4.869ff.; Apollodorus, *Library*, 3.13.6.

64   Statius, *Achilleid*, 1.133–4, 1.268–70, 1.480–8.

65   *Thetis Dipping Achilles in the River Styx*, https://collections.vam.ac.uk/item/ O66199/thetis-dipping-achilles-in-the-statue-group-banks-thomas-ra/.

66   Homer, *Iliad*, 21.166–7, 568–70.

67   Madeline Miller, *The Song of Achilles* (Bloomsbury, [2011] 2017), p. 336.

9. PENTHESILEA: WARRIOR

1   Georgij Nioradze, 'Zemoavchalis Samare [Das Grab von Semoawtschala]', *Bulletin du Musée de Géorgie*, 1931, pp. 139–40.

2   Skull: ibid., p. 224; rings: p. 221; carnelian beads: p. 145, fig. 8; spear and horse: p. 144, fig. 6.

3   Adrienne Mayor, *The Amazons: Lives and Legends of Warrior Women Across the Ancient World* (Princeton University Press, 2014), p. 72.

4   Nioradze, 'Zemoavchalis Samare', pp. 180–82, 226–7.

5   Mayor, *The Amazons*, pp. 41–3.

6   Homer, *Iliad*, 3.189, 6.186.

7   Homer, *Iliad*, 3.184–9; the epic is unclear as to whether the Amazons are regarded as allies or enemies of Priam.

8   Now fully digitized by the British Library and publicly available: https://www.bl.uk/manuscripts/Viewer.aspx?ref=burney_ms_86

9   Homer, *Iliad*, 24.804.

10 Schol. (T) *Il.* 24.804a; my translation.

11 Josine H. Blok, *The Early Amazons: Modern and Ancient Perspectives on a Persistent Myth* (Brill, 1995), pp. 21–143.

12 'Hysteria' itself, however, is a nineteenth-century term (used for a then-diagnosable women's condition with symptoms ranging from anxiety to sexual voraciousness) that isn't present in the ancient Hippocratic texts.

13 'Mythologische Wesen': Karl Otfried Müller, *Prolegomena zu einer Wissenschaftlichen Mythologie* (Vandenhoeck und Ruprecht, 1825), p. 276.

14 Mayor, *The Amazons*, p. 38.

15 Nioradze, 'Zemoavchalis Samare', p. 225.

16 Cat Jarman, *River Kings: The Vikings from Scandinavia to the Silk Roads* (William Collins, 2021), pp. 141–4.

17 Emilian Teleaga, 'Die Prunkgräber aus Agighiol und Vraca', in *Amazonen: Geheimnisvolle Kriegerinnen* (Historisches Museum der Pfalz Speyer Minerva, 2010), pp. 78–85.

18 Nurida Ateshi, *The Amazons of the Caucasus: The Real History behind the Myths* (Azerbaijan National Academy of Sciences, Nizami Ganjavi Cultural Institute, 2011), pp. 12–13.

19 *Hambastegi News* [Tehran] 2004, cited in Mayor, *The Amazons*, p. 73.

20 Anna Liesowska, 'Ancient Girl Amazon Warrior No Older than 13 is Confirmed by Modern Scientific Techniques', *Siberian Times*, 16 June 2020, https://siberiantimes.com/science/casestudy/news/ancient-girl-amazon-warrior-no-older-than-13-is-confirmed-by-modern-scientific-techniques/.

21 Mayor, *The Amazons*, pp. 357–429.

22 Ibid., pp. 63–4.

23 Ibid., p. 82.

24 Ibid., pp. 414–16.

25 Ibid., pp. 220–22.

26 Ibid., p. 65.

27 John Man, *Amazons: The Real Warrior Women of the Ancient World* (Transworld, 2017), p. 64.

28 Eileen M. Murphy, *Iron Age Archaeology and Trauma from Aymyrlyg, South Siberia* (BAR Publishing, 2003), pp. 97–9.

29 Homer, *Odyssey*, 12.69–72.

30 Caucasus tradition, *Nart Saga* 26, translated by John Colarusso: see Mayor, *The Amazons*, pp. 17–18.

31 Hellanicus *FGrHist* 4 F 107: see Mayor, *The Amazons*, pp. 85–6.

32 Hippocrates, *Airs Waters Places*, 17; Diodorus Siculus, *Library of History*, 2.45.3, 3.53; Strabo, *Geography*, 11.5.1; Apollodorus, *Library*, 2.5.9.

33 Quintus of Smyrna, *Posthomerica*, 1.654–74.

34 Antiope: Diodorus Siculus, *Library of History*, 4.28.1; Plutarch, *Theseus*, 26, 28; Pausanias, *Description of Greece*, 1.2.1, 1.41.7; Seneca, *Phaedra*, 927–9; Hyginus, *Tales*, 30; Apollodorus, *Library*, 1.16; John Tzetzes, *Scholia to Lycophron*, 1329. Hippolyta: implied in Euripides, *Hippolytus*; Isocrates, *Orations*, 12.193; Plutarch, *Theseus*, 27, citing Simonides and Clidemus; Justin, *Epitome*, 2.4; Orosius, *Histories*, 15.8.

35 Plutarch, *The Lives of the Noble Grecians and Romans*, translated by Thomas North (1579): *The Tudor Translations* (AMS Press, [1895] 1967), vol. 1, p. 116.

36 Hesiod, *Theogony*, 1287–94, *Catalogue of Women*, fr. 73 M-W; Apollonius of Rhodes, *Argonautica*, 1.768–73; Diodorus Siculus, *Library of History*, 4.34, 41–8; Ovid, *Metamorphoses*, 10.560–707; Pausanias, *Description of Greece*, 8.45; Apollodorus, *Library*, 1.8.2–3, 1.9.16, 3.9.2; Hyginus, *Tales*, 185; Aelian, *Historical Miscellany*, 13.1: see Mayor, *The Amazons*, pp. 1–11.

37 William G. Cavanagh and Christopher Mee, *A Private Place: Death in Prehistoric Greece* (Paul Åström, 1998), pp. 127–8.

38 Apollodorus, *Library*, 1.9.16; for the Argonauts and Amazons, see Apollonius of Rhodes, *Argonautica*, 2.966–1001.

39 Mayor, *The Amazons*, p. 3.

40 Colin Renfrew et al. (eds), *The Marble Finds from Kavos and the Archaeology of Ritual* (McDonald Institute for Archaeological Research, 2018), pp. 35–6, 224–5.

41 Hariclia Brecoulaki et al., 'An Archer from the Palace of Nestor: A New Wall-Painting Fragment in the Chora Museum', *Hesperia*, vol. 77, no. 3 (2008), pp. 363–97.

42 John Younger, 'Minoan Women', in *Women in Antiquity: Real Women across the Ancient World*, edited by Stephanie Lynn Budin and Jean Macintosh Turfa (Routledge, 2016), p. 587.

43 Scholars have presented a myriad of possible explanations for these white-skinned bull leapers: see, for a summary, Younger, 'Minoan Women', p. 578–9.

44 Alana N. Newman, 'Queering the Minoans: Gender Performativity and the Aegean Color Convention in Fresco Painting at Knossos', *Journal of Mediterranean Archaeology*, vol. 30, no. 2 (2017), pp. 232–3.

45 Kalliopi Efkleidou, 'Looking for Houses in the Tombs: The Evidence for House Societies in the Mycenaean Argolid', in *Oikos: Archaeological Approaches to House Societies in the Bronze Age Aegean*, edited by Maria Relaki and Jan Driessen (Presses universitaires de Louvain, 2020), p. 298.

46 Kristin Leith, *Expressions of Gender in Mortuary Behaviour from Middle Helladic and Mycenaean Burial Samples in the Aegean* (Institute of Archaeology, UCL, 2013), p. 68.

47 Georgios E. Mylonas, *Mycenae and the Mycenaean Age* (Princeton University Press, 1966), p. 98: see the comments by John G. Younger in Paul Rehak, 'Some Unpublished Studies by Paul Rehak on Gender in Aegean Art', in *Fylo: Engendering Prehistoric 'Stratigraphies' in the Aegean and the Mediterranean. Proceedings of an International Conference, University of Crete, Rethymno, 2–5*

June 2005, edited by Katérina Kopaka (Université de Liège/University of Texas at Austin, 2009), p. 14.

48   Georgios E. Mylonas, *Ο Ταφικός Κύκλος Β των Μυκηνών*, vol. 1 (Archaeological Society of Athens, 1973), p. 109.

ODYSSEY: WOMEN AT HOME AND AWAY

10. ATHENA: SHAPESHIFTER

1   Jack L. Davis and Sharon R. Stocker, 'The Lord of the Gold Rings: The Griffin Warrior of Pylos', *Hesperia*, vol. 85, no. 4 (2016), pp. 627–55.

2   Ibid., p. 630.

3   Iosif Lazaridis et al., 'The Genetic History of the Southern Arc: A Bridge between West Asia and Europe', *Science*, vol. 377, no. 6609 (2022), Supplementary Information, p. 134.

4   Tobias M. R. Houlton and Lynne Schepartz, 'Facing Ancient Civilisation: The Craniofacial Reconstruction of the "Griffin Warrior"', 5 May 2021, https://drive. google.com/file/d/1QZciwzTAY50ENT7lMMOvpphsNUND5ffW/view?pli=1.

5   Stacy Liberatore and Shivali Best, 'The Face of Bronze Age Fighter Revealed: Scientists Reconstruct Face of the "Griffin Warrior" Who Was Part of an Elite Group 3,500 Years Ago', *Daily Mail*, 14 October 2016, https://www.dailymail.co.uk/ sciencetech/article-3839092/The-face-Bronze-Age-fighter-revealed-Scientists-reconstruct-face-Griffin-Warrior-elite-group-3-500-years-ago.html; Nicholas Wade, 'Grave of "Griffin Warrior" at Pylos Could Be a Gateway to Civilizations', *New York Times*, 27 October 2015, https://nytimes.com/2015/10/27/science/a-warriors-grave-at-pylos-greece-could-be-a-gateway-to-civilizations.html.

6   'What is Collins Dictionary's 2019 word of the year?', *BBC News*, 7 November 2019, https://www.bbc.co.uk/news/uk-50327046.

7   Ovid, *Metamorphoses*, 3.316–38; Callimachus, *Hymns*, 5.57–136.

8   Homer, *Odyssey*, 11.90–151.

9   Charles Halton and Saana Svärd (eds), *Women's Writing of Ancient Mesopotamia: An Anthology of the Earliest Female Authors* (Cambridge University Press, 2018), p. 83 = *ETCSL* 4.07.3, lines 115–68.

10   Silimabzuta: the translation is mine with help from (and much gratitude to) Evelyne Koubková.

11   Chris Johnstone, 'Grave of Stone Age "Gender Bender" Excavated in Prague', *Lidovky.Cz*, 20 April 2011, https://www.lidovky.cz/ceska-pozice/grave-of-stone-age-gender-bender-excavated-in-prague.A110405_175644_pozice_10810/.

12   Plato, *Symposium*, 189e.

13   Davis and Stocker, 'The Lord of the Gold Rings', p. 650.

14   Sharon R. Stocker and Jack L. Davis, 'An Early Mycenaean Wanax at Pylos? On Genii and Sun-Disks from the Grave of the Griffin Warrior', in *Current Approaches and New Perspectives in Aegean Iconography*, edited by Fritz Blakolmer (Presses universitaires de Louvain, 2020), pp. 293–99.

15   Louise Hitchcock, 'Knossos is Burning: Gender Bending the Minoan Genius', in *Fylo: Engendering Prehistoric 'Stratigraphies' in the Aegean and the*

Mediterranean. Proceedings of an International Conference, University of Crete, Rethymno, 2–5 June 2005, edited by Katérina Kopaka (Université de Liège/University of Texas at Austin, 2009), pp. 97–102.

16 Davis and Stocker, 'The Lord of the Gold Rings', p. 627.

17 Ibid., p. 649.

18 Sharon R. Stocker and Jack L. Davis, 'The Combat Agate from the Grave of the Griffin Warrior at Pylos', in *Hesperia*, vol. 86, no. 4 (2017), pp. 583–605.

19 Ibid., p. 602.

20 Jack L. Davis and Sharon R. Stocker, 'The Gold Necklace from the Grave of the Griffin Warrior at Pylos', *Hesperia*, vol. 87, no. 4 (2018), pp. 619–20.

21 Homer, *Odyssey*, 1.1; my translation.

22 Hesiod, *Theogony*, 886–900; fr. 343 M-W.

23 Pindar, *Olympian Odes*, 7.35–8; *Homeric Hymn to Athena*, 4–16.

24 Note also, though, Athena's wrath against the Greeks: Homer, *Odyssey*, 3.135 and 5.105–11.

25 Homer, *Odyssey*, 1.81–95.

26 Homer, *Iliad*, 5.733–7 and 8.384–8.

27 Homer, *Iliad*, 5.738–42, cf. 21.400–402; for the chariot, 5.837–9.

28 Homer, *Odyssey*, 1.101; my translation.

29 Ibid., 1.103–5, 127–9.

30 Ibid., 1.122: I owe the translation, and observation, to Peter Gainsford, 'Translating Gender', *Kiwi Hellenist*, 22 February 2023, https://kiwihellenist.blogspot.com/2023/02/gender.html.

31 Homer, *Odyssey*, 3.41–61.

32 Lynne A. Schepartz et al. 'No Seat at the Table? Mycenaean Women's Diet and Health in Pylos, Greece', in *Anthropology à la Carte: The Evolution and Diversity of Human Diet*, edited by Lynne A. Schepartz (Cognella, 2011), p. 364.

33 Though not in the form it takes today: see Eberhard Zangger et al., 'The Pylos Regional Archaeological Project. Part II: Landscape Evolution and Site Preservation', *Hesperia*, vol. 66, no. 4 (1997), pp. 558–9.

34 Homer, *Odyssey*, 3.38.

35 Homer, *Odyssey*, 7.20.

36 Hesiod, *Theogony*, 585.

37 Hesiod, *Works and Days*, 373–4; my translation. Paraphrase of Semonides 7.57–70.

38 Hesiod, *Works and Days*, 67–8; my translation.

39 Costume: Hesiod, *Theogony*, 573–84, cf. *Works and Days*, 72. Art of weaving: *Works and Days*, 63–4.

40 Homer, *Iliad*, 14.178–9.

41 Homer, *Odyssey*, 5.51–3, 59–73; Calypso weaving: 61–2.

11. CALYPSO: WEAVER

1 Andrew Koh et al., 'Organic Residue Studies', in *Alatzomouri Pefka: A Middle Minoan IIB Workshop Making Organic Dyes*, edited by Vili Apostolakou et al. (INSTAP Academic Press, 2020), pp. 112–13, fig. 88a.

2   Kn X976, *wa-na-ka-te-ro po-pu-re-[ ]*, 'purple befitting the *wanax*' or 'royal purple' (Greek *porphuros*).

3   Koh et al., 'Organic Residue Studies', pp. 117–18.

4   Marie Nicole Pareja et al., 'Aegean Dyes: Unearthing the Colors of Ancient Minoan Textiles', *Expedition Magazine*, vol. 58, no. 3 (2017), pp. 24–6.

5   Sarah Bond, 'Whitewashing Ancient Statues: Whiteness, Racism and Color in the Ancient World', *Forbes*, 27 April 2017, https://www.forbes.com/sites/drsarahbond/2017/04/27/whitewashing-ancient-statues-whiteness-racism-and-color-in-the-ancient-world/?sh=32d28c9f75ad.

6   Donna Zuckerberg, *Not All Dead White Men: Classics and Misogyny in the Digital Age* (Harvard University Press, 2018), pp. 6, 19–20.

7   Kasia Weglowska, 'Paint and the Parthenon: Conservation of Ancient Greek Sculpture', *British Museum*, 23 May 2018, https://www.britishmuseum.org/blog/paint-and-parthenon-conservation-ancient-greek-sculpture.

8   Tim Whitmarsh, 'Black Achilles', *Aeon*, 9 May 2018, https://aeon.co/essays/when-homer-envisioned-achilles-did-he-see-a-black-man.

9   Mark Bradley, 'Colour as Synaesthetic Experience in Antiquity', in *Synaesthesia and the Ancient Senses*, edited by Shane Butler and Alex Purves (Acumen, 2013), pp. 132–3.

10   Homer, *Odyssey*, 16.175–6; my translation.

11   James H. Dee, 'Black Odysseus, White Caesar: When Did "White People" Become "White"?', *Classical Journal*, vol. 99, no. 2 (2004), pp. 157–67; Sarah F. Derbew, *Untangling Blackness in Greek Antiquity* (Cambridge University Press, 2022).

12   Homer, *Iliad*, 6.289; my translation.

13   Literally, 'violet-looking' (*ioeidēs*): Homer, *Odyssey*, 5.56.

14   Homer, *Iliad*, 3.126.

15   Elizabeth Wayland Barber, *Women's Work: The First 20,000 Years* (W. W. Norton, 1994), p. 127.

16   Homer, *Odyssey*, 5.61–2, 82–4.

17   Circe weaving: Homer, *Odyssey*, 10.222.

18   Homer, *Odyssey*, 5.258–9.

19   'Gender', *Labour Behind the Label*, 5 October 2015, https://labourbehindthelabel.org/our-work/gender/.

20   Manirul Islam, *Mind the Gap: A Study on Garment Workers in Bangladesh* (Bangladesh Institute of Labour Studies, 2023), pp. 13, 23–4.

21   *The True Cost*, documentary film directed by Andrew Morgan (Untold Creative, 2015), 11:50–55.

22   Islam, *Mind the Gap*, pp. 24, 31–2.

23   'Putting the Brakes on Fast Fashion', *United Nations Environment Programme*, 12 November 2018, updated 28 June 2021, https://www.unep.org/news-and-stories/story/putting-brakes-fast-fashion.

24   Homer, *Odyssey*, 2.89–110, 19.137–56, 24.126–46.

25   Martin Litchfield West, *Indo-European Poetry and Myth* (Oxford University Press, 2007), pp. 26–74.

26   Homer, *Iliad*, 3.125–8.

27 I owe the example of Myrtos to Barber, *Women's Work*, pp. 104–9.

28 Peter Warren, *Myrtos: An Early Bronze Age Settlement in Crete* (British School at Athens, 1972), pp. 27, 255–65; on wethers, Barber, *Women's Work*, p. 216.

29 Warren, *Myrtos*, p. 27.

30 Barber, *Women's Work*, p. 113.

31 Ibid., p. 104.

32 Elizabeth Wayland Barber, 'Minoan Women and the Challenges of Weaving for Home, Trade, and Shrine', in *TEXNH: Craftsmen, Craftswomen and Craftsmanship in the Aegean Bronze Age*, edited by Philip P. Betancourt and Robert Laffineur (Université de Liège/ University of Texas at Austin, 1997), p. 515.

33 Homer, *Odyssey*, 6.53, 306.

34 Barber, *Women's Work*, p. 214.

35 Canan Çakırlar and Ralf Becks, ' "Murex" Dye Production at Troia: Assessment of Archaeomalacological Data from Old and New Excavations', *Studia Troica*, vol. 18 (2009), pp. 87–104.

36 Barber, *Women's Work*, p. 107.

37 Stella Spantidaki et al., 'Interdisciplinary Perspectives on the Sails of the Athenian Trireme', in *Archaeology and Economy in the Ancient World 55: Sessions 6–8, Single Contributions*, edited by Martin Bentz and Michael Heinzelmann (Propylaeum, 2023), p. 34.

38 Marie-Louise Nosch and Eva Andersson, 'With a Little Help from My Friends: Investigating Mycenaean Textiles with the Help from Scandinavian Experimental Archaeology', in *Metron: Measuring the Aegean Bronze Age. Proceedings of the 9th International Aegean Conference, Yale University, 18–21 April 2002*, edited by Karen Polinger Foster and Robert Laffineur (Université de Liège/University of Texas at Austin, 2003), p. 201.

39 Homer, *Iliad*, 12.432–6.

40 Sevasti Triantaphyllou, *A Bioarchaeological Approach to Prehistoric Cemetery Populations from Western and Central Greek Macedonia*, British Archaeological Reports International Series 976 (BAR Publishing, 2001), p. 153.

41 Calypso's enslaved attendants are mentioned once (Homer, *Odyssey*, 5.199), setting the table for Odysseus and Calypso to eat; they are not engaged in weaving.

42 Homer, *Odyssey*, 5.167, 321.

43 Barbara Ann Olsen, *Women in Mycenaean Greece: The Linear B Tablets from Pylos and Knossos* (Routledge, 2014), pp. 42, 104, 106; for the count of women at Knossos, see p. 164.

44 Ibid., pp. 99, 106. Miletus: pp. 75, 98 and 282; Halicarnassus: pp. 98 and 300; Knidos: p. 96, n. 246; Chios: pp. 96 and 274.

45 Homer, *Odyssey*, 7.103–11.

46 Olsen, *Women in Mycenaean Greece*, p. 86.

47 Barber, *Women's Work*, p. 216.

48 Homer, *Iliad*, 6.289–92.

49 Ibid., 9.270–71.

50 Ibid., 6.456–61.

51 There is one exception in property ownership: the finishers/decorators

(*a-ke-ti-ri-ja*) – as Olsen, *Women in Mycenaean Greece*, notes (p. 84), the only group of all the lower-status female workers to receive allotments of property.

52   Barber, *Women's Work*, p. 218.

53   Olsen, *Women in Mycenaean Greece*, pp. 61, 65–6.

54   Ibid., p. 109; only five tasks are shared between men and women (p. 78), but even then men and women do not occupy analogous positions.

55   Ibid,. pp. 64–5, 79, 83–4.

56   Homer, *Odyssey*, 7.97.

57   Ibid., 7.83–90.

58   Cécile Michel, *Women of Assur and Kanesh: Texts from the Archives of Assyrian Merchants* (Society of Biblical Literature, 2020), pp. 255–6.

59   Ibid., pp. 274–5 (no. 170); I have removed the brackets from Michel's translation for ease of reading.

60   Ibid., pp. 371–2 (no. 252).

61   Ibid., p. 263.

12. NAUSICAA: BRIDE

1   LH 117: see Trevor Bryce, *Babylonia: A Very Short Introduction* (Oxford University Press, 2016), p. 23. The original number of laws is uncertain, as one of the Elamite kings scraped off some of them to write his name.

2   Susan Brownmiller, 'In the Beginning was the Law', in *Against Our Will: Men, Women and Rape* (Simon and Schuster, 1975), pp. 18–19.

3   LH 143, LH 141, LH 138, LH 129.

4   For the crime of committing adultery and murdering her husband: LH 153.

5   Raymond Westbrook, 'Penelope's Dowry and Odysseus' Kingship', in *Women and Property in Ancient Near Eastern and Mediterranean Societies*, edited by Deborah Lyons and Raymond Westbrook (Center for Hellenic Studies, 2005), pp. 3, 6. For a wife getting her dowry back on termination of marriage, see, for example, LH 137–8, LH 142, LH 149.

6   Ibid., pp. 3–4.

7   My loose paraphrase of Homer, *Odyssey*, 6.25–40.

8   Homer, *Odyssey*, 6.180–81.

9   Homer, *Odyssey*, 7.311–15.

10   Ibid., 8.461–2.

11   Westbrook, 'Penelope's Dowry and Odysseus' Kingship', p. 2.

12   Hesiod, fr. 204.47–9 M-W.

13   Homer, *Iliad*, 11.243–5.

14   Homer, *Iliad*, 18.593; my translation.

15   Westbrook, 'Penelope's Dowry and Odysseus' Kingship', p. 6.

16   Joanne Cutler, 'Arachne's Web: Women, Weaving and Networks of Knowledge in the Bronze Age Southern Aegean', *Annual of the British School at Athens*, vol. 114 (2019), pp. 86–8.

17   EA 25: William L. Moran (ed. and trans.), *The Amarna Letters* (Johns Hopkins University Press, 1992), pp. 72–84.

18   Westbrook, 'Penelope's Dowry and Odysseus' Kingship', p. 3.

19   Homer, *Iliad*, 22.51.

20   LH 137–8; Homer, *Odyssey*, 2.132–3, 20.341–2.

21   Westbrook, 'Penelope's Dowry and Odysseus' Kingship', p. 7.

22   Homer, *Odyssey*, 4.735–6, 23.227–8.

23   PY Ub 1318: Barbara Ann Olsen, *Women in Mycenaean Greece: The Linear B Tablets from Pylos and Knossos* (Routledge, 2014), pp. 150–53.

24   Homer, *Odyssey*, 7.68; my translation.

25   Homer, *Odyssey*, 1.249–50; my translation.

26   LH 143: translation from Martha Roth, 'The Laws of Hammurabi', in *The Context of Scripture: Canonical Compositions from the Biblical World*, edited by William W. Hallo and K. Lawson Younger Jr, vol. 1 (Brill, 2000), p. 344.

27   LH 134: ibid., p. 344.

28   Homer, *Odyssey*, 18.269–70.

29   LH 135: translation from Roth, 'The Laws of Hammurabi', p. 344.

30   Homer, *Odyssey*, 2.337–47, cf. 19.16–30 and 21.380–87 (Eurycleia locks the women's quarters).

31   LH 172.

32   Homer, *Odyssey*, 2.132–3; my translation.

33   Ibid., 18.158–62.

34   Ibid., 18.276–9.

35   Ibid., 18.291–303.

36   Ibid., 19.525–7; my translation.

37   Samuel Butler, *The Authoress of the Odyssey: Where and When She Wrote, Who She Was, the Use She Made of the Iliad, and How the Poem Grew under Her Hands* (Longmans, Green & Co., 1897), pp. 105–14.

38   Ibid., pp. 142–3, 154.

39   Ibid., p. 105.

40   Ibid., p. 106.

41   Paul O'Prey (ed.), *Between Moon and Moon: Selected Letters of Robert Graves, 1946–1972* (Hutchinson, 1984), p. 127.

42   Chloe Koutsoumbeli, 'Penelope III', translated by A. E. Stallings, in *Austerity Measures: The New Greek Poetry*, edited by Karen Van Dyck (Penguin, 2016), pp. 315–18.

43   Homer, *Odyssey*, 7.69–77.

44   My paraphrase of Homer, *Odyssey*, 6.310–15.

13. ARETE: HOST

1   Ralph Pedersen, '1980s', and Elizabeth Greene, '1990s', in 'Faith Hentschel: INA Archaeologists Pay Tribute', *INA Quarterly*, vol. 43, no. 1–2 (2016), p. 21.

2   George F. Bass, 'Oldest Known Shipwreck Reveals Splendors of the Bronze Age', *National Geographic*, vol. 172, no. 6 (1987), p. 709.

3   Cemal Pulak, 'The Uluburun Shipwreck and Late Bronze Age Trade', in *Beyond Babylon: Art, Trade and Diplomacy in the Second Millennium B.C.*, edited by Joan Aruz et al. (Metropolitan Museum of Art, Yale University Press,

2008), p. 288; Cemal Pulak, '1980s', in 'Faith Hentschel: INA Archaeologists Pay Tribute', p. 21.

4   Sturt W. Manning et al., 'Absolute Age of the Uluburun Shipwreck: A Key Late Bronze Age Time-Capsule for the East Mediterranean', in *Tree-Rings, Kings and Old World Archaeology and Environment: Papers Presented in Honor of Peter Ian Kuniholm*, edited by Sturt W. Manning and Mary Jaye Bruce (Oxbow Books, 2009), pp. 163–87.

5   Pulak, 'The Uluburun Shipwreck and Late Bronze Age Trade', pp. 290, 299.

6   Yuval Goren, 'International Exchange during the Late Second Millennium B.C.: Microarchaeological Study of Finds from the Uluburun Ship', in *Cultures in Contact: From Mesopotamia to the Mediterranean in the Second Millennium B.C.*, edited by Joan Aruz et al. (Metropolitan Museum of Art, 2013), pp. 54–61.

7   The area later associated by the Greeks with Phoenicia: Josephine Crawley Quinn, *In Search of the Phoenicians* (Princeton University Press, 2018), pp. 48–9.

8   Francisco W. Welter-Schultes, 'Bronze Age Shipwreck Snails from Turkey: First Direct Evidence for Oversea Carriage of Land Snails in Antiquity', *Journal of Molluscan Studies*, vol. 74, no. 1 (2008), pp. 79–87.

9   Pulak, 'The Uluburun Shipwreck and Late Bronze Age Trade', p. 292.

10   Wayne Powell et al., 'Tin from Uluburun Shipwreck Shows Small-Scale Commodity Exchange Fueled Continental Tin Supply Across Late Bronze Age Eurasia', *Science Advances*, vol. 8, no. 48 (2022), pp. 1–10.

11   Pulak, 'The Uluburun Shipwreck and Late Bronze Age Trade', pp. 300–301.

12   Eric H. Cline and Assaf Yasur-Landau, 'Musings from a Distant Shore: The Nature and Destination of the Uluburun Ship and Its Cargo', *Tel Aviv: Journal of the Institute of Archaeology of Tel Aviv University*, vol. 34, no. 2 (2007), p. 125.

13   Pulak, 'The Uluburun Shipwreck and Late Bronze Age Trade', pp. 302–4.

14   Eric H. Cline, 'Egyptian and Near Eastern Imports at Late Bronze Age Mycenae', in *Egypt, the Aegean and the Levant: Interconnections in the Second Millennium BC*, edited by W. Vivian Davies and Louise Schofield (Meretseger Books, 1995), pp. 91–115.

15   Homer, *Iliad*, 11.19–28.

16   Cline, 'Egyptian and Near Eastern Imports at Late Bronze Age Mycenae', p. 91.

17   Thomas Cucchi, 'Uluburun Shipwreck Stowaway House Mouse: Molar Shape Analysis and Indirect Clues about the Vessel's Last Journey', *Journal of Archaeological Science*, vol. 35, no. 11 (2008), pp. 2953–59. On the east–west route, see Pulak, 'The Uluburun Shipwreck and Late Bronze Age Trade', p. 288.

18   Powell et al., 'Tin from Uluburun Shipwreck', p. 1.

19   Homer, *Iliad*, 2.576–8.

20   Ibid., 16.168–70.

21   Homer, *Odyssey*, 7.108–9, 8.557–63.

22   Ibid., 7.71–4.

23   Ibid., 7.81–107.

24   Ibid., 8.389–93, 430–32.

25   Ibid., 8.438–41.

26   Additions to Odysseus' gifts: Homer, *Odyssey*, 13.13–19.

27   Homer, *Iliad*, 6.215–36.

28   Homer, *Odyssey*, 21.11–41.

29   EA 16: William L. Moran (ed. and trans.), *The Amarna Letters* (Johns Hopkins University Press, 1992), pp. 38–41.

30   EA 17: 36–45, EA 19: 80–85: see ibid., pp. 42, 45.

31   EA 369: see ibid., p. 366.

32   EA 33 (200 talents), EA 34 (100 talents), EA 35 (500 talents): see ibid., pp. 104–9. A talent is roughly equivalent to the weight of one of the oxhide copper ingots on Uluburun.

33   Mario Liverani, 'The Late Bronze Age: Materials and Mechanisms of Trade and Cultural Exchange', in *Beyond Babylon: Art, Trade and Diplomacy in the Second Millennium B.C.*, edited by Joan Aruz et al. (Metropolitan Museum of Art, Yale University Press, 2008), pp. 162–3.

34   *AhT* 8 §5 (rev. 11–17): Gary M. Beckman et al., *The Ahhiyawa Texts* (Society of Biblical Literature, 2011), p. 147.

35   Jorrit M. Kelder, 'Royal Gift Exchange between Mycenae and Egypt: Olives as "Greeting Gifts" in the Late Bronze Age Eastern Mediterranean', *American Journal of Archaeology*, vol. 113, no. 3 (2009), pp. 339–52.

36   Carlos Varias García, 'Mycenaean Terms with the Stem /xenwos/: "Foreigner, Guest, Host"', in *Aegean Scripts: Proceedings of the 14th International Colloquium on Mycenaean Studies, Copenhagen, 2–5 September 2015*, vol. 1, edited by Marie-Louise Nosch and Hedvig Landenius Enegren (Istituto di Studi sul Mediterraneo Antico, 2017), pp. 417–28.

37   EA 11: 19–23. Translation in Liverani, 'The Late Bronze Age', p. 165.

38   EA 9: 6–18: see Amanda Podany, *Brotherhood of Kings: How International Relations Shaped the Ancient Near East* (Oxford University Press, 2010), p. 243.

39   Homer, *Odyssey*, 4.126–9; 589–92.

40   Homer, *Iliad*, 9.262–72.

41   Ibid., 9.288–9.

42   EA 4: 36–50: Moran, *The Amarna Letters*, p. 9.

43   EA 1: 61–2: translation in Liverani, 'The Late Bronze Age', p. 164.

44   EA 12: translation in Moran, *The Amarna Letters*, p. 24.

45   EA 26: 58–63: see ibid., p. 85.

46   Translation in Gary Beckman, *Hittite Diplomatic Texts*, edited by Harry A. Hoffner Jr (Scholars Press, 1996), p. 123, letter 22b §4 (obv. 12–19).

47   Homer, *Odyssey*, 4.125–6, 130–2.

48   Jak Yakar, 'Presumed Social Identity of the Occupants of Late Third Millennium BC Alacahöyük and Horoztepe "Royal Tombs"', *Journal of Archaeomythology*, vol. 7, 2011, pp. 1–8.

49   Homer, *Odyssey*, 15.102; 4.615–19 = 15.115–19.

50   Ibid., 15.104–29: my translation, based on Melissa Mueller, 'Helen's Hands: Weaving for *Kleos* in the *Odyssey*', *Helios*, vol. 37, no. 1 (2010), pp. 1–21.

51   Mueller, 'Helen's Hands', pp. 8, 14.

52 Homer, *Odyssey*, 8.564–9.

53 Ibid., 13.146–87.

54 My paraphrase of Homer, *Odyssey*, 8.573–6.

14. CIRCE: WITCH

1 Gypsy C. Price et al., 'Stable Isotopes and Discriminating Tastes: Faunal Management Practices at the Late Bronze Age Settlement of Mycenae, Greece', *Journal of Archaeological Science: Reports*, vol. 14 (2017), p. 123, fig. 4.

2 Daisy Dunn, *The Missing Thread: A New History of the Ancient World Through the Women Who Shaped It* (Weidenfeld & Nicolson, 2024), p. 31.

3 Aristophanes, *Acharnians*, 801; Aristotle, *History of Animals*, 8.21.

4 Price et al., 'Stable Isotopes and Discriminating Tastes', p. 123.

5 Françoise Rougemont, 'Les porcs dans la documentation mycénienne', in *De la domestication au tabou: le cas des suidés dans le Proche-Orient ancien*, edited by Brigitte Lion and Cécile Michel (De Boccard, 2006), pp. 119–20, 123–4.

6 At Ayios Konstantinos: Yannis Hamilakis and Eleni Konsolaki, 'Pigs for the Gods: Burnt Animal Sacrifices as Embodied Rituals at a Mycenaean Sanctuary', *Oxford Journal of Archaeology*, vol. 23, no. 2 (2004), pp. 135–51. At the Cult Center at Mycenae: Price et al., 'Stable Isotopes and Discriminating Tastes', p. 119. Eleusis: Michael B. Cosmopoulos and Deborah Ruscillo, 'Mycenaean Burnt Animal Sacrifice at Eleusis', *Oxford Journal of Archaeology*, vol. 33, no. 3 (2014), pp. 257–73. Palace of Nestor at Pylos: Valasia Isaakidou et al., 'Burnt Animal Sacrifice at the Mycenaean "Palace of Nestor", Pylos', *Antiquity*, vol. 76, no. 291 (2002), pp. 86–92.

7 Price et al., 'Stable Isotopes and Discriminating Tastes', pp. 121–4.

8 Jacqueline S. Meier et al., ' "Well" off in Animals: A Taphonomic History of Faunal Resources and Refuse from a Well Feature at Petsas House, Mycenae (Greece)', *PLOS ONE*, vol. 18, no. 3 (2023), pp. 6, 19.

9 Francesca G. Slim et al., 'Pigs in Sight: Late Bronze Age Pig Husbandries in the Aegean and Anatolia', *Journal of Field Archaeology*, vol. 45, no. 5 (2020), p. 316.

10 Ibid., p. 315.

11 Meier et al., ' "Well" off in Animals', p. 19.

12 Rougemont, 'Les porcs dans la documentation mycénienne', p. 126.

13 Homer, *Odyssey*, 14.15–19, 107–8.

14 Ibid., 13.409–10.

15 Ibid., 14.72–81.

16 Price et al., 'Stable Isotopes and Discriminating Tastes', p. 116.

17 Homer, *Odyssey*, 10.276; my translation.

18 Homer, *Odyssey*, 10.136; cf. 10.228, where Odysseus' crew are unsure whether she is 'a woman, or a goddess'.

19 William B. Stanford (ed.), *Homer: Odyssey I–XII* (Bristol Classical Press, 1996), *ad* 10.305.

20 Homer, *Odyssey*, 10.471–4.

21 Ibid., 4.227–30.

22 Ibid., 10.234–6.

23 PY Ua 25: see Rougemont, 'Les porcs dans la documentation mycénienne', pp. 118.

24 PY Vn 1314: see Robert Arnott, 'Healers and Medicines in the Mycenaean Greek Texts', in *Medicine and Healing in the Ancient Mediterranean*, edited by Demetrios Michaelides (Oxbow Books, 2014), p. 47.

25 Lindsay C. Watson, *Magic in Ancient Greece and Rome: The Sorcery and Divination of Classical Antiquity* (Bloomsbury, 2019), pp. 60–75.

26 The conjecture that *a-ke-ti-ri-ja* on PY Aa 815 may mean 'healer' is uncertain, and may be more related to spinning/textile working: see Arnott, 'Healers and Medicines in the Mycenaean Greek Texts', p. 51.

27 Paul Rehak, 'Imag(in)ing a Women's World in Bronze Age Greece: The Frescoes from Xeste 3 at Akrotiri, Thera', in *Among Women: From the Homosocial to the Homoerotic in the Ancient World*, edited by Nancy Sorkin Rabinowitz and Lisa Auanger (University of Texas Press, 2002), pp. 34–59.

28 Root-cutting: Sophocles, *Root-Cutters*, F534–6 *TrGF*. Rejuvenating Aeson: Ovid, *Metamorphoses*, 7.159–351. Hercules' madness: Diodorus Siculus, *Library of History*, 4.55.

29 Euripides, *Medea*, 789, 806, 1126, 1201.

30 Lucan, *The Civil War*, 6.507–87.

31 Madeline Miller, *Circe* (Bloomsbury, 2018), p. 172.

32 Heraclitus, *Homeric Problems*, 72.2–3; Xenophon, *Memorabilia*, 1.3.7. Translation in Michiel van Veldhuizen, 'Back on Circe's Island', *Ramus*, vol. 49, no. 1/2 (2020), pp. 217–18.

33 José L. García Ramón, 'Mycenaean Onomastics', in *A Companion to Linear B: Mycenaean Greek Texts and Their World*, edited by Yves Duhoux and Anna Morpurgo Davies (Peeters, 2011), p. 235.

34 *Homeric Hymn to Aphrodite*, 68–74.

35 *Gilgamesh*, VI.58–63.

36 Homer, *Odyssey*, 10.238. Homer doesn't mention her eating any of the pigs, but Apollonius does: *Argonautica*, 4.700–717.

37 Walter Burkert, *Greek Religion*, translated by John Raffan (Harvard University Press, 1985), pp. 242–6.

38 Cosmopoulos and Ruscillo, 'Mycenaean Burnt Animal Sacrifice at Eleusis', pp. 257–73.

39 Burkert, *Greek Religion*, p. 13. For the likelihood of a long shared tradition behind the Thesmophoria linking the Anatolian and Mediterranean regions, see Max D. Price, *Evolution of a Taboo: Pigs and People in the Ancient Near East* (Oxford University Press, 2020), p. 86.

40 Gary Beckman, 'The Hittite "Ritual of the Ox" (*CTH* 760.1.2–3)', *Orientalia*, vol. 59, no. 1 (1990), p. 54.

41 Ibid., pp. 53–4.

42 Billie Jean Collins, 'Pigs at the Gate: Hittite Pig Sacrifice in Its Eastern Mediterranean Context', *Journal of Ancient Near Eastern Religions*, vol. 6 (2006), pp. 174–5.

43 Ibid., p. 174.

44 For another example of pigs as substitutes, see the Greek custom of purification

of murder by sprinkling piglets' blood: e.g. Circe's absolution of Medea and Jason at Apollonius of Rhodes, *Argonautica*, 4.700–717.

45 Homer, *Odyssey*, 10.509; my translation.

46 *Homeric Hymn to Demeter*, 6–8.

47 Miller, *Circe*, pp. 164–5, 172.

48 Margaret Atwood, *Selected Poems 1965–75* (Houghton Mifflin, 1976), p. 221.

49 Nikita Gill, *Great Goddesses: Life Lessons from Myths and Monsters* (Ebury Press, 2019), p. 32.

50 Judith Fletcher, 'Signifying Circe in Toni Morrison's *Song of Solomon*', *Classical World*, vol. 99, no. 4 (2006), pp. 405–18.

51 Homer, *Odyssey*, 8.447–8.

52 Louise Glück, *Meadowlands* (Ecco Press, 1996), p. 46.

15. EURYCLEIA: HANDMAID

1 Werner Hieke et al. (eds), *Meteor-Berichte 94–3: Mittelmeer 1993, Cruise No. 25, 12 May – 20 August 1993* (Institut für Meereskunde der Universität Hamburg, 1994), pp. 22–40.

2 Kay-Christian Emeis et al., 'Temperature and Salinity Variations of Mediterranean Sea Surface Waters over the Last 16,000 Years from Records of Planktonic Stable Oxygen Isotopes and Alkenone Unsaturation Ratios', *Palaeogeography, Palaeoclimatology, Palaeoecology*, vol. 158, no. 3–4 (2000), pp. 259–80.

3 Brandon L. Drake, 'The Influence of Climatic Change on the Late Bronze Age Collapse and the Greek Dark Ages', *Journal of Archaeological Science*, vol. 39, no. 6 (2012), p. 1864.

4 Ibid., pp. 1865, 1867 (fig. 3), citing E. J. Rohling et al., 'Holocene Atmosphere–Ocean Interactions: Records from Greenland and the Aegean Sea', *Climate Dynamics*, vol. 18 (2002), pp. 587–93.

5 Soreq Cave: Miryam Bar-Matthews et al., 'Sea–Land Oxygen Isotopic Relationships from Planktonic Foraminifera and Speleothems in the Eastern Mediterranean Region and Their Implication for Paleo Rainfall during Interglacial Intervals', *Geochimica et Cosmochimica Acta*, vol. 67, no. 17 (2003), pp. 3181–99. Mavri Trypa Cave: Erika Weiberg and Martin Finné, 'Resilience and Persistence of Ancient Societies in the Face of Climate Change: A Case Study from Late Bronze Age Peloponnese', *World Archaeology*, vol. 50, no. 4 (2018), pp. 584–602.

6 Eric H. Cline, *1177 B.C.: The Year Civilization Collapsed*, 2nd edition (Princeton University Press, 2021), pp. 158–62. Syria: David Kaniewski et al., 'Late Second–Early First Millennium BC Abrupt Climate Changes in Coastal Syria and Their Possible Significance for the History of the Eastern Mediterranean', *Quaternary Research*, vol. 74, no. 2 (2010), pp. 207–15. Egypt: Christopher E. Bernhardt et al., 'Nile Delta Vegetation Response to Holocene Climate Variability', *Geology*, vol. 40, no. 7 (2012), pp. 615–18. Cyprus: David Kaniewski et al., 'Environmental Roots of the Late Bronze Age Crisis', *PLoS ONE*, vol. 8, no. 8 (2013), e71004. Israel: Dafna Langgut et al., 'Climate and the Late Bronze Collapse: New Evidence from the Southern Levant', *Tel Aviv*, vol. 40, no. 2 (2013), pp. 149–75. Greece: Susanne Jahns, 'The Holocene History of Vegetation and Settlement

at the Coastal Site of Lake Voulkaria in Acarnania, Western Greece', *Vegetation History and Archaeobotany*, vol. 14, no. 1 (2005), pp. 55–66.

7   There are, of course, instances of free women drawing water: for instance, the Laestrygonian woman at Homer, *Odyssey*, 10.105, or Athena with her water pitcher at *Odyssey* 7.20.

8   Andromache: Homer, *Iliad*, 6.457–8. Nausicaa's *amphipoloi*: Homer, *Odyssey*, 6.84, 99 (*dmōiai*), 109 etc. Eurycleia: Homer, *Odyssey*, 19.353–507. On *amphipoloi* as likely referring to enslaved people, see Emily Wilson, 'Slaves and Sex in the *Odyssey*', in *Slavery and Sexuality in Classical Antiquity*, edited by Deborah Kamen and C. W. Marshall (University of Wisconsin Press, 2021), p. 16 with n. 5.

9   Homer, *Odyssey*, 1.428–35.

10   Ibid., 1.432: see Wilson, 'Slaves and Sex in the *Odyssey*', p. 15.

11   Eurycleia nursing Odysseus: Homer, *Odyssey*, 19.354, 482–3; Telemachus: 1.435. The bath: 19.353–507.

12   Homer, *Odyssey*, 19.474.

13   Other moments of recognition include those of Argos the dog and Laertes, Odysseus' father, at Homer, *Odyssey*, 24.320–61.

14   Albert Severyns, *Homère: le cadre historique*, 2nd edition (J. Lebègue & Cie, 1945), p. 19.

15   PY Aa 783, PY Ab 553: see Barbara Ann Olsen, *Women in Mycenaean Greece: The Linear B Tablets from Pylos and Knossos* (Routledge, 2014), pp. 89–90. *Loetrochooi* as bath pourers in Homer: *Odyssey*, 20.297.

16   Homer, *Odyssey*, 3.464–8.

17   Homer, *Odyssey*, 19.570–5. It's been suggested, ingeniously, that this rather bizarre axe-shooting competition may be a Homeric misrepresentation of Egyptian depictions of pharaohs firing arrows – in a vigorous display of manly strength – into metal ingots, that would have looked to a Greek eye remarkably similar to double axe-heads: see Sarah P. Morris, 'Homer and the Near East', in *A New Companion to Homer*, edited by Ian Morris and Barry B. Powell (Brill, 1997), pp. 621–2.

18   Homer, *Odyssey*, 22.417–32.

19   Ibid., 22.443–5.

20   Ibid., 22.37.

21   Emily Wilson, 'Translating Homer as a Woman', in *Homer's Daughters: Women's Responses to Homer in the Twentieth Century and Beyond*, edited by Fiona Cox and Elena Theodorakopoulos (Oxford University Press, 2019), pp. 288–9.

22   Ibid., p. 289.

23   Margaret Atwood, 'The Myths Series and Me', *Publishers Weekly*, 28 November 2005, http://www.publishersweekly.com/pw/by-topic/columns-and-blogs/soapbox/article/37037-the-myths-series-and-me.html.

24   Homer, *Odyssey*, 22.468–72.

25   Ibid., 22.468–72: see Wilson, 'Slaves and Sex in the *Odyssey*', pp. 31–4.

26   Wilson, 'Slaves and Sex in the *Odyssey*', pp. 30–31, 36.

27   Ibid., p. 30: Homer, *Odyssey*, 18.320–42, 19.63–97.

28   Ibid., pp. 30–31: Homer, *Odyssey*, 22.432, cf. 22.424.

29 Ibid., pp. 31, 36. As Wilson points out (pp. 29–30), the fact that this is not just about being a woman but about enslaved people and their threat to power is demonstrated by the similarly gruesome fate of the goatherd Melanthius, brother of Melantho, trussed up to the rafters while the suitors are slaughtered, and gorily dismembered.

30 Wilson, 'Slaves and Sex in the *Odyssey*', p. 36.

31 Thomas G. Palaima, '*Basileus* and *Anax* in Homer and Mycenaean Greek Texts', in *The Cambridge Guide to Homer*, edited by Corinne Ondine Pache et al. (Cambridge University Press, 2020), p. 302.

32 Natalie Haynes and Emily Wilson, 'The *Iliad*: How Modern Readers Get This Epic Wrong', *BBC Culture*, 5 October 2023, https://www.bbc.com/culture/article/20231004-the-iliad-the-ultimate-story-about-war.

33 Cline, *1177 B.C.: The Year Civilization Collapsed*, p. 2: translation of Ramesses III inscription at Medinet Habu.

34 Ibid., p. 6 (Medinet Habu); see further pp. 1–9.

35 Ibid., p. 2.

36 RS 20.238 (*Ugaritica* 5.24): translation as in Cline, *1177 B.C.: The Year Civilization Collapsed*, p. 9.

37 RS 94.2169: translation as in ibid., p. 108.

38 Ibid., p. 144.

39 Ibid., p. 135.

40 Translations in this paragraph from Cline, *1177 B.C.: The Year Civilization Collapsed*, pp. 154–6.

41 Ibid., p. 140.

42 Ibid., p. 145.

43 Manfred Korfmann in 'The Truth of Troy', BBC Two, 2004, https://www.bbc.co.uk/science/horizon/2004/troytrans.shtml.

44 Eric H. Cline, *The Trojan War: A Very Short Introduction* (Oxford University Press, 2013), pp. 93–4, 99–101, and *1177 B.C.: The Year Civilization Collapsed*, p. 122.

45 Cline, *1177 B.C.: The Year Civilization Collapsed*, p. 125.

46 Carl W. Blegen and Marion Rawson, *The Palace of Nestor at Pylos in Western Messenia*, vol 1: *The Buildings and Their Contents* (Princeton University Press, 1966), pp. 27, 40, 62, 421–2.

47 Erika Weiberg and Martin Finné, 'Resilience and Persistence of Ancient Societies in the Face of Climate Change: A Case Study from Late Bronze Age Peloponnese', *World Archaeology*, vol. 50, no. 4, pp. 584–602.

48 Meirav Meiri et al., 'Eastern Mediterranean Mobility in the Bronze and Early Iron Ages: Inferences from Ancient DNA of Pigs and Cattle', *Scientific Reports*, vol. 7, no. 1 (2017), pp. 701–11; Suembikya Frumin et al., 'Studying Ancient Anthropogenic Impacts on Current Floral Biodiversity in the Southern Levant as Reflected by the Philistine Migration', *Scientific Reports*, vol. 5, no. 1 (2015), p. 13308.

49 Cline, *1177 B.C.: The Year Civilization Collapsed*, pp. 134–80.

50 Ibid., p. xv.

51 Water: 'Water – at the Center of the Climate Crisis', *United Nations Climate Action*, https://www.un.org/en/climatechange/science/climate-issues/water.

Food: 'A Global Food Crisis', *World Food Programme*, https://www.wfp.org/global-hunger-crisis.

52 Cline, *1177 B.C.: The Year Civilization Collapsed*, p. xv.

53 Mario Liverani, 'The Collapse of the Near Eastern Regional System at the End of the Bronze Age: The Case of Syria', in *Centre and Periphery in the Ancient World*, edited by Michael J. Rowlands et al. (Cambridge University Press, 1987), pp. 66–73.

16. PENELOPE: THE END

1 For the metaphor, see the observation on the August 1953 earthquake by Maurice Grandazzi in 'Le tremblement de terre des Isles Ioniennes (août 1953)', *Annales de Géographie*, vol. 340 (1954), p. 432, quoted and translated in Robert Bittlestone, *Odysseus Unbound: The Search for Homer's Ithaca*, with James Diggle and John Underhill (Cambridge University Press, 2005), p. 395.

2 Vassilis Sakkas and Evangelios Lagios, 'Fault Modelling of the Early-2014 ~ M6 Earthquakes in Cephalonia Island (W. Greece) Based on GPS Measurements', *Tectonophysics*, vol. 644/645 (2015), pp. 184–96.

3 Homer, *Odyssey*, 9.19–26; my translation.

4 Bittlestone, *Odysseus Unbound*, pp. 23–47.

5 James Diggle, 'A Philologist Reflects', in Bittlestone, *Odysseus Unbound*, p. 520.

6 Bittlestone, *Odysseus Unbound*, p. 75.

7 Ibid., pp. 77–8 (two Palikians, Gerasimos Volterras and Evangelos S. Tsimaratos) and 551.

8 Emily Hauser, 'Putting an End to Song: Penelope, Odysseus, and the Teleologies of the *Odyssey*', in *Helios*, vol. 47, no. 1 (2020), pp. 43–5.

9 Homer, *Odyssey*, 11.161–2.

10 Ibid., 22.322–4.

11 She is not the last to recognize him in the poem: Laertes, Odysseus' father, has a recognition scene at Homer, *Odyssey*, 24.320–61; there was, however, an ancient tradition of ending the *Odyssey* at 23.296, after the reunion of Odysseus and Penelope.

12 Homer, *Odyssey*, 19.137–56.

13 Elizabeth Wayland Barber, *Women's Work: The First 20,000 Years* (W. W. Norton, 1994), p. 154.

14 Homer, *Odyssey*, 19.358–9.

15 Homer, *Odyssey*, 23.184, 203–4.

16 Froma Zeitlin, 'Figuring Fidelity in Homer's *Odyssey*', in *The Distaff Side: Representing the Female in Homer's Odyssey*, edited by Beth Cohen (Oxford University Press, 1995), pp. 121–3.

17 Homer, *Odyssey*, 1.334, 16.416, 18.210, 21.65.

18 Ibid., 13.194–6.

19 Strabo, *Geography*, 10.2.15 (translated by H. L. Jones).

20 Bittlestone, *Odysseus Unbound*, p. 365.

21 John Underhill, 'The Geology and Geomorphology of Thinia', in Bittlestone, *Odysseus Unbound*, pp. 530–33.

22 Bittlestone, *Odysseus Unbound*, pp. 3–7, 96.

23 Timo Willershäuser et al., 'Holocene Tsunami Landfalls along the Shores of the Inner Gulf of Argostoli (Cefalonia Island, Greece)', *Zeitschrift für Geomorphologie Supplementary Issues*, vol. 57, no. 4 (2013), pp. 105–38.

24 Peter Styles et al., 'The Palaeo-Geographic Development of Livadi Marsh, Paliki: Implications for the Detection of an Ancient Harbour and Anthropogenic Settlement', in *Archaeology of the Ionian Sea: Landscapes, Seascapes and the Circulation of People, Goods and Ideas from the Palaeolithic to End of the Bronze Age*, edited by Christina Souyoudzoglou-Haywood and Christina Papoulia (Oxbow Books, 2022), pp. 137–51.

25 Bittlestone, *Odysseus Unbound*, pp. 119–29.

26 Ibid., pp. 437–41.

CODA

1 Hyginus, *Tales*, 43.

2 Sextus Pompeius Festus, *On the Meaning of Words*, 18.27–30 (s.v. *Aegeum*); cf. Diodorus Siculus, *Library of History*, 3.52–5, though there the queen is called Myrina, not Aegea. See Adrienne Mayor, *The Amazons: Lives and Legends of Warrior Women Across the Ancient World* (Princeton University Press, 2014), p. 431.

3 Helen Carr and Suzannah Lipscomb (eds), *What is History, Now? How the Past and Present Speak to Each Other* (Weidenfeld & Nicolson, 2021), pp. 5–16.

4 Adrienne Rich, 'Reading the *Iliad* (As If) for the First Time', in *Tonight No Poetry Will Serve: Poems 2007–2010* (Norton, 2011), pp. 15–16; *Homer: The Iliad*, translated by Emily Wilson (W. W. Norton, 2023), p. lix.

BIBLIOGRAPHY

Below you will find the books and articles I have found particularly indispensable in researching this book. There is a vast ocean of literature on Homer and ancient history, and this bibliography cannot hope to survey it; what follows is therefore necessarily a selection. I hope the resources listed will be useful to readers who are interested in delving more into the fascinating topics covered here – and that they prove, like any good book should, to be a starting point for a voyage of your own.

Alexandri, Alexandra. 'Envisioning Gender in Aegean Prehistory'. *Fylo: Engendering Prehistoric 'Stratigraphies' in the Aegean and the Mediterranean. Proceedings of an International Conference, University of Crete, Rethymno, 2–5 June 2005*, edited by Katérina Kopaka, Université de Liège/University of Texas at Austin, 2009, pp. 19–24.

Alexiou, Stylianos. 'Contribution to the Study of the Minoan "Sacred Knot"'. *Studien zur Geschichte und Epigraphik der Frühen Aegaeis: Festschrift für Ernst Grumach*, edited by William C. Brice, Walter de Gruyter, 1967, pp. 1–6.

Andreadaki-Vlazaki, Maria. 'The Arrival of the Mycenaeans at Kydonia: Ancient Tradition and Archaeological Evidence'. *One State, Many Worlds: Crete in the Late Minoan II–IIIA2 Early Period. Proceedings of the International Conference Held at Khania, Μεγάλο Αρσενάλι, 21st–23rd November 2019*, edited by Anna Lucia D'Agata et al., Edizioni Quasar, 2022, pp. 193–212.

Archi, Alfonso. 'Aštata: A Case of Hittite Imperial Religious Policy'. *Journal of Ancient Near Eastern Religions*, vol. 14, no. 2, 2014, pp. 141–63.

Arnott, Robert. 'Healing and Medicine in the Aegean Bronze Age'. *Journal of the Royal Society of Medicine*, vol. 89, no. 5, 1996, pp. 265–70.

—— 'Healers and Medicines in the Mycenaean Greek Texts'. *Medicine and Healing in the Ancient Mediterranean*, edited by Demetrios Michaelides, Oxbow Books, 2014, pp. 44–53.

Arthur, Marylin B. 'The Divided World of *Iliad* VI'. *Women's Studies*, vol. 8, no. 1–2, 1981, pp. 21–46.

Aruz, Joan, et al., eds. *Beyond Babylon: Art, Trade and Diplomacy in the Second Millennium B.C.* Metropolitan Museum of Art, Yale University Press, 2008.

Ateshi, Nurida. *The Amazons of the Caucasus: The Real History behind the Myths.* Azerbaijan National Academy of Sciences, Nizami Ganjavi Cultural Institute, 2011.

Atwood, Margaret. *Selected Poems 1965–75.* Houghton Mifflin, 1976.

—— 'The Myths Series and Me'. *Publishers Weekly*, 28 November 2005, http://www.

publishersweekly.com/pw/by-topic/columns-and-blogs/soapbox/article/37037-the-myths-series-and-me.html.

—— *The Penelopiad*. Canongate, 2005.

Bachvarova, Mary. *From Hittite to Homer: The Anatolian Background of Ancient Greek Epic*. Cambridge University Press, 2016.

Balter, Michael. 'New Carbon Dates Support Revised History of Ancient Mediterranean'. *Science*, vol. 312, 2006, pp. 508–9.

Bar-Matthews, Miryam, et al. 'Sea–Land Oxygen Isotopic Relationships from Planktonic Foraminifera and Speleothems in the Eastern Mediterranean Region and Their Implication for Paleo Rainfall during Interglacial Intervals'. *Geochimica et Cosmochimica Acta*, vol. 67, no. 17, 2003, pp. 3181–99.

Barber, Elizabeth Wayland. *Women's Work: The First 20,000 Years*. W. W. Norton, 1994.

—— 'Minoan Women and the Challenges of Weaving for Home, Trade, and Shrine'. *TEXNH: Craftsmen, Craftswomen and Craftsmanship in the Aegean Bronze Age*, edited by Philip P. Betancourt and Robert Laffineur, Université de Liège/University of Texas at Austin, 1997, pp. 515–19.

Barker, Pat. *The Silence of the Girls*. Hamish Hamilton, 2018.

—— *The Women of Troy*. Hamish Hamilton, 2021.

Bass, George F. 'Oldest Known Shipwreck Reveals Splendors of the Bronze Age'. *National Geographic*, vol. 172, no. 6, 1987, pp. 693–734.

Beard, Mary. *Women and Power: A Manifesto*. Profile Books and London Review of Books, 2017.

Beckman, Gary M. 'The Hittite "Ritual of the Ox (*CTH* 760.1.2–3)'. *Orientalia*, vol. 59, no. 1, 1990, pp. 34–55.

—— *Hittite Diplomatic Texts*. Edited by Harry A. Hoffner Jr, Scholars Press, 1996.

—— et al., eds. *The Ahhiyawa Texts*. Society of Biblical Literature, 2011.

Bennet, John. 'Homer and the Bronze Age'. *A New Companion to Homer*, edited by Ian Morris and Barry B. Powell, Brill, 1997, pp. 509–34.

Benson, Fiona. *Ephemeron*. Jonathan Cape, 2022.

Bernhardt, Christopher E., et al. 'Nile Delta Vegetation Response to Holocene Climate Variability'. *Geology*, vol. 40, no. 7, 2012, pp. 615–18.

Bida, Constantine. *Lesya Ukrainka: Life and Work*, translated by Vera Rich, University of Toronto Press, 1968.

Bittlestone, Robert, with James Diggle and John Underhill. *Odysseus Unbound: The Search for Homer's Ithaca*. Cambridge University Press, 2005.

Blegen, Carl W., and Marion Rawson. *The Palace of Nestor at Pylos in Western Messenia*, vol 1: *The Buildings and Their Contents*. Princeton University Press, 1966.

Blok, Josine H. *The Early Amazons: Modern and Ancient Perspectives on a Persistent Myth*. Brill, 1995.

Blondell, Ruby. ' "Bitch that I Am": Self-Blame and Self-Assertion in the *Iliad*'. *Transactions of the American Philological Association*, vol. 140, no. 1, 2010, pp. 1–32.

Bond, Sarah. 'Whitewashing Ancient Statues: Whiteness, Racism and Color in the Ancient World'. *Forbes*, 27 April 2017, https://www.forbes.com/sites/drsarahbond/2017/04/27/whitewashing-ancient-statues-whiteness-racism-and-color-in-the-ancient-world/?sh=32d28c9f75ad.

Bouwman, Abigail S., et al. 'Kinship between Burials from Grave Circle B at Mycenae Revealed by Ancient DNA Typing'. *Journal of Archaeological Science*, vol. 35, no. 9, 2008, pp. 2580–84.

—— 'Kinship in Aegean Prehistory? Ancient DNA in Human Bones from Mainland Greece and Crete'. *Annual of the British School at Athens*, vol. 104, 2009, pp. 293–309.

Bradley, Mark. 'Colour as Synaesthetic Experience in Antiquity'. *Synaesthesia and the Ancient Senses*, edited by Shane Butler and Alex Purves, Acumen, 2013, pp. 127–40.

Brecoulaki, Hariclia, et al. 'An Archer from the Palace of Nestor: A New Wall-Painting Fragment in the Chora Museum'. *Hesperia*, vol. 77, no. 3, 2008, pp. 363–97.

Bridges, Emma. *Warriors' Wives: Ancient Greek Myth and Modern Experience*. Oxford University Press, 2023.

Brown, Ann, and Keith Bennett, eds. *Arthur Evans's Travels in Crete: 1894–1899*. BAR Publishing, 2001.

Brownmiller, Susan. *Against Our Will: Men, Women and Rape*. Simon and Schuster, 1975.

Bryce, Trevor. *The Kingdom of the Hittites*. Oxford University Press, 2005.

—— *The Routledge Handbook of the Peoples and Places of Ancient Western Asia: From the Early Bronze Age to the Fall of the Persian Empire*. Routledge, 2009.

—— *Babylonia: A Very Short Introduction*. Oxford University Press, 2016.

—— 'The Role and Status of Women in Hittite Society'. *Women in Antiquity: Real Women across the Ancient World*, edited by Stephanie Lynn Budin and Jean Macintosh Turfa, Routledge, 2016, pp. 303–18.

Budin, Stephanie Lynn. 'Maternity in the Bronze Age Aegean'. *Women in Antiquity: Real Women Across the Ancient World*, edited by Stephanie Lynn Budin and Jean Macintosh Turfa, Routledge, 2016, pp. 595–607.

Burkert, Walter. *Greek Religion*, translated by John Raffan, Harvard University Press, 1985.

Butler, Judith. *Gender Trouble: Feminism and the Subversion of Identity*. Routledge, 1999.

Butler, Samuel. *The Authoress of the Odyssey: Where and When She Wrote, Who She Was, the Use She Made of the Iliad, and How the Poem Grew under Her Hands*. Longmans, Green & Co., 1897.

Çakırlar, Canan, and Ralf Becks. '"Murex" Dye Production at Troia: Assessment of Archaeomalacological Data from Old and New Excavations'. *Studia Troica*, vol. 18, 2009, pp. 87–104.

Canevaro, Lilah Grace. *Women of Substance in Homeric Epic: Objects, Gender, Agency*. Oxford University Press, 2018.

Carr, Helen, and Suzannah Lipscomb, eds. *What is History, Now? How the Past and Present Speak to Each Other*. Weidenfeld & Nicolson, 2021.

Carson, Anne. *Norma Jeane Baker of Troy: A Version of Euripides' Helen*. Oberon, 2019.

Carter, Jane B., and Sarah P. Morris, eds. *The Ages of Homer: A Tribute to Emily Townsend Vermeule*. University of Texas Press, 1995.

Catling, Hector W., and Helen Cavanagh. 'Two Inscribed Bronzes from the Menelaion, Sparta'. *Kadmos*, vol. 15, no. 2, 1976, pp. 145–57.

Cavanagh, William G., and Christopher Mee. *A Private Place: Death in Prehistoric Greece*. Paul Åström, 1998.

Chadwick, John. *Reading the Past: Linear B and Related Scripts*. British Museum Publications, 1987.

—— 'The Women of Pylos'. *Texts, Tablets and Scribes: Studies in Mycenaean Epigraphy and Economy Offered to Emmett L. Bennett, Jr*, edited by J.-P. Olivier and T. G. Palaima, Ediciones Universidad de Salamanca, 1988, pp. 43–95.

Christensen, Joel. *The Many-Minded Man: The Odyssey, Psychology, and the Therapy of Epic*. Cornell University Press, 2020.

Cline, Eric H. 'Egyptian and Near Eastern Imports at Late Bronze Age Mycenae'. *Egypt, the Aegean and the Levant: Interconnections in the Second Millennium BC*, edited by W. Vivian Davies and Louise Schofield, Meretseger Books, 1995, pp. 91–115.

—— *The Trojan War: A Very Short Introduction*. Oxford University Press, 2013.

—— *1177 B.C.: The Year Civilization Collapsed*. 2nd edition, Princeton University Press, 2021.

—— *After 1177 B.C.: The Survival of Civilizations*. Princeton University Press, 2024.

Cline, Eric H., and Assaf Yasur-Landau. 'Musings from a Distant Shore: The Nature and Destination of the Uluburun Ship and Its Cargo'. *Tel Aviv: Journal of the Institute of Archaeology of Tel Aviv University*, vol. 34, no. 2, 2007, pp. 125–41.

Collins, Billie Jean. 'Pigs at the Gate: Hittite Pig Sacrifice in Its Eastern Mediterranean Context'. *Journal of Ancient Near Eastern Religions*, vol. 6, 2006, pp. 155–88.

Cosmopoulos, Michael B., and Deborah Ruscillo. 'Mycenaean Burnt Animal Sacrifice at Eleusis'. *Oxford Journal of Archaeology*, vol. 33, no. 3, 2014, pp. 257–73.

Coulmas, Danae. *Schliemann und Sophia: Eine Liebesgeschichte*. Piper, 2002.

Crielaard, Jan Paul. 'Basileis at Sea: Elites and External Contacts in the Euboean Gulf Region from the End of the Bronze Age to the Beginning of the Iron Age'. *Ancient Greece: From the Mycenaean Palaces to the Age of Homer*, edited by S. Deger-Jalkotsy and I. S. Lemos, Edinburgh Leventis Studies 3, Edinburgh University Press, 2006, pp. 271–97.

Cucchi, Thomas. 'Uluburun Shipwreck Stowaway House Mouse: Molar Shape Analysis and Indirect Clues about the Vessel's Last Journey'. *Journal of Archaeological Science*, vol. 35, no. 11, 2008, pp. 2953–59.

Cutler, Joanne. 'Arachne's Web: Women, Weaving and Networks of Knowledge in the Bronze Age Southern Aegean'. *Annual of the British School at Athens*, vol. 114, 2019, pp. 79–92.

Davis, Jack L. *A Greek State in Formation: The Origins of Civilization in Mycenaean Pylos*. University of California Press, 2022.

Davis, Jack L., and Sharon R. Stocker. 'The Lord of the Gold Rings: The Griffin Warrior of Pylos'. *Hesperia*, vol. 85, no. 4, 2016, pp. 627–55.

—— 'The Gold Necklace from the Grave of the Griffin Warrior at Pylos'. *Hesperia*, vol. 87, no. 4, 2018, pp. 611–32.

Dee, James H. 'Black Odysseus, White Caesar: When Did "White People" Become "White"?' *Classical Journal*, vol. 99, no. 2, 2004, pp. 157–67.

Derbew, Sarah F. *Untangling Blackness in Greek Antiquity*. Cambridge University Press, 2022.

Dickinson, Oliver. 'Homer, the Poet of the Dark Age'. *Greece & Rome*, vol. 33, no. 1, 1986, pp. 20–37.

—— 'The Will to Believe: Why Homer Cannot Be "True" in Any Meaningful Sense'. *Archaeology and Homeric Epic*, edited by Susan Sherratt and John Bennet, Oxbow Books, 2017, pp. 10–19.

—— et al. 'Mycenae Revisited Part 4: Assessing the New Data'. *Annual of the British School at Athens*, vol. 107, 2012, pp. 161–88.

Diggle, James. 'A Philologist Reflects'. *Odysseus Unbound: The Search for Homer's Ithaca* by Robert Bittlestone, with James Diggle and John Underhill, Cambridge University Press, 2005, pp. 505–29.

Doumas, Christos G. *Prehistoric Thera*. John S. Latsis Public Benefit Foundation, 2016.

Drake, Brandon L. 'The Influence of Climatic Change on the Late Bronze Age Collapse and the Greek Dark Ages'. *Journal of Archaeological Science*, vol. 39, no. 6, 2012, pp. 1862–70.

Dunn, Daisy. *The Missing Thread: A New History of the Ancient World Through the Women Who Shaped It*. Weidenfeld & Nicolson, 2024.

Easton, D. F. 'Priam's Gold: The Full Story'. *Anatolian Studies*, vol. 44, 1994, pp. 221–43.

Efkleidou, Kalliopi. 'The Status of "Outsiders" within Mycenaean Pylos: Issues of Ethnic Identity, Incorporation and Marginality'. *Minos*, vol. 37, 2002, pp. 269–92.

——'Looking for Houses in the Tombs: The Evidence for House Societies in the Mycenaean Argolid'. *Oikos: Archaeological Approaches to House Societies in the Bronze Age Aegean*, edited by Maria Relaki and Jan Driessen, Presses universitaires de Louvain, 2020, pp. 289–308.

Eller, Cynthia. 'Two Knights and a Goddess: Sir Arthur Evans, Sir James George Frazer, and the Invention of Minoan Religion'. *Journal of Mediterranean Archaeology*, vol. 25, no. 1, 2012, pp. 75–98.

Emeis, Kay-Christian, et al. 'Temperature and Salinity Variations of Mediterranean Sea Surface Waters over the Last 16,000 Years from Records of Planktonic Stable Oxygen Isotopes and Alkenone Unsaturation Ratios'. *Palaeogeography, Palaeoclimatology, Palaeoecology*, vol. 158, no. 3–4, 2000, pp. 259–80.

Espaillat, Rhina. 'On the Walls'. *Gods and Mortals: Modern Poems on Classical Myths*, edited by Nina Kossman, Oxford University Press, 2001, p. 219.

Evans, Arthur J. *The Palace of Minos at Knossos*, 4 vols. Macmillan, 1921–35.

Evans, Joan. *Time and Chance: The Story of Arthur Evans and His Forebears*. Longmans, Green, 1943.

Faraone, Christopher A. 'Aphrodite's ΚΕΣΤΟΣ and Apples for Atalanta: Aphrodisiacs in Early Greek Myth and Ritual'. *Phoenix*, vol. 44, no. 3, 1990, pp. 219–43.

—— *Ancient Greek Love Magic*. Harvard University Press, 1999.

Felson, Nancy and Laura M. Slatkin. 'Gender and Homeric Epic'. *The Cambridge Companion to Homer*, edited by Robert Fowler, Cambridge University Press, 2005, pp. 91–114.

Finkelberg, Margalit. 'Royal Succession in Heroic Greece'. *Classical Quarterly*, vol. 41, no. 2, 1991, pp. 303–16.

Finley, Moses I. 'The Trojan War'. *Journal of Hellenic Studies*, vol. 84, 1964, pp. 1–20.

—— *The World of Odysseus*, 2nd edition, Penguin, [1954] 1979.

Fitton, J. Lesley. *The Discovery of the Greek Bronze Age*. British Museum Press, 1995.

Fletcher, Judith. 'Signifying Circe in Toni Morrison's *Song of Solomon*'. *Classical World*, vol. 99, no. 4, 2006, pp. 405–18.

Ford, Andrew. *Homer: The Poetry of the Past*. Cornell University Press, 1992.

Fox, Margalit. *The Riddle of the Labyrinth: The Quest to Crack an Ancient Code and the Uncovering of a Lost Civilisation*. Profile Books, 2013.

Frumin, Suembikya, et al. 'Studying Ancient Anthropogenic Impacts on Current Floral Biodiversity in the Southern Levant as Reflected by the Philistine Migration'. *Scientific Reports*, vol. 5, no. 1, 2015, p. 13308.

Gainsford, Peter. 'Translating Gender'. *Kiwi Hellenist*, 22 February 2023, https:// kiwihellenist.blogspot.com/2023/02/gender.html.

Gallou, Chrysanthi. ' "What Would the World Be to Us If the Children Were No More?": The Archaeology of Children and Death in LH IIIC Greece'. *Aegis: Essays in Mediterranean Archaeology, Presented to Matti Egon by the Scholars of the Greek Archaeological Committee UK*, edited by Zetta Theodoropoulous Polychroniadis and Doniert Evely, Archaeopress, 2015, pp. 57–68.

García, Carlos Varias. 'Mycenaean Terms with the Stem /*xenwos*/: "Foreigner, Guest, Host" '. *Aegean Scripts: Proceedings of the 14th International Colloquium on Mycenaean Studies, Copenhagen, 2–5 September 2015*, vol. 1, edited by Marie-Louise Nosch and Hedvig Landenius Enegren, Istituto di Studi sul Mediterraneo Antico, 2017, pp. 417–28.

Gere, Cathy. *Knossos and the Prophets of Modernism*. University of Chicago Press, 2009.

Gill, Nikita. *Great Goddesses: Life Lessons from Myths and Monsters*, Ebury Press, 2019.

Glück, Louise. *Meadowlands*. Ecco Press, 1996.

Goldman, Hetty. 'Preliminary Expedition to Cilicia, 1934, and Excavations at Gözlü Kule, Tarsus, 1935'. *American Journal of Archaeology*, vol. 39, no. 4, 1935, pp. 526–49.

—— 'Excavations at Gözlü Kule, Tarsus, 1936'. *American Journal of Archaeology*, vol. 41, no. 2, 1937, pp. 262–86.

—— *Excavations at Gözlü Kule, Tarsus*, vol. 2: *From the Neolithic Through the Bronze Age*. Princeton University Press, 1956.

Goren, Yuval. 'International Exchange during the Late Second Millennium B.C.: Microarchaeological Study of Finds from the Uluburun Ship'. *Cultures in Contact: From Mesopotamia to the Mediterranean in the Second Millennium B.C.*, edited by Joan Aruz et al., Metropolitan Museum of Art, 2013, pp. 54–61.

Grandazzi, Maurice. 'Le tremblement de terre des Isles Ioniennes (août 1953)'. *Annales de Géographie*, vol. 340, 1954, pp. 431–53.

Graves, Robert. *Homer's Daughter*. Cassell & Company, 1955.

—— *The White Goddess: A Historical Grammar of Poetic Myth*. 6th edition, Farrar, Straus and Giroux, [1948] 1973.

Graziosi, Barbara. *Inventing Homer: The Early Reception of Epic*. Cambridge University Press, 2002.

Graziosi, Barbara, and Johannes Haubold, eds. *Homer: Iliad VI*. Cambridge University Press, 2010.

Greene, Elizabeth. '1990s', in 'Faith Hentschel: INA Archaeologists Pay Tribute'. *INA Quarterly*, vol. 43, no. 1–2, 2016, pp. 18–23. ·

Gumpert, Matthew. *Grafting Helen: The Abduction of the Classical Past*. University of Wisconsin Press, 2001.

Güterbock, Hans G. 'Observations on the Tarsus Seal of Puduḫepa, Queen of Ḫatti'. *Journal of the American Oriental Society*, vol. 117, no. 1, 1997, pp. 143–4.

Hall, Edith. *The Return of Ulysses: A Cultural History of Homer's Odyssey*. I. B. Tauris, 2008.

Hallager, Birgitta P., and Photini J. P. McGeorge. *Late Minoan III Burials at Khania: The Tombs, Finds and Deceased in Odos Palama*. Paul Åström, 1992.

Hallager, Erik, and Maria Andreadaki-Vlazaki. 'The Greek-Swedish-Danish Excavations 2014: A Preliminary Report'. *Proceedings of the Danish Institute at Athens*, vol. 8, 2017, pp. 280–92.

Halton, Charles, and Saana Svärd, eds. *Women's Writing of Ancient Mesopotamia: An Anthology of the Earliest Female Authors*. Cambridge University Press, 2018.

Hamilakis, Yannis, and Eleni Konsolaki. 'Pigs for the Gods: Burnt Animal Sacrifices as Embodied Rituals at a Mycenaean Sanctuary'. *Oxford Journal of Archaeology*, vol. 23, no. 2, 2004, pp. 135–51.

Hanink, Johanna. 'It's Time to Embrace Critical Classical Reception'. *Eidolon*, 1 May 2017, https://eidolon.pub/its-time-to-embrace-critical-classical-reception-d3491a40eec3.

Hartman, Saidiya. *Wayward Lives, Beautiful Experiments: Intimate Histories of Social Upheaval*. W. W. Norton, 2019.

Haubold, Johannes. *Greece and Mesopotamia: Dialogues in Literature*. Cambridge University Press, 2013.

Hauser, Emily. *For the Most Beautiful*. Transworld, 2016.

—— *For the Winner*. Transworld, 2017.

—— *For the Immortal*. Transworld, 2018.

—— 'Putting an End to Song: Penelope, Odysseus, and the Teleologies of the *Odyssey*'. *Helios*, vol. 47, no. 1, 2020, pp. 39–69.

—— *How Women Became Poets: A Gender History of Greek Literature*. Princeton University Press, 2023.

—— 'Women in Homer'. *The Cambridge Companion to Greek Epic*, edited by Emma Greensmith, Cambridge University Press, 2024, pp. 274–94.

Haynes, Natalie. *A Thousand Ships*. Pan Macmillan, 2019.

—— and Emily Wilson. 'The *Iliad*: How Modern Readers Get This Epic Wrong'. *BBC Culture*, 5 October 2023, https://www.bbc.com/culture/article/20231004-the-iliad-the-ultimate-story-about-war.

Heywood, Claire. *Daughters of Sparta*. Hodder & Stoughton, 2021.

Hieke, Werner, et al., eds. *Meteor-Berichte 94–3: Mittelmeer 1993, Cruise No. 25, 12 May – 20 August 1993*. Institut für Meereskunde der Universität Hamburg, 1994.

Hitchcock, Louise. 'Engendering Ambiguity in Minoan Crete: It's a Drag to be a King'. *Representations of Gender from Prehistory to the Present*, edited by Moira Donald and Linda Hurcombe, Macmillan, 2000, pp. 69–86.

—— 'Knossos is Burning: Gender Bending the Minoan Genius'. *Fylo: Engendering Prehistoric 'Stratigraphies' in the Aegean and the Mediterranean. Proceedings of an International Conference, University of Crete, Rethymno, 2–5 June 2005*, edited by Katérina Kopaka, Université de Liège/University of Texas at Austin, 2009, pp. 97–102.

—— 'Entangled Threads: Who Owned the West House at Akrotiri?'. *Journal of Prehistoric Religion*, vol. 25, 2016, pp. 18–34.

—— and Marianna Nikolaidou. 'Gender in Greek and Aegean Prehistory'. *A Companion to Gender Prehistory*, edited by Diane Bolger, Wiley-Blackwell, 2012, pp. 502–25.

Hood, Sinclair. 'The Bronze Age Context of Homer'. *The Ages of Homer: A Tribute to Emily Townsend Vermeule*, edited by Jane B. Carter and Sarah P. Morris, University of Texas Press, 1995, pp. 25–32.

Houlton, Tobias M. R., and Lynne Schepartz. 'Facing Ancient Civilisation: The Craniofacial Reconstruction of the "Griffin Warrior"'. 5 May 2021, https://drive.google.com/file/d/1QZciwzTAY50ENT7lMMOvpphsNUND5ffW/view?pli=1.

Hughes, Bettany. *Helen of Troy: Goddess, Princess, Whore*. Jonathan Cape, 2005.

Iezzi, Carina. 'Regional Differences in the Health Status of the Mycenaean Women of East Lokris'. *New Directions in the Skeletal Biology of Greece*, edited by Lynne A. Schepartz et al., American School of Classical Studies, 2009, pp. 175–92.

Immerwahr, Sara. 'The People in the Frescoes'. *Minoan Society: Proceedings of the Cambridge Colloquium*, edited by O. Krzyszkowska and L. Nixon, Bristol Classical Press, 1983, pp. 143–53.

Ingvarsson-Sundström, Anne. *Asine III: Children Lost and Found: A Bioarchaeological Study of Middle Helladic Children in Asine with a Comparison to Lerna*. Swedish Institute at Athens, 2008.

Isaakidou, Valasia, et al. 'Burnt Animal Sacrifice at the Mycenaean "Palace of Nestor", Pylos'. *Antiquity*, vol. 76, no. 291, 2002, pp. 86–92.

Islam, Manirul. *Mind the Gap: A Study on Garment Workers in Bangladesh*. Bangladesh Institute of Labour Studies, 2023.

Jahns, Susanne. 'The Holocene History of Vegetation and Settlement at the Coastal Site of Lake Voulkaria in Acarnania, Western Greece'. *Vegetation History and Archaeobotany*, vol. 14, no. 1, 2005, pp. 55–66.

Jarman, Cat. *River Kings: The Vikings from Scandinavia to the Silk Roads*. William Collins, 2021.

Jebb, Richard Claverhouse. 'Homeric Troy'. *Fortnightly Review* NS 35.208, 1884, pp. 433–52.

Johnstone, Chris. 'Grave of Stone Age "Gender Bender" Excavated in Prague'. *Lidovky.Cz*, 20 April 2011, https://www.lidovky.cz/ceska-pozice/grave-of-stone-age-gender-bender-excavated-in-prague.A110405_175644_pozice_10810/.

Jones, Tayari. *An American Marriage*. Algonquin, 2018.

Kakridis, Ioannis. 'The Role of the Woman in the *Iliad*'. *Eranos*, vol. 54, 1956, pp. 21–7.

Kanavou, Nikoletta. *The Names of Homeric Heroes: Problems and Interpretations*. Walter de Gruyter, 2015.

Kaniewski, David, et al. 'Late Second–Early First Millennium BC Abrupt Climate

Changes in Coastal Syria and Their Possible Significance for the History of the Eastern Mediterranean'. *Quaternary Research*, vol. 74, no. 2, 2010, pp. 207–15.

—— 'Environmental Roots of the Late Bronze Age Crisis'. *PLoS ONE*, vol. 8, no. 8, 2013, e71004.

Karanika, Andromache. *Voices at Work: Women, Performance, and Labor in Ancient Greece*. Johns Hopkins University Press, 2014.

Kelder, Jorrit M. 'Royal Gift Exchange between Mycenae and Egypt: Olives as "Greeting Gifts" in the Late Bronze Age Eastern Mediterranean'. *American Journal of Archaeology*, vol. 113, no. 3, 2009, pp. 339–52.

Kerényi, Carl. *Dionysos: Archetypal Image of Indestructible Life*, translated by Ralph Manheim, Princeton University Press, 1977.

Khromeychuk, Olesya, and Sasha Dovzhyk. 'Ukrainian Cassandras'. *London Ukrainian Review*, vol. 2, August 2022, https://www.londonukrainianreview.org/posts/editorial.

Kober, Alice E. ' "Total" in Minoan (Linear Class B)'. *Archiv Orientálni*, vol. 17, 1949, pp. 386–98.

Koh, Andrew, et al. 'Organic Residue Studies'. *Alatzomouri Pefka: A Middle Minoan IIB Workshop Making Organic Dyes*, edited by Vili Apostolakou et al., INSTAP Academic Press, 2020, pp. 111–18.

Korfmann, Manfred. 'The Truth of Troy'. BBC Two, 2004, https://www.bbc.co.uk/science/horizon/2004/troytrans.shtml.

Koutsoumbeli, Chloe. 'Penelope III', translated by A. E. Stallings. *Austerity Measures: The New Greek Poetry*, edited by Karen Van Dyck, Penguin, 2016, pp. 315–18.

Kramer-Hajos, Margaretha. 'Mourning on the Larnakes at Tanagra: Gender and Agency in Late Bronze Age Greece'. *Hesperia*, vol. 84, no. 4, 2015, pp. 627–67.

Kretschmer, Paul. 'Der Name der Lykier und andere kleinasiatische Völkernamen'. *Kleinasiatische Forschungen*, vol. 1, 1930, pp. 1–17.

Kuoni, Simone Zimmermann. 'The Obstetric Connection: Midwives and Weasels Within and Beyond Minoan Crete'. *Religions*, vol. 12, 2021, pp. 1–30.

Langgut, Dafna, et al. 'Climate and the Late Bronze Collapse: New Evidence from the Southern Levant'. *Tel Aviv*, vol. 40, no. 2, 2013, pp. 149–75.

Lapatin, Kenneth. *Mysteries of the Snake Goddess: Art, Desire, and the Forging of History*. Da Capo Press, 2002.

Latacz, Joachim. *Troy and Homer: Towards a Solution of an Old Mystery*, translated by Kevin Windle and Rosh Ireland, Oxford University Press, 2004.

Lazaridis, Iosif, et al. 'Genetic Origins of the Minoans and Mycenaeans'. *Nature*, vol. 548, no. 7666, 2017, pp. 214–18.

—— 'The Genetic History of the Southern Arc: A Bridge between West Asia and Europe'. *Science*, vol. 377, no. 6609, 2022, pp. 982–7.

Leith, Kristin. *Expressions of Gender in Mortuary Behaviour from Middle Helladic and Mycenaean Burial Samples in the Aegean*. Institute of Archaeology, UCL, 2013.

Lessing, Doris. *The Wind Blows Away Our Words*. Picador, 1987.

Liberatore, Stacy, and Shivali Best. 'The Face of Bronze Age Fighter Revealed: Scientists Reconstruct Face of the "Griffin Warrior" Who Was Part of an Elite Group 3,500 Years Ago'. *Daily Mail*, 14 October 2016, https://www.dailymail.

co.uk/sciencetech/article-3839092/The-face-Bronze-Age-fighter-revealed-Scientists-reconstruct-face-Griffin-Warrior-elite-group-3-500-years-ago.html.

Liesowska, Anna. 'Ancient Girl Amazon Warrior No Older than 13 is Confirmed by Modern Scientific Techniques'. *Siberian Times*, 16 June 2020, https://siberiantimes.com/science/casestudy/news/ancient-girl-amazon-warrior-no-older-than-13-is-confirmed-by-modern-scientific-techniques/.

Lipscomb, Suzannah. 'How Can We Recover the Lost Lives of Women?' *What is History, Now? How the Past and Present Speak to Each Other*, edited by Helen Carr and Suzannah Lipscomb, Weidenfeld and Nicolson, 2021, pp. 178–98.

Liverani, Mario. 'The Collapse of the Near Eastern Regional System at the End of the Bronze Age: The Case of Syria'. *Centre and Periphery in the Ancient World*, edited by Michael J. Rowlands et al., Cambridge University Press, 1987, pp. 66–73.

——— 'The Late Bronze Age: Materials and Mechanisms of Trade and Cultural Exchange'. *Beyond Babylon: Art, Trade and Diplomacy in the Second Millennium B.C.*, edited by Joan Aruz et al., Metropolitan Museum of Art, Yale University Press, 2008, pp. 161–9.

López, Guisela. 'Anti Penélope'. *Brujas*, Lunaria, 2006, p. 25.

Lord, Albert. *The Singer of Tales*, edited by David Elmer, 3rd edition, Center for Hellenic Studies, 2019.

Lorimer, Hilda L. *Homer and the Monuments*. Macmillan, 1950.

Maguire, Laurie. *Shakespeare's Names*. Oxford University Press, 2007.

———*Helen of Troy: From Homer to Hollywood*. Wiley-Blackwell, 2009.

Man, John. *Amazons: The Real Warrior Women of the Ancient World*. Transworld, 2017.

Manning, Sturt W. et al. 'Absolute Age of the Uluburun Shipwreck: A Key Late Bronze Age Time-Capsule for the East Mediterranean'. *Tree-Rings, Kings and Old World Archaeology and Environment: Papers Presented in Honor of Peter Ian Kuniholm*, edited by Sturt W. Manning and Mary Jaye Bruce, Oxbow Books, 2009, pp. 163–87.

——— 'Dating the Thera (Santorini) Eruption: Archaeological and Scientific Evidence Supporting a High Chronology'. *Antiquity*, vol. 88, no. 342, 2014, pp. 1164–79.

——— 'Severe Multi-Year Drought Coincident with Hittite Collapse around 1198–1196 BC'. *Nature*, vol. 614, 2023, pp. 719–24.

Mantel, Hilary. 'The Reith Lectures 1: The Day is for the Living'. BBC Radio 4, 2017.

Marinatos, Nanno. 'The West House at Akrotiri as a Cult Center'. *Mitteilungen des Deutschen Archäologischen Instituts, Athenische Abteilung*, vol. 98, 1983, pp. 1–19.

——— *Sir Arthur Evans and Minoan Crete: Creating the Vision of Knossos*. I. B. Tauris, 2015.

Marinatos, Spyridon. *Excavations at Thera, I–III: 1967–1969 Seasons*. 2nd edition, Archaeological Society of Athens, 1999.

Martino, Stefano de. 'Hurrian Theophoric Names in the Documents from the Hittite Kingdom'. *Theonyms, Panthea and Syncretisms in Hittite Anatolia and Northern Syria: Proceedings of the TeAI Workshop Held in Verona, March 25–26, 2022*, edited by Livio Warbinek and Federico Giusfredi, Firenze University Press, 2023, pp. 89–98.

Matney, T., et al. 'Understanding Early Bronze Age Social Structure through Mortuary Remains: A Pilot aDNA Study from Titriş Höyük, Southeastern Turkey'. *International Journal of Osteoarchaeology*, vol. 22, no. 3, 2012, pp. 338–51.

Matz, Friedrich. *Göttererscheinung und Kultbild im minoischen Kreta*. Wiesbaden, 1958.

Mayor, Adrienne. *The Amazons: Lives and Legends of Warrior Women Across the Ancient World*. Princeton University Press, 2014.

McGeorge, Photini J. P. 'Health and Diet in Minoan Times'. *New Aspects of Archaeological Science in Greece. Proceedings of a Meeting Held at the British School at Athens, January 1987*, edited by Richard E. Jones and Hector W. Catling, British School at Athens, 1988, pp. 47–54.

—— 'Intramural Infant Burials in the Aegean Bronze Age: Reflections on Symbolism and Eschatology with Particular Reference to Crete'. *Le mort dans la ville: pratiques, contextes et impacts des inhumations intra-muros en Anatolie, du début de l'Age du Bronze à l'époque romaine*, edited by Olivier Henry, Institut français d'études anatoliennes, 2013, pp. 1–20.

—— 'The Pit L Baby Burial – Hermeneutics: Implications for Immigration into Kydonia in MMIII/LMI'. *Proceedings of the Danish Institute at Athens*, vol. 8, 2017, pp. 293–304.

Meier, Jacqueline S., et al. ' "Well" off in Animals: A Taphonomic History of Faunal Resources and Refuse from a Well Feature at Petsas House, Mycenae (Greece)'. *PLOS ONE*, vol. 18, no. 3, 2023, pp. 1–26.

Meiri, Meirav, et al. 'Eastern Mediterranean Mobility in the Bronze and Early Iron Ages: Inferences from Ancient DNA of Pigs and Cattle'. *Scientific Reports*, vol. 7, no. 1, 2017, pp. 701–11.

Mellink, Machteld J., and Kathleen M. Quinn. 'Hetty Goldman (1881–1972)'. *Breaking Ground: Pioneering Women Archaeologists*, edited by Getzel M. Cohen and Martha Sharp Joukowsky, University of Michigan Press, 2004, pp. 298–350.

Meyer, Ernst, ed. *Briefe von Heinrich Schliemann*. Walter de Gruyter, 1936.

Michel, Cécile. *Women of Assur and Kanesh: Texts from the Archives of Assyrian Merchants*. Society of Biblical Literature, 2020.

Miller, Madeline. *The Song of Achilles*. Bloomsbury, [2011] 2017.

—— *Circe*. Bloomsbury, 2018.

Moran, William L., ed. and trans. *The Amarna Letters*. Johns Hopkins University Press, 1992.

Morgan, Lyvia. *The Miniature Wall Paintings of Thera: A Study in Aegean Culture and Iconography*. Cambridge University Press, 1988.

Morris, Ian. 'The Use and Abuse of Homer'. *Classical Antiquity*, vol. 5, no. 1, 1986, pp. 81–138.

Morris, Sarah P. 'A Tale of Two Cities: The Miniature Frescoes from Thera and the Origins of Greek Poetry'. *American Journal of Archaeology*, vol. 93, no. 4, 1989, pp. 511–35.

—— 'Homer and the Near East'. *A New Companion to Homer*, edited by Ian Morris and Barry B. Powell, Brill, 1997, pp. 599–623.

—— 'Potnia Aswiya: Anatolian Contributions to Greek Religion'. *Potnia: Deities and Religion in the Aegean Bronze Age*, edited by Robert Laffineur and Robin Hägg, Université de Liège, 2001, pp. 423–34.

—— 'From Kizzuwatna to Troy: Puduhepa, Piyamaradu, and Anatolian Ritual in Homer'. *Proceedings of the 24th Annual UCLA Indo-European Conference*, edited by Stephanie W. Jamison et al., Hempen, 2013, pp. 151–67.

—— and Robert Laffineur, eds. *EPOS: Reconsidering Greek Epic and Aegean Bronze Age Archaeology. Proceedings of the 11th International Aegean Conference, Los Angeles, UCLA – The J. Paul Getty Villa, 20–23 April 2006*. Université de Liège/ University of Texas at Austin, 2007.

Mountjoy, Penelope A. *Troy VI Middle, VI Late and VII: The Mycenaean Pottery*. Dr Rudolf Habelt, 2017.

Mueller, Melissa. 'Helen's Hands: Weaving for *Kleos* in the *Odyssey*'. *Helios*, vol. 37, no. 1, 2010, pp. 1–21.

—— *Sappho and Homer: A Reparative Reading*. Cambridge University Press, 2023.

Müller, Karl Otfried. *Prolegomena zu einer Wissenschaftlichen Mythologie*. Vandenhoeck und Ruprecht, 1825.

Murnaghan, Sheila. 'Penelope's *Agnoia*: Knowledge, Power, and Gender in the *Odyssey*'. *Homer's Odyssey*, edited by Lillian Doherty, Oxford University Press, 2009, pp. 231–46.

Murphy, Eileen M. *Iron Age Archaeology and Trauma from Aymyrlyg, South Siberia*. BAR Publishing, 2003.

Musgrave, Jonathan H., et al. 'Seven Faces from Grave Circle B at Mycenae'. *Annual of the British School at Athens*, vol. 90, 1995, pp. 107–36.

Mylonas, Georgios E. *Mycenae and the Mycenaean Age*. Princeton University Press, 1966.

—— *Ο Ταφικός Κύκλος Β των Μυκηνών*, vol. 1. Archaeological Society of Athens, 1973.

Nafplioti, Argyro. 'Mycenae Revisited Part 2. Exploring the Local Versus Non-Local Geographical Origin of the Individuals from Grave Circle A: Evidence from Strontium Isotope Ratio ($^{87}Sr/^{86}Sr$) Analysis'. *Annual of the British School at Athens*, vol. 104, 2009, pp. 279–91.

Nagy, Gregory. *Poetry as Performance: Homer and Beyond*. Cambridge University Press, 1996.

—— *The Best of the Achaeans: Concepts of the Hero in Archaic Greek Poetry*. 2nd edition, Johns Hopkins University Press, [1979] 1999.

—— 'Homeric Poetry and Problems of Multiformity: The "Panathenaic Bottleneck"'. *Classical Philology*, vol. 96, no. 2, 2001, pp. 109–19.

—— *Homer the Classic*. Center for Hellenic Studies, 2009.

—— *Homer the Preclassic*. University of California Press, 2010.

—— 'Observations on Greek Dialects in the Late Second Millennium BCE'. *Proceedings of the Academy of Athens*, vol. 86, no. 2, 2011, pp. 81–96.

Newman, Alana N. 'Queering the Minoans: Gender Performativity and the Aegean Color Convention in Fresco Painting at Knossos'. *Journal of Mediterranean Archaeology*, vol. 30, no. 2, 2017, pp. 213–36.

Nietzsche, Friedrich. *Beyond Good and Evil*, translated by R. J. Hollingdale, Harmondsworth, 1990.

Nikolaidou, Marianna. 'Looking for Minoan and Mycenaean Women: Paths of Feminist Scholarship Towards the Aegean Bronze Age'. *A Companion to Women in the Ancient World*, edited by Sharon L. James and Sheila Dillon, Wiley-Blackwell, 2012, pp. 38–53.

Nioradze, Georgij. 'Zemoavchalis Samare [Das Grab von Semoawtschala]'. *Bulletin du Musée de Géorgie*, 1931, pp. 139–228.

Nordquist, Güllog, and Anne Ingvarsson-Sundström. 'Live Hard, Die Young: Mortuary Remains of Middle and Early Late Helladic Children from the Argolid in Social Context'. *Autochthon: Papers Presented to O. T. P. K. Dickinson on the Occasion of His Retirement*, edited by Anastasia Dakouri-Hild and Susan Sherratt, British Archaeological Reports International Series 1432, BAR Publishing 2005, pp. 156–74.

Nosch, Marie-Louise. 'The Women at Work in the Linear B Tablets'. *Gender, Culture and Religion in Antiquity. Proceedings of the Second Nordic Symposium on Women's Lives in Antiquity, Helsinki, 20–22 October 2000, SIMA Pocket Book 166*, Studies in Mediterranean Archaeology, vol. 166, Paul Åström, 2003, pp. 12–26.

—— and Eva Andersson. 'With a Little Help from My Friends: Investigating Mycenaean Textiles with the Help from Scandinavian Experimental Archaeology'. *Metron: Measuring the Aegean Bronze Age. Proceedings of the 9th International Aegean Conference, Yale University, 18–21 April 2002*, edited by Karen Polinger Foster and Robert Laffineur, Université de Liège/University of Texas at Austin, 2003, pp. 197–205.

Ogden, Daniel. *Magic, Witchcraft, and Ghosts in the Greek and Roman Worlds: A Sourcebook*, Oxford University Press, 2002.

—— *Drakōn: Dragon Myth and Serpent Cult in the Greek and Roman Worlds*. Oxford University Press, 2013.

—— *The Werewolf in the Ancient World*. Oxford University Press, 2020.

Olsen, Barbara Ann. *Women in Mycenaean Greece: The Linear B Tablets from Pylos and Knossos*. Routledge, 2014.

O'Prey, Paul, ed. *Between Moon and Moon: Selected Letters of Robert Graves, 1946–1972*. Hutchinson, 1984.

Oreshko, Rostislav. 'In Search of the Holy Cube Roots: Kubaba – Kubeleya – Κύβεβος – Kufaws and the Problem of Ethnocultural Contact in Early Iron Age Anatolia'. *Linguistic and Cultural Interactions Between Greece and Anatolia: In Search of the Golden Fleece*, edited by Michele Bianconi, Brill, 2021, pp. 131–66.

Palaima, Thomas G. '*Basileus* and *Anax* in Homer and Mycenaean Greek Texts'. *The Cambridge Guide to Homer*, edited by Corinne Ondine Pache et al., Cambridge University Press, 2020, pp. 300–302.

Pareja, Marie Nicole, et al. 'Aegean Dyes: Unearthing the Colors of Ancient Minoan Textiles'. *Expedition Magazine*, vol. 58, no. 3, 2017, pp. 21–7.

Parmar, Sandeep. *Eidolon*. Shearsman, 2015.

Pedersen, Ralph. '1980s', in 'Faith Hentschel: INA Archaeologists Pay Tribute'. *INA Quarterly*, vol. 43, no. 1–2, 2016, pp. 18–23.

Philip, M. NourbeSe. *Zong! As Told to the Author by Setaey Adamu Boateng*, Wesleyan University Press, 2008.

Podany, Amanda. *Brotherhood of Kings: How International Relations Shaped the Ancient Near East*. Oxford University Press, 2010.

Powell, Wayne, et al. 'Tin from Uluburun Shipwreck Shows Small-Scale Commodity Exchange Fueled Continental Tin Supply Across Late Bronze Age Eurasia'. *Science Advances*, vol. 8, no. 48, 2022, pp. 1–10.

Prag, John. 'From the Caves of the Winds to Mycenae Rich in Gold: The Faces of Minoan and Mycenaean Women'. *Women in Antiquity: Real Women across the Ancient World*, edited by Stephanie Lynn Budin and Jean Macintosh Turfa, Routledge, 2016, pp. 561–72.

Price, Gypsy C., et al. 'Stable Isotopes and Discriminating Tastes: Faunal Management Practices at the Late Bronze Age Settlement of Mycenae, Greece'. *Journal of Archaeological Science: Reports*, vol. 14, 2017, pp. 116–26.

Price, Max D. *Evolution of a Taboo: Pigs and People in the Ancient Near East*. Oxford University Press, 2020.

Pulak, Cemal. 'The Uluburun Shipwreck and Late Bronze Age Trade'. *Beyond Babylon: Art, Trade and Diplomacy in the Second Millennium B.C.*, edited by Joan Aruz et al., Metropolitan Museum of Art, Yale University Press, 2008, pp. 288–310.

——— '1980s', in 'Faith Hentschel: INA Archaeologists Pay Tribute'. *INA Quarterly*, vol. 43, no. 1–2, 2016, p. 18–23.

Quinn, Josephine Crawley. *In Search of the Phoenicians*. Princeton University Press, 2018.

Raaflaub, Kurt A. 'A Historian's Headache: How to Read 'Homeric Society'?' *Archaic Greece: New Approaches and New Evidence*, edited by Nick Fisher and Hans van Wees, Duckworth with the Classical Press of Wales, 1998, pp. 169–93.

Rabinowitz, Nancy Sorkin. 'Christa Wolf's *Cassandra*: Different Times, Different Views'. *Homer's Daughters: Women's Responses to Homer in the Twentieth Century and Beyond*, edited by Fiona Cox and Elena Theodorakopoulos, Oxford University Press, 2019, pp. 73–88.

Ramón, José L. García. 'Mycenaean Onomastics'. *A Companion to Linear B: Mycenaean Greek Texts and Their World*, edited by Yves Duhoux and Anna Morpurgo Davies, Peeters, 2011, pp. 213–52.

Rehak, Paul. 'Imag(in)ing a Women's World in Bronze Age Greece: The Frescoes from Xeste 3 at Akrotiri, Thera'. *Among Women: From the Homosocial to the Homoerotic in the Ancient World*, edited by Nancy Sorkin Rabinowitz and Lisa Auanger, University of Texas Press, 2002, pp. 34–59.

——— 'Crocus Costumes in Aegean Art'. *Hesperia Supplements*, vol. 33: *ΧΑΡΙΣ: Essays in Honor of Sara A. Immerwahr*, American School of Classical Studies at Athens, 2004, pp. 85–100.

———'Some Unpublished Studies by Paul Rehak on Gender in Aegean Art', edited by John G. Younger. *Fylo: Engendering Prehistoric 'Stratigraphies' in the Aegean and the Mediterranean. Proceedings of an International Conference, University of Crete, Rethymno, 2–5 June 2005*, edited by Katérina Kopaka, Université de Liège/University of Texas at Austin, 2009, pp. 11–17.

Renfrew, Colin, et al., eds. *The Marble Finds from Kavos and the Archaeology of Ritual*. McDonald Institute for Archaeological Research, 2018.

Rich, Adrienne. 'Reading the *Iliad* (As If) for the First Time'. *Tonight No Poetry Will Serve: Poems 2007–2010*. Norton, 2011, pp. 15–16.

Rohling, E. J., et al. 'Holocene Atmosphere–Ocean Interactions: Records from Greenland and the Aegean Sea'. *Climate Dynamics*, vol. 18, 2002, pp. 587–93.

Roisman, Hanna. 'Helen in the *Iliad*: *Causa Belli* and Victim of War: From Silent Weaver to Public Speaker'. *American Journal of Philology*, vol. 127, no. 1, 2006, pp. 1–36.

Roller, Duane. 'When is a Queen Truly a Queen: The Term *Basileia* in Greek Literature'. *Society for Classical Studies 149*, 5 January 2018, https://classicalstudies.org/when-queen-truly-queen-term-basileia-greek-literature.

Roth, Martha. 'The Laws of Hammurabi'. *The Context of Scripture: Canonical Compositions from the Biblical World*, edited by William W. Hallo and K. Lawson Younger Jr, vol. 1, Brill, 2000, pp. 335–53.

Rougemont, Françoise. 'Les porcs dans la documentation mycénienne'. *De la domestication au tabou: le cas des suidés dans le Proche-Orient ancien*, edited by Brigitte Lion and Cécile Michel, De Boccard, 2006, pp. 115–29.

Rutherford, Ian. *Hittite Texts and Greek Religion: Contact, Interaction, and Comparison*. Oxford University Press, 2020.

—— 'Diplomatic Marriage as an Engine for Religious Change: The Case of Assuwa and Ahhiyawa'. *Linguistic and Cultural Interactions between Greece and Anatolia: In Search of the Golden Fleece*, edited by Michele Bianconi, Brill, 2021, pp. 167–81.

Saint, Jennifer. *Ariadne*. Wildfire, 2021.

—— *Atalanta*. Wildfire, 2023.

Sakkas, Vassilis, and Evangelios Lagios. 'Fault Modelling of the Early-2014 ~ M6 Earthquakes in Cephalonia Island (W. Greece) Based on GPS Measurements'. *Tectonophysics*, vol. 644/645, 2015, pp. 184–96.

Schepartz, Lynne A., et al. 'No Seat at the Table? Mycenaean Women's Diet and Health in Pylos, Greece'. *Anthropology à la Carte: The Evolution and Diversity of Human Diet*, edited by Lynne A. Schepartz, Cognella, 2011, pp. 359–74.

—— 'Mycenaean Hierarchy and Gender Roles: Diet and Health Inequalities in Late Bronze Age Pylos, Greece'. *Bones of Complexity: Bioarchaeological Case Studies of Social Organization and Skeletal Biology*, edited by Haagen D. Klaus et al., University Press of Florida, 2017, pp. 141–72.

Schironi, Francesca. *The Best of the Grammarians: Aristarchus of Samothrace on the Iliad*. University of Michigan Press, 2018.

Schofield, Louise. *The Mycenaeans*. British Museum Press, 2007.

Scully, Stephen. *Homer and the Sacred City*. Cornell University Press, 1994.

Seaford, Richard. *Reciprocity and Ritual: Homer and Tragedy in the Developing City-State*, Clarendon Press, 1994.

Seeher, Jürgen. 'After the Empire: Observations on the Early Iron Age in Central

Anatolia'. *Ipamati kistamati pari tumatimis: Luwian and Hittite Studies Presented to J. David Hawkins on the Occasion of His 70th Birthday*, edited by Itamar Singer, Institute of Archaeology, Tel Aviv University, 2010, pp. 220–29.

Severyns, Albert. *Homère: le cadre historique*. 2nd edition, J. Lebègue & Cie, 1945.

Shelmerdine, Cynthia W. 'Women in the Mycenaean Economy'. *Women in Antiquity: Real Women Across the Ancient World*, edited by Stephanie Lynn Budin and Jean MacIntosh Turfa, Routledge, 2016, pp. 618–34.

Shelton, Kim. 'Petsas House, Pottery Production, and the Mycenaean People in LH IIIA2'. *RA-PI-NE-U: Studies on the Mycenaean World Offered to Robert Laffineur for His 70th Birthday*, edited by Jan Driessen, Presses universitaires de Louvain, 2016, pp. 317–26.

Sherratt, Susan. 'Feasting in Homeric Epic'. *Hesperia*, vol. 73, no. 2, 2004, pp. 301–37.

—— and John Bennet, eds. *Archaeology and Homeric Epic*. Oxbow Books, 2017.

Skourtanioti, Eirini, et al. 'Ancient DNA Reveals Admixture History and Endogamy in the Prehistoric Aegean'. *Nature Ecology & Evolution*, vol. 7, 2023, pp. 290–303.

Slatkin, Laura M. *The Power of Thetis and Selected Essays*. Center for Hellenic Studies, 2011.

Slim, Francesca G., et al. 'Pigs in Sight: Late Bronze Age Pig Husbandries in the Aegean and Anatolia'. *Journal of Field Archaeology*, vol. 45, no. 5, 2020, pp. 315–33.

Spantidaki, Stella, et al. 'Interdisciplinary Perspectives on the Sails of the Athenian Trireme'. *Archaeology and Economy in the Ancient World 55: Sessions 6–8, Single Contributions*, edited by Martin Bentz and Michael Heinzelmann, Propylaeum, 2023, pp. 33–5.

Stager, Jennifer, M. S. 'Sophia's Double: Photography, Archaeology, and Modern Greece'. *Classical Receptions Journal*, 2022, pp. 1–42.

Stanford, William B., ed. *Homer: Odyssey I–XII*. Bristol Classical Press, 1996.

Stocker, Sharon R., and Jack L. Davis. 'The Combat Agate from the Grave of the Griffin Warrior at Pylos'. *Hesperia*, vol. 86, no. 4, 2017, pp. 583–605.

—— 'An Early Mycenaean Wanax at Pylos? On Genii and Sun-Disks from the Grave of the Griffin Warrior'. *Current Approaches and New Perspectives in Aegean Iconography*, edited by Fritz Blakolmer, Presses universitaires de Louvain, 2020, pp. 293–99.

Strasser, Thomas F., and Anne P. Chapin. 'Geological Formations in the Flotilla Fresco from Akrotiri'. *Physis: l'environnement naturel et la relation homme-milieu dans le monde égéen protohistorique*, edited by Gilles Touchais et al., Peeters, 2014, pp. 57–66.

Styles, Peter, et al. 'The Palaeo-Geographic Development of Livadi Marsh, Paliki: Implications for the Detection of an Ancient Harbour and Anthropogenic Settlement'. *Archaeology of the Ionian Sea: Landscapes, Seascapes and the Circulation of People, Goods and Ideas from the Palaeolithic to End of the Bronze Age*, edited by Christina Souyoudzoglou-Haywood and Christina Papoulia, Oxbow Books, 2022, pp. 137–51.

Tartaron, Thomas F. 'Aegean Prehistory as World Archaeology: Recent Trends in the Archaeology of Bronze Age Greece'. *Journal of Archaeological Research*, vol. 16, no. 2, 2008, pp. 83–161.

Teleaga, Emilian. 'Die Prunkgräber aus Agighiol und Vraca'. *Amazonen: Geheimnisvolle Kriegerinnen*, Historisches Museum der Pfalz Speyer Minerva, 2010, pp. 78–85.

Thomas, Bridget M. 'Constraints and Contradictions: Whiteness and Femininity in Ancient Greece'. *Women's Dress in the Ancient Greek World*, edited by Lloyd Llewellyn-Jones, Classical Press of Wales, 2002, pp. 1–16.

Traill, David A. 'Schliemann's Discovery of "Priam's Treasure": A Re-Examination of the Evidence'. *Journal of Hellenic Studies*, vol. 104, 1984, pp. 96–115.

Triantaphyllou, Sevasti. *A Bioarchaeological Approach to Prehistoric Cemetery Populations from Western and Central Greek Macedonia*. British Archaeological Reports International Series 976, BAR Publishing, 2001.

Tzedakis, Yannis, and Holley Martlew. *Minoans and Mycenaeans: Flavours of Their Time. National Archaeological Museum, 12 July–27 November 1999*. Kapon Editions, 1999.

Ukrainka, Lesia. *Cassandra*, translated by Nina Murray, Harvard University Press, 2024.

Underhill, John. 'The Geology and Geomorphology of Thinia'. *Odysseus Unbound: The Search for Homer's Ithaca* by Robert Bittlestone, with James Diggle and John Underhill, Cambridge University Press, 2005, pp. 530–47.

Veldhuizen, Michiel van. 'Back on Circe's Island'. *Ramus*, vol. 49, no. 1–2, 2020, pp. 213–35.

Ventris, Michael G. F. *Work Notes on Minoan Language Research and Other Unedited Papers* (*Incunabula Graeca*, vol. 90), edited by A. Sacconi, Edizioni dell'Ateneo, 1988.

Vermeule, Emily Townsend. *Greece in the Bronze Age*. University of Chicago Press, 1964.

—— 'The Promise of Thera: A Bronze Age Pompeii'. *The Atlantic*, December 1967, https://www.theatlantic.com/magazine/archive/1967/12/the-promise-of-thera/303778/.

Wade, Nicholas. 'Grave of "Griffin Warrior" at Pylos Could Be a Gateway to Civilizations'. *New York Times*, 27 October 2015, https://nytimes.com/2015/10/27/science/a-warriors-grave-at-pylos-greece-could-be-a-gateway-to-civilizations.html.

Warren, Peter. *Myrtos: An Early Bronze Age Settlement in Crete*. British School at Athens, 1972.

Watkins, Calvert. 'The Language of the Trojans'. *Troy and the Trojan War: A Symposium Held at Bryn Mawr College, October 1984*, edited by Machteld Johanna Mellink, Bryn Mawr Commentaries, 1986, pp. 46–62.

Watson, Lindsay C. *Magic in Ancient Greece and Rome: The Sorcery and Divination of Classical Antiquity*. Bloomsbury, 2019.

Weglowska, Kasia. 'Paint and the Parthenon: Conservation of Ancient Greek Sculpture'. *British Museum*, 23 May 2018, https://www.britishmuseum.org/blog/paint-and-parthenon-conservation-ancient-greek-sculpture.

Weiberg, Erika, and Martin Finné. 'Resilience and Persistence of Ancient Societies in the Face of Climate Change: A Case Study from Late Bronze Age Peloponnese'. *World Archaeology*, vol. 50, no. 4, 2018, pp. 584–602.

Welter-Schultes, Francisco W. 'Bronze Age Shipwreck Snails from Turkey: First Direct Evidence for Oversea Carriage of Land Snails in Antiquity'. *Journal of Molluscan Studies*, vol. 74, no. 1, 2008, pp. 79–87.

West, Martin Litchfield. 'The Rise of the Greek Epic'. *Journal of Hellenic Studies*, vol. 108, 1988, pp. 151–72.

———— *The East Face of Helicon: West Asiatic Elements in Greek Poetry and Myth*. Oxford University Press, 1997.

———— 'The Invention of Homer'. *Classical Quarterly*, vol. 49, no. 2, Jan. 1999, pp. 364–82.

———— *Indo-European Poetry and Myth*. Oxford University Press, 2007.

Westbrook, Raymond. 'Penelope's Dowry and Odysseus' Kingship'. *Women and Property in Ancient Near Eastern and Mediterranean Societies*, edited by Deborah Lyons and Raymond Westbrook, Center for Hellenic Studies, 2005, pp. 1–18.

Whitley, James. 'Homer and History'. *The Cambridge Guide to Homer*, edited by Corinne Ondine Pache et al., Cambridge University Press, 2020, pp. 257–66.

Whitmarsh, Tim. 'Black Achilles'. *Aeon*, 9 May 2018, https://aeon.co/essays/when-homer-envisioned-achilles-did-he-see-a-black-man.

Willershäuser, Timo, et al. 'Holocene Tsunami Landfalls along the Shores of the Inner Gulf of Argostoli (Cefalonia Island, Greece)'. *Zeitschrift für Geomorphologie Supplementary Issues*, vol. 57, no. 4, 2013, pp. 105–38.

Wilson, Emily. 'Translating Homer as a Woman'. *Homer's Daughters: Women's Responses to Homer in the Twentieth Century and Beyond*, edited by Fiona Cox and Elena Theodorakopoulos, Oxford University Press, 2019, pp. 279–98.

———— 'Slaves and Sex in the Odyssey'. *Slavery and Sexuality in Classical Antiquity*, edited by Deborah Kamen and C. W. Marshall, University of Wisconsin Press, 2021, pp. 15–39.

———— trans. *Homer: The Odyssey*. W. W. Norton, 2018.

———— trans. *Homer: The Iliad*. W. W. Norton, 2023.

Winckler, Hugo. 'Die im Sommer 1906 in Kleinasien ausgeführten Ausgrabungen'. *Orientalistische Literaturzeitung*, vol. 9, no. 1–6, 1906, pp. 621–34.

Wolf, Christa. *Kassandra*. Deutscher Taschenbuch Verlag, [1983] 1998.

Wood, Michael. *In Search of the Trojan War*. Guild, 1985.

Woodard, Roger D. 'Linear B *po-re-na, po-re-si*, and *po-re-no*-'. *Classical Inquiries*, 4 February 2018, https://classical-inquiries.chs.harvard.edu/linear-b-po-re-na-po-re-si-and-po-re-no/.

Woolf, Virginia. *A Room of One's Own and Three Guineas*, edited by Anna Snaith, Oxford University Press, [1929] 2015.

Yakar, Jak. 'Presumed Social Identity of the Occupants of Late Third Millennium BC Alacahöyük and Horoztepe "Royal Tombs"'. *Journal of Archaeomythology*, vol. 7, 2011, pp. 1–8.

Younger, John G. 'Waist Compression in the Aegean Late Bronze Age'. *Archaeological News*, vol. 23, 1998–2000, pp. 1–9.

———— 'Minoan Women'. *Women in Antiquity: Real Women across the Ancient World*, edited by Stephanie Lynn Budin and Jean Macintosh Turfa, Routledge, 2016, pp. 573–94.

Zangger, Eberhard, et al. 'The Pylos Regional Archaeological Project. Part II:

Landscape Evolution and Site Preservation'. *Hesperia*, vol. 66, no. 4, 1997, pp. 549–641.

Zeitlin, Froma. 'Figuring Fidelity in Homer's *Odyssey*'. *The Distaff Side: Representing the Female in Homer's Odyssey*, edited by Beth Cohen, Oxford University Press, 1995, pp. 117–54.

Zuckerberg, Donna. *Not All Dead White Men: Classics and Misogyny in the Digital Age*. Harvard University Press, 2018.

ACKNOWLEDGEMENTS

Writing the acknowledgements (and reading those of others) is one of my favourite parts of any book; and nowhere have acknowledgements been more due than in this one. This book has depended on the knowledge and generosity of so many brilliant scholars, writers, friends – all of whom, without fail, have exercised immeasurable patience in my attempts to get my head around their many fields and ideas, and to bring them together into *Mythica*. Any and all errors that remain are, of course, my own. My gratitude goes to you all for the brilliant work you do and for your generosity, which have not only made this book possible but have made writing it a pure pleasure and one of the most exciting privileges.

To Emily Wilson, for so generously being willing to share early proofs of her *Iliad* translation, and for her immensely helpful feedback on my book. I feel very lucky to have benefited from her sharp and insightful comments, and am not sure what I would have done without her brilliant translations which form the bedrock of this book. To Greg Nagy, for so many years a treasured mentor and the warmest of supporters from before *Mythica* was even conceived. To Sharon Stocker and Jack Davis, for patiently answering my many questions about their work at Pylos, for reading the entire manuscript in its earliest form (which truly was above and beyond), and for their immensely detailed and valuable feedback – I am so grateful. To Kim Shelton, who not only generously gave her time to talk with me, but who, in addition, took the time to read through my work and clarify details of pig anatomy that were far beyond me. To Eirini Skourtanioti, whose expert insights into ancient DNA and corrections of my genetic stumbles were invaluable to this book, my thanks and admiration – and also to Philipp Stockhammer, who (along with Eirini) was kind enough to take a punt on a classicist. Similar thanks are owed to Abigail Nunes-Richards, for her work on Γ58; and to Andrew Koh, for his warm encouragement and shared passion for public-facing research, as well as his invaluable help in sharing more about the site at Pefka. To John Crawshaw of the Odysseus Unbound project (and the project's trustees), who so generously updated me on the current state of play in Paliki, and put me in touch with John Underhill, Peter Styles and James Diggle, all of whom were kind enough to offer their comments: I am indebted to you all for your generosity and expertise. To my facial reconstruction experts: Tobias Houlton for advice on facial reconstruction methods, and Juanjo Ortega G. for his willingness to work with me on the stunning digital AI facial reconstruction of Γ58 – my immense gratitude.

To the many exceptional Bronze Age archaeologists, historians and linguists who so kindly offered their guidance and indispensable recommendations on the archaeology of Bronze Age women across the Mediterranean world: Gary Beckman, John Bennet, Tom Brogan, Michael Cosmopoulos, Kalliopi Efkleidou, Florence Gaignerot-Driessen, Agnès Garcia-Ventura, Graciela Gestoso Singer, Evelyne Koubková, Tina McGeorge, Sarah Morris, Ester Salgarella, Anaya Sarpaki, Sofia Voutsaki and Rebecca Worsham. Particular thanks are due, above all, to Marie-Louise Nosch, for her hugely helpful insights into ancient weaving; to Lesley Fitton, for her encouragement, insightful feedback, and expertise; to Paul Cartledge, for putting me in touch with all the right people and for his tireless support; and to Trevor Bryce, who was so generous in giving such thoughtful and helpful feedback on my Hittite and ancient south-west Asian chapters – his kindness and collegiality are unparalleled. To the wonderful Homerists and Greek literature crew who read my work: among many others, particular thanks go to Peter Gainsford, Matthew Ward, Tim Whitmarsh; and especial thanks to Joel Christensen, a Homeric friend since Boston days. To Ivy Livingston and Alyson Lynch at Harvard, for archival images of Smyth to make sure I was getting the right busts; to Nina Murray for help with Lesia Ukrainka's *Cassandra*, and above all for her kindness in sharing her translation ahead of publication; and to Yuliya Kostyuk, for her help in translating Ukrainka's letters.

To the libraries, archives and their staff who made the research for this book possible: particularly to the British Library (especially Hadiya Abdinur and Lauren Cook) for their help with viewing the Townley

Homer; and to Andrea Gerriets at the Leitstelle Deutsche Forschungss-chiffe at Universität Hamburg's Institut für Geologie; above all, to the Fondation Hardt in Geneva, whose generous award of a fellowship (and the precious, precious gift of time away to think and write) was where the idea for all this came together.

To my colleagues at Exeter, in particular Francesca Stavrakopoulou for chats over coffee and for being a general star and inspiration; also to those who very generously read and gave feedback on the book – Lena Linne (an honorary Exonian), Daniel Ogden, Mathura Umachandran, Matthew Wright – and to all my friends and colleagues (and amazing strong women) whose ears I have bent on *Mythica* over the past few years and who have helped in more ways than they know: Fiona Cox, Katharine Earnshaw, Sharon Marshall, Rebecca Langlands, Muireann Maguire, Helena Taylor, Charlotte Tupman; as well as those at the Classical Reception Centre who listened to early ideas.

To my students, especially the first cohort of Women in Homer 2024 and my Writing Women class of 2023 – you have been an inspiration and a joy to teach. In particular, I want to thank Sarah Brown for her brilliant point about Briseis and Achilles' horse, and for kindly allowing me to share it; also, my former PhD student and fellow writer Sylvia Linsteadt, for her mutual love of all things Cretan and (also) weasels. Also, to my teachers: Bob Bass, for inspiring my love of the Greek myths and for teaching me Greek after school (what a hero); Janet Taylor, for first introducing me to Homer; Tim Chambers, for helping me learn to love dictionary entries. Teachers, you all make more of a difference than you know.

To my brilliant team at Transworld – team *Mythica*: I'm so grateful to you all. To my wonderful editor, Simon, for his Herculean efforts in making this book a reality: here's to over a decade of working together to retell Homer's women in all kinds of different ways – with so much gratitude. To my steadfast agent Roger Field: not only for being untiring in the call of duty, but also for his keen and helpful eye on everything from Snodgrass to Mycenaean battle gear – so many thanks, as always. To my amazing publicists, Chloë Rose and Ollie Martin, and my marketing gurus Lucy Upton and Melissa Kelly, who all shouted the *Mythica* news from the rooftops. To Katrina Whone for steering the *Mythica* ship throughout; Kate Parker for her careful copy-edit; Lorraine McCann for her thorough proofreading; and Caroline Hotblack for her dedicated search for all my (many) images; Vivien Thompson, for keeping the script on track; Lucy Oates for early reads, and Irene Martinez for what is my dream cover; Phil Lord for his shepherding of the interior design and images; and Liane Payne for the splendid maps. My sincere thanks to you all: it really does take a village to raise a book. Thanks are also due to my wonderful US team in Chicago who have brought *Penelope's Bones* to life – Karen Levine, Victoria Barry, Kristen Raddatz.

And, finally, to my much-loved friends and family, who have all supported me and cheered me on. To Helena and Loukas, Kim and Miguel, Helena and Dave, the BSA crowd (always) and especially Athena for being one of my first (and very generous) readers. To my grandparents, especially my grandmother Mama, to whom this book is dedicated – for encouraging my love of Classics, for giving me books on Linear B and the *Odyssey*, for listening to me recite Homer as a teenager (what a saint). To my family for patiently letting me talk about *Mythica* all the time and – most of all – for stepping in to help with the childcare that made any of this happen: above all my parents, parents-in-law and sister Katy – you have been tremendous. Finally, the people who are at the heart of it: my wonderful, inspirational husband Oliver, who, without a doubt, makes everything possible – I am so grateful, always; and our two little lights, Theo and Eliza, who are the reason for it all.

CHAPTER-OPENING ILLUSTRATIONS

page 27: *Sophia Schliemann wearing the erroneously named 'jewels of Helen' from c.2400 BCE, discovered (and stolen) by Heinrich Schliemann at Troy.*

page 53: *A Linear B tablet from Pylos (PY Ab 194) lists women weavers from Chios, their children and rations (c.1200 BCE).*

page 71: *This fresco of a young girl stands on the threshold of the West House, a Minoan townhouse in Akrotiri (c.1600 BCE).*

page 91: *The seal of Puduhepa, the real Late Bronze Age Queen of the Hittites, appeared on the world's earliest peace treaty; this example comes from Tarsus and dates to c.1220 BCE.*

page 109: *Waving the soldiers off to Troy? A vase from Mycenae (c.1200 BCE) shows a woman waving farewell on the left, as warriors march off to battle.*

page 125: *An oracle tablet from Late Bronze Age Hattusa, capital of the Hittite Empire (c.1310 BCE). Now referred to as AhT 20, it seeks the advice and expertise of female seers and dream interpreters, as well as a Hittite princess.*

page 145: *One of the two so-called Snake Goddesses discovered by Sir Arthur Evans in the Bronze Age palace at Knossos, Crete (c.1600 BCE).*

page 169: *Skeleton of a baby boy from ancient Cydonia (modern Chania) dating from the seventeenth to sixteenth century BCE.*

page 193: *The sword of a real Amazon, dating to c.1000 BCE and discovered in modern Georgia alongside a woman warrior's skeleton.*

page 215: *Bronze mirror from the tomb of the Griffin Warrior, Pylos (1500–1450 BCE).*

page 235: *Complete shell of a murex snail: these sea snails held the key* *to the ancient trade in 'royal purple', in a gland that secreted the pigment used to create the dye.*

page 259: *Hammurabi's law code, one of the most complete collections of ancient Babylonian laws (c.1750 BCE).*

page 277: *A modern reconstruction underwater of the Uluburun ship that sank near the southern coast of Turkey around the end of the fourteenth century BCE.*

page 305: *The Lion – or, more properly, Lioness – Gate: the entrance to the citadel of the Late Bronze Age city of Mycenae.*

page 327: *The Late Bronze Age Mycenaean palace at Pylos, said by Homer to be the seat of Nestor: an ancient bathtub is still visible at the site.*

page 349: *The Poros rock off the coast of Cephalonia: notches on the rock demonstrate the island's uplift over millennia due to major seismic activity.*

PICTURE ACKNOWLEDGEMENTS

MAPS AND TIMELINE

Liane Payne

PLATE SECTIONS

First section

1:1 Lyre player. Watercolour reconstruction by Piet de Jong. (Courtesy of The Palace of Nestor Excavations, The Department of Classics, University of Cincinnati)

1:2 *Iliad.* Book 1 397–520, Karanis, Egypt, second century CE. Papyrus. P. Mich. Inv. 2810. University of Michigan Library. (University of Michigan Library, Papyrology Collection)

2:1 The Trojan Horse on the Mykonos Vase. Archaeological Museum, Mykonos, Greece. (Luisa Ricciarini/Bridgeman Images)

2:2 Close-up of the Ship Frieze from Akrotiri, Thera. National Archaeological Museum, Athens, Greece. (G. Dagli Ort/© NPL – DeA Picture Library/ Bridgeman Images)

3:1 Troy, reconstruction. Watercolour by Peter Connolly, 1986. (Peter Connolly/ akg-images)

3:2 Linear B tablet. Ashmolean Museum, Oxford. (© Ashmolean Museum, University of Oxford)

4:1 A woman of Mycenae. Reconstruction of fresco from Tiryns. National Archaeological Museum, Athens, Greece. (Lisa Ricciarini/Bridgeman Images)

4:2 Grave Circle B digital reconstruction by (and courtesy of) Juanjo Ortega G., popularizer of Ancient Rome. (Instagram: @imperiumromanum_27ac)

5:1 A young woman from a fresco in the West House, Akrotiri, Thera. National Archaeological Museum, Athens, Greece. (DEA/G. Nimatallah/DeAgostini/ Getty Images)

5:2 West House, Room 5. Digital reconstruction by Apostolis Kassios. (Apostolis Kassios, https://cad-monkeys.com)

6:1 and 6:2 Naval expedition. Minoan fresco from Akrotiri, Thera, Santorini. National Archaeological Museum, Athens, Greece. (Luisa Ricciarini/Bridgeman Images)

6:3 Gold signet ring. Ashmolean Museum, Oxford. (© Ashmolean Museum, University of Oxford)

7:1 'The Queen's Megaron'. Watercolour by Émile Gilliéron from *The Palace of Minos at Knossos* Volume 3 by Sir Arthur Evans, 1930

7:2 Ladies of the Minoan Court. Archaeological Museum of Heraklion, Crete. (Ancient Art and Architecture Collection Ltd./Bridgeman Images)

8:1 The rape of Cassandra by the lesser Ajax. The British Museum, London. (© The Trustees of the British Museum)

8:2 Warrior woman's skeleton, fourth century BCE, kurgan 1, burial 6, Kazakhstan. (Photo by James Vedder, Center for the Study of Eurasian Nomads, 1992, colour plate 3, Adrienne Mayor, 'The Amazons: Lives and Legends of Warrior Women across the Ancient World' (Princeton University Press, 2014))

Second section

1:1 Penelope and Telemachus. Museo Archeologico Nazionale, Chiusi. (Granger/ Bridgeman Images)

1:2 Tomb of the Griffin Warrior during excavation, Pylos. (Courtesy of The Palace of Nestor Excavations, The Department of Classics, University of Cincinnati)

2:1 Hatshepsut. The Metropolitan Museum of Art, New York. (The Metropolitan Museum of Art, New York. Rogers Fund, 1929)

2:2 Pylos combat agate sealstone. From tomb of the Griffin Warrior. (Courtesy of The Palace of Nestor Excavations, The Department of Classics, University of Cincinnati)

2:3 Gold necklace with beads of faience and agate. From tomb of the Griffin Warrior. (Courtesy of The Palace of Nestor Excavations, The Department of Classics, University of Cincinnati)

3:1 Gold ring with shrine scene. From tomb of the Griffin Warrior. (Photograph by J. Vanderpool. Drawings by T. Ross. Courtesy of The Palace of Nestor Excavations, The Department of Classics, University of Cincinnati)

3:2 Veiled girl 'Adorant'. Detail of fresco from Xeste 3, Akrotiri (Thera), Santorini. Museum of Prehistoric Thera, Santorini. (Luisa Ricciarini/Bridgeman Images)

3:3 Phases of weaving. Detail of black-figure terracotta lekythos. The Metropolitan Museum of Art, New York. (The Metropolitan Museum of Art, New York. Fletcher Fund, 1931)

4:1 Uluburun III, replica of the fourteenth century BCE Uluburun shipwreck, Kaş Underwater Archaeopark, Turkey. (© Guzden Varinlioglu)

4:2 Archaeologist at Uluburun carrying an oxhide ingot. (© Institute of Nautical Archaeology)

4:3 Aegean islander bringing ingot of metal. Detail of a facsimile painting of a scene in the tomb of Rekhmire at Thebes c.1479–1425 BCE. Tempera and ink painting by Nina de Garis Davies (1881–1965). The Metropolitan Museum of Art, New York. (The Metropolitan Museum of Art, New York. Rogers Fund, 1931)

5:1 Circe turning a man into a pig. Staatliche Kunstsammlungen, Dresden. (bpk/ Staatliche Kunstsammlungen Dresden/Hans-Peter Klut)

5:2 Saffron gatherers. Museum of Prehistoric Thera, Santorini. (Luisa Ricciarini/ Bridgeman Images)

6:1 Bathtub, Palace of Nestor, Pylos, Greece. (Erin Babnik/Alamy Stock Photo)

6:2 Myrtos. (© Oliver Hauser)

7:1 Seated goddess from Çatalhöyük. Archaeological Museum, Ankara. (DEA/G. DAGLI ORTI/deAgostini/Getty Images)

7:2 Odysseus returning to Penelope. The Metropolitan Museum of Art, New York. (The Metropolitan Museum of Art, New York. Fletcher Fund, 1930)

8 Homer flanked by Dante Alighieri and Virgil. Detail from *The Parnassus* by Raphael. Palace of the Vatican, Rome. (Album/Alamy Stock Photo)

IN-TEXT ILLUSTRATIONS

page 11: Helen of Troy from the earliest complete manuscript of Homer's *Iliad*. Venetus A, fol. 1v (detail); Marciana 822 (= Graecus Z. 454). Biblioteca Nazionale Marciana, Venice, Italy. (© Center for Hellenic Studies, Washington, DC)

page 27: Mme. Schliemann in the parure of Helen of Troy. (Chronicle/Alamy Stock Photo)

page 40: Walls and battlements of Troy VI. (© Oliver Hauser)

page 49: Facial reconstruction of a Late Bronze Age woman from Grave Circle B, Mycenae by Richard Neave. Manchester Museum, The University of Manchester. (© Manchester Museum, The University of Manchester/Bridgeman Images)

page 53: A Linear B tablet from Pylos (PY Ab 194). (Photograph by Emile Serafis. Courtesy of The Palace of Nestor Excavations, The Department of Classics, University of Cincinnati)

page 59: Drawing of a Linear B tablet from Pylos. (Drawn by the author)

page 71: A young woman from a fresco in the West House, Akrotiri, Thera. National Archaeological Museum, Athens, Greece. (DEA/G. Dagli Orti/De Agostini via Getty Images)

page 74: The Bronze Age city of Akrotiri, Thera, Santorini, Greece. (Gonzalo Azumendi/Getty Images)

page 77: The West House at Akrotiri, Thera, Santorini, Greece. (DEA/G. Dagli Orti/ De Agostini via Getty Images)

page 86: Electrum face mask. National Archaeological Museum, Athens, Greece. (DEA/G. Dagli Orti/De Agostini via Getty Images)

page 91: Seal of Puduhepa, Queen of the Hittites. From *Excavations at Gözlü Kule, Tarsus, Volume* 2 by Hetty Goldman, Princeton University Press, 1956

page 100: The Great Queen Puduhepa, making a libation to the Sun Goddess Arinna Hebat. Fraktin Hittite rock relief, Central Anatolia. (Carole Raddato Collection, American Academy in Rome, Photographic Archive)

pages 109 and 118: Mycenaean krater. National Archaeological Museum, Athens, Greece. (Zev Radovan/Alamy Stock Photo)

page 112: Teeth from XAN023. (Photograph courtesy of M. Vlazaki, T. McGeorge and E. Kataki)

page 120: The 'Siege Rhyton' (detail). Line drawing after E. Gilliéron from *The Arts in Prehistoric Greece* by Sinclair Hood, 1978. (Courtesy of Penguin Random House)

page 125: An oracle tablet from Late Bronze Age Hattusa. AhT 20 = KUB 5.6 = Bo 2044 + 7094. Vorderasiatisches Museum, Berlin. (Vorderasiatisches Museum, SMB/bpk)

TEXT ACKNOWLEDGEMENTS

Quotations from *The Odyssey* by Homer, translated by Emily Wilson. Copyright © 2018 by Emily Wilson. Used by permission of W. W. Norton & Company, Inc.

Quotations from *Homer's Iliad* by Homer, translated by Emily Wilson. Copyright © 2023 by Emily Wilson. Used by permission of W. W. Norton & Company, Inc

page 10: from Diane Arnson Svarlien's 1995 translation of 'Poem 7' by Semonides of Amorgos, first published in Diotima (http://www.stoa.org/diotima/anthology/).

page 45: from 'On the Walls' by Rhina Espaillat, in *Gods and Mortals: Modern Poems on Classical Myths*, edited by Nina Kossman, Oxford University Press, 2001.

page 166: Fiona Benson's 'Pasiphaë on her Last Newborn', from her cycle 'Translations from the Pasiphaë', in the collection *Ephemeron*, Jonathan Cape, 2022.

page 274: from Chloe Koutsoumbeli's 'Penelope III', translated by A. E. Stallings, in *Austerity Measures: The New Greek Poetry*, edited by Karen Van Dyck, Penguin, 2016.

page 324: from Margaret Atwood's poem cycle 'Circe/Mud Poems' in her *Selected Poems 1965-75*, Houghton Mifflin, 1976.

page 325: from 'Circe's Grief' by Louise Glück, from the collection *Meadowlands*, Ecco Press, 1996.

INDEX

Page numbers in *italics* refer to pages with illustrations.

ABOUT THE AUTHOR

DR EMILY HAUSER is an award-winning classicist and historian and the author of an acclaimed trilogy of novels retelling the stories of women of Greek myth: *For the Most Beautiful, For the Winner* and *For the Immortal.*

She read Classics at Cambridge, where she received a double first with distinction and won the Chancellor's Medal for Classical Proficiency. She has a PhD in Classics from Yale, and was a Junior Fellow at the Harvard Society of Fellows. She is now a Senior Lecturer in Classics and Ancient History at the University of Exeter, and teaches and researches on Homer and women's writing, ancient and modern.

Her recent publications include *How Women Became Poets: A Gender History of Greek Literature,* which was shortlisted for the Seminary Co-Op's best books of 2023.

Emily lives in Exeter.

To find out more, visit: www.emilyhauser.com

@emilyhauserauthor